The organic growth of an asset management system

Case: ProRail

The Rail Infra Manager
in the Netherlands

Jan Swier

Translated by Shivani Saxena (Lucknow, India) and Jan Swier

The organic growth of an asset management system

Case: ProRail
The Rail Infra Manager in the Netherlands

Explanation of the cover.
The figure on the cover is formed by a golden rectangle, subdivided into a square and a smaller golden rectangle. The ratio is the basis of a logarithmic spiral. It can be found everywhere in nature. The shape combines strength, size, regularity and compactness. The most impressive appearance is in galaxies and a wonderful example on Earth is the Nautilus shell in which lives a kind of squid, a living fossil. The shell contains a series of air chambers that the animal uses to control its buoyancy. The rooms grow in phases and dimensions, and offer living space and protection.

The Nautilus shell is used by me as a symbol for asset management: a well-organized system that organically grows in phases and offers work to motivated people who work in an exciting balance with their environment to deliver the desired assets to the stakeholder with the expected quality .

Original title: *De organische groei van een assetmanagementsysteem.*
Autor: Jan Swier
Dutch editions 2017 and 2019 (1st and 2nd print),
© 2017 / 2019 Jan Swier, all rights reserved

English edition, 2019
Translated by Shivani Saxena (Lucknow, India) and Jan Swier
© 2019 Jan Swier, all rights reserved
Publisher: Jan Swier.
Website: janswier.com
POD publishers: Ingram Spark (figures in color) and KDP Amazon (entirely in black & white)

Cover design: Peter Swier
Illustrations: all by Jan Swier with the exception of the SAM circle (ProRail), the nautilus shell (pixabay, 3dman_eu), OCCR (Wikipedia) and the Leonardo da Vinci Vitruviusman (Wikimedia)

ISBN: 9789083015415

Keywords: Asset Management, ProRail, Organization, Performance, Cost, Risk, Outsourcing

Index

Preface

This book is about the development of an asset management system at the Infra Manager ProRail. The organisation evolved from a radical reform of the rail sector in the Netherlands. It put an end to rapidly increasing losses of the Netherlands Railways. In order to relieve the Netherlands Railways (NS) of the infrastructure development and maintenance responsibilities, rail infrastructure was split off and made independent, with the government taking over the financing responsibility of development, maintenance and renewal needs. In addition, competition was introduced for rail transport service on lines, train operators had to pay for the use of the infra and all executive infrastructure activities were privatised. Within a four-year period, the infrastructure organisation shrank from 4000 seated employees to 800. In this period, the train continued to run but service was less reliable due to an increase in the number of failures of train operation and rail infrastructure. This was a price paid for the radical reform of a monopolistic, internal-oriented railway company with technical focus. The reform produced administrative chaos for a certain period of time, bringing in uncertainty, confusion, sub optimisation, conflicts and emotional turmoil among people and organizations. However, slowly and surely, it gave way to a new order, stability and collaborative corporate culture. After about ten years, performance returned to the level before the separation and privatisation of service provider activities; thereafter, it started getting better.

I have experienced the reforms and consequences of change from the beginning and in close proximity. In 1975, I started as a steel bridge engineer at NS's engineering office. It was an aging organisation that needed rejuvenation. There were no managers but bosses, engineers designed on a drawing boards and they made their calculations with the help of a slide-rule or a pocket calculator. Cultures clashed regularly. The young guard wanted to produce and create, while the old colleagues slowed down.

After five years, I made the switch to bridge maintenance. Something attracted me there, but I did not exactly know what it was. I followed my heart and never regretted it because I got opportunity to develop my skills and had colleagues and chefs who were dependable and stimulating. In 1989, I was selected with two other NS colleagues, to take part in the McKinsey & Company study for developing a new organisational structure of NS. It was an enriching experience to formulate strategy with premiere consultants for six months. I learned a lot and it took a while to find my way again after I returned. I became a staff manager and got involved in all the changes that occurred in the years to come. These included privatisation of the engineering agency, separation of train operations and infrastructure, and outsourcing of maintenance. The infrastructure organisation had to be built from the ground. At my request, I was appointed consultant and project manager in the field of maintenance and renewal, which is now called asset management. I worked on the development of the organisation and new tools, and thereafter was selected as the Dutch representative in the UIC benchmark study, known as the Lasting Infrastructure Cost Benchmark (LICB). In this role, I learned about costs, cost differences and cost drivers. I have good memories of the inspirational meetings and discussions, especially with Heiner Bente (BSL, now Civity) and Oskar Stalder (SBB). Our company visits to Hong Kong, Japan and the United States are unforgettable because they were instrumental in development of my understanding of asset management and its need.

CEO Bert Klerk and first Director Asset Management Anthonie Bauer, the founders of ProRail and the current asset management system, gave me the opportunity and confidence to apply my knowledge and experience in this area. Our bilateral communication was always open, constructive and, in my memory, enjoyable. Both of these people have encouraged me to share my experiences at congresses, in international workgroups and with other infra managers. This book about this is mainly due to stimulating talks with Bart Smolders and Paulien Herder, a former director of ProRail Asset Management and a professor at the university of Delft. By the end of 2010, I started writing a dissertation at TU Delft guided by Paulien. Due to illness, progress stalled. After my recovery, Paulien suggested that I write a book and not the dissertation. I followed that advice and soon writing began to flow abundantly with scientific approach no longer limiting a man of practice.

When the first draft of the book was completed, I asked colleagues to read and comment on the text with suggestions for improvement and additions. They immediately agreed without exception. I am grateful to the reviews of Rolf Post, Piet van der Hoorn, Hans Gosliga, Ronald van Meren, Anton Lamper, Johan Schouten, Marjolein van Breukelen, Martijn van Noort, Ted Luiten, Anthonie Bauer, Mark Beuk, Raymond Geurts by Kessel, Peter Booij, Paul Cartsens and Klaas Hofstra. I remember our plenary sessions and bilateral talks with great pleasure. It was rethinking and reflection which we all found helpful and pleasant. For me, it was not only inspiring and stimulating, but also necessary to understand the view of the reader and structure the content of the book. Part of it was confrontational but it led to adjustments and improvements. The final product is developed with the support of many comrades but I bear full responsibility for it.

It is my privilege to have worked for more than forty years in the rail sector; in many different organisations and functions, in very different places. The rail sector is socially relevant with dedicated and skilled colleagues and service providers who stand for their work. The circumstances and organisation are complex, developments are often slow, but always move forward in a constructive atmosphere. At the core, it is not about power and ego but about the business and people, connection and cooperation, and the development of individual qualities, which cannot be cherished and appreciated enough.

I cannot complete the book without gratitude for my family: my wife, Adri, and children Babs, Irene, Paul, Peter and Boudewijn. They have made me experience what really matters in life. It, therefore, means a lot to me that the cover of this book is designed by one of my children.

Jan Swier
Leusden, August 2017

Extension of the English version of the preface
This English translation would never have been possible without the help of Shivani Saxena from India. We got to know each other mid-2018; Shivani contacted me by email. She was looking for someone who could guide her in developing her knowledge about asset management (AM) and she asked if I wanted to help her. I sent her some information, including a few sections from my book that I translated. That eventually led to the agreement that, if I would translate the book completely into English, she would improve the draft translation manuscript. Through this exchange, she learned wisely what AM is about and I got translation suitable for publishing, with the commitment that I will continue to help her develop her AM knowledge. A win-win situation based on mutual trust. A stimulating cooperation that bridges gaps of culture, distance, age, race and gender. A great experience with a great outcome.

Leusden, July 2019

Introduction and structure book

Trains run on rail infrastructure, a means of production that makes rail transport possible and costs a lot of money. From the beginning of the railways, the rail infrastructure was a heavy financial burden for all the railway companies in the beginning. Scaling up by mergers and acquisitions was the answer and resulted in the formation of one national railway company: the Netherland Railways (NS). Due to the competition of road transport and unprecedented economic growth, costs increased faster than revenues. Only a government subsidy could save the railway company from bankruptcy. In order to make NS a healthy commercial transport company, the rail infrastructure was split off and housed in an independent company, the current ProRail, funded by the government. In order to be a business operating infrastructure manager, all executive engineering-, contractor- and supplier activities were privatized. The infra structure organization had to be built from the ground a skill now known as asset management. This book is about the development of the asset management system at ProRail. Not based on the implementation of a standard, but a practice case that shows how a well-functioning asset management system has evolved in an organic way driven by the circumstances, technological capabilities and a focus on controlling the process, performance, risks and cost, and stimulate continuous improvement.

The concept of asset management, often abbreviated as AM, was used for the first time in 2002 at NS Railinfrabeheer, the organization from where ProRail has emerged. The following was stated in a policy memorandum: *'Even though Railinfrabeheer already manages its assets, it is not yet professional. This means that the management of assets, the objects, lacks the tools needed for this, which also does not develop the culture aspect associated with asset management'.* The policy note stated that asset management is not just about improving care for the existing assets but also, in particular, to optimize their costs and performance throughout the whole life cycle. This requires all business- and chain partners, which imposes high demands on the administrative- and organizational skills of the infrastructure manager. It is a complex change process that affects the entire sector. The timing of milestones, keeping up the cohesion and choosing the right speed of change are crucial. It sets high demands on leadership. ProRail's development shows that asset management is not implemented so much, but it is more or less an organic growth on the basis of very small cohesive changes under the influence of changing circumstances, demands and opportunities. It affects the organizational preconditions of all involved organizations; the structure, tools, strategy, people, leadership and culture, in short, everything needed to make an organization work well.

The book describes the growth stages that the organization has gone through, what was needed and what the cohesion is. It describes the transformation of a traditional, technically oriented, task-based and internally-managed maintenance organization into a professional operating, external, process and result-oriented infrastructure manager, together with chain partners, and provides insight into the following themes:

- the influence of the governance model on the AM system;
- the organic way in which the AM system develops;
- the development begins with making *"house in order"* of the maintenance & renewal organization;
- what core skills are needed to achieve results;
- what core qualities are needed to manage the processes optimally;
- why the safeguarding and sharing of knowledge and information is key;
- that man is the measure, the journey is the goal and good leadership crucial.

The structure of the book is derived from the asset management model that Pro-Rail used since 2005 and is depicted in Figure 1. It describes the essence of asset management. It shows that the costs and performance of infrastructure are managed optimally and sustainably by controlling risks with activities which cost money and the amount of money depends on the work- and system conditions, and the quality of the organizations involved. The results achieved depend of the social, economic and political circumstances in which the organization operates. They are almost always the explanations for differences in performance between infrastructure managers in, for example, former Western or Eastern Europe, the United States and Japan.

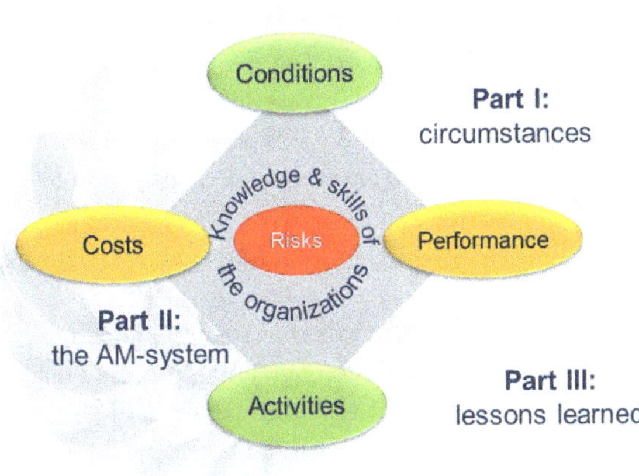

Figure 1   *The main structure of the book plotted in an AM-model developed by the author*

The figure shows that the book is made up of three parts: the conditions (part I), the AM system (part II) and the lessons learned (part III).

The first part describes the developments of the circumstances, the role distribution and organization. These were very important conditions for the way the AM system developed. Four developments have been analysed in just as many chapters in Part I:

1. ***The development of roles and relationships in rail transport.*** After more than 150 years, Transport and Infrastructure has been split, ProRail became an independent infrastructure manager and the government got an influential role in the Dutch Railways Administration.
2. ***Development of one business model for rail transport.*** By cutting up rail transport in multiple roles and companies, there is no longer one organization that optimizes its rail transport costs and performance. Therefore, a business model has been developed that provides insight into the correlation between usage, revenue and costs of transport and infrastructure, and what are the higher goals that connects both.
3. ***Development of the infrastructure organization.*** It consists of several business units operating in different life cycle phases and value chains. They determine together the quality of the AM system.
4. ***Development of outsourcing of maintenance.*** The outsourcing of maintenance has greatly influenced the development and organization of the AM system.

The second part describes the AM system that manages costs and performance explicitly and in coherence and it gives a detailed insight in how the system has evolved. This section describes all relevant aspects: models, systems, organization, control, performances, costs, activities, conditions and realized results.

The third part concludes with a reflection on the development of the asset management system and a future forecast. It is a summary in the lessons learned and an outlook for developments that will be possible and will affect the further development of rail infrastructure and asset management system.

The book concludes with a part with explanations and background information. It starts with the annexes referred to in the text.
Then an index is included with keywords that together with the book index discloses the content of the book in a systematic and structured way.
After the keyword register there is an alphabetical list with all abbreviations used in Dutch and then the translation in English between brackets.
The book concludes with an overview of the cited sources referred to in the text. The internal sources are marked with an asterisk at the year. They are collected in a file folder on ProRail's network, so they are not accessible for readers outside.

The book describes the past, present and future of rail asset management at ProRail. That knowledge and experience, combined with asset management guidelines and standards such as the PAS 55, ISO 55000 and EN50126, can inspire other organizations to start the growth of an asset management in an organic way. The book is not one continuous story. It is modularly built. Each chapter and each (sub) section deals with an issue that forms a part of the asset management system. In order to read the sections and chapters separately, the context is often briefly described which has already been described in detail before. Therefore there are doubles in the text of the book, but so it is consciously chosen.

The book is written for those who want to know more about asset management, what is needed, how it develops and where to start. It is intended for people who work in the asset management sector, not only the rail but also other means of production, and not only in the Netherlands but also abroad. The book is of special interest for education and research, not only from a technical or business perspective but also from a transformational perspective.

First part

The development of the circumstances and organisation of ProRail

Discover your strategy

The Danish philosopher Søren Kierkegaard said, "Life is lived forward, but understood backwards." In other words, we only know what we are doing after we have done it. Therefore, it is advisable for companies to take a break occasionally and discover the pattern in their operations. Often, this keeps track of the strategy that has been adopted. The role of a manager is to strengthen what's functioning well. Sometimes leadership is just following the facts (Starren, 2016, p. #12).

Part I: CIRCUMSTANCES and ORGANISATION

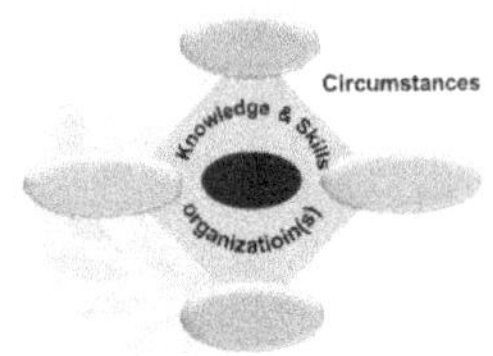

The circumstances affect development of the organisation and functioning of an infrastructure manager. This first part describes four developments that have determined the circumstances under which asset management developed within ProRail. It begins with the development of roles and relationships in rail transport which have been decisive in the development of ProRail and the role of government in rail transport.

1 Rail transport and government

In the Netherlands, train service started in 1839. Transport service and rail infrastructure were inseparable but, in 1995, they were split. After that, the professionalisation of the management and maintenance of rail infrastructure began and transformed into what is now called asset management. All these changes are not independent but are the result of changing circumstances in organisation, economy, politics and technology, each of which vary from country to country.

To understand the how and why of the development of AM system in the Netherlands, it is necessary to return to the history of rail transport. This chapter describes the history from the opening of the first railway line. At that time, there was already tension between rail transport, rail infrastructure and the government, a tension related to the mix of public- and private interests and money. This tension increased after the Second World War because rail transport costs rose faster than revenues due to strong growth in road transport, competition and prosperity. The direct and structural interference of the government with the financing and management of rail transport was inevitable as was the split between transport and infrastructure.

Let's start at the beginning: the development of the railways in the Netherlands. This is described in the following section briefly and in more detail in the book '*De Spoorwegen in Nederland*' by Guus Veenendaal (Veenendaal, 2004) on the railways in the Netherlands or the book '*Het spoor*' by Faber on the completion of 150-year existence of the railways in the Netherlands (Faber, 1989). The book '*Geschiedenis der Nederlandsche Spoorwegen 1832-1938*' (Jonckers Nieboer, 1938) describes the history of Netherlands Railways in the period 1832-1938; causes of entry and exit of railway companies; influence of the government; as well as facts and figures about the size, utilisation, costs and revenue of the network.

1.1 The development of rail transport in the Netherlands

The Netherlands is a country with a lot of water, rivers and canals. Water transport was the most important form of public transport for a long time. The pull boat was a unique phenomenon in Europe and famous for its reliability and comfort. It was in use since the seventeenth century and provided frequent service between cities. An Englishman who travelled through Holland wrote: *'Her draws one horse as much freight in one boat as else fifty horses on their carts.'*

Public transport by road was ensured horses and stagecoach before the rise of the railways. For a long time, the quality of surface transport lagged that of successful water transportation system because the former was slower, more expensive, simpler, fragmented and uncomfortable. Until the arrival of the Batavian Republic in 1795, there were almost no paved roads in the country. This began to change when the French secured influence over the country in the period 1795-1813, and even ruled it for some time. During the French period, centralised government was introduced for uniform administration of justice, currency, measures, weights and taxation. This ended old regional provisions that had frustrated interregional freight transport. After the departure of the French, development of a robust road network started to connect provinces and cities. The construction was delayed because of high cost of Belgium's separation in 1830 but was completed in early 1840. This substantially increased the speed, comfort and capacity of road transport with horses. On some routes, road transport even became a competitor of water transport. However, the arrival of the steam train brought about a bigger transformation.

Phase 1832-1860: private initiative

The rise of the railways is a direct consequence of the industrial revolution. The first steam train ran in England in 1804 and the first railway line was opened in the Netherlands in 1839 between Amsterdam and Haarlem, a distance of about 18 km.

The construction and exploitation of railways in the Netherlands was very slow because the government completely left it to the private sector functioning within the limits of concessions. The private sector was not prepared to bear the financial risk of construction and operation. In the Netherlands, the government did not offer any support, certainty or cooperation, even though, in other countries, it was the driving force for rapid growth. As noted by Jonckers Nieboer: *"What was done was making plans, corresponding, debating, criticizing; almost nothing came about."* For example, in 1841, an expropriation act was issued, which did not provide sufficient assistance to unwilling landowners, and concession conditions were changed during implementation, which led to additional costs for private companies.

In the first railway law of 1859, the government's position was not properly regulated. According to Jonckers Nieboer, the law was almost exclusively intended as a police act and gave insufficient power to the state vis-à-vis the railway companies even though there was need for it. The government interfered with safety and finance for construction but left operations entirely to private companies.

Phase 1860-1890: state construction and unhealthy competition

Until 1860, no more than 350 kilometers of railway lines were build. However, it became increasingly clear to the government that national economies in neighbouring countries were stimulated by the construction of railways. Therefore, in public interest, it decided in 1860 to fund building of ten main railway lines. Jonckers Nieboer quotes: *"The government believed that, taking into account the generally existing conviction of the necessity of railways, the so far unsuccessful attempts to obtain this through concessions already sufficiently justified the principle of State railways. In addition, the advantages of this would be: multiple integrity and safety, less costly and speedy implementation."*

After years of wait and discussion, the government decided to establish a nationwide rail network based on the following principles: construction by government, operation through concessions by private companies and competition on railway lines. P.J. Groote of the University of Groningen states that *"The paradox of Dutch railway history: construction and exploitation were in principle the responsibility of private companies, but by far the largest part of the network was built by the government."* Two main lines were added in 1873 and another eight in 1875. Around 1890, the railway lines had length of about 2,650 kilometres and formed the main network structure of present time. Figure 2 illustrates the development.

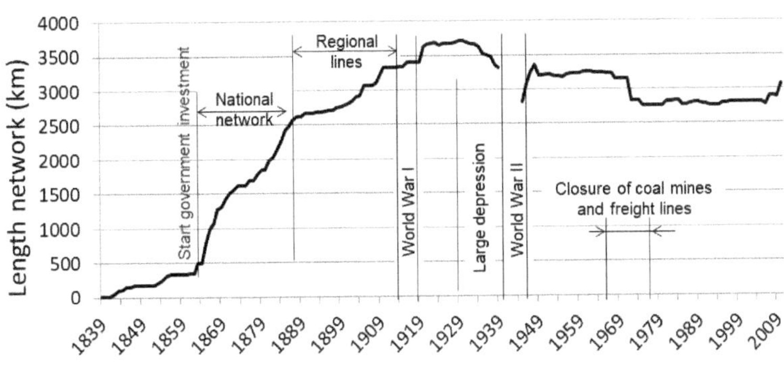

Figure 2   Development of the Dutch rail network (1839-2013).
Sources: (Jonckers Nieboer, 1938) (Veenendaal, 2004) (CBS, 2001) and annual reports.

The concession terms of 1863 assumed that capital investment by the government could be recovered from a (substantial) share of gross income after deduction of a fixed percentage for operations and payment for renewal fund and extraordinary repairs. However, the conditions proved to be very unfavourable for the operator: when the gross income increased, government benefits grew faster than the operator's income because of rising operating costs. As a consequence, despite growth in income, the operator could not pay dividend. The concession conditions were modified in 1876 such that the government shared operator profit less in quantity and frequency.

In 1875, a law was adopted which gave government more power over the railways but was still insufficient. The interference with or management of operations and the initiative for new regulations remained beyond government's control. The government could participate in operations, but only as a competitor. As a result, traffic interests were not properly managed and the rail network was built piece by piece, often based on political considerations instead of planned coordinated national network. In a speech in the Lower House on December 5, 1874, Mr van Naamen of Eemnes states, *"One of the characteristics of successive governments for almost 40 years with regard to the railways was that they did not have a good understanding of the railways and much less had a fixed system for the roads that were generally needed. The consequence of this has been that we, either in terms of operation or in relation to lines, have a desired whole, or in operation or consistency of the lines, and that the railways have cost the State much more than would have been necessary, without achieving the desired outcomes "*.

That situation was troubled for a long time as noted in an article by J.P. Bordes in the Economist of June 1890: *"Our rail system is spoiled, partly because the State has built railways that are out of use and some of which are competitors of their own lines, but companies have stimulated this approach because they agreed to operate at each other's area. Wasting money and forces is the consequence and it is inevitable disadvantageous to the economic situation of our country."*

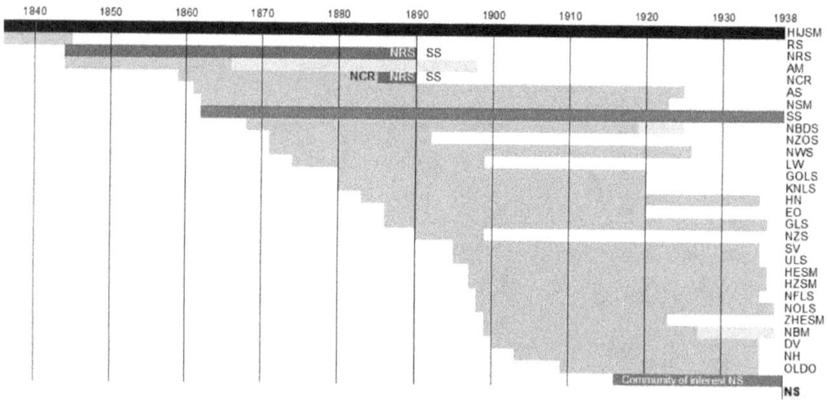

Figure 3   Rise and fall of railway companies.
Sources: (Jonckers Nieboer, 1938) (Graaf, 2006-12)

Many railway companies, including three big and many small private companies, were active over a period of about 100 years as illustrated in Figure 3 (Swier J. ,

2016-2*). However, cooperation and coordination was impossible because of general situation described as follows: *"A war of all against all, with as a consequence destruction and damage, capital destruction, disturbance in the regular development of traffic, sacrifice of public interest to the often changing insights from these or other warring parties, wasting money on a large scale".* Rail companies also speak of *'unhealthy competition'*, *'hopeless confusion'* and *'abuse of power to manipulate each other's destruction'*.

Between 1839 and 1890, two main deficiencies grew in the rail transport system. These included fragmentation of the operations of lines and unhealthy competition. In 1890, the government decided to disband the 'Nederlandsche Rhijn Spoorwegmaatschappij' (NRS) and divide their main lines between 'Staats Spoorwegen' (SS) and 'Hollandsche IJzeren Spoorweg Maatschappij' (HIJSM or HSM). The conditions were as similar as possible and operations were based on competition and consolidation with broad application and common use of lines, stations and transhipment facilities.

Phase 1890-1914: awareness about disadvantages of competition

After lifting of the NRS, it was evident that restructuring did not give the desired improvement. Prof. M. M.W.F. Treub published the following objections in 1898:

- Competition is artificial, unhealthy and leads to grumpy discussions.
- The position of the country vis-à-vis other countries has weakened.
- Competition exists partially and is even absent in the north and south.
- Competition on lines is uneconomical and doubles operating cost.
- The companies themselves determine the profit payed to the state.
- The companies themselves determine amortisation of assets and trains.
- Lines that yield insufficient profits are transferred to the state.

The conclusion drawn by Treub was as follows: *"The 1890 Railroad Agreement was concluded by the Government, with an unauthorized borderless lightness and lack of business knowledge. In doing so, nothing was done to overcome or reduce the disadvantages of private railroad exploitation".* Not everyone in the Lower House agreed with him; however, in 1908, a state committee was established to investigate whether and how policy should be changed. The committee provided important financial data and insights in its conclusions in 1911 but did not provide a specific reorganisation plan. The conclusions were as follows:

- Overall, the system has been conducive to traffic.
- Operating expenses are too high compared to gross revenues.
- Operating coefficient[1] is not expected to improve.
- The state has lost NLG 45 million on track capital over a period of eighteen years.

---

[1] Relationship between business expenses and business income.

- There is a risk that companies may no longer bear costs for operations and development of rail traffic.

From the beginning of the railways, market organisation received attention and concern. In Europe, there was vast difference in markets. In England, competition was on track, while in Germany, rail transport was a state affair. In the Netherlands there was uncertainty for a long time until 1890 when it was decided to opt for competition on lines, so according to the English model. This competition lead to rigidity which made the system inadequate in fulfilling wishes of the traveller and meeting the increasing demand for transport services.

Due to the low transport tariffs and (relatively) high train frequencies, the companies did not earn enough to do the necessary depreciation and the State did not take care of it. On the contrary, government tax revenue rose from railways, chamber debates and motions increased, but policy remained unchanged. It was a positive development that majority of the state committee members recommended consolidation, i.e., private operations by one railway company. Partly due to the outbreak of the First World War, the merger of the two largest competitors (HSM and SS) was delayed, but politics were ready for it.

Phase 1914-1921: Community of Interests
The outbreak of the First World War led to an accelerated change of political views and stimulated sustainable cooperation between HSM and SS. The railways gained strategic (military) significance and focus changed from commercial to national throughout Europe. At the end of July 1914, the government claimed use of railways and equipment for defence and awarded the highest authority over railways to the military authority. The operations were left to the companies themselves as much as possible. Initially the government funded the operations but at the end of 1914 was chosen for a compensation schema and all parties was satisfied with this. The three operating companies were guaranteed profit on the shares held by the government, and the 'Noord-Brabant-Duitsche-Spoorweg-Maatschappij' (NBDS) a coverage of the fixed costs. This scheme continued until January 1, 1920.

In 1916, the main operators, SS and HSM, formed a community taking the first step towards a merger. In 1911, it had already started by aligning the most important passenger tariffs, which significantly reduced competition. The passenger had benefited from competition but now the price was too high. The companies could not bear the financial costs and their survival was at risk.

In the first few years, the collaboration between SS and HSM was not smooth because culture of both companies was very different: the HSM system was rigid and the SS system was flexible. This provoked opposition and impacted service delivery leading to major delays and disruption of the timetable in 1920. The government appointed a commission but the chaos disappeared just as rapidly as they had arisen. By early 1921, all trains were running on time, and slowly but certainly, staff of both companies learned to appreciate each other. Because the prices of coal and raw materials increased during the war, the transport service was reduced and the tariffs increased. Bus transport also grew and there were radical reforms in labour legislation (known as: RDV 1920) including introduction of shorter working hours and higher rewards. As a result, revenues decreased and operating expenses increased. The capital cost for bond loans soared, as did the interest rates. The government and distressed rail companies became increasingly interlinked financially but the policymakers were not ready for a merger.

The merger gained prominence when the government's claim on rail transport ended on January 1, 1920. The businesses had to function on their own but needed state aid because operating expenses had increased more than income. The solution was found in 1920 by a statute amendment to the agreement among the government, SS and HSM, with government becoming a majority shareholder. The scheme was weak because the company's balance sheet had not been cleaned up and the government soon had to bear the financial consequences of this by the unstoppable rise of a competitor: the car.

The automobile first appeared at the end of the nineteenth century and by 1920s, it gained importance over horse-drawn cars, and later reduced market share of rail transport. The downside of this success was that the neglected, old and narrow roads could not cope with the growth. The road law adopted in 1926 obliged the state and provinces to align their plans as well as bear construction and maintenance costs through road user tax. While passenger transport was regulated, freight transport was unregulated and benefited from competition and inherent flexibility of road transport. Road transport for freight grew faster than rail transport. Even in the great depression, growth of road traffic did not stop and negatively impacted rail- and water transport.

Phase 1921-1938: Operations with state guarantee
In the years after World War I, rail transport was in trouble. In 1921, the loss was NLG 33.1 million on revenue of NLG 194.2 million. The deficit was covered by the state because of the guaranteed dividend. However, it became difficult when the economic crisis hit in 1921. There was increasing competition from automobiles and extension of the telephone network reduced need to travel.

Demand for freight and passenger transport declined further, which also caused income to fall, which led to measures to control costs. The remedial measures that were implemented included reduction in wages, partially lifting of guarded level crossings, postponement of project, closing of stations, modernising of trains and mechanisation of administration. As a consequence, expenditure and revenues were in balance by 1924 and government support was no longer needed.

A tariff reduction in 1926 stimulated the use in such a way that there was again growth in revenues, but shortly after this revival, things got worse again.

The government understood that rail company had to be strengthened. Rail transport was declining due to competition from the automobile, increase in depreciation backlog and inadequate payment from the government for transport services availed. With the new measures, there was no loss and costs of debt and depreciation could be sustained. However, the structural financial problems remained and, in 1928, an agreement was undertaken to clear debt position. This approach was limited and the backlog in depreciation continued to grow in the long term, especially with the rise of alternatives for steam engines. In 1929, the trend of falling revenue and rising loss restarted. In the period 1920-1938, revenue fell by about 50% even though costs had reduced by about 40%. Despite significant cost cuts, loss of about 23% was recorded in 1938 on an income of NLG 100.9 million.

To enable financial clean-up, a milestone law was adopted in 1934 that expanded rights of nationalisation. The construction costs no longer had to be refunded to the investor but could be reimbursed as capitalised net income of the railway line. As a consequence, eleven unprofitable local rail- and tram-lines were closed after settlement with the investors in 1934. Although this strategy was an effective means of improving the financial results, it caused massive capital destruction.

The consequences of the economic crisis were transient but the competition with automobile increased. The railways were hard to get used to the competition from car transport and the new market conditions that resulted from it. Not completely incomprehensible. The railways lost monopoly on fast transport and witnessed virtually unlimited competition from a large number of private companies that were not as regulated and needed little start-up capital. The railways had to fulfil transport- and operating obligation with rules and tariff arrangements, while road transport had a privileged position of choosing the most cost-effective transport business. There was anarchy and no fair competition. The government contributed to the malaise of rail transport by adhering to the mirage of an independent and self-supporting railway sector, and not launching a traffic vision. Car traffic was not regulated for a long time and the government continued to build unprofitable railways, roads and canals that often also competed with each other. As per the 1935 NS Annual Report: *"The state pays the new channels now twice: first in interest and repayment of construction costs and in maintenance and operation of the channels, and second in higher railway shortages."*

Something had to happen. The government launched a traffic policy in 1930s to align all modes of transport, induce fair competition and regulate behaviour. In 1937, the law 'Regelement Autovervoer Personen' (English: 'Regulation Car Transport Passengers) was adopted with a licensing system for taxis and buses. However, the freight cars remained in a privileged position and vagueness in the law led to 'wild' buses operating without permission and control. This led to adoption of the law 'Autovervoer Personen' (English: Car Transport Passengers) in 1939. A reorganisation of the railway company was now inevitable and timing was appropriate for merger of HSM and SS into a single company. On June 8, 1937, a bill was submitted to the Lower Chamber with measures to adopt a new and business-oriented solution by restructuring debt and securing settlement of harmful and loss-making contracts from the past. As a result, debt was restructured in 1937. Of the total railway debt of more than NLG 411 million, approximately NLG 235 million of depreciation backlog was cancelled, shares were exchanged for government bonds and remaining debts for construction of railways were cancelled.

On August 2, 1938, a notarial document was signed and on January 1, 1938, the HSM and SS were liquidated. Jonckers Nieboer writes: *"By the merger of companies into a body, the factual unity, which existed since the 1917, was confirmed by legal unity; the state is the only financially interested and governs the new Ltd fully. The company has become a state-owned company, although it is not a train exploitation by the state. The new Ltd will be in essence not different from a government administration, which is in the form of a Ltd for historical, commercial and other reasons."* Overall, restructuring of the balance sheet and establishment of the 'Nederlandse Spoorwegen' (NS) was an important step and start of further reorganisations for better alignment and coordination of traffic in the country. Finally, there was an end to cost reductions, indecision, organisational chaos and financial uncertainty.

Phase 1938-1969: stabilisation, recovery and financial dependency

The financial reorganisation enabled functioning of NS as an independent organisation. The NS centralised financial return but was entirely dependent on the government, which was now the concessionaire, legislator, law enforcement officer, and owner.

After May 1940, NS was no longer governed by the Dutch government but had the German occupier control of the company. The NS management opted for cooperation with the occupier, ie collaboration, in order to keep control over the company, which was hardly the case in practice. The scarcity in wartime made many people dependent on the train. This led to record number of passenger kilometres in 1943 realised with fewer train kilometres because of equipment scarcity. Just two years later, transport service collapsed because of bombardment, sabotage and a major railway strike. The strike had started after a call from the government in London and lasted from September 1944 to May 1945. During that period, many staff members hid themselves and there was no train service in most parts of the country

The war caused major damage to the rail network. The cost, estimated at NLG 708 million, was reimbursed 50% by the Dutch government and covered through final settlement of claims and debt restructuring in 1951. After a temporary recovery, the railway network became mostly normal in 1948 and, thanks to an urgent programme, fully restored in 1953. Hard work, economical lifestyle, better connectivity and increase in international trade led to economic prosperity and greater need for transport. In the 1960s, the economic growth was so strong that even foreign workers were attracted to the country. The price index rose sharply. Two oil crises, in 1973 and 1979, hardly caused any impact and the stock crash in 1987 was only a short-term interruption. The overall mobility increased rapidly with economic growth. Soon after the Second World War, there was tremendous growth in automobiles. In the period 1960-1980, the number increased from 0.7 million to 4.5 million, and in 2010, it reached 8.7 million, see Figure 4.

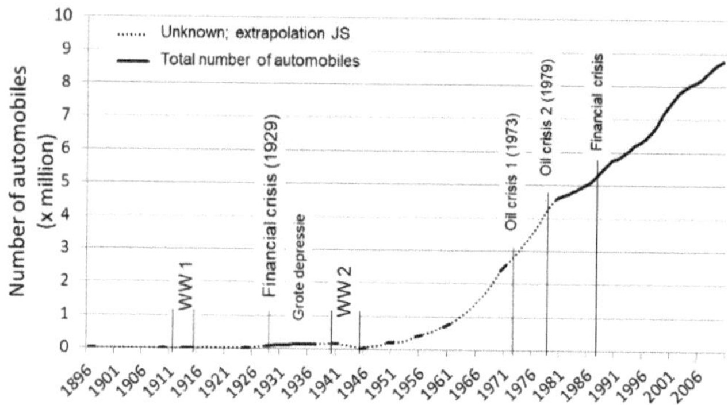

Figure 4   Development of road transport. Sources: (Jongma, 1992), (CBS, 2001)

The growth curve of the car park is similar to that of post-war economic growth and price index. There was only a slight decline after the second oil crisis in 1979 but growth resumed. Rail transport grew but less rapidly than road transport, see Figure 5.

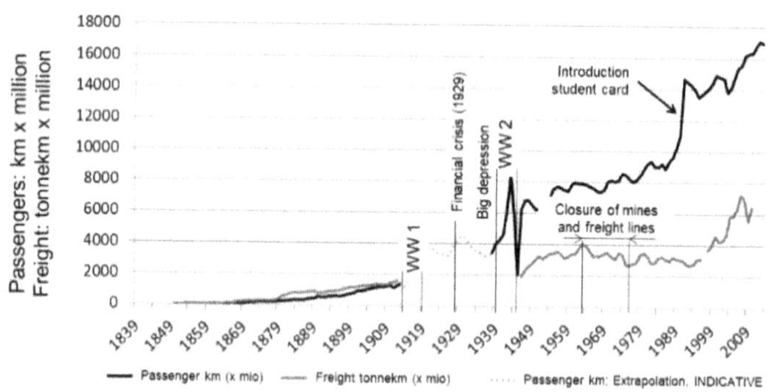

Figure 5   Development rail transport. Sources: Annual reports and (CBS, 2001)

In World War II, rail ridership peaked because of fuel scarcity but then stopped suddenly due to war operations. The recovery after war was used to substantially modernise railways as well as supply new security system, large-scale electrification, equipment for higher speeds, etc. The growth of rail transport not only slowed because of rise of automobiles but also because the Dutch economy switched from coal to gas in the late 1960s. With loss of coal transport business, decline in freight transport market share because of road transport competition and sharp rise in labour costs, the NS struggled to make a reasonable profit. Figure 6 illustrates the timeline of these developments.

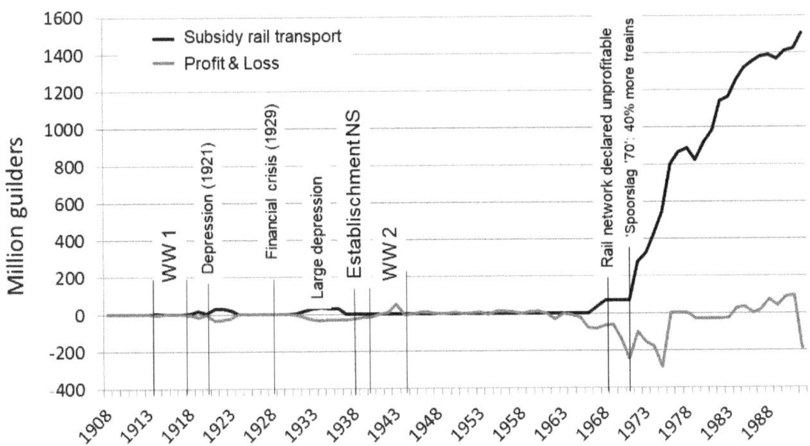

Figure 6   Development in rail transport of profit and loss.
Sources: (Faber, 1989), (Jonckers Nieboer, 1938)

The result of post-war attention was slightly positive though profits were not made by the transport company but by its subsidiaries. The situation was worse because there was a growing wage lag[2] and investment in expansion was no longer affordable. In 1967, NS proposed to close fifteen unprofitable lines unless the government provided subsidy to keep them open. Choices had to be made. In addition, the government received support of the EU Directive 1191/69 (EU, 1969-6*), which required national governments to compensate the losses of public passenger transport. In 1969, NS reported the entire passenger transport unprofitable and the government accepted the consequences thereof by structurally supplementing deficits. It was a fundamental change in the relationship between government and NS. For the first time, it was debatable that the government compensate the transport company for difference in infrastructure costs between rail, road and water transport. Road and waterways were already paid for by the government but railways was not.

---

[2] For example, wages in the metal industry were about 25% higher at the time.

Freight transport was also addressed. An accounting separation in 1969 illustrated that freight transport was also facing losses. NS decided to close many loading and unloading locations in 1969 because freight business was labour intensive and structurally loss-making. As per an observation, *"In 1969, the NS estimated that in this sector, 1.75 guilders were at a cost to each guilder."* (Veenendaal, 2004, p. 512). The focus was wagon transport, especially of containers. The entire freight sector shrunk with closing of marshalling yards and reduction of staff. The subsidiary 'Gend & Loos' was extensively cleaned up and sold in 1986.

These measures returned profit at NS Freight Transport in 1985 but soon, in 1988, losses grew again. Profit recovery remained an ongoing concern. The freight company proved too small to survive independently and was sold in 2000 to Railion, a company formed by the merger of DB Cargo and NS Cargo. The freight market grew again, as indicated in Figure 5, and Railion expanded in Europe through mergers and acquisitions. The parent company, Deutsche Bahn, rebranded the company as DB Schenker Rail in 2009.

Phase 1969-1990: revaluation and investment

To give a new impetus to rail transport, NS launched a new long-term vision 'Spoor naar 75' (English: 'Track to 75') and accompanying action programme 'Spoorslag 70' (English: 'Track stroke 70') in 1969. The plan put rail transport back on the political agenda. There were more trains in service and a new corporate identity was introduced. This attracted passengers and increased ridership. However, costs increased rapidly with economic growth. Road transport was threatened by traffic jams and parking problems, and the social utility of rail transport was recognised. In order to improve rail transport, the government decided, in the end of eighties, to invest heavily in rail transport. The NS presented future vision 'Rail 21' in June 1988 for long-term development up to 2015.

The former NS president, L. Ploeger, called it a *'God send'* solution for the growing and seemingly insoluble traffic problem. He understood well that the government, and not NS, decides about rail transport policy because the government was financing rail infrastructure and "who pays decides". This principle is stated in the book published on the occasion of Ploeger's farewell (Beckum, 1992): *"When the plan (Rail 21) was on the table, it was said, that should be in the strategy. I said no, it should not be in our strategy at all. That is not in our hand. We need to get along with other political circuits, such as Spatial Planning and Transport & Water Management, until we have so much political support that it gets a certain reality value. Only then you can put it in our planning for a reasonable period of time and follow it also strategically."* In another quote *"And then there was a piece of a solution for the traffic issue. If we had done it a few years earlier, the surrounding would not be ready for it. Then it was swept away as a nice brainwave. Such requires political support, a certain political maturity. And then the timing, the moment you come up with this kind of thing, is extremely important."* It is an example of good leadership.

The 'Rail 21' vision translated a social analysis into a new timetable model: two trains per hour for the Euro-/Intercity network between the five major cities in the Netherlands and European capital cities, the Inter-region network between fifty-six major intercity stations and the Agglo/Region network for regional and urban transport. It required infrastructure investment, mainly for improvements to and extensions of the existing rail network. The cost was estimated at NLG 9 - 10 billion over a period of approximately 25 years. Due to disappointments and changing circumstances, the plan was discontinued in 1997. However, in around 1990, it motivated many people to work hard for improving the capacity and quality of transport service and infrastructure.

Due to major investments in Rail21 and the anticipated increase in transport, the board of NS started to realise that changes were needed in the organisation of rail infrastructure management, which was too fragmented and lacked capacity to realise the goals. In 1989, the consulting firm McKinsey & Company recommended a new organisation structure of the Infra Process based on the following adjustments:

- Combining disparate operating maintenance and renewal departments;
- Separating all engineering agency activities;
- Vigorously decentralising the maintenance & renewal process.

The reorganisation in 1990 resulted in development of a single infrastructure organisation such that it was independent within the NS organisation and maintenance management was decentralised. This was the beginning of a major change in the country's rail transport industry. The separation of transport and infrastructure created an institutional triangle in which the government had a role in rail transport management.

Reflection

Socio-economic changes have a major influence on the development of railways. When we consider the rise of and competition caused by road transport and telephone, economic crises, closure of coal mines, welfare growth and traffic jams, we observe that rail infrastructure has always been expensive for railway companies.

The government paid off the national network investment and railway companies did not earn enough to cover the necessary depreciation cost for renewals. The government became more involved in the administration of railways because of growing financial interest. This influence was not always constructive and regularly caused half-hearted, political wrangling with slow and sometimes counterproductive decision-making. The involvement and influence of the government were inevitable because the government had secured a role in the governance of the railways. Annexure 14.1.1 provides a coherent overview of the influences and consequences that led to the separation of transport and infra and the emergence of an administrative institutional triangle in which the government has a role. The following chapter describes development of the triangle and is concludes with an analysis of the causes and consequences.

1.2   The institutional triangle

Reason for the separation; the origin of the institutional triangle

The interaction and tension between the railways and government results from combination of public and private interests. The government wants affordable public rail transport, but the size and price of transport are insufficient to cover all costs.

Until the Second World War, it was possible to complete bookkeeping with creativity but after the war, this was not possible anymore. Figure 7 illustrates the trend of total rail transport costs and revenue in the Netherlands. From the 1960's, the government was required to provide annual grants to maintain unprofitable lines (blue area).

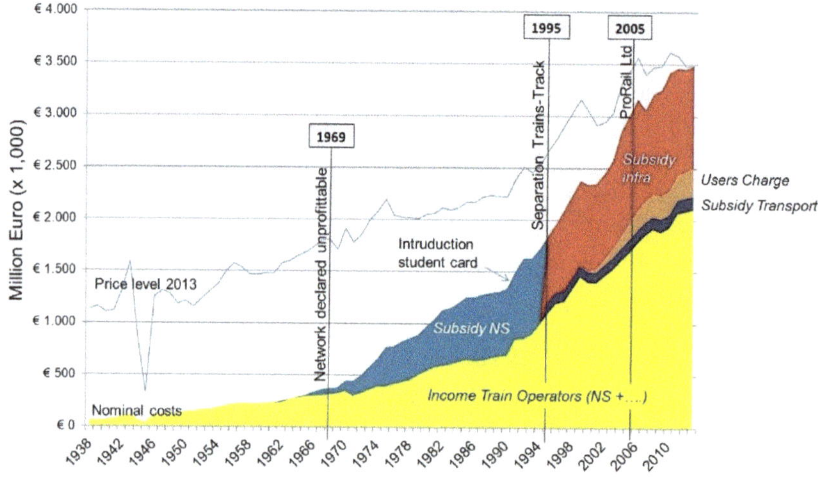

Figure 7   Development of costs and income of rail transport (1938-2013). Sources: Annual reports, (Faber, 1989) and (Swier J. , 2016)*

Despite mechanisation, remediation and reorganisation, the deficit continued to grow because of rapidly rising wages and gradual introduction of fortnightly work week. The costs increased in 20 years to approximately the same level as revenue from transport, and about the same level as total rail infrastructure maintenance costs. It was, therefore, inevitable that the government, as owner of rail infrastructure, would play a greater role in the administration of public rail transport.

The European Directive 91/440 (EU, 1991*) describes how the Member States should handle their railways: administrative independence of railway companies with the accounting as a minimum separation between infrastructure and transport, financial clean up, and admission of new operators to the rail network. Initially, accounting of Transport and Infrastructure were separated. After the split of Transport and Infrastructure business units in 1995, the subsidy was for rail infrastructure (dark red area) and maintenance of unprofitable passenger lines (dark blue area). In 1999, a user charge was slowly introduced (light brown area) up to a maximum of the variable cost, well over € 300 million in 2015. The user charge are costs for the operators but revenue for the infrastructure manager so they overlap each other in the figure.

The rising blue line in the figure is the nominal cost trend corrected by the CBS price index for cost increases and inflation. The increase is due to growth of passenger transport with investments to improve service quality, introduction of the student card and increasing congestion on the roads. The growth led to structural increase in transport revenues. As infrastructure stabilised, the ratio of government funding to transport revenue became more favourable. In the period 1970-1990, the ratio grew to over 0.9 but, in 2000, it fell to about 0.5 (Swier J., 2016*) and remained at that level.

Development of the institutional triangle

The reason for separation and origin of the institutional triangle was growing financial shortages in rail transport. The actual initiation of the split began in 1992 when, at the request of the government, the commission Wijffels recommended restructuring of the relationship between the government and NS. The committee advised a holding structure and administrative separation, but the government selected full economic- and legal separation for the long term.

As a result of this decision, NS started distinguishing three types of activities at the top level: commercial core activities, non-core activities and non-commercial tasks. The non-commercial tasks included infra activities, better known as task organisations, namely, NS Rail Infrastructure, NS Traffic Control and Capacity Manager Railned. Figure 8 illustrates the division of NS.

The restructuring of the company was completed in 1995. The three task organisations were housed in the holding company NS Railinfratrust Ltd (RIT), an independent company owned by the national government and juridical owner of the Dutch rail infrastructure[3]. The task organisations started to work on the account and behalf of the Minister of Traffic & Water Management (V&W) but

---

[3] NS remained the economic owner of infra until the Railinfratrust was acquired from the NS Holding in 2002 and ProRail became independent. The economic owner can own a property but only the legal-owner, the government in this case, may sell it.

continued to be part of NS Holding until there was more clarity about the final position and status.

NS Railinfrabeheer joined this NS-wide reorganisation with its own reorganisation, 'Infra '96'. This included not only the separation of Transport and Infrastructure, but also the division of the Infra Process into a management- and maintenance organisation, with the intention to privatise maintenance in the long run. In addition to the separation of Trains and Track, the NS Engineering firm was privatised in 1994. It started with the name Holland Railconsult and is now called Movares. Some of the engineering activities were earlier housed in the NS subsidiary Articon and are now part of Arcadis.

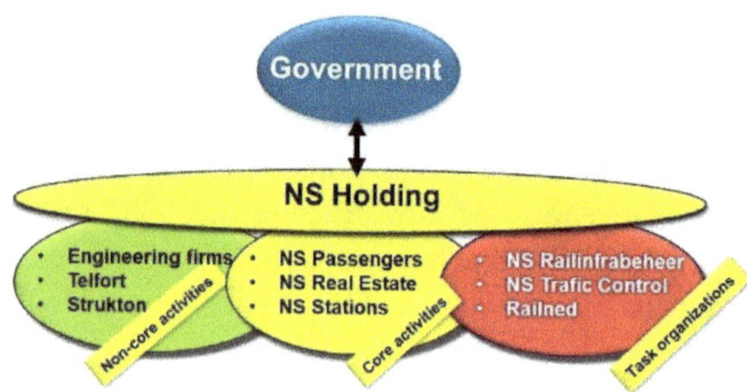

Figure 8   Division of NS in 1995 in type of activities

Following the Wijffels restructuring proposals, the former minister of V&W suddenly and unexpectedly announced in 1993 the declaration to privatise NS and launched experimental competition on a line by granting a license to Lovers in 1996 to operate a main rail network line. An effect was that the NS management got a strong focus to reduce costs, strengthen the financial base and improve quality. This worked until 2000 but in the two years thereafter punctuality collapsed fully due to rigorous cuts in train maintenance, late ordering of new trains, staff shortages and pushing of an unsupported timetable known as *'het rondje om de kerk'* (English: 'the circle around the church').

The average annual punctuality decreased from more than 86% in early 2000 to less than 80% in 2002[4]. Workers, unions and management were in conflict and witnessing strikes, sick staff, disruptions, delays and dissatisfied travellers (Wessels, 2003). The minister eventually intervened and the NS executive and supervisory boards resigned in early 2002. A new management team worked slowly but certainly to restore communication and trust with the staff by cancel the unsupported service schedule and solving issues with the train equipment. As a result, punctuality reached former levels around 2004.

---

[4] The development in punctuality is illustrated in Figure 63.

NS Railinfrabeheer had very different concerns at that time. Its focus was on the development of its own organisation. Because of the split and privatisation of executive activities, the entire process had to be built up largely from the bottom. About 1000 employees moved to independent engineering firms and about 2800 maintenance employees moved to the three existing rail contractors: Strukton, Volker Stevin and BAM/NBM. The contractors were experienced in construction and renewal of rail infrastructure. There was no market for maintenance so the client and contractors had to learn how to manage costs and performance through a maintenance contract. This made the initial years after privatisation quite difficult.

The infra organisations had to give form and content to very new roles and tasks, and thereby develop a new identity. For many years, they focussed internally on developing new skills and instruments, managing maintenance contracts and regaining performance. Later, the attention shifted to the external environment. This was necessary because on July 1, 2002 the Railinfratrust (RIT) was removed from NS Holding and from January 1, 2003, the three task organisations started cooperating under the trade name ProRail. They merged on January 1, 2005 and became the existing infrastructure management organisation ProRail Ltd[5].

The loosening, cooperation and merger took place after the politicians had opted for a governance model based on concessions. A new railroad law passed in 2003 and became effective on January 1, 2005. The government was the sole shareholder of ProRail Ltd through the RIT with a Supervisory Board to supervise policy implementation, including the general course of affairs within the company and associated companies. With the new Railways Act, the legislation and regulations concerning the rail sector were modernised and the relationship between government and rail sector was finally regulated in accordance with the EU Directive 91/440.

Since 2005, the government, transport companies and ProRail are inextricably linked in an administrative form known as the institutional triangle, illustrated in Figure 9. The relationships are based on concessions, performance agreements and two supervisory boards acting on behalf of the government and overseeing the implementation of agreed policy at NS and ProRail[6]. The NS remained an NV with a Supervisory Board and with the Ministry of Finance as the sole shareholder. ProRail became a Ltd, also with a Supervisory Board and the government

---

[5] Incidentally, without the safety task of Railned, because it went to the Transport, Public Works and Water Management Inspectorate (IVW), the current Human Environment and Transport Inspectorate (ILT).

[6] Alternatives that were not chosen were an Independent Administrative Body (ZBO) or Agency. A ZBO is an organisation that executes government tasks but does not fall directly under the authority of a minister. Examples are: Land Registry, Dutch Bank, ACM, Air Traffic Control and Staatsbosbeheer. An Agency is an independent part of a ministry that has its own management, budget and financial administration. Examples are: Rijkswaterstaat (RWS), Buildings Department, KNMI and ILT.

('the State of the Netherlands') as sole shareholder and the Ministry of Infrastructure & Environment (I&E) as the largest client. Both companies are therefore not fully state-owned but semi-governmental.

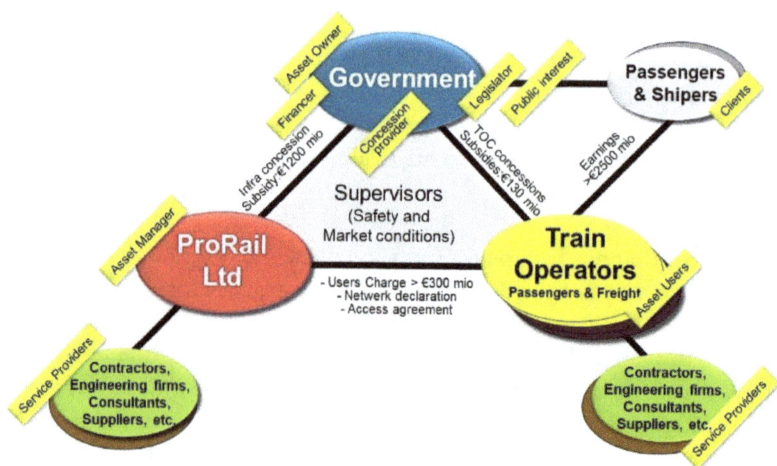

Figure 9   The institutional triangle; administrative context of rail transport in the Netherlands

From the position of the infrastructure manager ProRail, there are five separate roles: infrastructure owner ('asset owner'), infrastructure users ('asset user'), infrastructure manager ('asset manager'), service providers and transport users, the clients. The roles are fulfilled by the government, train operators, ProRail, contractors and passengers/shippers, respectively. The government performs more than one role. It is the owner of the rail network, financier, concession provider, legislator and guardian of the public interest. These roles have always existed but their importance and interpretation changed after introduction of the institutional triangle.

The government became part of rail transport management as owner and financier of rail infrastructure, and the infrastructure organisation became independent for the first time. Freight transport was fully privatised and liberalised, competition was introduced on regional lines[7] and train operators were to pay for use of rail infrastructure. The number of train operators increased from one (the NS) to more than thirty. Liberalisation and competition improved operations and transport quality in both passenger and freight.

Government and ProRail have a business relationship. The Minister is ultimately responsible for the rail network and has delegated management to ProRail through a concession with term of ten years. The concession covers maintenance,

---

[7] In case of competition around lines only one train operators gets a concession instead of competition on lines where there are more.

36

renewal, expansion, capacity distribution and control. Each year, ProRail prepares a management plan that is approved by the Minister. The contract states which performances are to be delivered and the budget available. The performance concerns network capacity, availability, reliability and safety, quality of capacity distribution, adjustment and information provision, cleanliness, accessibility and social safety of transfer facilities. The funding is from the infrastructure fund, a component of the national budget, which covers national roads-, rail- and water infrastructure. Together with the user charge, it covers operating costs for management of existing rail infrastructure. Investments in network extensions are paid for by the government through separate multi-year Infrastructure, Space and Transport (MIRT) programme. In addition, there are investment projects for and at the expense of third parties such as provinces and municipalities.

The government and train operators for passenger transport have a business relationship as a concession agreement, which stipulates performances to be delivered, such as punctuality and capacity of trains. In accordance with the European regulations, the government pays the PSO subsidy for keeping unprofitable lines open. The business relationship has been arranged between the infrastructure manager and train operators through an access agreement and a network statement. The Access Agreement contains general conditions, requirements for railway vehicles, use, services provided and user charge. The network statement contains practical information about functionality and capacity of the railway network; access conditions for railway and the process how to get capacity on the network.

1.3   Analysis reason and consequences of the split

The reorganisation of rail transport in the Netherlands was achieved in 2005 after fifteen years of separation, privatisation and stabilisation. This period lasted far too long due to slow and sloppy steering and decision-making by the national government and the NS (Veraart M. , 2007). For more than ten years, there was uncertainty about the organisation of the company. In Appendix 14.1.2, a summary overview is provided of the most important milestones in that period[8]. There was labour unrest and uncertainty in the entire sector which caused poor performance in both transport and infrastructure. Delays, disruptions and accidents led to strong criticism and suggestions to re-join transport and infrastructure. After the government opted for a governance model based on concessions in an institutional triangle, there was peace and stability. The industry performed better than before the split, but criticism continued. It shows that an industry does not lose negative image quickly, and that passengers, politicians and media

---

[8] An alternative is the weekly comic *'Donald Duck'* Nr.3-2016 (Duck, 2016-1*). It contains a comic strip about Dagobert and Donald Duck that is based on the separation of NS, the outsourcing of maintenance and the problems it has given.

have become more critical. The requirements and expectations regarding quality of rail transport have increased such that it is to be improved continuously and the industry is working on it. It is no longer possible to return to the old situation because the world and circumstances have changed; and the organisations have adapted and are better than ever.

This chapter is concluded with a summary of the fundamental changes resulting from the separation of transport and infrastructure and a brief explanation of the causes and consequences.

a. ***Risky separation that works out well.*** There was a period of at least ten years in which there was uncertainty about the organisation of the rail sector. It started with the sudden announcement in 1994 by the government to privatise the NS. This caused uncertainty and tension among staff as well as increase in train failures because of reduction in maintenance expenses. The results were instability, decline in performance, strikes, and, finally, resignation of the NS board. The new board regained confidence by blowing off of the Initial Public Offering. The adoption of a new railway and concession law in 2003 started a period of stability. In this period, customer service and performance were central and driven by an institutional triangle based on concessions and well-crafted division of roles.

b. ***Cultural change.*** McKinsey advised in 1989 to turn around the fragmented, technical and task-oriented infra organisations within the NS into a more professional and transparent infra-process (McKinsey, 1989-1, pp. 1-I). This led to the privatisation and outsourcing of all engineering activities, merger of organisations and decentralisation of maintenance. The recommendations of the Wijffels commission in 1992 led to the split of Transport and Infrastructure as well as privatisation of maintenance. The split and privatisation of all executive activities led to a new division of roles, far-reaching organisational changes and business relations based on agreements about costs and performance. As the organisations became more performance- and customer-oriented, the entire company culture changed.
Until 2002, the infrastructure organisations were mainly focused on survival, damage control and development of new roles. The organisation structure, function and instrumentation received full attention. However, when the most important basic organisational conditions were fulfilled and the governance model for rail sector became clear, there was capacity and motivation to introduce new management techniques and collaborate for optimal and sustainable management of results for passengers and shippers. The cultural change was slowly but surely visible to the companies and customers involved: customer and performance were central, and operations became professional.

c. ***Separation of the funding sources and decision making.*** The split of transport and infrastructure was to ensure transparent and legal separation of two large sources of finance and decision-making processes. The NS and other transport companies were liberated from the financial burden of rail infrastructure and related involvement of the government. The train operators are now independent commercial companies. They may receive a PSO reimbursement[9] from the government for maintenance of loss-making lines but such compensation is fixed during the term of the concession for a contractually stipulated performance. For the use of infrastructure, train operators pay an access charge lower than variable costs of the infrastructure, as per conditions in European regulations. In the institutional triangle, the government acquired a meaningful role in the management of rail transport as owner and financier of rail infrastructure; concession provider; and sole shareholder in the supervisory board of NS and ProRail.

d. ***Transparency in the mix of public and private interests.*** By separating the two funding sources, social and commercial interests became transparent. The public interest is primarily served by the government because it oversees the need for rail transport and invests in it. The commercial exploitation for transport companies operating within concession agreements. These companies are private, risk-bearing, and profit-oriented. The government has delegated to ProRail the task to permanently optimise costs and performance of rail infrastructure over the life cycle, control the network and divide the capacity, all per strategic decisions of the central government. ProRail is an independent company with a profit-and-loss account but it does not bear risk because it is financed at the expense and risk of the government. Thus, transport and infra are separate companies which aim to optimally optimise their respective results. If there is tension in the distribution of benefits and claims then everyone can see it and the government is the decision maker. Even when transport and infrastructure were a single company, there was tension but it was not obvious and not within the influence of the government.

e. ***More interfaces, more commercial operation.*** Until 1990, the NS was the only train operator on the Dutch railway network, responsible for both transport and infrastructure. A cohesive company with history of more than sixty years (NS was founded in 1938) was split into several independent companies within a period of seven years. An informal network based on collegial contacts changed into a formal network based on contracts in a relatively short period of time. This caused sub-optimisation and coordination problems as well as impact on the

---

[9]According to an EU directive, freight transport cannot be subsidised but certain unprofitable passenger lines can be subsidised by the Public Service Obligation (PSO).

quality of transport and rail infrastructure due to rapid change. The interfaces, however, also forced the organisations to make explicit agreements about performance and costs, and the process to manage them. All companies involved were required to work on commercial basis. Initially, the companies focused on optimising their own results but after some time they realised their interdependencies and need to collaborate. This takes time, causes friction but leads to success.

f.   ***One network, multiple train operating companies.*** Since the split of NS, the network is open to new train operators and the number of operators has grown from one (the NS) to more than thirty: passenger operators, freight operators, contractor equipment, inspection trains, etc. A single coherent network is used by several train operators on the basis of a reasonable usage fee. Because ProRail, an independent company, is responsible for management of rail infrastructure[10], it is able to optimally manage costs and performance of the entire life cycle on behalf of the government. If management of infrastructure were task of a certain train operator then it may cause tensions among other infra users and reduce transparency in disagreements (between public and private interests) and fragmentation of infra tasks. In such circumstances, optimal management of performance and costs would be difficult. The option to divide the network and place it under the management of different train operators may compromise network cohesion cause tensions with operators have nationwide service.

g.   ***Better results.*** The split between transport and infrastructure in 1995 initially caused worse punctuality, more failures and tensions between companies. This may well be expected given that a railway company with a long history was split in a short period of time. From 2002-2005, however, there was improvement with performance back to pre-split level and parties accustomed to their role, task and each other. For details on performance, please refer section 7.3 (punctuality) and section 7.4 (infra failures). Since 2005, the results and business operations have improved and ProRail is one of the best performing infra managers in Europe and the world. For more details and background information about the realised results, please refer chapter 0 which provides international benchmark context to compare results.

Ultimately, the split and outsourcing of tasks had a positive outcome. However, this became visible only after more than ten years of uncertainty, unrest and deteriorating performance and relationships. The necessary cooperation that was needed among government, train operators and infrastructure manager became possible when the new railroad law was enforced in 2003/2005 and the institutional triangle was realised. The potential benefits of outsourcing maintenance

---

[10] Development, expansion, maintenance, renewal, operations and capacity allocation.

were visible only after the first performance contract (PGO) was tendered in 2008. Since then, the turnaround began from OPC-contracts to PGO-contracts, from input- to output management and from price negotiation to tendering. This turnaround was planned to be fished in 2015 but has problems of its own and, therefore, the last PGO-contract will be tendered in 2019. Due to the long duration and major impact of the change from input- to output, this book devotes a separate chapter to outsourcing of maintenance and its influence on the development of the asset management system.

At the end of this chapter, an analysis is provided of the development of conditions in five countries to understand differences, similarities and coherence with division of roles and role fulfilment. The role change and task distribution in the Dutch rail transport sector is not unique but also present in other countries in- and outside Europe (Velde, 2012-11*). There are interesting parallels and differences between the countries and companies based on changes in socio-economic circumstances and the response of the companies and government to it.

1.4 Development of rail transport in five other countries

For the purpose of illustration, the development of rail transport is described for countries on three continents and facing different circumstances. The cases are: Great Britain, France and Poland in Europe, a large freight company in the United States of America, and Japan in Asia. The circumstances and developments in these countries are very different and yet there are many parallels. A brief introduction is provided into the rationale for selection of these five cases.

The development of rail transport began in Great Britain but was uncontrolled and fragmented. It experienced closures, acquisitions and eventual nationalisation because of heavy competition by road transport. This created a coherent network but witnessed decline of the network because of constant rebalancing of private initiative and government intervention.
The development of rail transport in France has many similarities with that in the Netherlands but differs fundamentally in the role of government, financing and the partial split of transport and infrastructure. This has resulted today in poor performance and a maintenance backlog on the traditional network.
The case of US focuses on restructuring of rail transport in the period 1960-1990. It demonstrates the influence of government on both the downfall and restructuring of what was then the largest company in the US, the Pennsylvania Railroad, and loss due to self-enrichment and mismanagement of the board.
In Poland, the development of rail transport has been strongly influenced by the changes in national boundary, political system and socio-economic condition.
Japan illustrates that nationalisation and privatisation of railway companies is strongly determined by the circumstances and reaction of the government to it.

1.4.1 **Great Britain**

Britain was at the forefront of the development of the railways. George Stephenson started construction of the first locomotive in 1825. Four years later, the first railway line opened between Liverpool and Manchester, and it was successful. The rail network then expanded rapidly: 160 kilometers in 1830, 11,000 kilometers in 1852, about 25,000 kilometers in 1870 and about 37,500 kilometers in 1917. Figure 10 illustrates this growth. The growth seemed unlimited and share price of railway companies were increasing. There was enough money for construction of new lines until the bubble burst and prices plummeted. Small railway companies went bankrupt and were taken over by larger ones. Until the First World War, however, there were more than one hundred and twenty active companies competing with each other, often on parallel lines. The system was inefficient, expensive and financially unsustainable, especially with the rise of road transport.

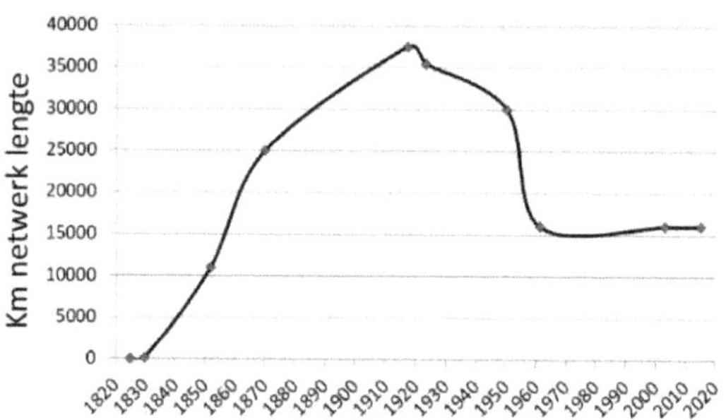

Figure 10   Development of the rail network in Britain

During the First World War, the government took control of all railway companies. Up to 1921, costs decreased due to cooperation. In 1923, the Railway Act of 1921 was launched and all existing companies were merged and grouped into four new ones. With the closing of unprofitable and secondary regional lines, the network length reduced by more than 2,000 kilometers.

During the Second World War, the network was used intensively for the war industry. However, there was little time, money and attention for maintenance and the network quality degraded to a poor state after the war. In 1948, British Railways (BR) was established by nationalising the four existing railways companies. Approximately, 5,300 kilometers of railway lines were closed to clear the maintenance backlog and reduce competition from road transport. An ambitious modernisation plan started in 1955 but failed, partly because investments were made in projects that were unnecessary and because road transport offered better alternatives. The heavy interest costs of the failed mitigation plan further increased transport costs. BR was in a downward spiral. The government realised need for drastic remediation and appointed Richard Beeching, a powerful director, as chairman in 1961. His reorganisation plan led to the abolition of steam trains, closure of 26,000 kilometers of track and 2000 stations, as well as the modernisation of around 5,000 kilometers of railway lines. The number of jobs decreased by 70,000.

In the 1980s, Britain faced economic challenges. Inflation was high, industry was outdated and labour disputes prevented innovation. Margaret Thatcher embarked on a rigorous recovery policy that consisted mainly of privatising state-owned companies and breaking conservative power of the trade unions. BR was one of the last to transform[11]. The company was divided in 1994 into transport concessions that were put out to private companies. There was one infra organisation, Railtrack, which went public in 1996. The execution of infrastructure maintenance and renewal was split off and privatised. However, due to political instability and forthcoming elections, privatisation was too fast and rigorous. The services decreased, prices increased, transport companies went bankrupt, and infrastructure was neglected. The government had to intervene; more tax money was spent than before privatisation and quality deteriorated. The chaos climaxed when a train accident occurred in Hatfield in 2000 because of bad state of the track, and four people were killed. More than 1,200 speed restrictions were enforced across the country and Railtrack's losses increased sharply. In order to protect it from bankruptcy, Railtrack was taken over in 2001 by Network Rail Ltd, a company set up by the government to manage infrastructure. The Office of Rail Regulation (ORR) was also set up to monitor performance and financing as well as regulate access to the rail network. In 2003, Network Rail put an end to outsourcing of maintenance for the approximately 16,000 kilometers network[12].

The transport companies benefited from privatisation. They invested in new equipment, increased train frequency, opened new stations and improved services. The number of passengers increased by more than 50% over a period of twenty years. Network Rail also changed for the better and network performance demonstrably improved. However, the company is troubled by the fact that costs to maintain the outdated network are increasing.

1.4.2 France

The first railway line in France opened in 1827. From 1859, concessions were in the hands of six large companies. The government financed building of the substructure including earthwork, bridges and buildings. The companies that built the superstructure (rail, switches, signalling, facilities, etc.) got monopoly in exploitation of 'their' lines. The government provided subsidy for interest guarantees on invested new capital. After a somewhat slow start, the expansion was rapid

---

[11] Margaret Thatcher seems to have been fiercely opposed to the privatisation of BR. Only under her successor, John Major, BR could be privatised.
[12] The lines have a total track length of approximately 33,800 kilometers and, in 2013, Network Rail had about 37,000 employees.

as indicated in Figure 11 (Caralp, 1951*). The growth of the network is comparable to that of the Netherlands.

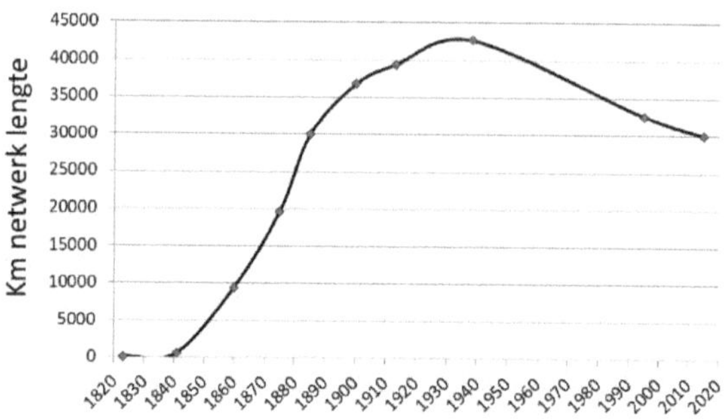

Figure 11   Development of the rail network in France

As a result of rapid growth in road transport, cost increase and large recession after the First World War, profitability of the companies deteriorated. The five loss-making private railway companies were nationalised in 1938 and transferred to the newly formed SNCF; a scenario similar to the Netherlands. The state started with a share of 50% but gained full ownership. In 1983, the status of the company was converted to that of a public institution with an industrial and commercial character (French: EPIC). This provided protection from bankruptcy. The nationalisation and increase in government subsidy also has similarities with the Netherlands. A huge difference is that the total subsidy is much higher, covers not only infrastructure but also transport, government contributes to pensions, and debt is significant and rising because deficits are covered by loans. The separation of infra and transport imposed by the EU was minimal in France in 1997. The Reseau Ferré de France (RFF) became the owner and manager of the entire network. It was owned by the French state and had an EPIC status. It was obliged to purchase all maintenance and renewal activities from SNCF Infra, which employed maintenance and renewal staff. In addition to the fact that EU directive on competition was ignored, this obligation made RFF highly dependent on SNCF and this was reinforced by the fact that traffic control also stayed with SNCF.

In 1997, the French rail system had a debt of around € 35.5 billion. The RFF took over a debt of € 20.5 billion from SNCF, which itself remained with a debt of about € 10 billion. Approximately € 5 billion was allocated to a special debt restructuring group, the SAAD (Gomez-Ibanez, 2006, p. 92). According to Gomes-Ibanez, debt restructuring was influenced by legal consideration of debt being classified as government deficit. According to the Maastricht Treaty, this has macro-economic consequences if the debt is greater than 50% of the gross domestic product (GDP), deficit is greater than 3% of the GDP, and micro-economic consequences are interest payments for borrowing. The French government opted to not classify railway debt as government deficit. The debt of the French railways is great because deficit in pension fund is supplemented by the government through an annual contribution to SNCF until 2007 and to an independent railway pension fund thereafter.

In 1999, the High Council for Public Transport by Rail (CSSPF) was set up to monitor the RFF and SNCF as well as promote integration of public services. After the split, debts continued to increase because shortfalls were covered with loans. The performance of the classic rail network decreased because there was insufficient money to maintain the system given high investment in high-speed lines. A growing number of regional lines faced lower speed limits because of the poor state of the track and lack of funds for maintenance. More loans were needed to close other financial deficits. Debt increased to around € 40 billion in 2013 and is expected to continue to increase by € 1-1.5 billion annually if borrowing is used to cover deficits (Dehornoy, 2011*, p. 17). It was, therefore, no surprise that RFF and SNCF announced a merger in 2013. The merger includes capacity management at RFF and is expected to end unproductive rivalry, lack of clarity and uncoordinated duplication. The reform has four objectives: performance improvement, structural stabilisation of finances, readiness for competition and collective labour agreement with profit sharing for the employees.

1.4.3   United States

The Pennsylvania Railroad (PRR) was a US Class I railroad company founded in 1846. It was the largest railroad company in terms of traffic and sales in the United States (US) in the first half of the twentieth century, becoming the largest listed company in the world. At its peak (around 1920), PRR controlled approximately 16,000 kilometers of railway. PRR still holds the record for the longest uninterrupted dividend payments: more than a hundred years. At one point, PRR had annual budget bigger than the US government, and had 250,000 employees. This enormous company with long illustrious history went bankrupt in the seventies. It was impacted by the extent of the influence of changing circumstances, mismanagement and wrong influence of the government. A special feature of this case is that in a country such as America, which is averse to government intervention, the government played an important and decisive role in bankruptcy, rescue, restructuring and again becoming independent of the railway company.

Railway companies in the US transport freight and only Amtrak provides passenger transport. However, this was not the case always. Passenger transport was extensive and profitable around 1900 and even had a glamorous appearance (Loving, 2006). Slowly but surely circumstances changed. In the northeast, there was an unfavourable combination of cost-increasing conditions and far-reaching macro-economic changes. Passenger and freight transport were severely affected by competition from aviation and road transport. This had bigger consequences for passenger transport because freight trains only drive when there is cargo, but passenger trains follow a timetable irrespective of the number of passengers. Less passengers meant less revenue and operating costs of passenger transport were significantly higher than that of rail freight transport. In his book 'The Men Who Loved Train', Rush Loving Jr. states the causes of higher operating costs as higher train weight, higher speed, higher technical complexity and specialised personnel (Loving, 2006, p. 121). Costs also increased because of the extra track required for passenger transport as well as maintenance and exploitation of large stations constructed in the heydays of passenger transport. An illustrative example in the book by Loving Jr. is the operation of the New York-Chicago Broadway Limited sleeper train. In 1968, it transported only sixty passengers per trip, while seventy people were needed to run the train. As a result, at the end of the 1960s, Penn Central had annual loss of USD 100 million. Nevertheless, the Interstate Commerce Commission (ICC) [13] demanded that all railway companies continue to operate loss-making passenger trains. It was a lost battle. Passenger transport was making increasingly large losses, and these losses weighed heavily on PRR's operating results. With income from freight transport also declining, the market was getting smaller but the organisation did not respond - whether or not forced by the circumstances - to work more efficiently by, for example, stopping train services or reducing the network. Instead, losses were disguised with questionable and creative accounting practices. This was unsustainable and in 1968, PRR merged with its rival, the New York Central Railroad (NCR). Together, they formed the Penn Central Transportation Company. The ICC also demanded in 1969 that the ailing company New York New Haven & Hartford Railroad be added to the merger. A string of events caused by inflation, abnormally bad weather conditions, poor management and withdrawal of government-guaranteed operating loan forced Penn Central to apply for bankruptcy protection on June 21, 1970. The railways in the northeast had to be restructured and the government had contributed to the downfall.

In 1971, passenger transport was taken over from nineteen of the twenty-two railway companies by the newly established Amtrak company that was subsidised by the government. The companies transferred equipment, capital and personnel and, in return secured permission from the ICC to stop the operation of low profitable passenger trains. In Washington, it was believed that the 'experiment' would not last long. The government saw Amtrak as a politically advantageous way of giving one last chance to the diminishing passenger transport in accordance with the wishes of the people. They expected Amtrak to disappear quietly as public interest in the issue diminished. At the same time, proponents of the system hoped that Amtrak would soon be financially viable. Neither predictions

---

[13] The ICC was the first independent, regulatory government agency of the US for railways initially and road freight transport later. The agency was abolished in 1995 because of its poor reputation. Its powers were transferred to the Surface Transportation Board (STB), which now monitors tariffs, services, construction, purchase, cancellation and mergers of railways.

proved correct: the support for Amtrak was not reduced and financial independence was not feasible. The company was relatively successful in rebuilding passenger transport with number of passengers increasing from 16.6 million in 1972 to 21 million in 1981.

The restructuring of freight transport started after Amtrak took over loss-bearing passenger transport. The federal government intervened because the economy would have suffered major damage if rail freight stopped. A law was passed in 1974 to keep bankrupt companies functional and the Unites States Railway Association was set up for this purpose. It served as an investment bank and determined which lines had to be closed and which parts of Penn Central were to be transferred to a new railway company, namely the Consolidated Railroad Corporation, better known as Conrail, in 1976. After restructuring loss-making lines and improving operations, Conrail became profitable in 1981. The government withdrew from the company and sold shares in 1987 for an amount of USD 1.9 billion. The railway companies, CSX and Norfolk Southern (NS), tried unsuccessfully for years to fully take over Conrail and finally formed a joint plan in which NS got about 9,500 kilometers and CSX 5,700 kilometers. On June 1, 1999, both companies took over respective operations of Conrail and ended the struggle that drastically changed rail transport in the US.

The main players in and around railways in northeast US had the biggest difficulty in adapting themselves to changing circumstances. Changes led to power struggle with clashing egos, waste and mismanagement. The result was a painful clean-up, separation and privatisation of passenger transport, and revaluation of the role of the government. The events in the period 1960-2000 has been extensively described by Rush Loving Jr. in his book *The Men who Loved Trains* (Loving, 2006). The book describes what transpired behind the scenes and shows how changing circumstances, mismanagement and improper government intervention formed a negative mix that led to bankruptcy of one of the largest companies in the US. It is similar to what happened years later with ENRON, an American energy company that went bankrupt in 2001 because it spent more than earned and masked its earnings through mismanagement, tax evasion and accounting tricks. It is painful to note that history was repeated after thirty years. At present, rail freight transport in the US has returned to profitability

1.4.4 Poland

In 1795, Poland was divided among Russia, Austria and Prussia. With the arrival of the railways in the nineteenth century, each of these areas developed differently. The densest railway network was created in the Prussian part, while development lagged and track gauge was 1,524 millimetres in the Russian part. When Poland regained its independence in 1918, the national railway company Polskie Koleje Państwowe (PKP) was established and given priority task of harmonising the three railway networks. The former Russian gauge tracks were rebuilt to gauge of 1,435 millimetres and new equipment was added. A major economic crisis in 1930 forced the government to reduce investment and PKP profits fell by 50%. More than 23,000 employees were dismissed and there was labour unrest. In 1937, the crisis ended and freight transport increased again.

In the Second World War, the PKP was under the supervision of the German and Russian occupiers. After the Second World War, the Polish territory 'shifted' to the west due to border changes. The eastern part was annexed by the Soviet Union and all German territories east of the Oder-Neisse border were assigned to Poland. The PKP lost the rail infrastructure it had and gained new one.

In the communist period (1945-1989), Poland again became an important transit country. Because Soviet Union doubted reliability of Poland as a partner, alternatives were also developed for transport through Poland. For military transport from the Red Army to the East Germany (GDR), the Linia Hutnicza Szerokotorowa (LHS) was specially constructed in 1979. The LHS was Russian gauge freight line of length about 400 kilometres from Sławków Południowy in southern Poland (near Katowice) to the Russian border. Russia also provided ferry connections between Lithuania and the GDR for military purpose.

In 1989, Poland became the first Eastern Bloc country to have a democratically elected parliament. Its socialist economy initially experienced negative effects when shock therapy was applied largely recovered around 1995. In 2000, the monopolistic railway organisation was restructured as a holding company with separate companies for transport, infrastructure and services. Each company was legally autonomous and had its own profit-and-loss account.

Today, the Polish railway network spans around 18,500 kilometers and is the third largest in Europe, after Germany and France. After the fall of communism, traffic increased but railways faced competition from fast-growing road transport. In the period 1990-2012, rail-based freight transport fell by about 40% and passenger transport by about 65%, see Figure 12.

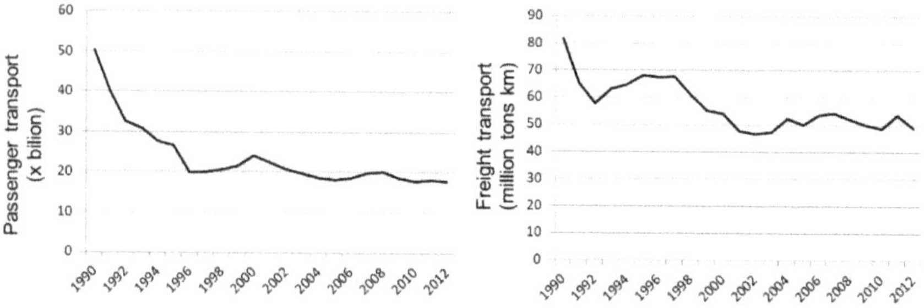

Figure 12   Development of passenger- and freight rail transport in Poland (Eurostat, 2014)*

These sharp declines transformed PKP from a profit-making company in 1990 to a loss-making company. The PKP became dependent on government subsidies for both rail infrastructure and passenger transport as was the case with railway companies in the former Western Europe. The cause was the same but the result came thirty years later due to differences in political, social and economic circumstances. Due to shortage of financial resources, a backlog developed in maintenance and renewal of rail infrastructure. This caused failures, speed restrictions and train delays, thereby decreasing the quality of rail transport. The development of rail transport in Poland is more or less a model for other former Eastern European countries with the difference that Poland has witnessed the greatest economic growth among all countries in Europe; therefore, the decline is relatively less than in other former Eastern European countries.

In 2004, Poland became a full member of the European Union. With the PKP-group having implemented most of the provisions of the EU Railway guidelines, transport and network comply with most important EU directives and there is an open rail transport market with following characteristics:

- Accounting separation at PKP between transport and infrastructure.
- No cross subsidy between PKP companies.
- Transport realised on a commercial basis, driven by market demand, and independent of the state.
- Non-discriminatory access to the rail infrastructure.

Since 2007, railway lines are being modernised and renewed under national programmes partly financed by EU's Trans-European Transport Network (TEN-T) programme. The aim is to improve accessibility and quality of main transport corridors to create an integrated rail system in Europe. The results are now visible. The share of tracks and switches in good technical condition increased from 37% to 51% in the period 2010-2015. However, there is one hidden problem: loans are deferred payments which have to be repaid. They do not provide a structural solution to solve the financial deficits. The situation in France shows that this can lead to an annually growing debt burden. Given the political and economic situation in Poland, it is understandable that debt has been selected as a short-term solution.

On lines that are not covered by the TEN-T programme, the maintenance and renewal backlog continues to grow and results in an increasing number of speed restrictions and failures. In 2013, it was decided to suspend transport services on 10% of the regional network to save costs. Altogether, approximately 2,000 kilometers of railway lines have been taken out of service to structurally save € 14 - 19 million annually. A minimal staff continues to monitor these lines because infrastructure exists.

1.4.5 **Japan**

Until the arrival of the Meiji Emperor in 1868, Japan was governed by an aristo-
cratic and bureaucratic system that emphasised tradition and seclusion. This period is known as the Edo period. It ended because of threat of occupation by the
West. There was a revolution by the nobility, supported by Emperor Meiji. In the
Meiji period (1868-1912), borders were opened, industrialisation was promoted
and a new socio-economic system was introduced. The first railway line opened
in 1872 and was operated by the state-owned Japan National Railways. The expansion of the network was slow because of insufficient finances and left to private initiative from 1881 onwards. Ippon Railway was the first private railway
company and soon more followed. The network grew fairly quickly but not fast
enough. In 1892, the Railway Construction Act was adopted to construct thirty-
three railway lines by government and private companies.

After the first Chinese-Japanese war (1894-1895) and the Russian-Japanese war
(1904-1905), the Japanese government decided to nationalise railway companies
of the main network. The Railway Nationalisation Act was adopted in 1906. The
Light Railway Act of 1910 stipulated that expansion of regional and international
lines be left to private companies and that light rail companies develop their own
business models. The railway companies in Japan had the advantage that competition from road transport did not start until after 1950, which was much later
than 1910 for US and 1920s for Europe. The Japanese railway companies gained
stable foothold and survived competition from road transport, which also faced
challenges due to unfavourable geographical conditions inhibiting road development.

In the second Chinese-Japanese war (1937-1945) and the Pacific war (1941-1945),
the railways came under military control. Small private regional companies
merged into larger ones. In the period 1943-1944, another twenty-two private
companies were nationalised because they had lines important for military purpose. In order to prioritise military transport, passenger transport was reduced
1943 onwards and railway companies cannibalised lines to meet military's demand for steel.

After the Second World War, the rail network was badly damaged by US bomb-
ing and cannibalisation of lines. It took many years to repair the damage given
lack of raw material, maintenance and fuel. The government encouraged private
companies to develop their own heavily-used railway lines and this promoted a
quick recovery.

In the period 1945-1951, the Allies controlled the occupied Japan. A board decided in 1949 to reorganise the Japanese Government Railways and merge all
existing companies into a single national railway company: the Japanese National
Railways (JNR). In the years after 1960, economic growth was rapid and demand

increased. To accommodate this growth, the five main lines in the Tokyo agglomeration were expanded into four-track lines.

Due to the construction of new lines, including the first high-speed line between Tokyo and Osaka in 1964, JNR's debt grew rapidly. This led to labour unrest and strikes. In 1987, the government decided to privatise JNR and split it into seven separate companies: six for passengers and one for freight, now known as the Japan Railways Group (JR Group). After privatisation, the four JR companies were listed on the stock exchange and became profitable by improving service. Private companies were encouraged to compete with each other and the JR companies on the basis of quality because the government regulated tariffs. The competition between railway companies improved efficiency, punctuality and passenger demand. By developing real estate in the vicinity of new lines, private railway companies expanded and diversified their offerings. This made them profitable and financially independent.

Conclusion based on the five cases

The five cases illustrate that circumstances have major impact on the development of rail transport and railway companies in a country and that government plays an important role. The role of the government may be incidental or structural, but it concerns costs of rail infrastructure, balance between costs and revenues and tension between public and private interests. In Europe, the separation of transport and infrastructure has created open market competition for train operators. In Japan, productivity of rail transport increased after privatisation and, thanks to intensive use and real estate development, revenues were sufficient to cover the costs of infrastructure. The case of US makes painfully clear the effects of negative government influence and mismanagement, even with listing of independent freight companies on the stock exchange.

The separation of transport and infrastructure suits the European conditions but is often unthinkable on other continents. Yet, this separation is not unusual in other industries. For example, airports and airplanes; power stations and electricity network; and independent car factories (VDL in Born, the Netherlands) which produce cars for multiple brands such BMW and Mitsubishi.

The means of production and products can co-exist but operate independently. In a healthy industry, the income from sale of product must cover the costs of production. This is not the case with rail transport in Europe. Cost, income and use form a complex and often unclear combination. Chapter 2 provides insight into the logic of bringing costs and revenue of transport and infra in one business model so it becomes clear what comes from where as well as mutual connections and influence realised.

2   Business model of rail transport

Rail infrastructure and rail transport are inextricably linked. Infra is the means of production and rail transport the product. The product costs money and its sale generates revenue. The income depends on the number of passenger- and freight kilometers and the price for it. If the income is higher than the expense then profit is booked and vice versa.

Today, no railway company in Europe earns enough to cover all costs. The fact that these companies do not face bankruptcy is true because government cover deficits. In order to stimulate market forces and liberate transport companies from financial burden of rail infrastructure, monopolistic railway companies have been split into Transport and Infrastructure companies. Train operators pay access charge for the use of rail infrastructure. The split, government funding and user fee have positive effects on the rail transport business in Europe but made its business model more complex.

No one has complete insight into and responsibility for the total costs and benefits of rail transport in an area so optimisation is difficult. A single business model is needed to understand coherence and dependencies, and identify what binds the various businesses. ProRail developed a model based on the Dutch conditions but the model is universal applicable for Europe. It combines all costs and revenues of rail transport with utilisation, based on realisation information. Coherence is therefore transparent. The model provides insight for decision-making to all parties in the railway industry and for the politicians who decide about the organization and management of the railways, both at the national and European level.

Preface

The business model for rail transport comprises business models of several train operators and a model for rail infrastructure. With the availability of new knowledge and information, ProRail has modelled total costs and revenues of rail transport in a single business model, calibrated to the situation in the Netherlands.

The model provides insight into relationship among utilisation, costs, revenues and social benefits of rail transport. Its structure and background are described in this chapter but have previously appeared as a paper for CRNI-Congress in Brussels (Swier J. , 2012*) and published in the Railway Gazette International journal (Swier J. , 2012-4*). In this chapter the articles have been copied and supplemented with a description of the role that central government, train operators and infra manager play in uniting what was once separate but is inextricably linked. By taking the interests, demands and wishes of the passengers, shippers and other stakeholders as the starting point, the parties have forged a common and binding higher goal, from where individual business goals and contributions can be derived and tested.

The model

For rail infrastructure, an earlier model described the relationship between costs and utilization as well as the influence of the most important cost drivers (Swier J. , 2004*). The model is described in sub-section 8.2.6 at page 235. This model provided new knowledge but was limited to rail infrastructure. In order to cover the entire rail transport system, the infrastructure model had to be expanded to include costs and revenues of train operators.

The new information was provided as an annexure of an internal ProRail report covering costs and profits of the Dutch railway system (Hofstra, 2005*). The report was part of a new railway vision in which the cost effectiveness of lines was an important part. It provided costs, revenues and a ratio of the cost coverage for Dutch railway network as a whole and various line sections. For the purpose of analysis, the network was divided into line sections to which all costs and revenues of transport and infrastructure were allocated. These included:

- Operating costs and revenues for passenger train operators;
- Operating costs and revenues for freight operators;
- Rail infrastructure maintenance costs;
- Rail infrastructure depreciation (= renewal) costs;
- Traffic control costs;
- ProRail organization costs;
- Government financial contributions to the railway industry

The data and results per line were considerable reliable because they matched figures stated in official sources such as annual reports and data files. The costs and utilisation information per line from the report were used to model a business model for the entire rail transport in the Netherlands. That was information from 2005 and was updated to the situation in 2008. (Swier J. , 2016*). The modelling began by choosing the right starting points and the development of cost/benefit graphs for transport and infrastructure.

Principles for the business model of rail transport

Wherever possible, existing information was used for the model. ProRail has good insight into the costs and revenues of rail infrastructure. All management information on objects, costs, performance and utilisation is available for the approximately 95 lines into which the entire network is divided. Because the information was accessible via the web application RailFocus in one coherent database, a wealth of information and insights were produced.

ProRail had no insight into the costs and revenues of train operators but the annual reports proved to be a valuable source to start with. The information from the reports was combined with detailed transport information per line that ProRail had from Traffic Control databases and the QuoVadis system, which measures utilisation for access charge payment. Additional insights and information came from forecasting models for infrastructure development and transport protocols, as well as models testing new timetables.

For the business model, the costs and revenues of transport and infrastructure were plotted in relation to utilisation. The selected unit for utilisation had to be related to the commercial value of rail transport. This resulted in the selection of passenger kilometres for passenger transport and net tonne-kilometers for freight transport. Both of these parameters form the universally-accepted Transport Unit (TU) and can be added together (UIC, 2007*). For example, in the Netherlands in 2008, passenger transport produced about 17.8 million passenger kilometres and freight transport about 7.4 million net tonne-kilometres, adding to about 25.2 million TUs.

To combine the costs and benefits of different railway lines into one relationship graph, they are divided by the line kilometers. An alternative was track kilometres but the model concerns rail transport which is realised between two junctions regardless of the number of tracks and driving direction. With these starting points, the two axes were defined for the graphs of rail infrastructure, passenger transport and freight transport. The structuring of the three relation graphs is explained in the following (sub) sections.

Relationship chart costs rail infrastructure

For the rail infrastructure graph, the financial- and asset information in ProRail's SAP information system was used: costs incurred per line for maintenance, renewals, stewardship and the ProRail organisation. For consistency, the classification of railway lines was adopted from the Hofstra report, in which cost information was allocated to 70 lines instead of the 95 lines at the time.

For renewals, depreciation costs were used and not the realisation figures because realisation fluctuates widely and may deviate strongly from the average annual depreciation costs per line. The share of organisation costs, including traffic control, were allocated to railway lines on the basis of train kilometres. This resulted in the relation graph of Figure 13 in which small yellow triangles indicate the infrastructure costs per line and the red rectangle the national average. The graph area is limited by the trend line drawn through the line costs ($R^2 = 0.7$). The spread is due to differences in the complexity of the lines.

The costs are low for lines with low use because infrastructure of these lines is often single-track and simple. The costs are higher for lines that are used intensively because they often have more than two tracks and contain often complex yards with or without tunnels and/or flyovers.

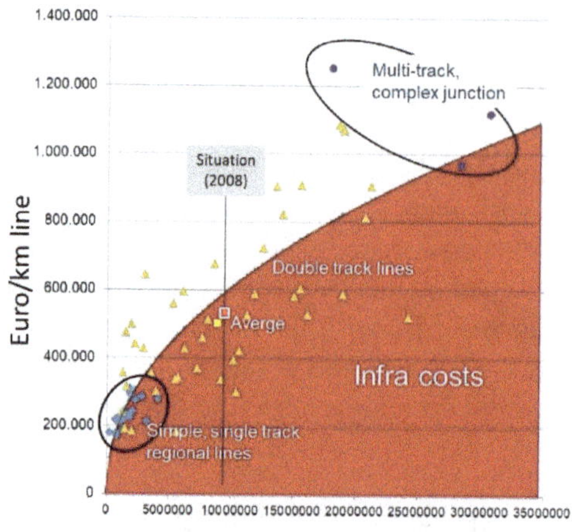

Figure 13   Utilisation versus costs per line in the Netherlands (2008)

Relationship chart costs/benefits of passenger transport

ProRail does not have detailed information about the costs and revenues of train operators but it has estimated the figures reasonably well based on available information. The results of an internal ProRail study on system costs and revenues per line made the task rather easy (Hofstra, 2005*). The train and tonne-kilometres per line were known because of detailed capacity management information for planned time tables. However, no realisation information was available about passenger kilometres per line. Hofstra estimated this parameter by combining train kilometres per line with the average train occupancy and then calculated the operating costs, revenues and depreciations using the TRANS and EKOM models.

Quote (Hofstra, 2005 *): *'TRANS is a model with which a set of train journeys from origin to destination (station-relation matrix) is allocated to the train series in a timetable. It is known how many passenger kilometres is made on each line section. Upon multiplication by the average price per passenger kilometre, this provides revenue per line section. It takes into account the fact that not every passenger kilometre yields the same amount.'*

Quote (Hofstra, 2005 *): *'EKOM is a model that calculates operating costs and revenues on train service levels. For this purpose, the number of wagons required per train is calculated on the basis of the busiest rush hour, combined with the thinning pattern for off-peak hours. The number of compositions required is also calculated on the basis of the driving time'.*

All cost items for personnel and material are then calculated on the basis of wagon kilometres, compositions and driving times. The type of equipment also plays a role. The item 'depreciation of equipment' is included in this calculation but is also provided separately.

The figures from Hofstra's report have been extrapolated for the development of the business model to the situation in 2008 by dividing the (small) differences between the three years evenly across the lines. For input details see Appendix 14.2. The relationship graph for passenger transport in Figure 14 was developed by plotting costs and revenues of train operators in relation to passenger kilometres per line.

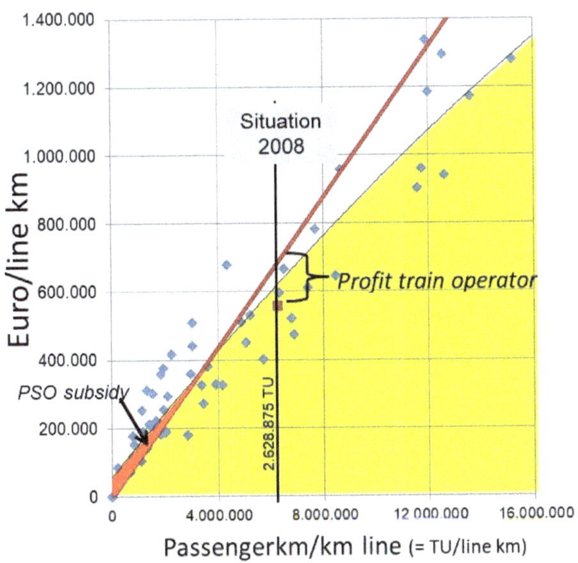

Figure 14   Cost versus benefit of passenger transport in the Netherlands (2008)

The small blue squares in the graph indicate cost per line kilometre and the small red rectangle is the national average. The yellow graph area is limited by the trend line ($R^2 = 0.92$) that runs through costs. The straight red income line is modelled by multiplying passenger kilometres with the average revenue of € 0.11 per passenger kilometre, a figure obtained from the NS annual report by dividing ticket sale revenue by the number of passenger kilometres. NS also had the following other sources of income in 2008 (NS, Jaarverslag 2008 (NS09), 2009*):

- Passenger transport abroad: costs € 697 million, profit € 19 million;
- Station development and operation: costs € 629 million, profit € 120 million;
- M&R rail infra and construction: costs EUR1,249 million, profit € 29 million

These costs and revenues are not included in the business model because they do not have direct relationship with rail transport on the Dutch network. While profit from station development and operation could have been included as income from transport, it was excluded. It was also decided not to divide the relationship chart for passenger transport into transport- and train costs because both are an integral part of rail transport and separation would make the model complex. In this context, it is notable that lease of equipment is now. For example, rolling stock of operating companies (ROSCOs) have been set up in the United Kingdom for leasing equipment to passenger- and freight operators. These companies lease the rolling stock to the train operating companies (TOCs) who then deploy it on their services. In this construction the TOCs do not need own capital and receive tax benefits for lease.

In the relationship graph for passenger transport, the costs and income of all passenger operators are taken into account. NS Passengers serves approximately 90% of that market and the remaining 10% is served by several small regional operators. The graph has been elaborated for both type of lines, those of NS Passenger operates and of regional operators. Both receive the Public Service Obligation (PSO) subsidy from government (national or regional) for operating unprofitable lines. In 2008, subsidy of € 77 million was granted to NS Passenger but that of various regional carriers could not be traced. The model accounts for the PSO subsidy as income, marked as a narrow red triangle in Figure 14. The PSO subsidy must at least cover the part that exceeds the income from ticket sales in the graph.

The relationship graph indicates cost differences per line. It also demonstrates that, on average, revenues (red, straight line) increase faster than costs (yellow area), and thus the cost-coverage ratio grows with utilisation. It is evident that NS Passenger is profitable on heavily used lines. The regional train operators have revenues lower than costs on some lines and depend on a PSO fee to pay all the costs. They have to keep costs low and maximise transport growth because, on average, income from ticket sales rises faster than costs.

The business model illustrates why competition works around the use of lines and not between companies on the same lines: the utilization intensity per line and subsequent income is too low for competition on lines. For example, if a competing train operator is admitted on an intensively used line then use and revenue per operator reduces by 50%. The model shows that profit for both parties will disappear because revenues fall faster than the costs. To avoid loss, the costs have to go down or the income has to go up. Because the costs have to decrease, quality improvement is unlikely, and performance of both companies declines.

Cost-benefit relationship of freight transport

The least is information available about freight transport because the sector is fully liberalised. In order to establish the relationship among costs, revenues and utilisation thereof, annual report figures from DB Schenker Rail and utilisation information from ProRail capacity management were used. Indicators for the costs and income of DB Schenker: cost per net tonkm are € 0,041 and the profit at about 6.6% in 2008. Appendix 14.2 provides input data which yields the relationship graph in Figure 15. Because there are no cost and revenue figures available per line, the relationship graph is constructed by drawing an almost straight line from the origin through the derived transport costs for average annual transport. The fixed costs are rated low because practice shows that small freight operators can exist by taking benefit of lease or use of old amortised equipment.

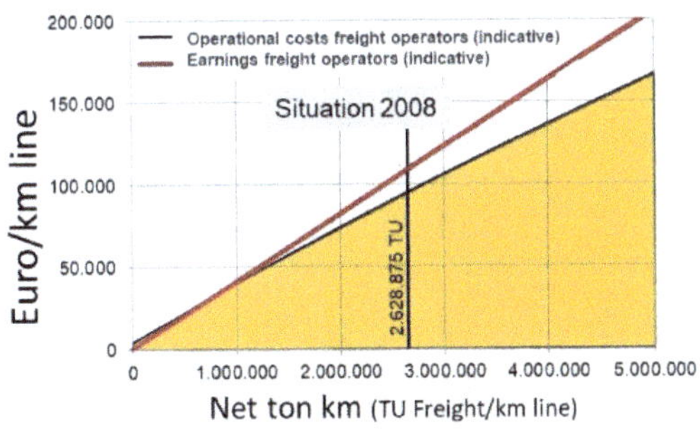

Figure 15   Relationship graph cost/benefit of freight transport in the Netherlands (2008)

In the Netherlands, freight transport accounts for around 30% of the total TUs and passenger transport for the remaining 70%. The relationship charts for passenger and freight transport have been drawn up by dividing the trend lines per modality over the total annual use and using the freight graph as a basis. According to the modelling data, the total cost of freight transport is a factor of 2.7 (= 0.11 / € 0.041/TU) lower than that of passenger transport. The relationship chart for freight transport is much less steep than that of passenger transport. This has been attributed to lower cost of equipment and less staff. The small freight operators are profitable only if they succeed in keeping the fixed costs very low.

Access charge

The European regulations require train operators to pay an access charge for use of rail infrastructure. These are costs for operators and income for infrastructure manager, which reduces government subsidy. The access charge calculation in the Netherlands is based on several factors: train kilometres, tonne-kilometres, number of stops per type of station, energy consumption and some specific services.

For the business model in use, the average price for access charge is estimated at €0.0086/TU and this corresponds to revenue of approximately € 199 million in 2008. The per TU cost difference for each type of transport is considerable; passenger operators pay € 0.0104 and freight operators € 0.0019 per TU. Thus, on average, freight operators pay 5x less per TU. This is because train kilometres of relatively light passenger trains is charged more heavily than the net tonnes of freight. This seems reasonable because freight revenue per TU is 2.7 times lower than passenger transport, and profit margins of freight are small because of the intense competition with road and water transport.

Compared with other European countries, the access charges in the Netherlands are low. This is not expected because the Netherlands - together with Switzerland - has the most intensively-used network in Europe and NS is the largest train operators making a profit and using relatively small PSO subsidy for unprofitable lines. There are three possible explanations for a relatively high access charge in other European countries:

- The revenues of carriers are higher because of more expensive train ticket or higher freight price. Example includes € 0.16 /km in Great Britain versus € 0.12 in the Netherlands (SMC, 2014*, p. 3).
- The costs are lower for infrastructure and/or transport. Examples are Sweden and Finland
- The government subsidy for infrastructure goes (at least partly) to train operators and comes back to the infra manager via a much higher access charge. Example are Germany, Belgium and France.

The last explanation often applies: high PSO subsidy = high access charge = low infra subsidy, and vice versa. A benchmark performed by SMC Consultants on behalf of the Belgian railways (SNCB) confirms this logic (SMC, 2014*, p. 2).

The access charge tells nothing about the business without insight into PSO subsidy and profit of train operators. The access charges vary much among European countries even though the same EU rule is implemented because total income from access charges may not exceed the usage dependent (read: variable) costs.

Generic relationship graph for rail transport

By combining the relationship graphs previously described, a single relationship chart is created that describes all costs/benefits of rail transport in the Netherlands, see Figure 16. The costs as well as use of passenger and freight transport are plotted for each line. The weighted average of passengers and freight income is € 0.089/TU[14] (= € 2,245 million / (25,240 million TU / 2,831 line km)). The coloured areas represent development of transport and infrastructure costs in relation to utilisation. The access charge is a cost item for the carriers and an income for the infrastructure manager ProRail. In the model, the total infrastructure costs are, therefore, a sum of the infrastructure costs (dark red area) and the access charge (orange area). The little light brown triangles below are the freight transport costs per line and form the basis. The blue balls are the added passenger transport costs and the yellow squares the added infrastructure

---

[14] The profit from station development and exploitation is considered a second line of business but has been excluded. Its linear relationship line in the graph would run from EUR 0 / TU at zero use to EUR 0.0048 / TU (= EUR 120 million / 25,240 million TU / 2,831 line km) for national average use.

costs. The white line illustrates revenue from passenger and freight transport. The dashed white line in the bottom left corner delineates passenger transport revenue from PSO subsidy (hard to see but corresponds to the upper boundary of the red area in Figure 14 at page 57, left under).

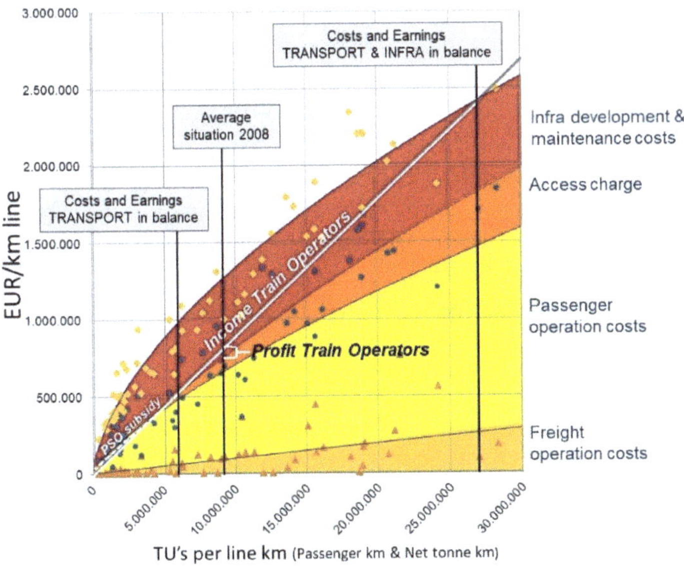

Figure 16   Business model for rail transport in the Netherlands

The model provides a number of interesting insights:
- The model describes the average situation, cost per line may differ substantial.
- Rail infrastructure has higher fixed costs than transport.
- For passenger transport lines, average costs of non-intensively used lines are higher than average revenues; a PSO subsidy is needed.
- If transport use increases, transport revenues grow faster than the costs.
- At current kilometre rates (= ticket prices), transport is cost-effective but not enough to cover rail infrastructure costs.
- The access charge increases costs of the train operators and reduces their cost coverage.
- Transport volume growth is need to make transport and infrastructure cost-effective. Profitable secondary businesses, such as station operation and real estate development, have positive influence on the business model but are not included.

The Netherlands has large-scale public rail transport because of the high population density and the fact that social benefits for 'Ltd Netherlands' are higher than costs of rail infrastructure construction and maintenance. When social benefits are added to the model then a complete business-economic picture is given of an industry that serves both private and public interest.

Social cost/benefits

With growing prosperity, transport demand and consequent traffic jams have increased considerably. Rail transport reduces traffic jams, accidents and environmental pollution. To fully capture positive effects of public transport on social and environmental well-being, social costs and benefits are also included in the business case through a Social Cost Benefit Analysis (MKBA = Maatschappelijke Kosten Baten Analayse). The crux of MKBA is expressing the social effects in monetary terms for addition to the economic costs and benefits. The European directive, Guide to Cost-Benefit Analysis of investment projects (EU C. , 2008*), enumerates the following benefits:

- Travel time savings by reduction of traffic jams;
- Lower air pollution;
- Fewer accidents;
- Lower damage to the landscape;
- Lower production costs; and
- Economic stimulus.

In 2005, ProRail estimated the social benefits of rail transport at network level at minimum of € 1,200 million and maximum of € 2,400 million annually (Dalen, 2005*), respectively € 0.424 and € 0.848 per line kilometer. Rail transport in the Netherlands is cost-effective because benefits outweigh the costs, see Figure 17.

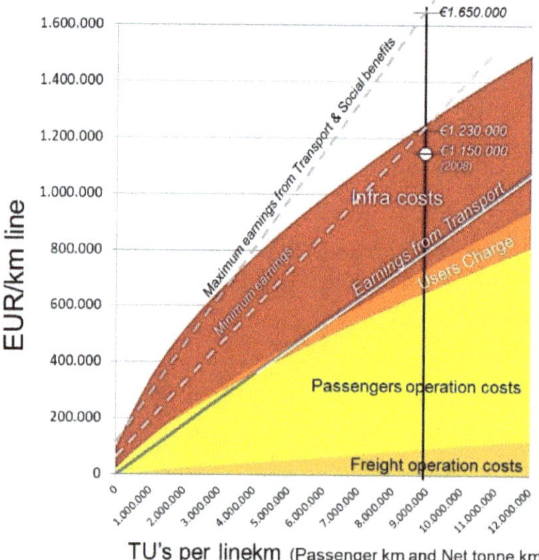

Figure 17   Influence of the social costs/benefits on the business model (situation 2008)

New relationships and roles

With the split of transport and infrastructure, two large flows of money are fully separated in the Netherlands, along with their associated roles, tasks and focus of the main actors: government, train operators and infrastructure manager. It is now evident that the government fulfils several essential roles in the management of rail transport. It is the owner and financier of rail infrastructure, concession provider and the guardian of public interest. Without government policy and financing, there would be very little left of rail transport in the Netherlands (and all other countries in Europe). With the use of performance agreements and financial targets, the government stimulates the train operators and infra manager to improve results. It no longer subsidises a monopolistic transport company but has an explicit and active role in the management of public rail transport in the Netherlands.

Without responsibilities of rail infrastructure, the train operators focus on their core task: efficient and effective transport of passengers and freight. ProRail manages, on behalf of the government, not only construction and maintenance of rail infrastructure, but also traffic control and capacity allocation. It adds value in the interaction between train operators and government. From an independent position, ProRail advises on optimisation of rail transport. If the infrastructure manager and the train operator(s) do not work out together the best solution, the government will make the best choice for the benefit of the country and customers. In order to prevent sub-optimisation, the main players must have the same main objective and the government should represent requirements and wishes of the customer: passengers and shippers (I&M M. , 2012). This common objective unites all actors in the industry and directs their activities.

Common goals and achievements

The goal of rail sector is efficient and effective rail transport service. The average passenger and shipper may not be interested in train operations and rail infrastructure as long as service is safe and reliable. The government formulated the following main objectives in 2012 (I&M, 2012*):

- *Safety.* Safe transport, safe working and safe living with rail;
- *Reliability.* Minimising disruptions and impact;
- *Mobility.* Growth of passenger and freight transport while protecting the environment;
- *Actual travel information.* Correct, timely, consistent and up-to-date information is a basic passenger need today;
- *Travel convenience and comfort.* Improvement of travel time and experience with door-to-door service and accessible stations and trains;
- *Efficiency.* Affordable rail transport by improvement in cost-effectiveness of both train operation and rail infrastructure;
- *Sustainability.* Maintaining leading position with innovation

Figure 18 provides a coherent overview of the roles, goals and achievements of the parties delivering the aforementioned goals. The goals do not differ from the advertising slogan of NS in the seventies and are still important to the customer today: 'Vlug, Veilig, Voordelig' (= in English: 'Fast, Safe and Affordable').There are now new goals and performances added to it regarding travel information, comfort and sustainability, factors which were of little concern in the seventies.

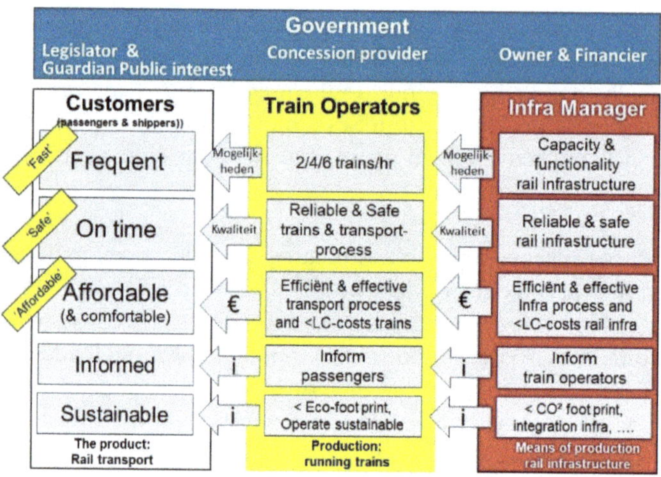

Figure 18   Performance matrix of railway sector: roles, goals and performance

Train operators and infrastructure manager each make their own and coherent contribution to realise goals that the government has formulated for transport users. In practice, rail infrastructure is a prerequisite for train operators because it is a means of production with a long lifespan. That has always been the case, regardless of the split between transport operation and rail infrastructure..

There were tensions in the industry when the split happened between transport and infrastructure. With the passage of time, the parties involved have matured in their respective roles and understand each other better. The government stimulates this cooperation by formulating goals for the entire rail sector. This is illustrated by the context that ProRail not only reduces infrastructure failures but also the impact of disruptions on punctuality (ProRail, 2011*). The rail sector players collaborate to achieve common goals by improving performance cost effectively.

Optimal and sustainable performance and life cycle costs
When transport and infrastructure are separated, the one company managing costs and revenues of rail transport is replaced with three entities: government, train operators and infrastructure manager. None of these has the integral responsibility for sustainable and optimal management of costs and performance of rail transport. This is complicated by the fact that there are several train operators and

multiple ministries and local authorities. For example, the ministries of Finance and Infrastructure & Environment (I&M), provinces and municipalities each have their own goals, budget responsibility and agenda. They all form part of the institutional triangle. In order to perform better for less money, there are four options:

- Increasing efficiency: *'do things right'*
- Increasing effectiveness: *'do the right things'*
- Improve the system: *'increase capabilities'*
- Improve the use: *'optimise timetables and track use'*

Doing things right involves operations, which is the responsibility of the service providers. However, it also depends on infra manager because train free periods for maintenance put transport out-of-service. Effectiveness is particularly influenced in the strategy and planning phase. It determines what needs to be done and how to do it. A good (technical) assessment is important for life cycle costs analyses of project alternatives.

The largest life cycle cost reductions can be realised in the development phase, the stage in which demand is set for new capabilities and functionalities. Thereafter, choices are made that determine life cycle costs in the future. It is in this phase that biggest savings or mistakes are realised with impact on entire lifetime.

Experience has shown that it is wise to regularly involve a plan developer and schedule maker in assessing the capability and functionality of the existing infrastructure. Infra was built a long time ago but circumstances and use continue to change drastically over the years. The Dutch rail infrastructure was built almost entirely in the period 1860-1910, as indicated in Figure 2 at page 21. Since then, there have been changes and increase in use and performance requirements. Nevertheless, train service is still largely delivered on the same infrastructure. This is why ProRail started to systematically analyse how capacity of the existing old network can be increased without additional network extensions. The project 'Benutten & Bouwen' (= Utilize and Construct') (Spoorsector, 2003*) has taken an important first step towards this goal.

The programs 'High Frequency Rail Transport' program (= PHS) (I&M M. , 2011-9) and 'Improvement Program 2012-2015' aim to create a robust rail system by adding capacity and quality in consultation with train operators and other stakeholders (ProRail, 2012*). For example, ProRail and NS have various inspiring and concrete ideas to improve punctuality, quality and capacity of rail transport, often for lower life cycle costs (Hofstra, 2005*), (Swier J. , 2006*), (Swier J. , 2010*), (Hofstra, 2010*). To illustrate this, a few examples of collaboration between operators and the infra manager to improve rail transport results:

- Disconnection of lines increases capacity and makes the time table less vulnerable to the secondary consequences of disruptions.
- Change of infrastructure strategy from 'maximising flexibility'[15] to 'maximising performance' increases capacity and quality while lowering costs. This is because of reduction in number of switches as well as maintenance and renewals because of simpler catenary, signalling and traffic control system.
- No longer using 'double diamond switch'[16] and replacing these with switch type 1:15. This lowers infrastructure costs, reduces failures, increases track section speed, increases capacity and shortens travel-/ driving time, which increases the turnover rate of train equipment and thereby reduces transport costs.
- Reduction of double-single track signalling[17] to make the signalling system simpler, cheaper and more reliable.
- Reduction of signal distance to increase capacity in disturbance and reduce headway and follow-up delays.
- Utilising professional risk management to reduce costs and improve quality through utilisation- and condition-based maintenance, differentiate maintenance frequencies, realise longer life and steer performance.

The examples indicate measures to increase capacity and quality at lower costs. The separation of transport and infrastructure enables the development of new measures from different perspectives and makes evident the conflicts of interest caused by unbalanced distribution of costs and benefits. Improvements are achieved only when all parties are aware of others' possibilities and limitations, and collaborate for a shared, optimal and sustainable solution. The main objectives formulated by the government for rail transport provide the common point that connects disparate organisations.

The infra manager contributes to realising demands and wishes of passengers and shippers while balancing performance and costs of rail infrastructure. The effectiveness and efficiency of this task depends on the quality of cooperation in the institutional triangle, its own organisation and the service providers. Asset management is a professional technique to manage costs and performance of rail infrastructure optimally and sustainably over the entire life expectancy of the assets taking into account the stakeholders' interests. It is a new, powerful and rather complex technique that influences orientation, structure and operations of the entire railway industry. The development of an asset management organisation is

---

[15] Before the nineties, the 'open end layout' was discussed, which implied that every timetable and track plan was possible on the available rail infrastructure.

[16] The 'double diamond switch' combines possibilities of four separate switches in a much smaller space. It is a crossing of two tracks with capability to change track from any direction.

[17] One can use a track in two directions.

described in the two chapters that follow: Chapter 3, which covers the development of infrastructure organisation, and chapter 4, which covers outsourcing of maintenance.

In the second part of the book, the development of the asset management system is described. It includes organisation and management principles; management of performance and costs; and influence of conditions, activities and risks. For now, we move to the development of the infrastructure organisation.

3 Infra manager ProRail

The management of maintenance and renewal (M&R) of rail infrastructure has long been an inseparable part of the rail transport companies. Socio-economic developments prompted drastic changes in an apparently stable situation. This chapter describes how the NS infrastructure organisation developed into an independent, professional infra manager (ProRail Ltd) that is capable of optimally managing the performance and costs through the entire life cycle in accordance with requirements and wishes of the stakeholders. The organisation was not created from a visionary master plan but rather evolved organically by continuously anticipating changing circumstances, meeting new needs and exercising will to fully control performance, risks and costs.

3.1 Development organisation

Not too long ago, maintenance was considered a craft that costs money. This has changed with the influence of mechanisation (Appendix 14.1.3), rise of information and computer technology (Appendix 14.1.4) and availability of powerful management techniques (Appendix 14.1.5). The aircraft and oil industry were at the forefront of these changes. The railway companies in Europe were conservative and awaiting. They were mostly traditional and internally oriented monopolists, dependent on government subsidy. These characteristics were also applicable to the infrastructure departments within the Netherland Railway (NS). The management and maintenance & renewal of rail infrastructure were carried out by NS Infrastructuur (Is) and NS Exploitatie Onderhoud (Ep Od), as indicated in Figure 19. Both organisations were technical, task oriented and centrally managed.

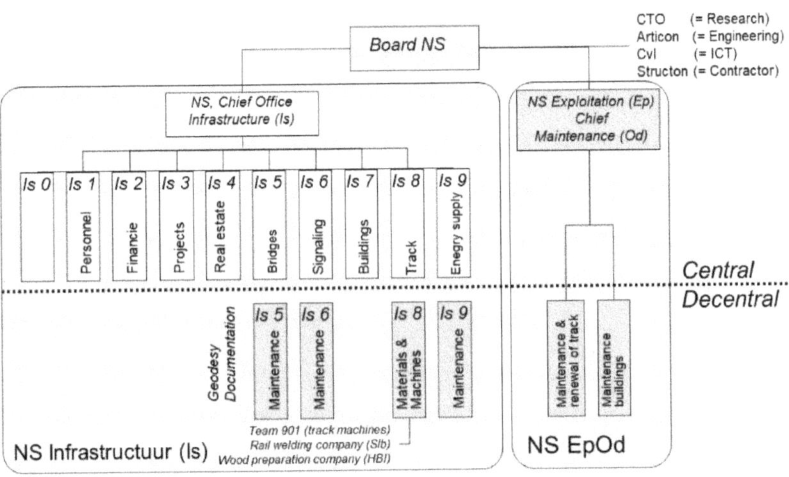

Figure 19   NS infra organisations within the railway company NS up to 1990

The regional maintenance organisations of Is (the grey blocks) fell under the centrally organised new construction departments (white bocks). It was striking that there was a split in the management of the superstructure; this includes track, switches and level crossings. Infrastructure was responsible for technical policy, heavy equipment and material supply, while EpOd was responsible for the execution of maintenance and renewal of superstructure.

Upon the advice of an internal steering committee, the NS board of directors decided in April 1988 to study the organisation of the infra process. The steering committee had concluded that the organisation was not suitable for an optimal infra process, particularly in the areas of management and maintenance. McKinsey was commissioned for an in-depth study. In hindsight, one can say that this was the beginning of a period of 15-20 years in which the organisation underwent changes in position, structure, working methods and culture because of drastic changes in the entire rail transport sector.

Period 1990-1994; reorder

McKinsey recommended a new organisational set-up of the infra process within the NS in January 1989. The title of the report accurately summarises purpose of the recommendations: *'Naar een meer Bedrijfsmatig en Doorzichtig Functionerend Infra-Proces'* (In English: 'Towards a more Operational and Transparent Functioning Infra Process') (McKinsey, 1989-1). Three organisation adaptations formed the core of the recommendations:

- Combine scattered maintenance and renewal departments.
- Separate all engineering activities.
- Fully decentralise the maintenance and renewal process.

The major reorganisation that resulted in 1990 was known as ODIS, an anagram of the two organisations merged: Ep Onderhoud (Od) and Infrastructuur (Is). Figure 20 described the structure of the new organisation formed, NS InfraBeheer (If). The reorganisation caused a lot of emotional turmoil, especially among managers in Utrecht who were specialists responsible for the technical system. The employees were unhappy about the fragmentation of infrastructure activities and technical division. The new organisation structure was based on integrated business management and decentralisation. Many managers did not see the usefulness and necessity of this restructuring; however, the board stood firm and new management was appointed. The time was right to combine coherent tasks and de-specialise management.

With the merger of Od and Is, all engineering tasks were combined in a new NS Engineering department, which from then on delivered projects of NS If. This opened access to external engineering firms, which were expected to increase capacity and flexibility for improved effectiveness and efficiency and allow better and faster implementation of rail infrastructure expansion projects. In retrospect, it can be concluded that these expectations have been fulfilled.

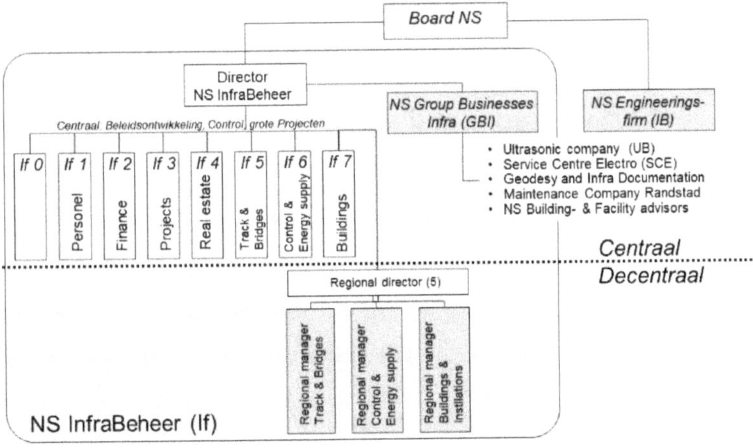

Figure 20   NS Infra organisation (1990-1995)

The impact of the separation of engineering activities was drastic. The role of the engineering organisation was integral in defining culture of the entire infrastructure organisation and determined, to a large extent, the identity of the employees. The construction of new railway lines, bridges and signalling systems involves high-quality engineering skills with tangible results that appeal to the imagination. This was the focus of the top management. The work in maintenance was considered traditional and less appealing because result were not tangible, as a new railway line, but rather had the character of a service which keep existing infrastructure functional and safe. In making the engineering firm independent, it was necessary to properly secure the technical knowledge and documentation necessary for the core tasks of NS If. Fortunately, this went well and did not lead to serious problems.

With the separation of engineering activities, the identity of the management organisation changed into a strong decentralised maintenance & renewal management organisation with growing awareness that the business performance of rail transport depends on management and maintenance of rail infrastructure. This was the beginning of a fundamental shift in management focus from design, building and maintenance of physical objects to a provider of a rail network with specified capability, functionality and quality.

The goal of decentralisation was to shift decision-making from central staff and to the regional areas of management and maintenance. The central staff had to conquer a new position in consultation with the regions but the regions were autonomous and did not need a national policy. Consequently, national policy was replaced with self-aware and integral maintenance management that responded more flexibly and commercially to local requirements. Later, it became clear that these effects were negative and decentralization was too powerful . However, it was a useful and necessary phase in organisational development to realise change in culture and customer focus.

Period 1994-1998; separate and outsource

From 1990 onwards, the engineering activities were set aside and the maintenance & renewal management was decentralised in five regions. The change was not only limited to organisational restructuring but also impacted attitude and working method of employees and managers. Hardly had the first development started or a new one already appeared.

The Wijffels commission came in 1992 with the recommendation to restructure the NS organisation and the relationship between the government and NS. The commission advised to split the NS organisation into a transport and infrastructure organisation. A distinction was needed between the three types of activities at the top level: commercial core activities, non-core activities and non-commercial tasks. The non-commercial tasks included all infra activities. The three task organisations were NS InfraBeheer[18], NS Traffic Control and Railned, an infrastructure organisation to manage capacity development and distribution. These three organisations were later housed in the NS Railinfratrust BV, an independent company owned by the government and legal owner of the entire rail network.

In order to realise the separation of transport and infrastructure, the operation *"Sporen naar '96"* (In English: 'Tracks to '96') was executed with an actual split in 1995. NS If joined this NS-wide reorganisation with its own reorganisation, *'Infra '96"*, which involved separation of transport and infrastructure as well as a split of the infrastructure process into a management and execution part, with the intention to privatise maintenance execution in the long term.

The split of transport and infra went much deeper than demanded by European regulations. While the European Union (EU) did not provide guidelines for the positioning of the maintenance organisation, the NS management decided that maintenance had to be outsourced to provide access to foreign contractors into the Dutch railway market. In order to maintain a strong market position, restructuring and privatisation of rail maintenance were necessary. In his dissertation, Maarten Veraart states that this misinterpretation of the EU directive was deliberate to cause change (Veraart M. , 2007, p. 145). The responsible change management considered privatisation a stepping-stone to enforce the envisaged organisational changes. The NS benefited from it because the sales of maintenance organizations generated income. In that period, NS was eagerly looking for

---

[18] The name changed later in NS Railinfrabeheer

money, because in 1994 the Minister had unexpectedly announced that NS would be privatized after 1998 and would go to the stock market.

The first step in restructuring of the infra process was resignation of approximately 600 employees in 1994 to increase the efficiency and effectiveness of the organisation. This happened after an overhead value analysis under the motto *'Snoeien om te groeien'* (In English: 'Prune to grow'). After shrinking size of the organisation, all rail maintenance units were concentrated in a new management organisation called NS Railinfrabeheer (RIB) and a separate business unit Execution (Uitvoering, 4-1994). The business unit Execution consists of NS Infra Services (IS) with three regional management companies for the execution of maintenance, six facility companies[19], a trade & industrial company[20], and a heavy equipment company, see Figure 21.

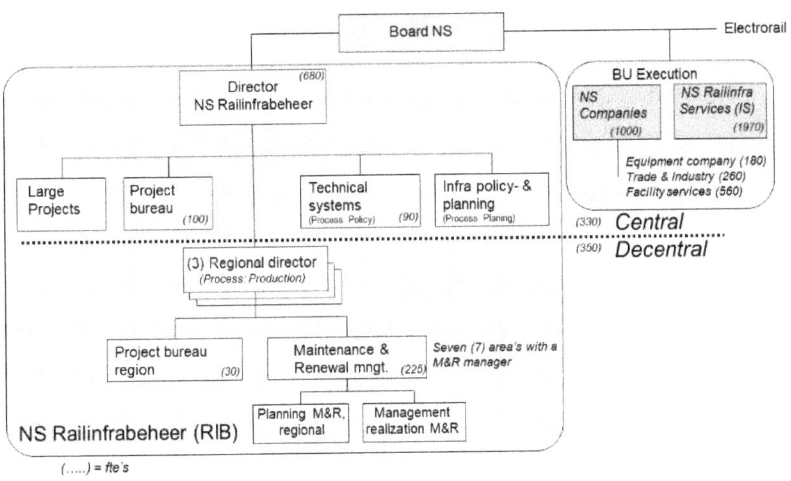

Figure 21   NS Railinfrabeheer organization (1995-1998)

The RIB consisted of a project organisation for new construction, technical staff for infrastructure policy and staff for national consolidation of decentralised maintenance and renewal planning. There were seven regional maintenance & renewal organizations and three regional project bureaus, spread over the three regions, each managed by a regional director.

In addition to the separation of infra management and execution, the NS also privatised the NS Engineering Office in 1994. It started under the name Holland Rail-consult and is now called Movares. After the consolidation in 1990, the

---

[19] Facility services included: Ultrasonic Company (UB), Data Telecom Services (DTS), Service Center for Electrical Engineering (SCE), Geodesy & Infra documentation (G&I), Maintenance Company Randstad (OBR) and Building & Facility Advisors (GFA).

[20] The trade and industrial companies were: Switch Building Company (WBB), Rail Welding Company (SLB), Wooden sleeper Company (HVB) and Central Stockroom Track components (CMB).

separation in 1994 was intended to be the last step to realise maximum benefit of market forces in construction of rail infrastructure. Safeguarding of the knowledge and information at the new Railinfra management organisation received a lot of attention and was arranged through an outsourcing policy, agreements on copyright, guarantee of design as well as agreements on rights of ownership and use of specific production tools. There was a division of technical expertise by quality and quantity, and a division of tasks for participation in international working groups and committees.

After the consolidation of companies in 1994 and privatisation of all engineering activities, the next step was regrouping through merger of NS Infra Services, NS ElectroRail[21] and three resistant Dutch rail contractors. By the end of 1997, this had resulted into the formation of three new and equivalent rail maintenance companies to carry out the entire work package required for rail infrastructure maintenance. Each company received a share of the total maintenance market: Strukton (50%), Volker Stevin (30%) and BAM/NBM (20%). The NS equipment company merged with Strukton's equipment department and became independent. ElectroRail was split up and divided among the three new maintenance contractors. The Trade & Industry business was privatised under the brand Railpro[22] and became the largest supplier of products and logistics services in the Dutch rail infrastructure market.

With this final restructuring, the outsourcing of all operational maintenance tasks became a fact in 1998 as did the supply of material and equipment. This was a drastic change for more than 4,000 civil workers but it was realised without any noteworthy labour unrest. This may have been possible because privatisation of maintenance was considered necessary and collective labour agreement for maintenance sector was financially attractive. A negative consequence of these far-reaching changes was a sharp increase in the number of technical train effecting irregularities (TAOs) in the period 1996-1998. These increased by more than 50%, from 5,600 to more than 8,400 and the increase has been attributed to uncertainty among executive staff and insufficient management attention to radical changes. After the reorganisation and privatisation were realised, the recovery was quick. From 2003 onwards, the number of technical TAOs fell below the levels before separation of transport and infrastructure. For more details on the development of the infrastructure performance, please refer section 7.4.

1995-2005; new railway governance model

At the end of 1995, RIB was a line organisation with decentralised maintenance & renewal (M&R). The infrastructure managers were fully responsible for personnel, costs, quality and planning of the M&R process in their area. In the central

---

[21] ElectroRail NV was a subsidiary of the NS from 1948 to 1999. It served train engines, switches, electronics, box construction, sheet metal and coatings.
[22] It is known as Voestalpine Railpro BV since 2002.

organisation in Utrecht comprised technical staff who drafted technical policy and regulations on behalf of the RIB board, supervised product development and conducted research and analyses.

The strategic part of the M&R process was hardly developed at the time and received little attention because maintenance management was not a specific task for NS infra management. There was a general and financial director and the responsibility for maintenance was delegated to the three regional directors. Not only were the instruments and information missing, but also the processes were underdeveloped and lacking balance between centralised and decentralised tasks. As a metaphor for the organisation, the Indonesian archipelago was used: *'beautiful islands without good connections'*. The following arguments were given to describe the necessity of having a vision on the design and control of the M&R process:

- The task of RIB was drastically changed after the split into maintenance management- and execution.
- After the reorganisations, NS consisted of several independent and result-oriented companies. The informal network disintegrated and relationships became formal.
- The national government and train operating companies got more attention for the costs and quality of rail infra. The output control shifted from implicit to explicitly defined and managed performance.
- Because all maintenance work had to be outsourced, controls such as contracts, specifications and quality measurements were needed.
- The possibilities and valuation of the maintenance sector changed. Maintenance was no longer seen as a craft and cost item, but as a management-intensive profession which influences results of rail transport.
- The intention to implement the integrated SAP information system meant that the information requirements of all processes had to be mapped out. The management wanted a clear picture of the desired situation.

Vision for the asset management organisation

In the vision that was elaborated, outsourcing of all executive engineering and maintenance tasks was decisive for the new position and task of RIB. The RIB became a client with role and task as the current concept of 'Asset Manager'. It was the link between the stakeholders who wanted something as well as the contractors and engineering firms who were to realise the requirements. The roles were described as 'Asset Owner', 'Asset Users' and 'Service providers'. For more information on the organisational conditions, please refer to section 1.2 and 6.1. For the positioning and relationships among units, a chain was used as the metaphor as shown in Figure 22 (Projectteam, 1995*). It is an appealing image that still applies.

The management process for which RIB was responsible had contracts and management of realisation as output. The core task was to translate the objectives of the national government and train operators into many executive assignments for contractors and engineering firms, and to manage the realisation of these contracts; *'from assignment to assignments'*. With this determination, the RIB defined its position and task in a simple and appealing way. This gave the employees something to hold on to, and it became the basis for a new identity and focus. The vision was elaborated in phases and recorded in four small books on A5 format with the titles:

1. *De plattegrond van Railinfrabeheer* (in English: 'The ground plan of Railinfrabeheer'), (Projectteam, 1995*);
2. *De rode draad van de besturing Instandhouding* (in English: 'The red thread of the maintenance management process'), (Projectteam, 1997*);
3. *De veelzijdigheid van instandhoudingsconcepten* (in English: 'The versality of M&R Concepts'), (Projectteam, 1997-4*); T
4. *Sturen op output. Samen werken aan kwaliteit (in English:* 'Manage on output. Work together on quality'), (Projectteam, 1998-1*).

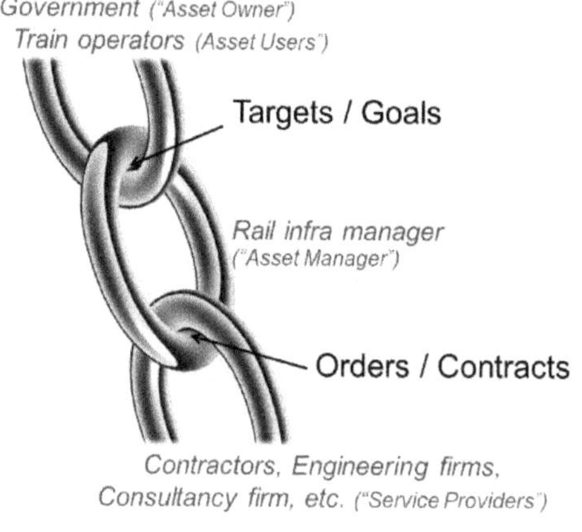

Figure 22   Positioning of the Asset Manager

In the booklet about the ground plan, an image is sketched for positioning and main structure of the new management organisation. The booklet about the red thread describes control of the maintenance & renewal process and instruments required. It discusses a fictitious example of introducing a plastic sleeper. The booklet on risk analysis and maintenance concepts provides knowledge and information for delivery and systematic recording of rail infrastructure maintenance. It introduces risk management instruments and shows its importance for management and execution of maintenance process. The last booklet was about the outsourcing of maintenance and its management by output or performance. It discusses various fictitious practical situations.

Vision for development of asset management organisation

When the position of RIB became clear, a management model was developed to serve as the starting point for structuring the organisation (Projectteam, 1997*). The organisation model comprised three basic control tasks, namely, Strategy, Tactics and Operations, and four coherent management activities, namely, Plan, Do, Check and Act, also known as PDCA- or Deming circle. This model is explained in section 6.7. The basic control tasks were called main processes at the time and the activities in the PDCA circle were the four elementary management processes. The process model was used as a work breakdown structure (WBS) for setting up the control process. The WBS is a matrix formed by the three main processes and the four management processes. Together they create 12 sub-processes as indicated in Figure 23.

Main processes	Management activities			
	Act	**Plan**	**Do**	**Check**
Strategy (Policy)	Identify demand/wish stakeholders	Plan Policy	Delegate realization policy	Evaluate Policy
Tactics (Planning)	Identify best solution	Prioritize & optimize solutions	Plan & delegate execution	Evaluate realized planning
Operate (Execution)	Choose best contract type	Tendering	Manage realization contracts	Evaluate contract realisation

Figure 23   Work Breakdown Structure (WBS) control proces of an Asset Manager

These are the essential building blocks of an organisation and the organizational conditions. To specifically develop and strengthen the 12 subprocesses, an insight was adopted that the results of an organisation are influenced by four conditions (Marcelis, 1984*), also known as the organisational conditions, namely:

1. Personnel: number and level of persons involved in the processes;
2. Organisational arrangements: appointments about functions, tasks, powers and responsibilities of staff members as well as course of processes;
3. Information: all recorded data required for a task and its control;
4. Control tools: all systems, methods, techniques and physical aids available to personnel.

When the WBS and conditions were used to map the situation at RIB, it appeared that policy process was hardly developed (10%), the planning process for around 30% and the operational process around 50%. Many tasks were performed, but they were incomplete and incoherent. This was also experienced by the employees and managers; therefore, the WBS analysis identified the missing part. Having obtained insight and by monitoring progress, the management got control on the development of the organisation.

The process model and WBS illustrate the relationship between subprocesses. Each subprocess makes a unique and indispensable contribution to another subprocesses. If any subprocesses does not produce the desired result then there is a negative effect on the quality of the contracts, their management and/or the realised performance. The quality and costs of rail infrastructure come under scrutiny as the organisation transitions from a technical and task-oriented focus to a performance and process-oriented focus. It involved development and implementation of instruments and processes as well as several organisational changes, with the first major one in 1998.

Period 1998-2002; stabilisation and development

The management model and WBS led to the insight that organisational adjustment was needed to improve the positioning and alignment of processes. The big difference from previous reorganisations was that this time the driving forces were internal and not external. The following adjustments were made in 1998:

- Management of NS Railinfrabeheer (NS RIB) was expanded with a Director for New Constructions.
- All expansion- and change projects were transferred to the New Construction department.
- The director responsible for Maintenance & Renewal got a staff group (named: technical systems) for policy development, policy control as well as development of new processes and steering instruments such as telematics control.
- The decentralised Maintenance & Renewal management reduced from seven management areas to four regions.
- Planning and realisation were organised in a central planning department and M&R management was decentralised with contract managers and technical experts in regions.
- Project leaders and trace managers in the regions became responsible for , respectively, managing new building projects and the day-to-day performance through maintenance (process) contracts.
- Technical experts started to project-based work relationships so they got a regional manager and consultation with centre-level system managers.

Figure 24 illustrates the results in the form of an organisation chart. It is worth noting that the main structure remained the same: a line organisation. That choice was undisputed at the time and not open to discussion. Later, it would appear that this structure is not optimal for an asset management organisation under development with many instruments and skills to be implemented.

The reorganisation started in January 1998 and by the end of June 1998 everyone had either completed or transferred the old tasks, moved or not, and taken on new tasks. In that period, all 700 RIB employees played a two-day management game to learn the value of collaboration in realising objectives as an organization. It is necessary to bridge differences, break the 'managerial clay layers' and eliminate contradictions. Only by improving internal cooperation and communication can the 'archipelago' Railinfrabeheer function as one organisation. It is essential to structure the organisation based on processes and results.

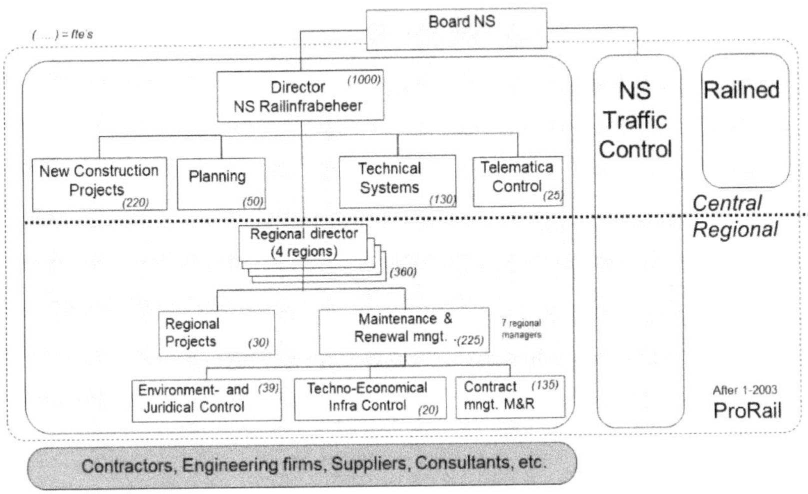

Figure 24   NS Railinfrabeheer organisation (1998-2002/2005)

With reorganisation of 1998 and experience with the RIB game, a new phase emerged in which splitting, cutting, regrouping and outsourcing ended to give way to a period of stability and improvement. Policy as well as skills for maintenance-, contract- and knowledge-management are skills were developed. An overview of the biggest improvement projects from 1998 gives a good picture of the level of organisational development at the time:

- Development of contract management skills;
- Award of multi-year maintenance contracts;
- Improvement in quality measurements and reports;
- Development of performance targets (KPIs) and related dashboards;
- Improvement of information provision;
- Strengthening of production planning process;
- Introduction of Life Cycle Management and Maintenance Management;
- Development of a cost indicator database;
- Development of risk analyses and Maintenance Concepts.

From 1998 onwards, all these developments started but they picked up speed after the three task organisations came off NS in 2003 and started to work together.

Period 2002-2005: privatisation

An agreement was made between the Minister and NS to postpone the three task organisations in 1995 but the first step was taken in 2002. On July 1, 2002, the three task organisations were taken out of NS Holding and from January 1, 2003, they started to cooperate under the brand ProRail. On January 1, 2005, the formal arrangements were achieved and ProRail became a private limited company with the government as sole shareholder. Incidentally, this was without Railned's railway safety task because that became part of the Inspectorate Traffic & Transport (IVW), an organisation known as ILT from 2012 onwards.

The privatisation lasted long because the national government kept changing ideas about the removal of task organisations and could not establish definite governance framework and supervisory policy. Soon after releasing the idea of privatizing NS, a railways act and concession law were finally adopted to definitively regulate positions and governance framework. Pursuant to this legislation, the Minister awarded a transport concession for the core network to NS and a rail infra-structure management concession to ProRail on January 1, 2005. Figure 25 illustrates the chronological developments that transformed a fragmented infrastructure organisation within the NV Nederlandse Spoorwegen into a coherent, self-employed infra manager which outsources all executive tasks to service providers.

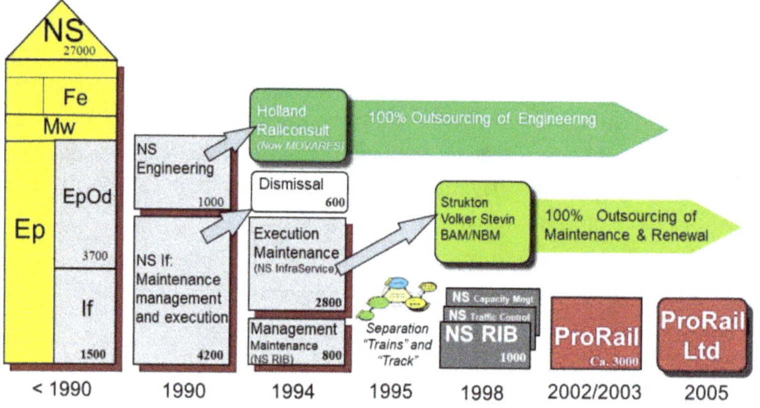

Figure 25   The development of the rail infra manager ProRail Ltd.

After 15 years of drastic changes, the non-commercial task organisations arrived at their destination and NS as well as other potential train operators learned how the competition on and around the rail infrastructure network would be regulated. The institutional triangle based on concessions became a fact.

With the merger of the three task organisations, a new organisation structure emerged in 2005, as indicated in Figure 26. There were six business units: Railway

Development, Projects, Infra Management, ICT Services, Traffic Control and Capacity Management. At Infra Management, managers supervised the main processes: Product-, Production-, Information-, Safety- as well as Environmental Management and Planning, and the contract management of stations was specialised. There were four M&R-regions, each responsible for the regional planning as well as management of maintenance contract and legal-, relationship-, environmental management, and regional information (ProRail, 2005-11*). More information about the underlying process model and the organisational structure is provided in sections 6.3 and 6.4.-

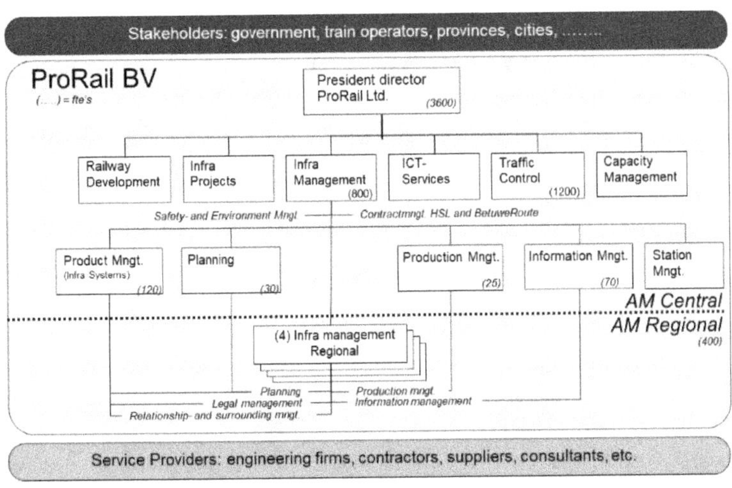

Figure 26   ProRail-organisation (2005-2009)

The long period between the advice of the Wijffels Commission (2002) and the start of ProRail Ltd (2005) had major consequences for the functioning of task organisations. In his thesis, Maarten Veraart states that these units were not only neglected managerially but also faced constant pressure from NS Passenger to give priority to transport over maintenance (Veraart M. , 2007, p. 122). This resulted in deterioration of rail infrastructure condition and weakening of infrastructure organisations. Even before ProRail started as an independent organisation, a recovery plan was prepared for the railways (ProRail, 2003*). For this purpose, RIB developed three result scenarios in 2003 to eliminate maintenance and renewal backlog and improve performance (Bauer, 2003*). The scenarios were as follows:

1. ***Scenario 1: 'Niet verder afglijden'*** ('Do not slip further'), € 1,000 million annually for management and maintenance aimed at reducing number of failures in the short term.
2. ***Scenario 2: 'Huis op orde'*** (= 'House in order'), € 1,350 million annually for management and maintenance aimed at improving basic quality by renewal of worn out infrastructure and making it robust.

3. ***Scenario 3: 'Benutten en Bouwen'*** (= 'Utilizing and Building'),
    € 1,450 million annually for management and maintenance aimed at
    simplifying infrastructure and transport process, combating noise pol-
    lution as well as increasing capacity (> 70%) and punctuality (> 90%).

For the first time, the government received a maintenance plan with options
based on scenarios, each with an action plan and a price tag. The discussion was
not only about money but also about the desired performance and approach. This
was a good start for the developing infrastructure organisation and this period
witnessed greater attention for management and maintenance. Various initiatives
were started to strengthen control and some of these were jointly launched by
ProRail and the Ministry. For example, a funding system was developed to efficiently use financial resources and a transparent and detailed long-range renewal
plan was developed for the period 2005-2025 (Swier J. e., 2004*). More and better
information became available for performance and technical quality. The KPIs
for control and dashboards improved. The management of ProRail and the government gained insight into the costs and performance of infra in the short and
long term as well as means to influence them.

The separation of task organisations from the NS was a long-awaited and necessary milestone. The merging of these organisations was a logical step and favourable condition for development of infrastructure manager ProRail. This is illustrated by the results achieved in the fields of technical policy, production and
train-free period planning, life cycle management and risk management. The improvement of the small-scale maintenance contract management process was difficult because management was fragmentated into four independent regions and
eleven trace managers. That changed after an organisational change in 2005.

Matrix organisation from 2005

After 2001, the development of management organisation picked pace but the
management determined that organisational strength was lagging because implementation and embedding of new skills and instruments was slow, volatile and
fragmented, and the maintenance process was ineffective in controlling costs and
performance.

In order to gain a better understanding of the underlying causes, the LREHC[23]
partnership was asked in 2003 to assess organisation functioning on the basis of
in-depth interviews and detailed information analyses. The assessment resulted in
four sub-reports: (1) Basic quality (LREHC, 2003*), (2) Efficiency (LREHC,
2004*), (3) Quality assurance and (4) Cost level (LREHC, 2004-12). The insights
from these reports were well-founded, illustrative and confrontational. In all areas, the organisation was making progress but anchoring of the results and

---

[23] LREHC = Lloyds Register en Horvat & Partners

coherence were missing. Everything seemed all right on paper but the reality was different. The management lacked insight, attention and focus to effectively manage the development and implementation of new tools and skills. Its focus was primarily on the operational process and strengthening of the organisation quality and control they added more or less. The puzzle pieces fell into place when, in 2005, the business units were formed within the new main structure of ProRail based, not on organogram and functions but on a blueprint of the various processes and their results. All business units - including Infra Management (IM) - developed a vision document that outlined their aim and approach of change operations. The Layout, Formation and Development plan (IFO-plan) was the outcome of this initiative.

The change of the IM organisation was described on the basis of four core processes and eight clusters of related activities. The core processes were: Product management (technical policy, frameworks and standards), Planning, Production management (management of maintenance) and Information management. The line organisation remained intact but a centre-level manager was appointed for each of the four core processes. The result was a matrix organisation, as illustrated in Figure 27, in which regional line managers and central process managers collaborated to realise the IM business plan. The regions are responsible for their operational results. The experts in the region have a functional manager in Utrecht, who is responsible for their professional development as well as the quality and uniformity of the process they adopt.

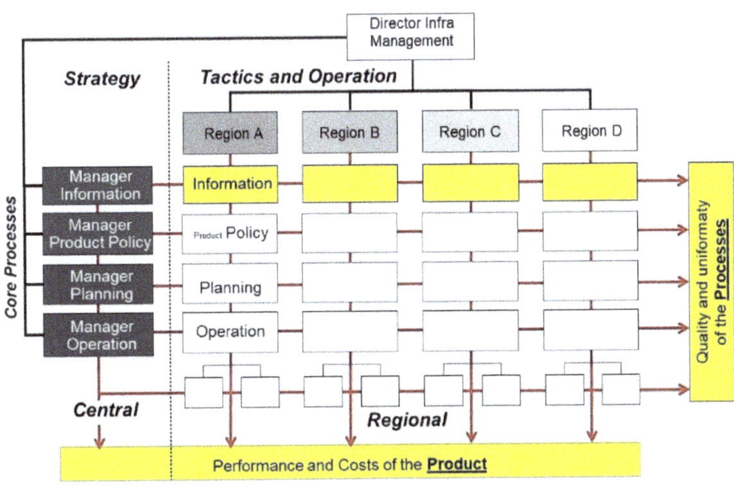

Figure 27   Matrix organisation of ProRail (2006)

In a matrix organisation, there is dual leadership. The product to be realised is managed from two perspectives: results of product or service and quality of processes. The line manager and process manager are responsible for this, respectively. A prerequisite for their functioning is good information and that was organised as a supporting main process. Together, the processes from both perspectives and information provision, formed the foundation on which the national infrastructure management organisation was built.

A matrix organisation is a logical choice for an organisation that has geographical spread, interest in uniformity of processes and in full development. The result-oriented line managers need support of many professional disciplines. The disadvantage of this structure is that more coordination is needed and employees face conflicting interests. The matrix structure is effective when managers and employees have sufficient process- and result orientation, and are not focused on maintaining or strengthening their own (power) position. From the smooth introduction of the matrix organisation and visible acceleration of improvements thereafter, it can be concluded that employees and managers at ProRail were ready for the new structure and handled it well.

The structuring of the organisation around four core processes and appointment of process managers had significant positive impact on functioning of the entire ProRail infra management organisation. In that period, the name was also changed to ProRail Asset Management, abbreviated as ProRail AM. To illustrate the type of improvements, two examples have been worked out – one each for Information and Production.

1. ICT was a staff organisation until 2005 but became a business unit with its own director in the management board. At the same time, there was a separate Information Management department at AM to translate the information needs of the business processes into information facilities. In addition, the AM Information had its own business information managers (BIMs) to bridge the gap between information users and ICT[24]. Soon after these organisational changes, developments in the area of ICT and information provision started and bridged the gap of missing functions such as improvement of information structures, linking of databases, online information exchange with contractors, introduction of business intelligence tools and better use of intranet. As a result, information flowed and connection was established between business units and employees. This enhanced effectiveness and efficiency of the entire infra process.

2. Production as a core process had major impact on the ProRail AM organisation. Until 2005, there was no central manager or staff group for production; therefore, maintenance contract changes were managed ad hoc by project managers who resigned after the end of their project. There was no ownership, continuity and knowledge transfer. This

---

[24] The other business units only organised the BIM function and not Information management because information requirement is less extensive and complex than that at ProRail AM.

condition changed with the introduction of a production process manager and a small central staff group, Central Regie team Contracting (CRC), was established to coordinate, support and improve regional contract management. The position of the contract managers was strengthened. The process manager and staff group ensured that policy, contract strategy, specifications and production plan were aligned with operational contract management process. As a result, the position of trace managers slowly but surely changed from *'the waste pit'*[25] to that of an internal customer and professional client. It took time and perseverance to heal frustrations and injuries but maintenance contract management became increasingly successful and professional with the support of CRC.

The two examples show that the matrix structure provided a stable foundation for further development of the organisation, knowledge, skills and instruments for well-functioning asset management system at ProRail AM.

Development organisation from 2009

The ProRail organisation was in full development after the separation from NS and privatisation. That was much needed but results were achieved. In April 2009, an article was published in the magazine *Binnenlands bestuur* (= Domestic Management) that describes the development process unapologetically. The article starts with the heading *"PotterRail becomes ProRail"* and opens with: *"ProRail changes. The first so bureaucratic track manager learns what customer friendliness is. Decentralized authorities are often enthusiastic about the implementation of large projects. But there is often still friction around rail maintenance and in the run-up to projects. Especially in the Randstad."* (Overdijk, 2009-4*).

The three technocratic and internally-oriented task organisations learned through trial and error to cooperate with stakeholders in customer-friendly manner. This was a huge change for the infrastructure organisation to work not only on behalf of the NS but also for other stakeholders such as train operators, government, municipalities, interest groups, etc. It took time, but the corporate culture demonstrably changed and for stakeholders to become externally focused and customer-friendly. change continued.

In 2009, the organisation structure of ProRail was changed to improve connections and better control on operations. The Board of Directors was replaced by a five-member board comprising chief executive officer (CEO), director Finance (CFO) and three company directors for Infra Projects, Operation and Transport & Timetable as indicated in Figure 28 (ProRail, 2010*, p. 62). Traffic Control, Asset Management and ICT Services are part of the business unit Operation.

---

[25] This is how the trace managers described their position at the time.

In mid-2012, ProRail launched a new vision for the period 2012-2015: *"In samenspel naar een vernieuwd Nederlands spoor"*(In English: In interaction to a renewed Dutch rail network) with seven change targets (ProRail, 2012*). The organisation had to become more efficient, decisive and customer-oriented. In addition, the Ministry of Infrastructure and Environment decided to reduce organisation expenses by making structural changes which led to loss of about 600 jobs. The management decided to execute this assignment such that efficient and effective operations keep infrastructure reliable and safe. The structure of the Asset Management business unit was changed in 2012 such that the matrix organisation is maintained but regional influence is strengthened. In the central staff, the Planning process manager became part of the Architecture & Technology policy staff group (A&T) and the function of Operation process manager was transferred to Maintenance & Operation regional managers. These were supported by the CRC-team and the Infra Availability staff group, which includes Operational Control Centre Infra (known as OBI), risk and incident management and train free period management. Station management moved from the AM business unit to Projects business unit because there were many, often large, station projects, and stations have a result focus and relationship very different from rail infrastructure.

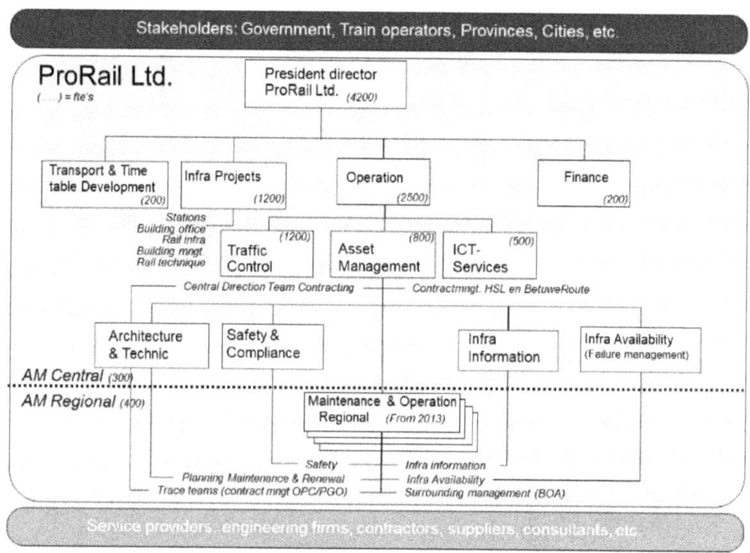

Figure 28   Infra organisation in the period 2009-2012, ……..

So far, the infrastructure organisation development under the influence of changing conditions and circumstances over the period 1990-2015. To conclude this chapter, a balance sheet of the development process of ProRail is prepared.

3.2   Balance sheet after twenty years of changes

ProRail will continue to develop and adapt itself to the circumstances but now it has suitable organisational structure and preconditions. The traditional maintenance organisation has developed into a professional infrastructure manager. The orientation and culture have changed dramatically from technical-, task- and internal-oriented to business-, process- and externally-oriented. Is it a success story? When we consider the results achieved after 2005, the answer is yes, but the years before witnessed loss of quality and reputation, long period of uncertainty and huge toll on employees in the form of insecurity, frustrations and stress. There was a period when employees were not proud of the company and avoided talking about it in their private lives. This was the price ProRail and the service providers paid to adapt to changing circumstances and improve results. It illustrates the saying: *no gain without pain.* After twenty years of change, the balance sheet looks as follows:

    a.   ***Bad starting position of infrastructure organisation.*** Nobody is positive about the change process. The result could have been very different. There were conscious and unconscious large risks involved in the realisation of ProRail. The NS knew in 1992 that task organisations would be relocated but actual event materialised around 2002/2003 and was formally ratified in early 2005. In the interim period, decisions were taken about RIB without any intention to create a strong asset management organisation. In fact, RIB was the remainder of a stripping operation after a long list of tasks were privatised: engineering, maintenance, fibre optic network, material purchasing & logistics, training, personnel safety and commercial station activities. The starting position of RIB in 1998 was such that elementary management skills and instruments were lacking. The organisation was not ready for the task of asset- and contract management and neither were the maintenance contractors, because maintenance was a new industry to be built from scratch and integrated into existing business operations. The development of infrastructure organisation flourished after the privatisation of ProRail. The national government and NS left the management and maintenance of rail infrastructure to their fate for a while. They did not used their influence to establish powerful rail infra management. RIB and the maintenance contractors were thrown in the deep without preparation. That it did not go wrong, as it did in the UK[26] at that time, is because transition to maintenance contracting was gradual, the executive staff was dedicated, and informal contacts remained between former colleagues at infra management and the

---

[26] Eight years after outsourcing, Railtrack restarted doing maintenance on its own. Please refer section 1.4.1 for more details.

service providers. The informal contacts bridged the gap when formal contracts were introduced but necessary instruments and skills were lacking. Since process of change started with a backlog, more time was needed to improve performance at lower costs.

b. ***Significant change of orientation and skills.*** Due to the separation of Transport and Infrastructure, and the outsourcing of maintenance, synergy benefits were lost. Relationships, processes, instruments and skills changed fundamentally. The cabinet full of organisational regulations was rendered waste and collaboration based on informal contacts changed into business relationship based on formal contracts. Companies withdrew within their organisation boundaries and had little attention for dependencies and co-operation. For example, the rail infra organisation was built from scratch while the trains continued to operate. The new roles and tasks required management and employees to use new management techniques such as contract-, risk-, lifecycle-, knowledge- and quality management. Existing and new information was recorded and managed through asset registration, KPIs, specifications, production plan, renewal plans, cost indicators, etc. In summary, all the organisational preconditions changed drastically: structure, processes, instruments, knowledge and training of people, business strategy and organisation culture. Table 1 shows the changes. The radical changes in the period 1995-2002 focused on survival. When that was successful, there was opportunity to connect with other business units and companies for developing skills and instruments.

Table 1   Changes in orientation and skills

NS Railinfrabeheer (<1998)	ProRail Asset Management (>2008)
Man hours and budgets	Costs
Technique	Price/Performance
Implicit output	Explicit output
Tasks	Processes
Activities	Risks
Rules and instructions	Specifications and contracts
Yearly budget	Long term production plan (10-25 yrs)
Personal knowledge	Shared knowledge and information

c. ***New roles and tasks are the drivers for cultural change.*** Splitting an organisation with long history and simultaneously outsourcing all executive and culture determining tasks created huge impact on the entire industry. The initial years after the split were difficult for all employees, particularly at the RIB. Every day they experienced that their organisation was the result of a strip operation. The consequences were visible in changing demands for knowledge, skills and orientation of

many employees as well as lack of effective organisational conditions
The task content shifted from an almost complete technical orientation
to a business orientation supported by technical specialists. Figure 29
illustrates how, in a period of ten to fifteen years, the 'colour' of the
functions in the organisation changed; from technical content (blue) to
a business result (yellow). Due to this 'discoloration' of functions and
people, there was initially a disengagement between technology and
management. This was reinforced in 1994 when integral maintenance management was decentralised and regional maintenance
managers increased from five to seven. Employees who have to fulfil new positions do not change 'colour' quickly. The management
and client tasks were built from scratch. The RIB was the client for
maintenance and renewal but the core skills, instruments and information required were largely lacking. New identity, culture, control
instruments and procedures were developed based on new tasks
and processes. An assessment of what was missing indicates RIB's
position at the beginning of 1998. The organisation did not have explicit M&R policy, production plan, planning organisation, experienced maintenance contract managers, management techniques
such as life cycle management and maintenance engineering, experience with maintenance contracting or outsourcing of maintenance.
The new maintenance companies were not fully equipped either but
they focused on development of their organisation, shielded by contract managers, and energetically structured the work order system
with standardised annual work plans and job descriptions. In the initial years after privatisation of maintenance, RIB was not leading
but following. This was difficult and frustrating. As the organisation
developed, the role and responsibility of an asset manager and client
gained form and content based not on power but professionalism.

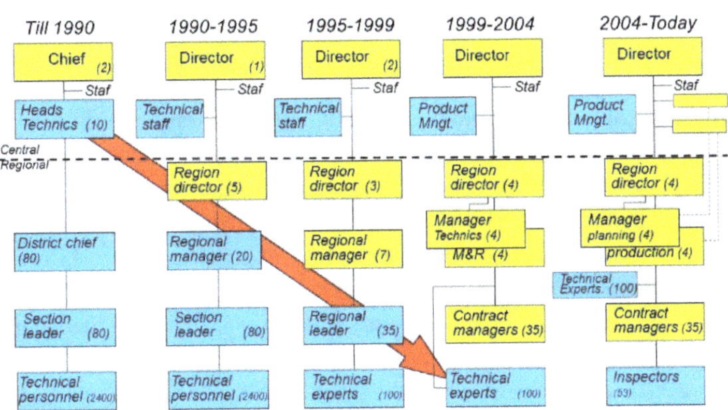

Figure 29   Shift from a technical to a business orientation

d. ***Man is the measure.*** The effort for continuous result improvement started after 2005. Decisive for success were the pragmatic and stimulating approach of ProRail management; focus and expertise at line managers and project managers, as well as recognition by employees. The change was not based on a well-considered master plan but on achieving challenging milestones and sub-goals with focus on costs and performance, specific- and necessary developments, and notion that cooperation is necessary; it all is a nice example of good, course-seeking leadership. The organic process of change was gradual and based on coherent improvement projects that employees realised when driven by circumstances and priorities. Maarten Veraart made several observations in his dissertation (Veraart M. , 2007) that illustrate learnings from this process:

- Beautiful plans are not decisive for success: the risk of 'blueprint thinking' and underestimation of process conditions is big.
- Externally desired changes require internal support.
- Mobilising the employees for change goals requires appeal to their professional pride and development of a new form of professionalism.
- Professionalism is necessary not only for public interest ('good public transport') but also for driving change.
- Trains and rail are interdependent and active collaboration prevents sub optimisation.

By starting from their own knowledge and experiences, and learning from mistakes every time, fundamental organisational changes and new high-quality management techniques were introduced. A lot of small development steps were taken because of the dedication, knowledge and skills of employees as they embarked on the path of organisational growth.

e. ***Leadership: results follow process quality.*** Successful changes are about leadership: setting appealing, clear and achievable goals and giving space to people to innovate. After separation and privatisation, the companies in the sector gradually developed themselves and established connection with other business units to make structural improvements for results. That really gained momentum after the government opted for governance model of concessions and ProRail was formed. ProRail worked on behalf of the government, within the framework of management concession and annual management plans. A stimulating effect on the organisational development of ProRail was created by the first management concession (2005) in which the government did not impose impossible result targets for ProRail but rather four constructive and challenging conditions to improve organisation quality for switch to output management in 2008. The four conditions, which are stated in Article 20 of the Management Concession 2005 (V&W, 2005*), are as follows:

1. Be familiar with the relationship between the resources at its disposal, activities, operation and outcomes thereof. (Freely translated: know the relation between costs and performance, and know how to influence it = master risk-, performance- and maintenance management techniques.)
2. Be familiar with the interaction effects between the activities, operational goals and outcomes of M&R and of the train operators. (Freely translated: know the relationship between infrastructure and train operation and know how to influence it = master how to optimise costs and performance of infrastructure and transport.)
3. Be familiar with the life-cycle effects on rail infrastructure network. (Freely translated: know the relationship between costs and performance in the investment and exploitation phases and know how to optimise performance).
4. Be able to direct business operations to the knowledge referred to under I, II and III. (Freely translated: structures and systems should use the insights gained under I, II, and III decisively = master quality- and information management techniques.)

The four conditions briefly describe the basic skills needed to become an asset manager with a professional asset management system. These are the conditions for managing performance and costs explicitly and in relation to each other over the entire lifecycle. The timing, content and coherence are examples of good leadership. The four requirements has helped ProRail to change and improve the organisation with more focus and speed. On January 1, 2008, the Minister determined that ProRail meets the requirements in the management concession to manage on output. This was a milestone in the process of restructuring rail infrastructure sector. However, many collaborators also realised that the organisation was only at the beginning of control and continuous improvement of the infrastructure and transport process, quality and results. Things are going in the right direction, the foundation is lain, and continuous improvement drives organisation development.

Finally

The organic growth of the asset management organisation and system at ProRail has been initiated and stimulated by the separation of transport and infrastructure, through leadership, and by setting challenging but achievable organisational development goals. The outsourcing of maintenance in 1998 was of great influence. The decision of the government and NS management to outsource rail infrastructure maintenance created conditions that were decisive for the development of

infrastructure organisation and asset management system. It forced the infrastructure organisation to specify, monitor and control the performance and technical quality explicitly and consistently. It succeeded because the processes were
well organised properly and bridges were built between business units and service
providers. Given its significance, the development of maintenance outsourcing is
described in a separate chapter of this first part and starts as the next chapter 4.

Final comment: outsourcing maintenance is not a condition for developing a professional asset management organization. It did help ProRail (ultimately) because
the roles, tasks, authorities and responsibilities were separated in such a pure and
fundamental way. It can therefore be an instructive case for other infrastructure
managers and service providers to improve their organizations.

4 Outsourcing maintenance

In 1994, Infra Management and Infra Execution were separated into two organisations, and in 1998, the execution of the maintenance was fully outsourced. The choice to outsource was not a textbook example of well-crafted policy because, in hindsight, a certain naivety and innocence is observed.

An explanation for this could be that in the nineties, at the time of Margaret Thatcher, it was fashionable to outsource. The NS board had confidence in the strength of the market and output steering without any knowledge how to do it and what the consequences are. At the time, there was no explicit idea on how to outsource and what preconditions are necessary to create an effective asset management organisation, the client. There was hardly any realisation that outsourcing of maintenance is a profession that places high demands on the management for control of performances, costs and processes, both on the part of the client and those of the contractors.

However, outsourcing in the Netherlands did not turn into a fiasco like that in Great Britain, where it was reversed after five years. This had various causes, including a difference in social system: the neo-liberal Anglo-Saxon model[27] in Great Britain versus the Rhineland consultative model[28] in the Netherlands. This partly explains why the Dutch approach to outsource maintenance was different than in Great Britain. This chapter provides insight into how ProRail dealt with important matters such as the development of contract skills, a differentiation in specification levels, cooperation in a contract relation and how the development of the AM-organisation and the contract management skills influenced and reinforced each other.

4.1 Development of AM organisation

Railways have existed for more than 175 years and are traditional in character. They place high demand on safety and control, and this is achieved through the use of robust technical systems, fail-safe security system as well as technical, well-trained and almost military-like organisation structure.

Worldwide, almost all railway companies are still doing maintenance themselves. It is difficult and risky to outsource maintenance even with a high admission threshold for market players. This is because railways operate in a niche market

---

[27] In the Anglo-Saxon model, the forces of free market operate with minimum influence of the government. In this case, liberal values such as self-reliance, private initiative, market forces, freedom and social security are central.

[28] In the Rhineland model, the government is actively engaged in matters such as environment, spatial planning, education and social issues. There is a relatively large public sector and heavy regulation. The model assumes cooperation among government, employers and employees.

with unique superstructure, security techniques, together with civil, high-voltage and low-voltage technologies.

The government and NS decided around 1994 to outsource process-based small-scale maintenance (Abbreviation in Dutch: KO). This was challenging because the result to be achieved was not tangible and hence difficult to specify and measure. Maintenance does not involve realisation of a concrete product, such as a new switch or preservation of a bridge, but rather performance in the form of reliability, availability, maintainability, safety, health and environment, summarised in the acronym RAMSHE. This is further complicated by the fact that the average lifetime of rail infrastructure systems is more than 50 years and the duration of a maintenance contract is always much shorter. Too little or poorly executed maintenance is difficult to determine and its effect often manifests itself later in the form of a shorter asset life, higher maintenance or renewal costs, increase in disruptions and/or unsafe situations.

About 60-70% of the maintenance costs consist of personnel costs. Maintenance is very labour-intensive with craftsmanship, experience and dedication of personnel being decisive in short-term and long-term effects of maintenance. The work of maintenance personnel may not look spectacular or appeal to imagination but the effect it produces is significant. Illustrative of this is the quote: *'If you think maintenance is expensive, try an accident'*. In order to outsource KO in a controlled, efficient and effective manner, a market is needed as well as knowledge and experience. The client and contractor must be able to:

- Specify, measure and evaluate performance;
- Identify, analyse and manage performance risks with maintenance activities;
- Identify deviations from specifications and translate them into efficient and effective maintenance actions;
- To carry out maintenance on time and only if really necessary;
- Ensure well-trained, experienced and dedicated staff;
- Assess long-term effects of maintenance on asset life, costs and performance.

These competences are not naturally present in an asset management and service provider organisation. Management of NS Railinfrabeheer was aware of this and intended to manage on output and from distance, but the industry had to be capable to work accordingly. In 1997, a project team was commissioned to develop a management philosophy with associated contract process and maintenance contract.

To clearly define the scope, a list of all maintenance and renewal activities was prepared. The list is known as the TESI-list. It indicates whether an activity is small-scale or large-scale maintenance, or a renewal. More information on this can be found in section 6.10 on the definition and coherence of M&R-activities. The starting point was management of KO on output and from distance; while it was unclear at the time how to do this, it was evident that contract specification would be decisive.

For inspiration, a work visit was made to Railtrack, the infrastructure manager of Great Britain. It had fully outsourced maintenance two years earlier and steered its contract for realisation of integral performance specifications with heavy penalties if insufficient performance was achieved. There were contract teams with contract managers but only a few technicians because according to Railtrack's management philosophy, technicians were no longer necessary for output-based contracts.

The visit was very informative and useful. On the return journey, the Dutch team discussed how it could maintain control over network safety if the maintenance contractor did not function properly. They could nod answer the question properly and concluded that Railinfrabeheer needed another approach: it would not immediately focus on integral RAMS output specifications, but first learn how to manage maintenance through a contract and start with what is known. Important was the determination that output can be specified, manages and controled at different levels; not only at the highest level of RAMS performance, but also at the level of quality indicators for systems, technical reject specifications for objects and components, as well as at an input level of prescribed maintenance activities. More details and background information on this is provided in section 6.8.

The management of Railinfrabeheer agreed with the proposal of the project team to start with specification and steering at the level of work plans and technical specifications; so a mix of input and low level output. A wise decision because there was no maintenance market for rail infrastructure in the Netherlands or Europe in 1998. The NS Railinfrabeheer and its three process contract contractors also did not have the tools and skills to outsource maintenance or manage publicly-tendered performance contracts.

Since 1998, both parties have slowly but surely grown in their new role and have actively collaborated on developing the missing management skills, tools and process structuring. This chapter describes the development based on the evolution of the maintenance contract. It started with the first generation contract in 1998, the Output Process Contract (OPC), followed by the second generation contract in 2002, the OPC +, and that led in 2008 to the third generation contract, the Performance Based Maintenance (Abbreviation in Dutch: PGO) contract. It took approximately ten years to learn how to outsource and switch from input-based OPC contracts with price agreements to the tendering of output-based PGO contracts.

Steering on input and/or output

The booklet by Hans de Bruijn on *'Performance measurement in the public sector'* (Bruin, 2002) was important for forming image and gaining knowledge for steering on input and output. The following quote has helped to find the right way: *'In case of input control (= steering on effort or activity) the contractor is more or less a temporary agency of hands and a rental company of machines. In the case of output control (= steering on performance or result), the client indicates which quality requirements the product or service must meet. The contractor must then have the knowledge and experience to choose the most effective and efficient working method to realise this. That seems simple and attractive, but it only works if the client and the contractor manage input and output control properly. Both need to know what the relationship is between activities and performance and how it should be controlled. The choice of management is thus determined by the level of development of the entire sector'.*

The following quotation from booklet of de Bruijn was also important for the development of the maintenance contract: *'Chosen form of control does not have to lead to exclusion of the other forms. You could say that the different control methods have a relative position with respect to each other''*(see Figure 30). *If output control is chosen then input control is given a (possibly) temporary peripheral position, but can always return to a more central location. Output or performance control can perform a beneficial function but must always be used in combination with other systems of judgment'.*

According to de Bruijn (Bruin, 2002): *'... the client who fully trusts on output/performance measurement will experience the perverse (negative) effects. The client who in response to this relies fully on the input control, will experience new and other perverse (negative) effects.'*

Railtrack and Railinfrabeheer have both experienced these phenomena. Railtrack fully relied on output control and lost control of performance, which became worse. Railinfrabeheer relied on input-driven OPC contracts for a long time, such that prices increased every year without any improvement in performance and management conditions became increasingly complex.

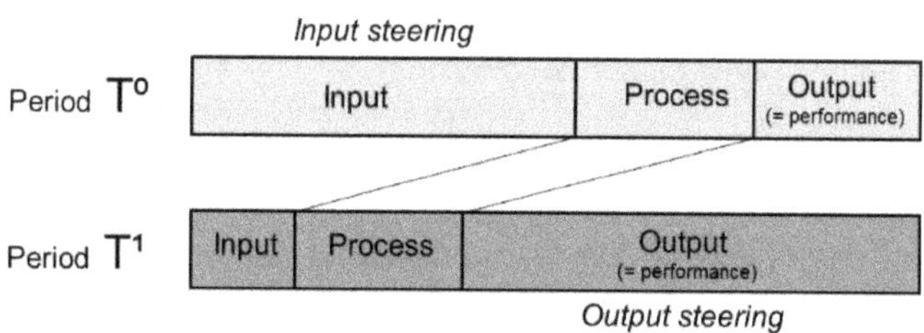

Figure 30   Input- and output steering can change over time

With the help of such insights, Railinfrabeheer learned what is required for management and control of maintenance contracts. Some of the lessons were:

* Input- and output control can co-exist.

- Steering on output (= performance management) is not a goal but a means to improve the results. It places high demands on process control and the availability of proper instruments.

- In the case of output control, the client and contractor need more knowledge and information to control and optimise costs and performance explicitly and demonstrably.

- Steering on output does not mean that the client can no longer have insight into what has been done to maintain (= input). Steering and knowing what has happened should not be confused with each other. They go together without problems.

- A client who does not know how to keep control over output-driven performance contracts is advised not to start.

Conclusion: for output-steering, the industry must be ready with knowledge, information and experience. Only an experienced professional asset manager and maintenance contractor can do it and a growth path is needed to develop those qualities.

First-generation maintenance contract: OPC (1998-2002)

The first OPC-contract was developed in 1998 and introduced step-by-step. The name 'Output Process Contract' is confusing because it was not an output contract but demonstrated intention to grow to that level.

For strategic reasons it was decided to call the contract OPC, because board members had been talking about managing on output and at a distance for years. But the first OPC maintenance contract was based on an annual work plan (= input), an open budget (= input) and maintenance & renewal specifications (= output). The management process comprised the following eight steps:

1. Collect data for the request;
2. Make a risk assessment;
3. Align risks;
4. Draft quality plan;
5. Select vendor and award contract;
6. Prepare and accept various plans;
7. Develop reports; and
8. Deal with deviations.

The contract consists of three parts:

I. Generic conditions (abbreviation in Dutch: AVPI);
II. Specific job description with information about contract area;
III. Generic specifications regarding technical condition, performance, contract process, etc.

The OPC setup requires uniformity, unambiguousness, well-developed contract processes and professional instruments. The features of OPC setup included the following:

- 39 contracts, geographically dispersed;
- Framework contract with a term of 5 years and annual agreements to address changes;
- Separate approval scheme for maintenance, including failure recovery;
- Integral contract for small-scale maintenance of track & switches, bridges & tunnels, telecommunication systems, signalling, energy supply and level crossings;
- Uniformity in contracts through single, standard model-OPC;
- Elaboration. of the eight contract process steps;
- Generic process risk analysis as the basis for specific risk distribution;
- Open budget based standard calculation model M31 as the basis of the offer;
- Start with specifications for level of work plans and that for maintenance & renewal (abbreviation in Dutch: IHS), and progress to RAMS performance steering;
- Preparation of risk inventory for safety and safety & heath plan, including railway safety; and
- Inspections linked to maintenance & renewal specifications.

After the contract was developed in 1998, all employees involved, at Railinfrabeheer and the three maintenance contractors, were informed about contract set-up and working through an extensive training program. Subsequently, 39 OPC contracts were introduced in tranches over a period of 5 years by a project team from Railinfrabeheer. An information booklet was published to outline principles of output control (Projectteam, 1998-1*).

An evaluation of the OPC in 2001 showed that the contract was satisfactory but suffered from shortcomings as follows:

- There was no market and no competition at the time of start.
- There was no insight into the relationship between costs and the (RAMS) performance.
- There were insufficient specifications instruments for output steering.
- The contracts were interpreted and arranged differently by the trace managers because there was no central, operational coordination for contract management.
- There was insufficient cooperation in the sector chain; the maintenance contractor was focused on its own operating result and Railinfrabeheer did not sufficiently specify the performance and cost results to be achieved.

The conclusion of the evaluation was that the contract was a good basis, but improvement was needed for cooperation among parties involved and insight into costs, performance and their relationship with each other. The OPC+ project was thus born as further development of the OPC contract. Its purpose was to manage smarter by detailing relationship between costs and performance as well as improving collaboration across the entire infrastructure chain.

Second-generation maintenance contract: OPC+ (2002-2008)

Collaboration and insight into realisation may seem to be in conflict with outsourcing and business contract relationship but it is not so as observed in the aerospace- and oil industry. These industries use a management technique that forms the basis of EN 50126, the European quality standard for management of RAMS over the life cycle. The standard provides railway authorities and rail supply companies in the European Union with a process to manage RAMS-performance effectively.

The processes for specification and measurement of RAMS requirements form the cornerstone of the EN 50126 standard and associated management techniques for maintenance and renewal. The standard provides a method to prevent failures by systematic mapping of the following in a risk analysis: potential failures (= risks), causes and effect on performance and costs. If the failure risks and their effects are significant then one can take preventive actions: inspect more or differently, replace a part sooner, increase lubrication frequency, renew asset, etc.. These management activities are recorded in a maintenance & renewal concept. Ultimately, three birds are beaten in one fell swoop:
1. a clear picture of the relationship between performance risks and maintenance activities emerges;
2. insight is gained into associated costs;
3. a structured recording develops for exchange of experiences.

The sharing of experiences, knowledge and information creates a climate for continuous improvement.

The insights from the EN50126 were used to improve the OPC contract process. An important starting point for OPC+ was creation of a better task- and role division. The result is elaborated in a branch process model indicated in Figure 31. The branch process model describes the entire process of concluding contracts with the national government and transport companies, through the process contract with the PCA to the work of the engineers. ProRail and the maintenance contractors had to work as one continuous process and thus performance risk management also became part of the contract process. The process to manage performance risks was called the IHM/OHM process[29].

---

[29] Dutch abbreviation: IHM = Instandhoudingsmanagement = Maintenance & Renewal Management.
   Dutch abbreviation: OHM = Onderhoudsmanagement = Maintenance Management

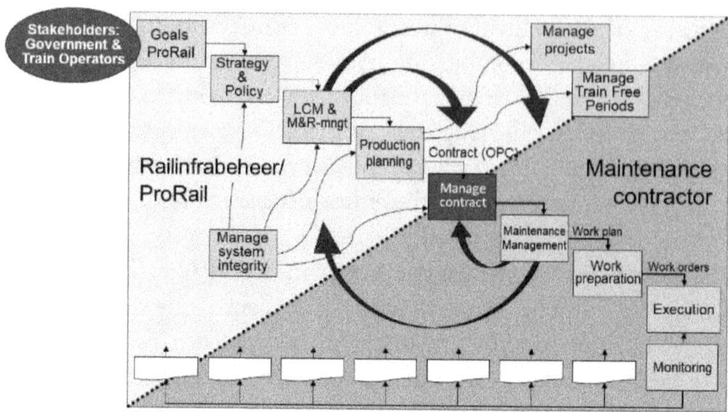

Figure 31   Branch process model: processes and products

The OPC contract remained unchanged but the following six new elements were added:

1. A cooperation agreement.
2. Performance risk analyses and M&R-concepts included in the contract as instruments of the IHM/OHM process.
3. A maintenance plan derived from M&R-concept, with standardised pre-calculation, known as the M31 format, based on standardised activities (units) and unit prices.
4. A new principle to control performance and settle units.
5. Improved management process based on RAMS-KPIs and standardised daily, weekly and monthly reports.
6. Continuous improvement of the M&R-management process through the IHM/OHM process.

A project manager was appointed in 2001 to add the new elements to the OPC+ contract and process. The concerned person had a strong focus on realising project results but was little interested in the effects of these elements on the organisations and relationships involved. There were many (drastic) changes without regard for operational effects. Within ProRail, opinions were divided on the working method and results of the project manager, also because contractors had major influence on the entire implementation process.

In 2005, the OPC+ project organisation was cancelled and balance was drawn up. Positive effects were performance improvement, better insights into maintenance plan and calculated maintenance costs; insight into relationship between risks and control measures; and better management reports. The negative effects were rising maintenance costs, heavy administrative burden with a lot of attention for input calculation, no insight into actual maintenance costs, a mix of input and output specifications, a fragmented and highly process-oriented management attention and, still, a fragmented contract management process across four regions and eleven trace managers who manage the maintenance contract. In addition, tasks and personnel members were transferred from ProRail to the PCAs, which was a radical change with uncertainty about usefulness and necessity.

Finally, the results from the regional contract managers at ProRail were perceived as insufficient with the following main objections:

- Complex and long-term reorganisation of the branch, with a lot of attention for the change process and little for a better control of the contract and contract process.
- Strong orientation on given confidence and little on how to earn and keep trust.
- Arbitrary and poorly substantiated task transfer resulting in dissatisfaction about the principle 'people follow work'.
- Insufficient grip on the results and organisational quality of the contractors.

The operational contract management process at ProRail was becoming increasing fragmented and the contract managers received insufficient support from specialist in other processes or their own managing board. The regional contract management identified its position as that of a *waste pit*, a worrisome signal that was taken seriously. It was evident that more was needed to improve performance and reduce costs than adjustment of the contract model or better cooperation.

Contract management at ProRail needed to be strengthened, insight into effectiveness and efficiency of maintenance was to be increased and greater focus was needed for continuous improvement in price/performance ratio. Upon stimulation from the Netherlands Competition Authority (NMa) to publicly contract maintenance, a plan was created to utilise possibilities of public tendering and performance-based contract. The industry seemed ready and a necessary first step was unification and strengthening of maintenance contract management.

Strengthen maintenance control in the period 2005-2008

Management and maintenance of rail infrastructure was the area of technicians until 1996. With the separation of NS into separate transport and infrastructure organisations, economists and business managers became involved. With the outsourcing of maintenance, contract managers were also added. Soon, technical knowledge and experience disappeared into the background even thoug this knowledge was the glue that kept the old maintenance organisation together and source of its strength. With loss of technical knowledge, there was fragmentation and sub-optimisation.

Economists, technicians and contract managers interfered with each-others' knowledge domain often overlooking the consequences. This was a potentially dangerous phenomenon that affected other industries as well. As an illustration, an article was cited from the Dutch paper NRC, which covered the disaster of Space Shuttle Challenger in an article *'That's how it goes without technicians at the top'* (Schöyer, 2006*). In short: we should let technicians decide on technical matters and economists on economic matters.

In order to achieve more control on operations and execution, the following two essential organisational changes were implemented at Pro-Rail IM in 2005: introduction of a matrix organisation by appointing process managers for the four main processes and set up of a Central Regie team for contracting (abbreviation in Dutch: CRC). More details on these is provided in section 3.1 in the sub-section about the matrix organisation being introduced in 2005.

The above-mentioned two changes aligned strategic goals with operational implementation and created bridges between technicians, contract managers and economists. This was necessary because an external study, based on in-depth interviews and detailed information analysis, indicated many demonstrable weaknesses in the control system. The main weaknesses and causes were as follows:

- ***Trace manager operated in isolation and received insufficient support.*** The trace managers did not have a formal consultation platform. They operated as individuals in a completely new, difficult and evolving field. Many ProRailers in other business units overlooked them, often unconsciously, and seriously weakened their position.

- ***Technical regulations did not adequately match the contracting method.*** The regulations and specifications in the product catalogue were not written from the point of view of a maintenance contract. New policy and regulations were often 'dropped' at the trace managers without explicit decision making about contractual and financial consequences.

- ***ProRail had no insight into the realised maintenance activities, performed inspections and object information.*** For a long time, the industry did not provide any insight to ProRail regarding maintenance activities and inspections. This was often not necessary for contract management but rather for the fulfilment of the role of asset manager. In addition, the object registration was unreliable. Therefore, ProRail was partially blind and could not fully perform core client tasks of risk-, life cycle- and contract management.

- ***Supervision was insufficiently guaranteed.*** Before outsourcing, ProRail had many experienced service technicians and team managers who knew what had to be done and registered activity information in their time sheets. They supervised contractors well, partly because they were themselves facing consequences of the contractor's poor performance. With the outsourcing of maintenance, ProRail lost that experience and insight. This could be compensated only by a robust quality assurance system that provides insight into organisation quality of the contractor and types of inspections and maintenance activities. Such a system was not arranged.

- ***Inadequate assurance of stewardship.*** The people in operation, both at ProRail and the maintenance contractors, felt responsible for the daily safety and reliability of rail infrastructure. By outsourcing, there was risk of inadequate care because ProRail had insufficient insight into the technical quality and realised maintenance history, while the contractor tended to manage maintenance as a project with result heavily dependent on individual initiatives, qualities and involvement of executive staff. An attitude of stewardship is needed for maintenance If stewardship is not present at a maintenance contractors, performance management is not an option.

- ***Anchoring a new unifying value in the industry.*** In 1996, technique was the unifying value and everyone used about the same language. The binding effect disappeared largely upon outsourcing of all in-house engineering and maintenance activities. A new unifying value was needed to realise the right cooperation and interaction but it was unclear what that new language and binding value may be.

- ***Insufficient assurance and transfer of professional knowledge.*** There were not many internal vocational training or management courses at ProRail to transfer and secure knowledge and skills. There were some initiatives on the technical side but none in the field of contract management.

With the arrival of the production process manager in 2005, the organisation of CRC and cooperation between the regional and central organisations improved such that there was increase in focus, unanimity and strength at ProRail Operations. Thereafter, a focused and decisive effort was made to address weaknesses. The tendering of the first performance contract in 2007 was a milestone that illustrated the progress.

Third-generation maintenance contract: PGO (2007-present)

According to agreements with the government and the NMa (now known as ACM), ProRail had to start in 2007 with the tendering of small-scale maintenance. Division and renewal of 39 maintenance contracts in one-on-one negotiations with the three maintenance contractors was completed over a period of 8 years such that the new maintenance market for rail infrastructure time has time to develop. Thereafter, the market was trusted to function effectively for improving price performance with competition.

In a market, competition requires presence of equivalent contractors, interest in procurement opportunity and ability of contractors to distinguish themselves. There must be something to improve and earn from. Unfortunately, no European maintenance market had developed at the time. The Netherlands, Finland and Sweden were the only countries in Europe that had outsourced all or part of rail infrastructure maintenance (situation in 2016). So for the time being ProRail had to deal with competition only in its own country. On the positive side, the number of certified maintenance contractors increased from three to four[30] after 2007, but the same pie had to be shared with more entities. In order to make the conditions for competition as favourable as possible, ProRail decided to reduce the number of maintenance contracts from 39 to about 20, i.e. a halving.

By combining two OPC contracts into a single new Performance contract (Dutch abbreviation: PGO), the situation was such that there was almost always one maintenance contractor that lost a contract and at least two that can acquire the contract. With the combination of contracts, the overhead cost fell, tendering frequency was reduced and contract volume doubled from around € 30 million (5 years * € 6 million) to € 60 million, making the opportunity attractive for market players.

The main structure of a PGO contract consists of three parts: specifications, generic contract conditions provided in the General Condition for Performance-related Maintenance Contract (abbreviated AVPO in Dutch) and specific process requirements described in the 'Statement of Work'. Incentives and payment conditions complement the whole, see Figure 32.

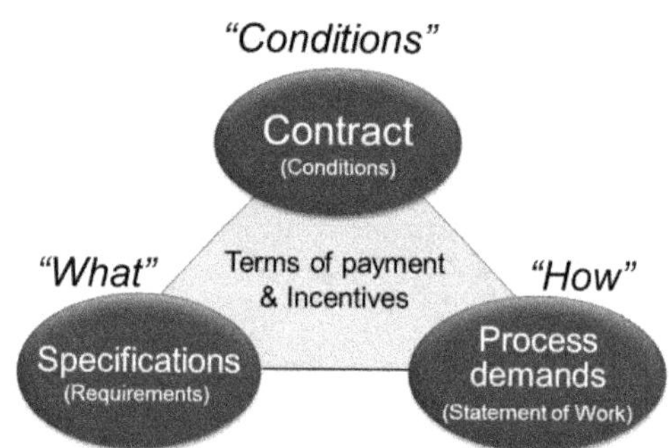

Figure 32   Main structure of the performance contract PGO

In order to give market parties the opportunity to improve price/performance and distinguish themselves from each other, the steering method had to change: from steering on realising a work plan (= input) to controlling the realisation of a desired performance (= output). Only then there was an incentive and

---

[30] In fact, there were five, but the fifth (Spitske) did not actively participate in tenders

104

opportunity for a maintenance contractor to distinguish itself from competitors. A condition was that the desired performance be well specified, measurable and manageable, because: *'Only if you can specify and measure something can you manage it'*. The specification was, therefore, completely redesigned in 2006 using the risk analyses available and based on 'system engineering' principles (GWW, 2013-11*).

The services to be delivered were divided into three types of specifications: one for RAM (reliability, availability and maintainability); one for railway safety and and one for durability. The former is a specification at the top-level of RAM and the latter are at the level of technical rejection criteria and, where necessary, even mandatory activities. For more information on this, please refer section 6.8. The specifications are structured as per a specification tree[31], which comprises a decomposition of generic system-specific performance requirements up to the level of technical condition, with reference to the relevant regulations of the system managers at Architecture & Techniques (A&T) Utrecht.

In addition to the specification of the PGO contract, the scope was changed such that the contract was no longer strictly limited to small scale (KO) activities but included specific large scale (GO) activities to give opportunity to the contractor to optimise the maintenance concept throughout the life cycle. Examples of added GO activities are replacement of insulated welds, exchange of switch tongues and frogs, tamping & lining of tracks and switches, and preventive grinding of rails.

The PGO contract included extensive requirements for process and process control in the 'Statement of Work'. These covered the risk management process, design of risk analyses and maintenance concepts, the maintenance process, quality control, railway safety, request for train-free periods, failure repair, failure registration, information delivery, audits and inspections.

The PGO contract award is not based on the lowest price but the 'economically most advantageous tender' (EMVI). To determine this contract price, an award model was developed to convert the monthly amounts in 8 steps into a cumulative amount:
1. Influence of changes in duration, scope and time on provided Train Free Period (TVP) schedule;
2. Influence of the reduction function of recovery time (FHT) and number of failures;
3. Rates for activities outside the scope of the contract;
4. Influence of changes in utilisation on the offered price;
5. Monthly amounts to be settled with contract transfer;
6. Costs of making a contract area free of specification deviations;

---

[31] Figure 73 is an example of the specification tree for Durability.

7. Settlement of costs/benefits as a result of a 'request for change' (VTW);
8. Fictitious discount at basic level on the CO_2 performance ladder.

For steps 1, 2, 4 and 8, values and amounts are fixed per contract. The values and amounts of the first two steps - offered TVP schedule, FHT and number of failures - are also used as incentives during the contract term. If the contractor performs better in a month then performance improvement is paid as a bonus on top of the fixed monthly amount and vice versa.

The first PGO contract put out to tender was Gelre in 2007. It was a combination of the OPC contracts 'Achterhoek' and 'Maas & Waal'. Prior to 2007, two new maintenance contractors had been certified: the German company Spitzke and Asset Rail. The last one is a combination of Arcadis, Imtech and Dura Vermeer. The first tender was won by Asset Rail. This tender was followed by another 7 PGO contracts, produced by combining 15 OPC contracts, in the period 2008-2012. The results of the new PGO contracts were positive (Factsheet, 2013*) and included:

- Less failures with impact on trains: on average -15%
- Failures resolved in a shorter time: on average -18%
- Less time for maintenance (= more capacity for trains): -40 to -60%
- Lower maintenance costs: -25 to -50%

The results were good but unrest and tension existed behind the scenes. The contractors saw market volume rapidly decline, faced threats of losing contracts and forced drastic change in working methods and personnel to fulfil performance contract obligations. The client expectations had deeply impacted the contractors.

PGO 2012-2015: unrest and tension

In 2012, the Human Environment and Transport Inspectorate of the government (ILT) conducted a Quick Scan into the functioning of the PGO contracts (ILT, 2012*). A quotation from the conclusion of the ILT report: *'The Inspectorate concludes that PGO can serve as a basis for subcontracting the KO, provided this is arranged in a different way. The formal and legal attitude and relationship between the contractor and ProRail, which impedes joint acceptance and shared responsibility with the contractors, regards the inspection as an undesirable situation. ProRail manages the contract tightly in a financial and legal sense. We find that less direct attention is given to safety aspects. PGO creates risks that affect safe driving ability''*. The inspectorate was concerned about the lack of availability of object data and poor visibility of the actual state of maintenance.

Upon review of the ILT report, ProRail concluded that quality and control of the PGO contracts be improved and the negative price spiral be broken. In April 2012, it decided to not award the (eighth) PGO contract 'Eemland' because the offered price/performance did not seem realistic anymore.

In previous invitations to tender, ProRail saw that quality offered always improved and quoted price became lower, but this could lead to unrealistic offers. ProRail launched a new tender to cease this trend. Asset Rail won the tender but competing bidder Strukton Rail raised dispute claiming that there was a non-commercially viable registration. Strukton wrote a letter of fire to the House of Representatives (In Dutch: 'Tweede kamer") at the end of November 2012 and went to court for a summary proceedings. The court ruled in favour of ProRail stating that the latter applied its tender conditions consistently and reasonably as per expectations of a normally circumspect bidder. It was determined that Strukton had a fair chance of winning the assignment and the tender was not to be repeated (Rechtbank d. , 2013).

ProRail was cleared by the judiciary but it did not feel like a winner. The rail infrastructure branch was divided and had to be aligned again. ProRail had to ensure that a realistic price would be offered for the performances offered and that the quality of the relationship with contractors would be improved. On August 26, 2013, a covenant (P/SA, 2013*) was concluded among ProRail and the four active PGO contractors to achieve stability in relationship. The trade unions and ILT also facilitated this development. The focus of all parties was on improving:

- Collaboration and knowledge sharing: setting up a knowledge centre and formulating 'Information delivery specifications' (ILS)
- Transparency in information: setting up a database management system
- Transition to a national PGO 3.0 contract model
- Co-operation in operations

A decision was also made to include a type of time-out in the tender. The four new PGO contracts were not put out to tender, but were awarded on a one-to-one basis of the contractors' tenders and a cost calculation test by ProRail. The duration of these four PGO 3.0 contracts was extended from 5 to 10 years.

At the end of June 2014, it was clear that two of the four offers could be accepted for contract award but that the remaining two offers far exceeded cost calculation of ProRail. This was a difficult situation because the latter two contractors were not able or willing to offer realistic price. The price was too low in case of public tender and too high in case of a direct award. Eventually, an agreement was reached but it became clear that not all maintenance contractors can adapt quickly to the new requirements of a performance contract.

On November 5, 2014, the compliance officer of ProRail informed the Supervisory Board (RvC) that ProRail did not comply with the procurement legislation. The Supervisory Board then assigned PricewaterhouseCoopers (PwC) the task to examine the tender and award of the four PGO pilot contracts. In June 2015, PwC delivered its findings (PwC d. A., 2015-6*) in which it stated that the longer duration of the contracts may be in conflict with the agreements made with the Minister to tender all maintenance contracts publicly in the period 2013-2017. PwC also noted that the Ministry and the Supervisory Board were not informed actively and adequately by ProRail management and that urgent internal warnings had been dismissed.

Upon receiving PwC findings, the Supervisory Board concluded that the situation was of *'once and never again'*. It handed over the file to the new president of ProRail, Pier Eringa, and instructed him to prepare an action plan. The term of the disputed contracts was to be reduced to 5 years. ProRail was required to tender these contracts publicly and improve the information provided to the Ministry of Infrastructure & Environment (I&M). The contractors were willing to cooperate. After dissolution of the direct awarded four PGO contracts they could be put out to tender at an appropriate time.

ProRail started tendering of three new PGO contracts in August 2015 but the procedure halted in November 2015 due to a lawsuit filed by three of the four contractors. The contractors claimed that tendering procedure was contrary to procurement law and put forth ten arguments for justification. The two main objections were that contractors received insufficient information to register properly and that risk distribution was disproportionate preventing discounting of risks in their offer. The facilities court rejected all ten claims (Rechtbank m. N., 2016*) and ProRail was proven correct even though dissatisfied. There was tension in a relationship that was to be based on trust and cooperation.

At the time, quick resumption of the tendering process was inevitable because of the agreement with the Ministry to have publicly procured all PGO before the end of 2017. Two contracts were awarded in May 2016, but the third contract faced a legal difference-of-opinion in its award. ProRail had rejected the winner's offer because of its 'Abnormally Low Tender' (ALI) and awarded the contract to number two. The case was taken to court and the judge ruled in favour of ProRail yet again (Rechtbank m. N., 2016-7*). The tendering of PGO contracts was delayed by litigation but resumed when ProRail developed an extensive package of measures to ensure that maintenance is carried out throughout the Netherlands on the basis of PGO contracts by the end of 2019. Finally, the four directly awarded PGO contracts were put out to tender.

Over a period of 10 years, the infra sector developed knowledge, experience and instruments to manage maintenance through contracts. It would take another ten years to fully switch from input- to output-based maintenance contracts. Figure 33 summarises the history of process development and section 9 provides details of managing the maintenance process through performance contracts on the side of the contractors.

The outsourcing of maintenance had a major impact on the development of the asset management system. It led to fundamental choices to optimally and coherently manage the costs and performance in the operating phase. The following section provides an overview comprising a final consideration as well as summary of experiences and insights in the development of maintenance outsourcing.

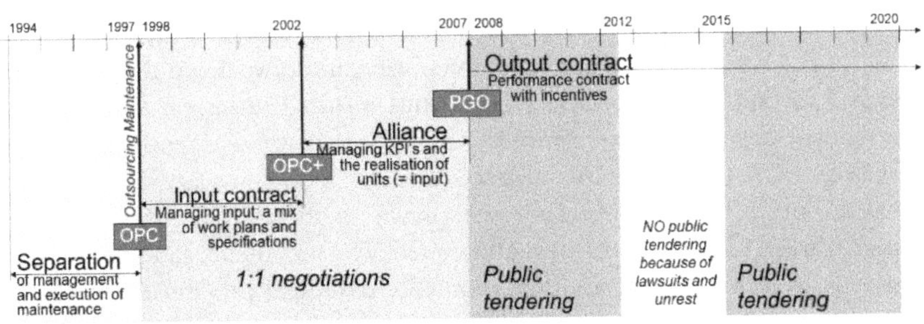

Figure 33   Development process of outsourcing Small Scale Maintenance (KO)

4.2   Consideration, experiences and insights

Consideration

The decision to outsource maintenance in the nineties was naïve and risky. The choice was not made by but for rail infrastructure sector even though real need, markets and expertise were lacking. While it was fashionable at the time, the split between Transport and Infra created a power vacuum and put Infra manager in a bad starting position. The unstable and uncertain situation that developed made the entire rail sector vulnerable. Fortunately, the decision was taken to not start with outsourcing output-driven contracts, but rather start with input-driven OPC contracts based on technical specifications, agreed work plans and price agreements.

The entire rail sector in the Netherlands was given the time to develop knowledge, experience and tools to steer and manage maintenance on the basis of contracts. The rationale was to switch to output-based performance contracts in the long term. As a result, the quality of rail infrastructure quickly stabilised and returned to the old level before the split and privatisation. However, the costs for maintenance gradually increased. This has been attributed to the contract form and changing conditions such as stringent safety measures, increase in night work, shorter train free periods, emergence of 'rail contract fatigue' (RCF) and intensive use.

The sector developed such that it was 2007 when the first output-based performance contract PGO was publicly put out to tender. A fourth new market party (AssetRail) won that tender and provided serious competition. The market was also stimulated because several OPC contracts were combined into a single new PGO contract. A review of tenders indicated that structural price reduction of more than 25% with corresponding improvement in performance quality. It also made evident that a performance contract places high demands on the organisations of contractors and ProRail because lot of new and different tasks had to be performed. The changes led to tensions in the sector.

In 2012, the bomb burst when a contract was withdrawn from the market because of an unofficial offer and subsequent lawsuit. There were investigations, new consultation structures, process improvements, private tendering of four PGO contracts, parliamentary questions, and two new summary proceedings at court. In just within 3 years of the withdrawal of the PGO contract from the market, three PGO contracts were contracted. The judgments all three summary proceedings indicated that the PGO contract, tendering process and tender are well organised but experiencing conflicting interests.

A number of contractors had interest in continuing the old OPC contracts as long as possible because they needed time to adjust their organisation and financial structure. From the perspective of contractors, the PGO tender harmed continuity and management of companies, increased risks, reduced prices and made ProRail unpredictable and ambiguous. The market forces released when performance contracts were publicly tendered taught lessons to ProRail and the contractors. The market gives you nothing for free. You really have to do something to achieve the best performance at the lowest cost in an optimal and sustainable way and then your work with pleasure, satisfaction and in harmony.

Experiences and insights

It is well understood that the outsourcing of maintenance places high demands on the quality and endurance of the entire sector, especially when the sector changes from directly awarded input contracts to publicly contracted performance contracts. The changes, risks and interests are significant, but if success is achieved then the entire sector gains the professionalism required to deliver better performance for lower costs, the holy grail for infrastructure managers and maintenance contractors.

The development in the Netherlands has yielded many insights that can benefit other infrastructure managers in rail transport or other sectors. Some of these insights are summarised as follows:
- **General:**
    - Market does not give anything for free.
    - Outsourcing is not a goal but a means to improve.
    - Outsourcing is not a solution for financial or management problems.

- o Realization is outsourced, not the final responsibility for the result.
- o Tendering and managing projects is less difficult than maintenance because projects deliver a tangible product and have a clear beginning and end. Outsourcing of maintenance is difficult and more risky because the result is a service and it is a continuous process.

- **Learning to outsource maintenance:**
  - o Grow from steering on activities (= input) to steering on performance (= output).
  - o Focus on performance to stay in control.
  - o Adapt the organisation for outsourcing: regulation, specifications, training, functions, tasks, responsibilities, etc.
  - o Outsourcing maintenance requires cultural change that takes time.
  - o Retrieving responsibilities or tasks is much more difficult than giving away.
  - o Transparency, trust and information are core requirements.

- **Client perspective on performance management and specification:**
  - o Performance management is top-class sport and sets high standards for organisations.
  - o Only what we can specify and monitor, we can manage.
  - o Performance can be specified and steered at different levels.
  - o Risk management is indispensable for performance management. It establishes relationship among performance, activities, specifications and costs.
  - o Process control depends on specification of requirements.
  - o Specify and organise information provision; in particular, quality of asset database, asset documentation, RAMS performance and technical condition of assets.
  - o Right incentives in the contract are essential to stimulate the desired behaviour.
  - o Co-operation and open communication create win-win conditions.

- **Contractor perspective on performance management:**
  - o The contract creates the framework to execute the work.
  - o Build a transparent process with clear distribution of FTBVs.
  - o Maintenance field teams should be fixed and led by dedicated chief mechanics per line.

- o For each contract area, the support team should be permanent with a maintenance engineer, a planner and a work preparer.
- Field and support staff should work coherently as one team. An effective and efficient PGO process is not commissioned from planning (= 'push') but demand-driven (= 'pull') based on need and execution.
- It is all about co-operation, trust, open communication and information.

Price and performance of rail infrastructure have demonstrably improved with the arrival of PGO contracts, and most people are happier. Nevertheless, there have been several developments that are risky for the long-term success of PGO, and require attention and/or a solution. These are summarised as follows:

- The aim is to reduce total number of train effecting failures (TAO) and their duration. But structural improvements realised in one system allow the contractor also to compensate for poor performance in another system. By abolishing this compensation option the continuous improvement of performance will be strengthened.
- PGO contracts are not directed at reducing TAO impact as a performance goal of the management.
- There is tension between technicians and contract experts due to differences of opinion in managing and controlling the PGO contract. The contract experts want no unannounced renewals or modifications over 7 years, while technicians sometimes want to deploy extra renewals to continuously improve results. This leads to disagreements in implementing policy changes, modifications, specifications and risk management. The contract and compliance rules often determine what the technician can do and this causes tension, emotional distance and finally disinterest.
- The risk management tool is not very effective in managing performance. The client and contractors conduct their respective risk analyses while the objects - and therefore the risks - are the same for all. The contractor often has too much freedom to decide what is safe and sustainable. For more information about this fundamental and high-risk problem, please refer section 0.
- The process of tendering brings inherent tension in the relationship between the client and the contractor. Maintenance requires continuity, an open and transparent relationship and creation of a win-win environment, but tendering puts this under stress. It is unclear how this will develop and what the consequences may be.
- Prices have fallen sharply under the influence of tendering and competition. It is unclear where the optimum lies. There are signs that the bonus/malus scheme may work out in negative for the contractors and cause loss to them. This would be undesirable in the niche market of rail infrastructure maintenance. ProRail has not yet formulated an approach for this.

112

- The rail maintenance market is stagnant, both nationally and internationally, which means that it is likely to remain a niche. The four rail infrastructure maintenance contractors can apply their rich and valuable knowledge and experience to other infrastructure sectors but there is no certainty.

The rail maintenance industry in the Netherlands has achieved a lot and it continues to develop further. With these observations, we have come to the end of the book's first part, which deals with the development of circumstances and organisation of the infra manager ProRail. The circumstances are the starting point and the organisation forms the basis for the asset management (AM) system. The development, arrangement and operation of the AM system are described in the second part.

Second part

The development, equipment and operation of an asset management system

Think in circles

There are three types of logic. We learn the first 'linear logic' in primary school. The logic of cause and effect, question and answer, as well as problem and solution. These are clear like black and white. Later, we learn that one consequence may have multiple causes and that one cause may have multiple consequences. This may be called 'multiple logic', which helps us understand complex situations. Finally, there is the 'circular logic', where is relationship between cause and effect such that cause becomes effect and effect becomes cause. Service is always relational and, therefore, benefits from mastery of the third logic. Like good students make teachers better, good audience benefits from a good performance system. (Starren, 2016, p. #32).

Part II: THE ASSET MANAGEMENT SYSTEM

5 Essence and growth model of an AM system

This part describes the asset management (AM) system that ProRail has developed. It provides insight into the organisational and management principles, and the required management techniques and instruments. A model is used to explain the essence of AM in a systematic way. The first chapter describes the model and provides insight into the growth phases of the organisation as it becomes able to optimally and permanently manage asset costs and performance over the entire life cycle. The AM-model that ProRail has developed is based on the European quality management model, EFQM.

5.1 The essence of asset management; the AM-model

A good definition for asset management is in the English standard PAS55: *"Asset management is the set of systematic and coordinated activities through which an organization optimally and sustainably manages its assets and asset systems and their coherent performance, risks and expenses over the entire life cycle, with the aim of implement the strategic plan of the organization in accordance with the requirements and wishes of the stakeholders".*(IAM, 2008*). This definition has helped ProRail in improving a model that was introduced in 2007 to make it clear to everyone what is needed to manage performance and costs of assets explicitly and in relation with each other. The model was known as the 'AM wybertje' (SPA, 2007-12*). It described in a simple way what the essence of asset management is, but at the beginning it was incomplete because the risk was missing. By adding risk, all aspects in the model were connected in a logical and consistent way, and the coherence and interaction between them became clear; see Figure 34.

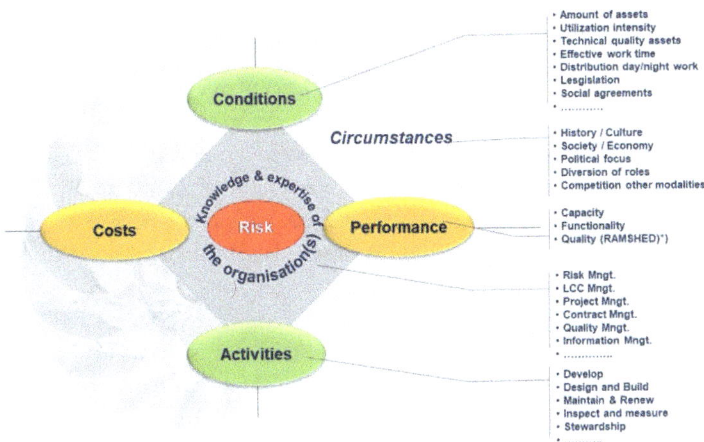

Figure 34   AM-model; the essence of asset management, develped by the author

To explain the model, let us start with *performance*. It is the purpose of the rail infrastructure and can be found in the business objectives of every infrastructure manager. There are three types of infrastructure performance: the network capabilities like capacity, the asset functionality and the RAMSHE quality with which the first two are made available to the train service. Non-delivery of performance is the *risk*. The performance risks are controlled with *activities*. Examples of activities are maintenance, renewal, construction and inspection, and these require people, material, machines and methods. The activities cost money, these are the *costs* or *expenses*. The amount of money needed to control the risks depends on the given *conditions*. The most important conditions are the size of infrastructure, type of infrastructure, intensity of use, actual working time, ratio of day-night work, and legislation such as the environment, safety and working conditions. The costs depend on the quality and experiences of the *organisation(s)* involved: organisational structure, process control, application of high-quality management techniques, the information provision, as well as knowledge and skills of employees. All the aspects are related and change in one may have consequences for the others with risks as the connecting links.

The AM model is placed in the environment where it functions, the *circumstances* in which the infra manager operates and that vary substantially by company, country and time period. It addresses differences in the socio-economic situation, competition by other modes of transport, political focus, governance model, division of roles, method of subsidising, as well as history and culture of the country. For example, the former Eastern Bloc countries have technicians that know very well how to maintain rail infrastructure but the government's financial resources are limited and have other priorities such as expansion of the road network. On the other hand, politicians in Switzerland and the Netherlands attach great importance to well-functioning rail transport to keep cities accessible and limit traffic congestion. They provide sufficient money to improve the performance of the network. The situation in France is different. It is known for high quality technicians, but the quality of its traditional network deteriorated because attention and investment went to the high-speed network at the expense of the traditional network. These examples illustrate the influence of circumstances on the effectiveness and efficiency of rail transport in general and of the infra manager in particular. It also shows that the government is always involved and has often a major influence on the results achieved. This is the reason development of the circumstances and organisation is described extensively in the first part of this book.

The AM model was developed by ProRail AssetManagement. This business unit is responsible for the performance of the rail infrastructure during operational phase. However, the AM-system includes optimisation over the entire life cycle, including the development, design and construction, that fall under the investment phase. With the AM model, the investment phase starts with a demand for transport performance and ends with new infra that provides for it. The exploitation phase is based on the available infrastructure and ends with the quality offered to the train operators. To clarify the difference, a further explanation is provided for use of the AM model.

AM model in the investment phase (new construction)

The investment phase of rail infrastructure starts because of changing circumstances in the short and/or longer term, and the causes of this change can be very different: new transport policy, growth of mobility, new technology, etc. The changes impose new demands on the performance of rail transport. This results in new performance requirements for rail infrastructure. These are potential infra performance risks that need to be controlled and cost money. When the financing is arranged, the performance requirements from transport are gradually developed into detailed infra solutions: network capabilities to system functionality, object types, components and material. By using proven standard solutions, the expected RAMS quality in the exploitation phase can be estimated. *In the investment phase, the requested network capabilities and functionality are realised by designing and building new infrastructure with a virtual, intended RAMS quality.*

Management of system integrity and RAMS quality of rail infrastructure structure is a responsibility of the Maintenance & Renewal Organization (Abbreviation in Dutch: B&I) of ProRail, especially the system managers of the Architecture & Technology department (A&T). They standardise design choices through 'design regulations' (Abbreviation in Dutch: OVS) and approve new design solutions through release procedures.

By applying OVS solutions, the M & R organization knows the RAMS risks related to design and the maintenance concept with which they can be managed. For new infra solutions, the design organisation must demonstrate potential RAMS risks through an initial risk analysis and maintenance concept as well as management of these risks. This is the beginning for an initial inspection and maintenance plan to be transferred to the manager.

AM model in the exploitation phase (management & maintenance)

The management organisation receives rail infrastructure from the design & building organisation with certain capabilities and functionality, and puts it into use. This is the point of departure for the M&R manager. In the AM model, it is mentioned the conditions: the size, type and configuration of the assets. The utilisation and aging creates risks that threaten RAMS performance of the infrastructure. These are risks resulting from wear and tear, weather influences, aging, vandalism, material defects, etc. They can lead to failures, unsafe situations and, in the worst case scenarios, derailments or collisions of trains. It is the task of the maintenance manager to control the RAMS risks through activities such as inspection, measurements, maintenance and renewal. These activities cost money and the costs depend on conditions such as the utilisation, working conditions, effective working time, manhour costs, etc. The effectiveness and efficiency of the maintenance organisation depends on the quality of the organisation. *In the exploitation phase, the RAMS quality is determined with which the capability and functionality of the railway infrastructure is made available to the carriers.*

The infrastructure organisation and service providers contribute to and are involved in the AM system. The M&R organisation is the continuous factor responsible for daily performance in the 24/7 operation. The business units that have developed, designed and built new infra according to the specifications are no longer involved. The infrastructure operational quality depends not only on the design & build quality but also on the quality of M&R management (= ProRail AM) and execution of maintenance activities (which ProRail has outsourced to service providers).

Resume

The AM model is applicable for the investment and exploitation phases but works differently. In the investment phase, the model is triggered by new performance requirements for the network because of changing circumstances. In order to design & build the necessary infra, activities are required which cost money and generate risks. This ultimately leads to new infrastructure capabilities, functionality and utilisation. In the exploitation phase, the AM model is triggered by the existence and use of the infrastructure. The technical quality decreases due to the use and thus increases the RAMS performance risks. To control this, activities and money are needed, and the amount depends on the conditions and circumstances.

The AM model describes the essence of asset management. ProRail has also developed a model that provides insight into the development phases that an organisation goes through to implement an AM system. The AM growth model is explained in the next section.

5.2   Growth model for an asset management system

The development of the circumstances and organisation of ProRail is described in the first part of this book. It is a tangle of development steps: forward, backward, sometimes goal-oriented but often searching and forced by the circumstances. The coherence is discovered by looking at it from the perspective of the 'quick scan' of the EFQM/INK[32]- model that ProRail has used as a structure for its own organisation development. The starting point of the EFQM model is that the organisation and results develop in successive orientation phases. Each phase

---

[32] EFQM = European Foundation for Quality Management. The Dutch version of this is INK, which is the Dutch abbreviation for 'Institute Dutch Quality'.

creates condition for the next one. It is possible to start a new phase earlier, but the growth is structural only possible if a certain degree of maturity was reached in the preceding phase.

The development phases of the EFQM model were taken as the starting point for the organic growth model developed for the implementation of asset management, see Figure 35. The EFQM model distinguishes five phases. In the AM growth model, these have been expanded to six phases to better connect with the development process of ProRail; the system orientation phase in the EFQM model has been divided into a product- and a life cycle orientation.

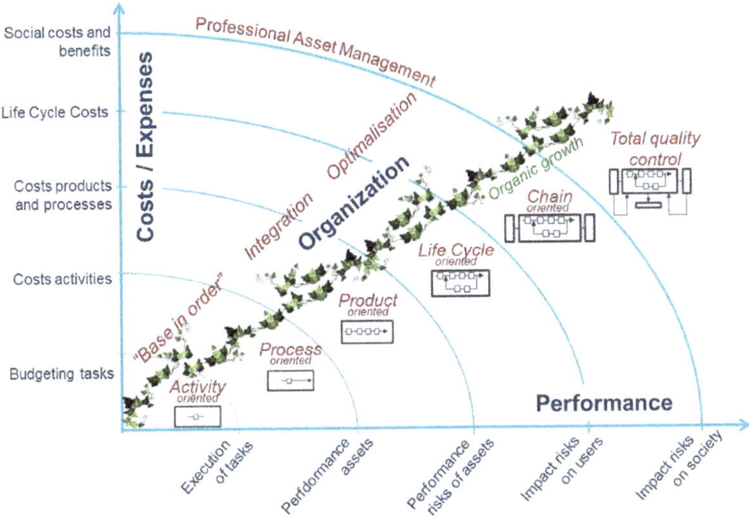

Figure 35   The implementation- or growth model for an asset management system (Source: Jan Swier/ EFQM)

For each orientation phase, the X and Y axes have been characterised as development trends in cost and performance. On the vertical axis (cost), development starts with 'Budgeting of tasks' and then goes from 'Cost of activities' to 'Costs of products and processes' and from 'Life cycle costs' to 'Social costs/ benefits'. On the horizontal axis (performance), development starts with the management of the 'Execution of tasks' and then goes from management of 'Performance of assets' to 'Performance risks of assets' and from 'Impact of risks on users' to 'Impact of risks on society '. The degree of control on costs and performance is related to the growth in orientation.

The development of asset management at ProRail had the characteristics of organic growth of the orientation. The development was driven by the circumstances and the results depended on the knowledge and skills of the people in the organisation at the moment. It started with the 'Basis is in order' of the B&I

organisation as an appealing way of prioritising tasks to control costs and performance of the AM organisation in the initial orientation phases. Only if the organizational basis is reasonably well organized, the organization can work effectively on an 'integration' over the life cycle and then on 'optimization' over the entire sector chain. (Lamers, 2003*). Orientation growth affects not only the core skills of individual employees, but also the culture, structure and systems of the entire organisation.

The organic growth model clearly shows that asset management is not a stand-alone management technique for a group of specialists in the B&I organisation, but that the entire infrastructure organisation is involved, including the value chain partners. In order to optimally and sustainably manage the performance, risks and costs of the existing assets over the entire life cycle, the AM organisation must cooperate with other business units of the infrastructure manager with the ultimate goal of full quality control over the entire value chain. Asset management is the core competency of the M&R organisation, but the entire organisation and chain make a contribution to it. The NEN-ISO 55002 formulates this process as follows: *The asset management system should not stand alone. Part of successful asset management is the ability to integrate processes, activities and data of asset management with those of other functions within the organization, such as quality, accounting, safety, risk and human resource management. Where possible, existing business processes should be optimally used to avoid unnecessary new work and duplication of existing work and existing data. These interactions with the existing processes should be clearly communicated to all parties involved* (NEN-ISO, 2014*, p. 11).

Structure second part (Part II)

The elements that make up the AM model form the main structure of this second part, which is structured as follows:

- Chapter 5: the essence of asset management, the AM model and the AM growth model
- Chapter 6: AM System and Organization.
- Chapter 7: Performance.
- Chapter 8: Costs.
- Chapter 9: Activities, Conditions and Risks.

In chapters 6 to 9, all aspects of the AM model are described in a systematic way, with the exception of the 'Circumstances', because they are already discussed in the first part.

6   Asset management system and organisation

The AM model shows how performance and costs are managed through the control of risks with activities, given the conditions that affect them. This chapter describes the organisation and the asset management system, and the evolution of both at ProRail.

The word asset management was used by ProRail AM for the first time around 2003. Until then, it was called Railinfrabeheer or Management, Maintenance & Renewal abbreviated respectively as RIB and B&I. In a first policy memorandum on asset management (Lamers, 2003*), an image is outlined of what is meant by asset management and its interpretation for ProRail. Quote: *Making improvements in the processes, organization, information provision and culture, in combination with the integral application of the management techniques and instruments of asset management, will lead to a substantial improvement of the relationship between costs and performance. The analysis of the existing situation shows that the required skills have been developed to a basic level. The improvement projects currently underway show the good intention. To ensure that the final results on the improvement projects are consistent and deliver the desired result on time, a degree of central coordination is necessary. The memorandum only deals with asset management in the perspective of RIB, as a pars pro toto for ProRail. Asset management for and by RIB alone does not make ProRail a fully-fledged asset management organization.*

The policy memorandum was written at a time when there was no PAS55. ProRail had found its own way to professionalise maintenance, forced by changing circumstances and conditions. Today, PAS55 and ISO55000 provide a good insight into what is needed to manage assets optimally and sustainably over the entire life cycle. Both norms have the character of a checklist and an inventory shows that the asset management system developed by ProRail (situation 2016) fully covers the checklist, see Appendix 14.3. What is not in the standards, but described in this book, is how to organise asset management, milestones, reason for doing what we are doing, where to start, results expected and so on. This book is, therefore, an addition to both standards. It is a practical case study that describes development of the asset management organisation and in the form of a coherent system of structures and techniques. It provides insight into the 'how' and 'why' of asset management and can be regarded as a paradigm for asset management to understand how performance, risks and expenses can be optimally, sustainably and coherently managed throughout the life cycle. The paradigm is made up of the following themes:

1. Role and task of the (rail) infrastructure manager.
2. The essence of managing.
3. Process model for an infrastructure manager.
4. Organisational structure of an infrastructure manager.
5. The asset management system.
6. Organisation conditions.
7. Process model for asset management.
8. Control of asset management.
9. Maintenance strategies.
10. Delineation and coherence between maintenance and renewal activities
11. Techniques needed for asset management.
12. Core skills and qualities of the organisation.
13. External AM standards, guidelines and techniques.

This chapter starts with the delineation of the role and task of the infrastructure manager and subsequent sections covers the remaining themes.

6.1   Role and task of the (rail) infrastructure manager

The delineation of the role and task of the asset manager is decisive for the development of the organisation and the asset management system of the infrastructure manager. This was done in phases at ProRail. In the nineties, the role of NS Railinfrabeheer changed drastically: all engineering activities were outsourced in 1994, Transport and Infrastructure were separated in 1995 and all executive maintenance activities were outsourced in 1998. All executive tasks disappeared from the task package and it was unclear what actually remained for people who had been responsible for those tasks. In a way, the infra management organisation lost its identity. A foothold was found at the time in the chain model: the Railinfrabeheer is the connecting link between the requirements and wishes of the government and train operators, as well as the contractors and engineering firms who realise them. Figure 22 at page 76 illustrates the chain. The model provided guidance to develop the management organisation. The links in the chain were elaborated in 2004 by a Railforum working group for asset management to delineate the task of an infrastructure manager (Capgemini, 2004*). These roles are: asset owner, asset manager and service provider, as indicated in Figure 36. Later, the role of asset user, the train operator, was added.

It is, of course, no coincidence that the four roles correspond with the organisations in the institutional triangle indicated in Figure 9 at page 36. The relationship between the roles starts with that of the train operator (asset users) who have the requirement of transport. ProRail (asset manager) divides the infrastructure capacity, translates it into a timetable and determines location of capacity bottlenecks. The national government (asset owner) is the financier of the rail infrastructure and determines goals with risk levels. The asset manager advises the asset owner upon the consequences of choices, determines path of achieving the goals, weighs risks and manages the realisation. Service providers realize what the asset manager has specified and planned.

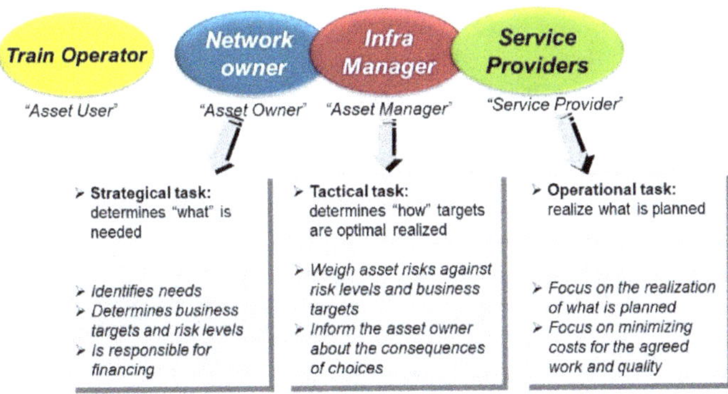

Figure 36   The four roles associated with those of an infrastructure manager

Each of the four roles has a unique Function, Task, Competency and Responsibility (FTBV). It does not mean that these roles have to be filled in by independent companies, as is the case in the Netherlands. They can also be combined in one organisation, as is the case with independent freight railways in the United States. These organisations unite the four roles into one organisation with roles recognised as separate business units.

The four roles are well aligned. An important starting point is: *who pays decides*. The train operators pay their own organisation and means of production from the transport revenues. The national government finances around 85% of the rail infrastructure costs and the remaining 15% comes from the user fee payed by the train operators to the infrastructure manager. The strategic infrastructures choices are not made by the train operators and infra manager but by the government. The role and role interpretation of the asset owner (national government) has a major impact on the performance of the infra manager. The following three examples provide an illustration:

1. At the request of the Dutch government, ProRail helped the Bulgarian infrastructure manager NRIC in the period 2006-2009 to develop a vision for asset management. The infrastructure was worn out and the performance was poor so a plan was necessary for structural improvements (Roest Crollius, 2010-1*). The backlog were caused by the socio-economic consequences after the fall of the 'iron-curtain'. When the vision and approach were presented in 2009, a new government with different political priorities emerged. All directors and top managers were replaced and the vision and plan disappeared in some file cabinet. The decline continued.

2. In France, the infra manager RFF and the train operator SNCF merged in 2015 through a holding company. The government wanted to put an end to the counterproductive relationship between the two entities, which was caused by improper division of roles at the time of separation[33]. RFF was completely dependent on SNCF because it employed all the maintenance staff and owned the engineering firm. The merger solved this problem but the government subsidizes now again a powerful monopolist. In addition, SNCF has already built up a debt of around 50 billion and it is fully dependent on the government for the repayment.

3. In Belgium, Transport and Infrastructure were separated in 2005, but both companies fell under a (much too) large and strong holding company, a tripartition of two roles that led to reduced transparency and counterproductive power politics. Quote: *'In 2008 it was clear that the three-way division in NMBS, Infrabel and NMBS Holding could not be maintained'* (Descheemaecker, 2014-3, p. 268). On January 1, 2014, the NMBS group disappeared, Infrabel became an autonomous public company and the NMBS Holding merged with the NMBS. This was an improvement but politics and trade unions still have too much influence on the business operations of both companies, as a result of which the rail system is still incapable of being run *'as a company with all that it implies in de-politicization, accountability and modernization, from supply to social status'* (Descheemaecker, 2014-3, p. 299)'.

An imbalance in the division of roles creates negative circumstances and conditions for the asset manager. A good delineation of the roles is essential for effective functioning of the rail transport system in general and for that of the infra manager in particular. The chosen division of roles in the Netherlands is clear and consistent, which undoubtedly has contributed to improvement of rail transport system management.

The following section describes the essence of managing, and the basic skills necessary for an infra manager and an asset management system.

6.2   The essence of managing

Projects and assets are managed. According to a definition in an old dictionary, managing is *"being the boss and ensuring that everyone does what he or she has to do"*. This definition no longer applies and may be substituted with *'Getting things done through people'*. Railinfrabeheer used the balance in Figure 37 as a metaphor for managing. The idea behind this is that the scope, time and conditions are on one side of the scale and the available budget on the other. A manager must maintain the balance.

---

[33] For more details see section 1.4

The quality of the organisation determines the degree of efficiency and effectiveness of the management. In a high-quality organisation, less money is needed to do more and vice versa.

The balance is a powerful metaphor for both project- and asset management. The scope and time period may differ of a project or an M&R-process but both aspects are to be managed by both, project manager and asset manager.

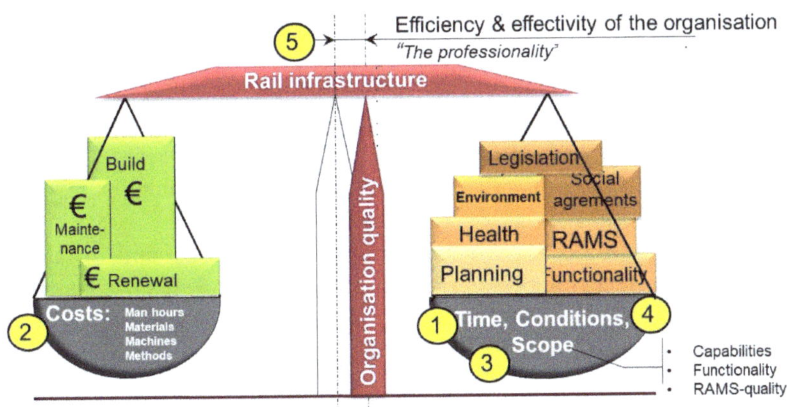

Figure 37   Balance as a metaphor for management (Source: Jan Swier)

The aspects that build the balance are explained in the Lamers' book about '*Expliciet werken*' (English: *Explicit working*) (Lamers, 2008) and the Prince2 method for project management. Lamers discusses in his book "the vital production triangle' that a project manager must control. It consists of three aspects: Time, Scope and Money. A further explanation of these aspects follows with the numbering used in Figure 37.

1. ***Time.*** Time is needed not only for the design and construction of infrastructure, but also for maintenance and renewal or for the lifetime that is or has to be realised. Planning is the instrument to control time.
2. ***Scope.*** Scope is the intended goal or result of a manager's assignment. For a project manager, it is the design and building of new assets, a visible and tangible product. For an asset manager, the scope is maintaining the intended RAMSHE performance (CENELEC, 1999*) for which the asset is built. The scope is controlled by a specification tree, an object tree, a drawing tree, work breakdown structure (WBS), etc.
3. ***Money.*** Money is needed to finance the construction and maintenance of the assets. It covers investment and operation for overhead and executive work, labour, material, equipment, methods and all related organisational and conditioning costs. The money is controlled through budget structure, cost structure, financial administration, cost calculations, etc.

Lamers captures the essence, but is not complete with his 'vital production triangle'. The project management method Prince2 discusses not three aspects but six tolerance areas: time, scope, money, project risks, product quality and business benefits (B.Hedeman, 2015). Prince2 not only discusses control of the substantive aspects of a project but also influence of the conditions for its realisation.

4. ***Conditions.*** Conditions are all circumstances and preconditions that affect a project and are starting point for the manager. They include specifications, quality requirements, collective labour agreement, hourly rates, legislation, working conditions, etc.

The four-unity forms a coherent framework for a manager. If one of the aspects changes, its effects on others and consequences must be managed. This is a general principle that applies not only to a project manager who realises new infrastructure but also to an asset manager who maintains the existing (rail) assets.

A professional project or asset manager delivers more, better and/or faster for less money. S/he makes the organisation more efficient and effective. In the metaphor of the balance, a professional project or asset manager shifts the pivot point of the scale to the right such that the balance can be maintained with less money. Organisational quality is better because the process is better controlled by using powerful organisational and management techniques. For projects, these techniques are the Prince2 method and principles of 'Explicit working' according to Lamers. For asset management, these techniques include Risk-, RAMS- and Life Cycle management, Reliability Centred Maintenance (RCM), etc. The shifting of the pivot point symbolises the quality of the organisation, the fifth aspect to be controlled by a manager.

5. ***Organisation quality.*** It includes the training and professional competence of co-workers, process control, quality and availability of information, deployment of high-quality management techniques, etc.

Management is control of the five aspects in conjunction. Asset management is a specific form thereof. The asset management model developed by ProRail, described in chapter 5, includes all five aspects of the scale, but these aspects are arranged in a different way. The time aspect and physical assets are part of the conditions, and asset performance is the scope. The rationale is that asset management is not about assets but about their performance. By constructing asset objects and systems smartly, a network of railway lines is created with desired capacity and functionality. The operational quality of this network is to be maintained by a process that manages all aspects of the life cycle optimally and sustainably. The principles and coherence of that process are described in the next section.

6.3   Process model for an infra manager

From its inception, ProRail has distinguished six main processes, each with their own core competencies and spread over two life cycle phases: investment and exploitation. In 2013, the LEAN program provided insight that within ProRail there are two value streams and each makes its own contribution to the realisation of customer value: a logistic-value stream and an asset-value stream. The logistic value stream realises customer value through rail traffic including network and timetable. The asset value stream realises customer value by building and managing infrastructure that forms the network. A control function must ensure optimal interaction between the two streams. The organisational building blocks of a rail infrastructure manager are indicated in Table 2.

Table 2   Organizational building blocks

Main processes	Core competences	LC-phase	Value chain
Development of new network capacity	Rail traffic technology, …….	Investment	Logistic
Design new assets	Project management, and system- and value engineering.		Assets
Build new assets	Project management, …		Assets
Maintain existing assets	Asset management (= management, maintenance, renewal	Exploitation (or Operation)	Assets
Operate Existing network	Process management, control, ……		Logistic
Divide existing network capacity	Rail traffic technology, system science, …		Logistic

These are the building blocks for the organisation of an infrastructure manager and they form a coherent whole. In Figure 38, these blocks come together in a process circle that traverses four quadrants by combining the two life cycle phases and two value streams. Thanks to this process circle, the infra manager is able to translate the requirements and wishes of train operators, government and other stakeholders into optimal logistics and asset solutions, which are then realised by service providers.

Train operators are not interested in infrastructure per se but in the performance of the network: capabilities, functionality and quality. Therefore, they have contact with the organisations in the logistics chain in particular developer of new capacity, distributor of existing capacity and the asset operator Traffic Control. These organisations speak the language of the train operators and are able to translate their requirements and wishes into infra solutions, which are then realised by designers and builders, and managed and maintained by the maintenance & renewal organisation.

In every quadrant, a product is realised that is input for a process in an adjacent quadrant. Each quadrant adds value and it all starts with the development process. This is where the decisions are taken that lead to the design, construction and maintenance of the current network. At ProRail, the total renewal value of assets is approximately € 36.6 billion (2015), and € 1.2 billion is the annual requirement for (asset) management, maintenance and renewal. The effectiveness and efficiency with which this is done is determined by the quality of the cooperation between the various business units in the four quadrants, and the quality of the relationship with the stakeholders and service providers.

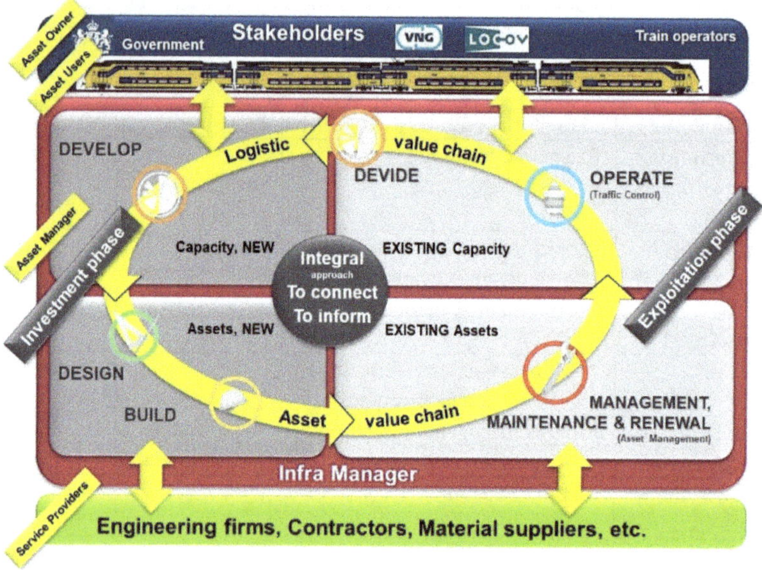

Figure 38   The process model of an infra manager (Source: Jan Swier)

Although asset management is the core competency of the management, maintenance and renewal organisation, the maximum value is generated when all processes in the asset life cycle work together to achieve a common goal. Therefore, the infra manager manages two very different cycles: the life cycle which runs from conception to demolition and the annual operating cycles which allow the network to operate as required and to distribute capacity.

In the 'Develop' quadrant, choices are made that, for a large part, determine the costs and performance over the entire life cycle. This task is carried out by the business unit ProRail Transport & Timetable (V&D). There is also a large potential for reduction in life cycle cost. This potential is encashed when the most optimal and sustainable variant is chosen. This is because every investment decision makes a trade-off between the costs and performances over the entire life cycle of different solutions and all business units must work together to achieve this.

ProRail stimulated and organised this process through a guideline for RAMS and LC management (Lamper, A, 2010*). This includes a checklist with requirements for maintenance & renewal provisions that must be account for in design. In 2013, a generic structure was made available for the preparation of a RAMSHE-LCM dossier (Werkgroep, 2013*). The file aims to provide relevant data to Pro-Rail AssetManagent for project management after completion of the project. It contains requirements not only regarding drawings, documentation and data, but also about the expected corridor and critical systems performance, points of attention for the management, maintenance and insight into project costs.

The RAMSHE-LCM dossier is part of the documentation to be provided for the provisional commissioning and ultimate transfer of the project to the asset management organisation. The procedure PRC00055 (ProRail, 2015*) describes step-by-step a method for a smooth transfer of a project from contractors to ProRail Projects and from ProRail Projects to ProRail AM. There have been many improvements in this area but it still requires constant attention.

The process model explains relationships between stakeholders and main processes of ProRail. It forms the basis of organisational structure of the infrastructure manager as is explained in the next section.

6.4   Organisation structure of an infra manager (ProRail)

The development of the rail infrastructure manager's organisation is described in detail in chapter 3. It shows how a fragmented and technically-oriented infrastructure management organisation transformed into a performance and process-oriented infrastructure manager over a period of fifteen years. The structural change was in phases and led to an organisation which features all identified main processes of the process model, see
Figure *39*.

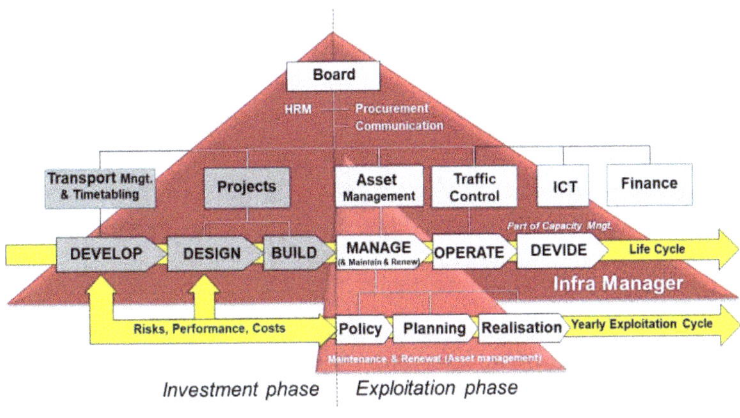

For example, the development and division of new and existing capacity is covered by Transport & Timetabling (V&D), management of design and building new asset is under the Projects business unit and the maintenance & renewal and asset operations are under the business units Asset Management and Traffic Control, respectively. Finance and ICT are housed in separate business units. HRM is a support staff as Communication, and purchasing & contracting are under Procurement.

The two cycles managed by the asset manager can clearly be distinguished in Figure *39* in the two triangles. The major triangle indicates the life cycle and the small one indicates the annual management cycle(s) in the exploitation phase. The management cycle shows only asset management for clarity but it also has annual cycles for traffic control and capacity allocation.

Since exploitation processes are repeated annually, they naturally involve an improvement cycle. This is not self-evident for the life cycle. To close it, the investment and exploitation phase must be brought into contact with each other and work together. The (yellow) relation arrow connects the Asset Management organisation with the Project organisation that develop and design new infrastructure. By exchanging knowledge and information about the consequences of a new asset development and its design, it is possible to choose the most optimal and sustainable solution with the best price/performance ratio over the entire life cycle. This is in essence the asset management system. The working of an AM system is described in the following section.

6.5   The asset management system

From the beginning, ProRail has chosen asset management as core competence of the Maintenance & Renewal organisation, later called ProRail AssetManagement. This business unit manages the daily RAMS performance in the exploitation phase. It guarantees continuity and knows the performance, risks and life cycle costs of installations. It is the task of the AssetManagement organisation to inform the developers, designers and builders of new infrastructure about requirements to meet in the investment phase to improve and optimise asset performance over the life cycle. Various tools and methodologies are used to facilitate and stimulate communication about this information sharing. These include:

- assessing project alternatives based on RAMS / LCC analyses,
- including well-substantiated M&R-costs in all investment proposals
- inclusion of M&R requirements in design and construction requirements.

The asset management system, therefore, includes a collection of specific management techniques necessary to bridge the gap between the people working in the exploitation and investment phases, and between the requirements and wishes of the stakeholders and the implementation, see Figure 40.

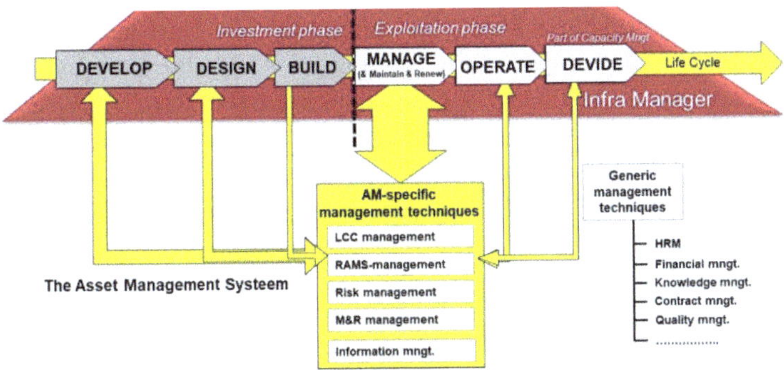

Figure 40   Asset Management System: optimising asset performance and costs over the life cycle

In order to manage costs and performance optimally and sustainably over the entire life cycle, the M&R organisation must be part of the asset management system. The following management techniques are deemed necessary and implemented by ProRail to establish connection between all processes and units in the life cycle:

- ***Life Cycle Cost Management (LCCM)*** supports decision-making by providing insight into the financial consequences of the entire life cycle for several solutions of an issue, including the cost of quality loss and social consequence. ProRail has developed its own analysis model that is available on the intranet, also available to the service providers.

- ***RAMS management*** is the process and method to manages RAMS performance over the entire life cycle, including project development and project realisation phases. ProRail uses the Cenelec standard EN50126 (CENELEC, 1999*).

- ***Risk management*** is a continuous process to identify risk with respect to the business objectives; assess consequences and risks; as well as manage and monitor risks. ProRail uses the RISMAN method (RISMAN, 1998).

- ***Maintenance & Renewal management*** chooses optimal maintenance and renewal strategy and plans measures to manage RAMS performance in the exploitation phase. ProRail uses in-service concepts with risk analyses and management activities (SAM, 2014*) and 'Yardstick' inspections (in Dutch: "Duimstok" inspecties) to determine the technical necessity of a renewal.

- ***Information management*** is the process to ensures that the information requirements arising from different work-, business- and supply chain partner processes (regarding the static and dynamic asset information) are translated into information provision. Each business unit does its own information management using the systems and services of ICT Services.

Asset management is the core competence of the (asset) management, maintenance & renewal organisation and ancillary task for other business processes with different core skills. At V&D, the core skill is rail traffic technology; at Projects, it is project management, system engineering and value engineering; and at Traffic Control, it is process management. All business units not only have core skills but also use generic management techniques such as human resource management' (HRM), financial management, contract management and quality management.

Asset management is, therefore, not a single technique but a combination of multiple techniques with aim to link business processes and organisations to sustainably optimise performance and costs throughout the life cycle. The verb 'connecting' is typical of asset management and ProRail AM used the quality model for organisational development at a time when PAS55 or ISO55000 did not exist.

Quality management aims to improve operating results by connecting the units that contribute to it. This connection is predetermined by anchoring AM techniques in the work processes of all relevant business units and chain partner organisations. It requires all involved business units to control the processes properly as well as establish and maintain necessary connections to optimise results over the entire life cycle. The organisational boundary conditions necessary for the optimal functioning of an organisation are described in the next section.

6.6   Organisational conditions

Asset management is a form of Total Quality Management (TQM). For a developing vision of the organisation, ProRail InfraManagement used the EFQM model at the time. The model consists of four result areas and five organisational areas, also called organisational conditions. These are fully controlled in an effective organisation. The four result areas are: personnel, customer, society and company performance. The five organisation conditions are:

- **Resources.** It includes all systems, techniques, instruments and information that serve the organisation.
- **Organisation.** It includes structure, processes, procedures and division of tasks and competences.
- **Culture/leadership.** It impacts how people interact with each other, the shared values and the management style.
- **People.** It includes knowledge, skills and personal development of people involved.
- **Strategy.** It is the method to realise set goals and balance goals with possibilities.

The organisational areas are not unique to EFQM and are also available in other models to analyse organisations. Some of the well-known examples are the McKinsey 7s model, the ISO 9000 and the Balance Score Card. The EFQM model has been applied by ProRail IM in an adapted form as illustrated in Figure 41. The model was developed around 2004 and consists of a universal framework of organisational conditions, processes and results that enable the organisation to effectively manage and share information. It allowed the organisation to check extent of the conditions for a high-quality organisation are and identify gaps. In the late nineties, NS Railinfrabeheer used such an organisation analysis model as part of a work breakdown structure, to identify what and where to develop in the twelve control processes of Railinfrabeheer. For more details on this, please refer Figure 23 on page 77 with the accompanying explanatory text.

By determining organisational preconditions for each process to realise intended results, an organisational change becomes much more than changing of an organogram. EFQM has also developed a handy assessment tool that enables an organisation to find out where it is in the development process for total quality management. The assessment always starts with the results and involves measures in at least one of the organisational areas to improve them.

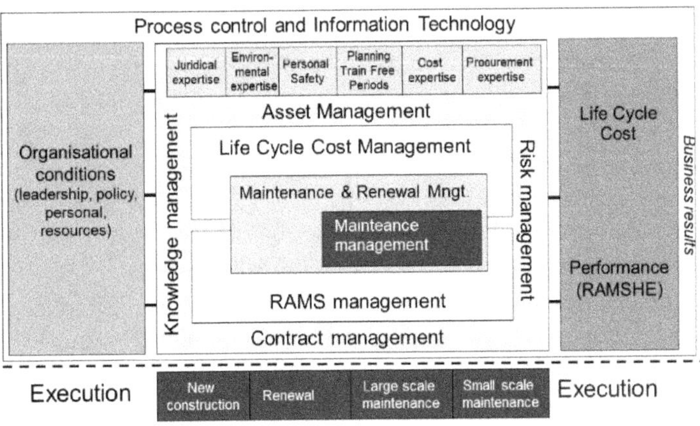

Figure 41   The EFQM-model such as NS Railinfrabeheer that used it at the time

The Dutch equivalent of EFQM is the Dutch Quality Assurance Institute (INK). It is an independent foundation, which was established in 1991 upon the initiative of the Ministry of Economic Affairs. It supports organisations as they travel on the road to excellent performance. The INK uses the nine focus areas of the EFQM model and has added a tenth area of attention: 'improving and renewing'. Similar to the EFQM model, the INK offers the option to make an inventory of the organisation quality with a 'quick scan'. It provides insight into the organisation's level of maturity represented on a scale of five orientation phases: activity, process, system, chain orientation and control of total quality. These phases provide a very powerful and appealing way to illustrate the development process of asset management.

The process models, organisations and organisational conditions covered so far apply to an infrastructure manager and asset management system. The following sections analyse the organisation and management of the Management & Conservation organisation, the business unit that ProRail branded ProRail Asset Management in 2005.

6.7 Process model of Asset Management

In around 1997, the role and position of NS Railinfrabeheer was clear and a management model was developed to serve as the starting point for design of the organisation. The model is described in a booklet in A5 format and was titled *"De Rode draad van de Besturing Instandhouding"* (Projectteam, 1997*) (In English: *"The Red Thread from the Control of Maintenance & Renewal"*). The principle of the model assumes that every organisation has three basic control tasks - strategic, tactical and operational) (Marcelis, 1984*) - and that each improvement process consists of the four elementary activities in the Deming process circle: Plan, Do, Check, Act, also known as the PDCA circle. The elementary control tasks were then called main processes and the activities in the PDCA were called the circle management processes. The main processes were characterised as follows:

- ***The strategic task*** of the organisation is to answer the 'What' question: 'What comes to us, what do we want to achieve and what resources are needed for this?' It is about analysing and choosing the right business objectives and the policy to realise the agreements made with the stakeholders. This is the main process POLICY and corresponds to the activity 'Act' in the PDCA circle.

- ***The tactical task*** of the organisation is to answer the 'How' question: 'How are we going to achieve the business goals and with what means and methods?' It is about planning the right projects and activities. It is the main process PLANNING and corresponds to the 'Plan' activity in the PDCA circle.

- ***The operational task*** of the organisation is to realise the plans within the framework of the policy. Because the infra manager ProRail has outsourced all executive activities, the process consists of delegating the realisation through contracts and managing them. It is the main process EXECUTE and corresponds to the activity 'Do' in the PDCA circle.

- ***The information and evaluation task*** was added later as the fourth task. This task is not only necessary to realise the above three control tasks, but also to continuously improve them. The fourth task involves measuring, analysing, checking and evaluating the business objectives, policy, plans and realisation. It is an integral part of the three control tasks and is seen as the fourth main process, INFO & EVALUATE. It corresponds to the 'Check' activity in the PDCA circle. In this way the asset management organisation has a closed quality circle as main structure such as ProRail Asset Management.

Based on the four main processes and four management processes, the process model of ProRail is developed as a universal model that has proven its value and continued relevance, see Figure 42. The Deming circle can be found not only at the organisational level, but also at the level of the main processes. This is because every main process produces a product that can be renewed, supplemented, updated and improved every year. With this relatively simple process model, it was possible to explain what NS Railinfrabeheer should do to realise the business objectives and how the employees can contribute . The model also provided a good understanding to the management about requirements for improving management control: the control of the control.

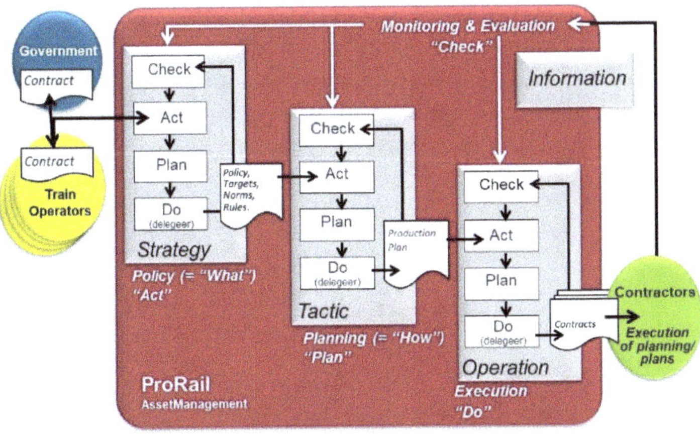

Figure 42   Universal process model for asset management (Source: Jan Swier)

At the time, the model was distributed to all RIB employees in the form of a printed plastic card in a wooden standard. It stood on their desk of many employees because it was decorative but it had no use value for them. The value of a management model for the employees in an organisation should, therefore, not be overestimated. It is far away from their daily work and very mechanistic representation of their reality. However, the combination of a process model, result areas and organisational preconditions is of value for managers to understand and manage their organisation as per the goals. The following section describes how the control of the AM process works.

6.8   Control of Asset Management

In the context of the UIC benchmark study, a work visit was made to the asset manager KCR in Hong Kong in the late 1990s. During an interview, the head of the asset management organisation made a comment which has always lingered in my memory: *"Only if you can specify and monitor it, you can manage it."* This sentence concisely summarises the importance of specifications and monitoring for the management and control of costs and performance. The infra management organisation was aware of this from the start of the split and the outsourcing of maintenance. This is illustrated in the concept developed for the specifications in the OPC contract and the control principles lain with it.

The specification of the OPC-contract (1998)

A work visit to the infra manager Railtrack was decisive in making the choice to not start with managing maintenance contract on output but rather on work plans and technical specifications. For more details on this, please refer to the text in the beginning of section 4.1. At the time, it was recognised that performance can be specified at various levels and that input and output control can co-exist. There is a coherent hierarchy that ranges from top specifications at the level of RAMS performance to input specifications at the level of work plans and process requirements. To make the connection clear, the specification triangle was developed as shown in Figure 43. It is a universal principle and is still in use.

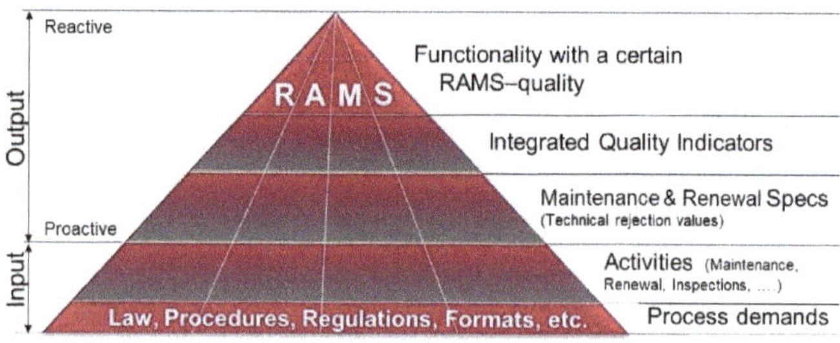

Figure 43   Specification triangle developed for OPC

The highest level that an infrastructure manager can manage is the functioning of the rail infrastructure with a certain RAMS quality. The lowest level is carrying out activities and meeting process requirements such as legislation, procedures and regulations. From control perspective, performance is 'output', and activities and process requirements are 'input'. Railinfrabeheer made a distinction between three output specification levels, and the control influence proceeds from reactive to proactive; from steering of performances to control of the technical condition degeneration that precedes failures and unsafe situations. A further explanation of the three output specification levels:

1. ***RAMS performance*** are the universal top performances that apply to all types of production equipment: rail, road, water, electricity, aircraft, machines in a factory, and so on. The importance can differ and there may be other performance requirements, but these four are always applicable. It is a reactive form of output control because it is directed at what has happened, so the performance experienced by the users.

2. ***Integrated Quality indicators*** (SKI) is a class of specifications that provides insight into the development of the technical quality of a system. It informs whether the whole system works better, worse or remains as is. We can compare it with the periodic measurement of heartbeat and blood pressure. An example of a SKI is the k-value for track quality. It informs about the quality of track geometry and comprises many underlying technical specifications. By determining the k-value periodically and plotting it on a time axis, the track geometry of a piece of track becomes apparent and one can estimate how it will develop. The SKI is a proactive form of output control, which provides insight into technical condition development on whole system level but only gives a limited insight into the underlying cause. It is particularly interesting for system managers and technical experts.

3. ***Maintenance & Renewal Specifications*** (IH-specs) are the technical rejection criteria. If we stick to them then we are assured that the object functions reliably and safely. These rejection criteria were included in the regulations of the old NS Infrastructure organisation but were brought together for the OPC contract in a specification document of around eighty pages (RIB, 2000*). This OPC-spec contains the following specifications for each object type:

    - Demarcation of the system according the object tree;
    - Function(s) of the object;
    - Theoretical lifetime of the object;
    - All quality specifications that apply to the object, each with a unique identification number, measurement method and reference to the source (old standards in regulations).

    It is arbitrary to drop the theoretical useful life under the M&R Specifications. At the time, it was decided to do so because maintenance contributes to the realisation of the intended life time of an object.

The OPC contract management was based on agreed work plans and the M&R specifications, set in one-to-one price negotiations. It gave Railinfrabeheer and the maintenance contractors time to build knowledge and experience in the field of maintenance management on the basis of a contract. Chapter

4 details the development of maintenance outsourcing. The government forced maintenance outsourcing and to make that happen the control, specification and financing had to change. Around 2006, it was decided to develop a performance-oriented maintenance contract, better known as a PGO contract. It was, among other things, to adjust the specification and even now the specification triangle again gave guidance on how this could be done best

The specification of the PGO contract (2007)

The crucial question for development of the PGO contract in 2005/2006 was what performance level the specification and control should be on: the level of RAMS performance or the level of Maintenance & Renewal specifications. The experiences gained during the period 1998-2005 also indicated that a specification had to be made for the contribution of the contractor to realise the longest possible life span and optimal life cycle costs. This top requirement is relevant because the contract duration of a maintenance contract is five years and the average lifetime of the rail infrastructure structure is more than 50 years. The contractor must be prevented from leaving infrastructure at the expense of a shorter lifespan and, thus, higher life cycle costs.

The level of specification was clearly decided when the then director of asset management, Anthonie Bauer, stated: *"I do not want to steer safety on the number of derailments and collisions. I want the contractor to show that it cannot happen"*. Bauer thus established that safety be steered at a proactively manageable level of specification. This can be done by M&R-specifications with rejection values for the minimum technical condition. However, if these specifications are not available then the only option is preventive maintenance activities, the input. The same conditions were also imposed on durability management because reactive control is unacceptable there as well. As far as Bauer is concerned, availability, reliability and maintainability can be specified and controlled on a reactive performance level because they are easy to specify, measure, manage and sanction. At the time, Bauer also wanted specifications for the management and control of the environment and personal safety performance.

As a result of these developments, the RAMS performance evolved into something indicated by the acronym RAMSHED performance[34]. Depending on the type of risk and the options of control, a choice was made regarding level be specified and controlled for each performance aspect. Figure 44 illustrates the principle. The green area defines the responsibility area of the contractor and the red of ProRail. The specification defines the boundary between both parties.

Starting point was that the client should, at all times, maintain control over the management of all performance risks. S/he should be able to determine whether

---

[34] RAMSHED = Reliability, Availability, Maintainability, Safety, Health, Environment, Durability

140

the contractor does the work well and adjust timing, if necessary. The following choices were made at the time:

- The starting point was the RAMS specification triangle of OPC. The top requirements availability and reliability (RA from RAMS) are easy to specify and control at the highest level using the numbers and duration of failures. It was expected that the failure impact[35] would be added to this specification later. The top requirement of maintainability (M of RAMS) can also be controlled at the highest level by using the number and duration of train free periods necessary for maintenance.

- It was not acceptable to manage railway safety (S of RAMS) at the top level by the number of collisions and derailments. The requirement was that safety should be managed on the level of demonstrably safe use of the rail infrastructure, i.e., on the level of condition-based M&R specifications, and if that is not possible then on the level of preventive maintenance activities.

- Specifications were added for Health and Environment in the form of process requirements as well as references to applicable legislation and regulations, Dutch Safety Framework (NVW), associated procedures for requesting train free periods and safety measures to secure workplaces.

- The top requirement Durability[36] has been added to RAMSHE to explicitly specify and control the demonstrable contribution of maintenance to the realisation of the intended theoretical life-time. It is a new kind of top requirement that was developed and has proven itself. In

- Figure 73 on page 220, there is an example of a specification tree that is used for Durability.

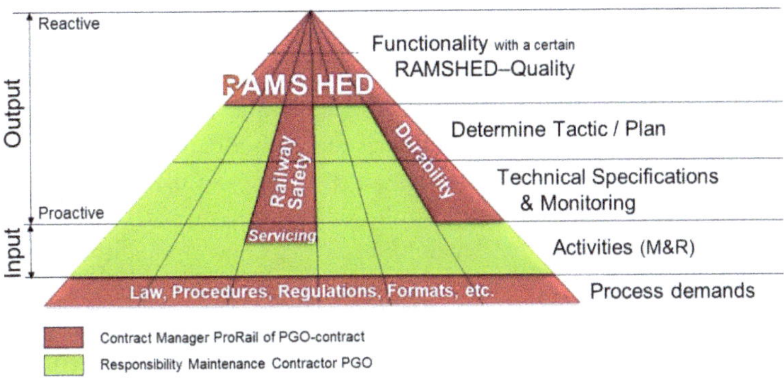

Figure 44   Specification triangle PGO: differentiated management responsibilities

---

[35] Amount of delayed trains because of a failure and added to that the amount of train delay minutes. Known within ProRail as TVTA = Te Verklaren Trein Afwijking = To Explain Train Deviation
[36] The English word 'Durability' is chosen because it also starts with a 'D'. The alternative was 'Sustainability' but it is not chosen because the first letter of it corresponds to that of 'Safety'.

Differentiating the specification level per RAMSHED performance spec made it possible to react either reactively or proactively, depending on where it can and should. It was an optimal solution but it required distinction between M&R specifications that relate to safety and durability, and other performances. Fortunately, the solution was available in the form of available risk analyses with control activities at that time. All risk rules therein are sorted by the type of performance risk. The specifications and control measures for the risks related to Availability, Reliability and Maintainability as well as those for Environment and Health were set aside. The remaining measures for railway Safety and Durability were grouped according to risk causes as well as specifications and control activities to create requirement trees (also mentioned specification trees): a systematic decomposition based on 'System Engineering' principles. Every requirement in the decomposition tree was given a unique number and functionally described with reference to binding documents including specific installation requirements where necessary. This systematic method resulted in a complete and clear specification structure.

However, the formulation of the RAMSHED specifications developed necessary tensions between system- and contract experts at ProRail AM. The technicians wanted to prescribe as much specific technical requirements as possible to which the contractor had to comply with, while the contract experts wanted to focus as much as possible on the functional specification of the performance requirements to give more responsibility to the contractors, which would break through traditional methods. This tension created a distance between the (technical) policy process and the operational (contract) process. Undesirable but not incomprehensible. A certain change started in 2012 as a result of critical research reports, safety incidents and improved information to specify and manage safety and durability risks. In short, an overview of the reports, recommendations and actions that gave rise to it:

- In 2012, a parliamentary inquiry was conducted by the "Kuiken committee" for maintenance and innovation on the railway (Kuiken, 2012*). It provided a number of recommendations for better quality assurance in the near and long term. For example, an annual overview must be conducted on the state of the infrastructure to provide insight into the development of (technical) quality in the longer term.

- In June 2012, there was a Quick Scan report from the Inspectorate of living environment and transport (ILT) on Management and Maintenance (ILT, 2012*). This report concluded that the contract is tightly controlled on the financial and legal aspects but less so on the safety aspects. Therefore, there was poor insight into the actual state of the infrastructure and the execution of the maintenance.

- Based on the Quick Scan, the ILT decided to carry out a further investigation into the PGO contracting. The report was published in early 2014 (ILT, 2013*). The inspectorate concluded that ProRail give more prominence to railway safety in the tendering and execution of small scale maintenance of railway infrastructure. This main conclusion was supported by a number of conclusions about specific subjects, such as: safe driving, ProRail standards and safety management.

- Three safety incidents in the first two months of 2014 prompted the management of ProRail to have Horvat & Partners investigate (Horvat, 2014*) whether there was a structural problem in the area of guaranteeing safe driving on rail infrastructure. The starting point for the investigation was the extent to which ProRail complied with the twelve guarantees that Horvat & Partners had formulated in order to manage safe driving practices. Horvat wrote in his report (Horvat, 2014*, p. 43): *'The railway is a complex technical system. A large number of technical- and organizational measures have been taken to prevent and combat accidents. The potential consequences of accidents are great, the chance of accidents occurring is small due to the presence of these measures. The case studies show that the chance of a derailment or collision with serious consequences for passengers is low, both in absolute terms and for example with respect to car traffic. However, the risk of accidents is not negligible. Paradoxically, the small chance of accidents makes it difficult to manage safety: we try to prevent something that happens rarely. The occurrence or absence of accidents is therefore a poor indicator of how safety is concerned (the safeguards that the organization has set up to prevent accidents). Controlling the quality of these guarantees is in our view the only way to structurally limit the chance of these accidents'.* The conclusion was that ProRail and the contractors manage safe driving ability for all twelve guarantees, but that seven of the twelve are insufficiently filled in and could be better controlled. The core of their recommendations:
  - *'Facts are the basis'* so send on measurements and specifications
  - *'The data is true'* so send on data from a single source
  - *'Continuously improve the quality of the data that is used for managing'.*

ProRail endorsed the conclusions of the ILT report and presented an action plan in March 2014 (Geerlings, 2014*) with primary focus on addressing the two main areas for improvement: (1) rejection values for all objects and (2) a control process if the values are exceeded. At the end of 2015, ProRail introduced improved rejection standards for rail and switches, the systems with greatest safety risks. For safety, rejection requirements were in the form of intervention values and immediate action values, and for durability maintenance values[37]. In 2016, the methodology was further developed and used to implement other systems. In 2013, ProRail had already begun the Spoordata.NL project, which aimed to provide digital access to correct, complete, current and consistent static and dynamic data of all assets to all employees in the ProRail value chain and partners by 2017. These developments strengthened control and management of infrastructure condition and performance. The development of the specification of the PGO contract has been described extensively in this chapter to show how big the influence is of the specification on the control system.

The management of maintenance and renewal (contracts)

The specification triangle of PGO determines the manner of control. The control system connects the requirements and wishes of train operators and passengers with the mechanics who ensure that they are actually realised. Figure 45 illustrates the principle. The control triangle is applicable not only for the small-scale maintenance process, but also for the large-scale project maintenance and renewals. It works as follows.

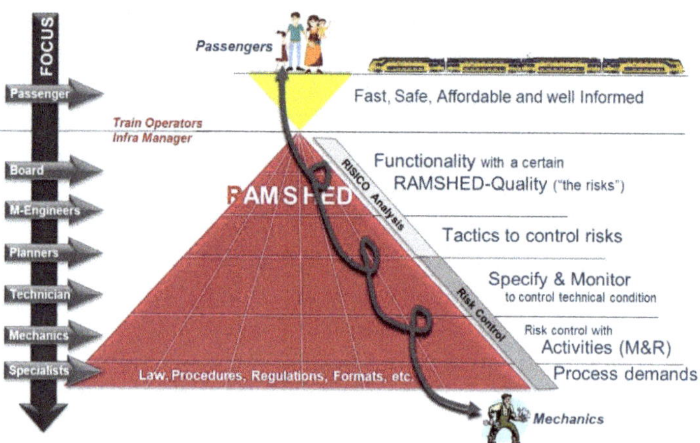

Figure 45   Control triangle

Passengers and train operators are not interested in the quality of the rail infrastructure but in fast, safe and affordable transport. The infra manager makes a contribution in the form of rail infrastructure with desired capabilities, functionality and (RAMS) quality. To proactively steer performance, one needs technical norms and measurements. The standards were in technical regulations initially and contract specifications at the time. They provide the minimum technical

---

[37] *Intervention Value:* technical value that, if exceeded, gives rise to a control measure, which brings risk caused by unsafe handling of the object / system to an acceptable level. *Immediate action value: technical* value that, if exceeded, leads to such high risks that direct train traffic is ceased immediately. *Maintenance value:* technical value that, if exceeded, reduces technical life of the object / system.

limits that an object must meet in order to function reliably and safely. By regularly inspecting and measuring pre-decided parameters, we can follow degeneration of the technical quality and carry out maintenance activity just before reaching the minimum technical limit. This principle always applies.

The specification triangle illustrates the coherent management levels needed to link the customer requirements to the operational activities realising them. None of these levels can be missed and the system works optimally only when each level is linked to the next one.

The control- and specification triangle are congruent. The first describes it in the form of a process to manage maintenance and renewal and the second in the form of related specifications that are related to this. A growing number of maintenance strategies make it possible to manage performance and costs more effectively and efficiently and these are described in the following section.

6.9   Maintenance strategies

A maintenance strategy is the way to realise the desired asset performance and costs. There are several strategies often used together and interchangeably. The number has grown in recent decades due to the rapid developments in the field of ICT, sensors and data analysis techniques. Figure 46 provides a coherent overview of the maintenance strategies.

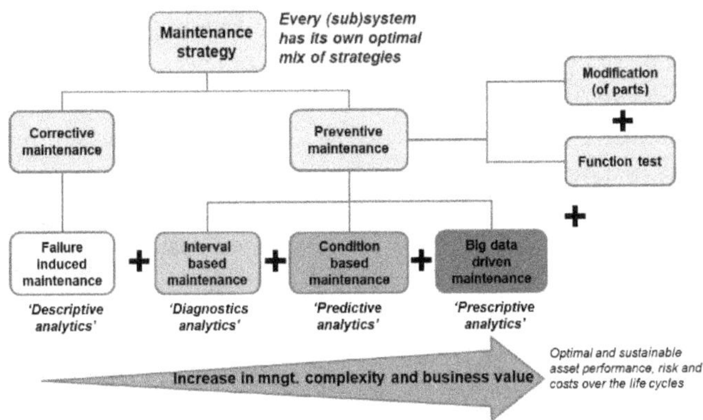

Figure 46   Decomposition and coherence of maintenance strategies

The most well-known categories of maintenance strategy are corrective maintenance, which means maintenance after a breakdown, and preventive maintenance, which means maintenance to prevent a breakdown. A less well-known additional strategy is the function test which experimentally establishes whether the installation is functioning properly. If it is not possible to deliver the desired performance with the aforementioned strategies, then the maintainer still has the possibility to adjust parts of the installation, i.e. conduct modification.

In the area of preventive maintenance, several strategies are possible depending upon the available data and analysis options. The most popular strategies are those that depend on frequency and condition. A new development, I call 'Big data driven maintenance', is where the installation and / or maintenance engineer is able to collect real-time data through sensors and other sources, and produce maintenance work order taking into account all requirements – safety, financial, environmental, etc.

Figure 46 is sourced from the System Asset Management (SAM) manual of Pro-Rail (SAM, 2014*) supplemented with the 'Big data driven maintenance' strategy and expanded with a characterisation of the required analytical skills. The skills are described as 'Descriptive-, Diagnostics- Predictive- and Prescriptive Analytics'. From left to right, the strategies and analysis are becoming increasingly complex and offering superior business results. An explanation of the maintenance strategies and analysis techniques follows:

- **Failure induced maintenance** (SAO) is a form of corrective maintenance and includes failure repair activities. For example, replacement of a broken lamp is an activity related to maintenance. To eliminate a malfunction, (maintenance) knowledge of the system / object is required. Failure repair and maintenance, therefore, form a two-unit.

- **Frequency based maintenance** (GAO) is a form of preventive maintenance, where maintenance is on the basis of a certain frequency and usage time. For example, renewal of the lubricating oil of an automobile engine after certain number of kilometers.

- **Condition based maintenance** (TAO) is a form of preventive maintenance where maintenance takes place on the basis of rejection values that provide insight into the technical condition of an installation. They are indicators of a function failure, i.e., a malfunction and/or end of life. This form of preventative maintenance is also called predictive maintenance. For example, determining the wear/tread depth of a car tire and renewing it when the 1 mm mark is reached.

- **Big data driven maintenance** is a form of preventive maintenance that goes beyond condition dependent maintenance and predictive analytics. On the basis of 'Big data' and prescriptive analysis, maintenance measures are proposed taking into account influences of the conditions and their implications.

- **Function test** is used to test the entire system periodically to check whether it is still functioning. It is the search of an invisible cause of failure. Depending on the result, failure repair may be undertaken if the test shows that a part is defective.

- *Modification* involves introducing improvement to an existing installation to help it perform better and/or more effectively.
- *Descriptive Analytics* involves aggregating and analysing data that provides insight into the past and answers the question "What happened?"
- *Diagnostics Analytics* involves aggregating and analysing data that provides insight into the causes of events and behaviour. It examines the question "Why did it happen?"
- *Predictive Analytics* uses statistical models and prognoses to understand the future and answers the question "What is going to happen?"
- *Prescriptive Analytics* uses optimisation and simulation algorithms to assess possible results of an action. It answers the question "How can we make it happen?". It is also seen as the 'final frontier of analytic capabilities'.

An installation is maintained through a mix of strategies depending upon chance, impact of risk, options and limitations of gathering information, costs and/or performance to be delivered. The condition based strategy (TAO) is often the highest possible. The organisation must be able to measure degeneration of technical parameters and determine timing of maintenance on the basis of rejection specifications. The biggest change with the introduction of asset management is often not in the transition from corrective to preventive maintenance but from frequency based (GAO) to condition based (TAO). At ProRail, this transition was stimulated by contracting performance-oriented maintenance PGO-contracts. It gave contractors the opportunity to deviate from the traditional fixed maintenance schedules in the ProRail regulations (GAO) and switch to risk-based predictive maintenance based on rejection standards and technical condition degeneration (TAO), where possible.

Another development is that the maintenance contractors also stopped carrying out maintenance that had very little or no risk-reducing effect, and that was more than expected. The latest development is that the maintenance contractors now also use big data analysis techniques to find specific combinations of circumstances that are the cause of failures for assets in specific conditions and / or circumstances..

Measuring and assessing technical asset condition

Traditionally, the condition of assets was assessed through inspections and manual measurements. That has changed with the mechanisation of rail maintenance and rise of ICT. For more details on this, please refer to Appendix 14.1.3 and 14.1.4

Measuring, assessing and reporting of technical condition of assets has developed into a high-quality profession and new industry. Before that happened, NS had already set up a laboratory in 1938, which became the centre for technical research (CTO) around 1975 and was privatised around 1995 when transport and infrastructure were separated. The work of the CTO was partly taken over by Eurailscout, a subsidiary of Strukton Rail, one of the maintenance contractors today. Railinfrabeheer was the client and formulated requirements that were used in measurements, methods and applicable national- and international standards. Within these requirement frameworks, private companies are free to offer their services to any organisation. For example, ProRail annually purchases a large package of measurement and reporting services for the management and control of maintenance contracts and the testing of policy implementation. The measurement information is also made available to the maintenance contractors and they can purchase additional measurements for their own use if required.

The privatisation of measurement has fostered development of measuring methods and reporting. Huge amount of measurement data are now compressed into user-friendly information that not only manages maintenance processes but also maintenance machines. As a result, the quality, efficiency and effectiveness of the measuring services and maintenance increases. A wide variety of measurements are possible and several specialised companies are active, each with its own methods and reporting techniques. Apart from Eurailscout (now owned by Strukton and SNCF), VolkerRail with Inspectation, and Fugro with RailData are also active in the Dutch market. Eurailscout and Inspectation work with own measurement trains while Fugro has developed the mobile measuring system RILA that can be placed on any train and conducts continuous laser scan of the environment. The companies often also offer telemonitoring systems to remotely monitor the condition of an installation and issue warning when a limit value is exceeded. The following list provides an indicative overview of the type of (tele)monitoring systems that are offered and parameters they measure:

Infra system	**Measurement**	**Parameters to be measured**
Track/Switches	Geometry	*Track, vertical position, horizontal position, cant, horizontal and vertical arc, equivalent conicity, desired profile.*
	Track width	*Distance between two rails.*
	Video footage	*Uninterrupted, high resolution film strip of rail construction and direct environment of the free train profile*
Rails	Rail profile	*Rail profile*
	Wave wear	*Rail head defects, short wave.*
	Vertical Split Head	*Cracks due to metallurgical defects*
	Squats	*Cracks rail surface.*
	Head check	*Open cracks in rail surface.*

Catenary	Overhead wire Location	*Height and horizontal position wire.*
	Impact detection	*Measuring incidents and incoming wiring.*
	Wire thickness	*Wire thickness / contact surface.*
	Position of poles	*Position of catenary poles*
	Video footage	*Uninterrupted, high resolution film strip of the current collector and the overhead wires.*
	Line scan overhead wire	*Location and thickness with high resolution camera.*
	Automatic inspection	*Image evaluation of damage and strange objects.*
Signalling	ATC- measurement	*Correct operation of code transmitter and receiver, ATC code, code level, quiescent current, symmetry and time ratio signal.*
	GSMR-measurement	*Field strength radio signal and strength and range changeover transmitters.*
	ERTMS-measurement	*In development.*
Telemonitoring	Switch	*Measuring function via current motor.*
	Signalling	*Measuring amperage isolated track section.*
	Level crossing	*Measuring amperage motor, relays, closing and opening time, passed trains, etc.*
	Switch heating	*Functioning, burning time, temperature, weather,.....*
	Track use	*Measuring axle load, passed tonnage, # trains*

Maintenance may be the main activity to manage asset performance during the exploitation phase, but supervision is also necessary to manage contracts but also to determine when objects or object parts are worn out, have reach the end of their life span and have to be renewed. The following section describes how various Maintenance & Renewal activities are defined by ProRail and what their consistency is.

6.10 Delineation and coherence M&R activities

For outsourcing maintenance, it was necessary to clearly define scope of the contract. For this purpose, a long list, known as the TESI-list, was prepared around 1998. It comprised all possible maintenance and renewal activities as per infrastructure system. These activities were allocated to small-scale maintenance (KO), large scale maintenance (GO), renewal and stewardship, see Figure 47.

Maintenance is maintaining performance over the lifetime and realising longest possible life span. The distinction between GO and KO was made on the basis of activity frequency. All work with frequency less than or equal to one year was called KO and that with frequency greater than one year GO; that is why KO is called process maintenance and GO project-based. An activity is called 'renewal' when the entire object needs to be replaced either because it is worn out or for other reasons.

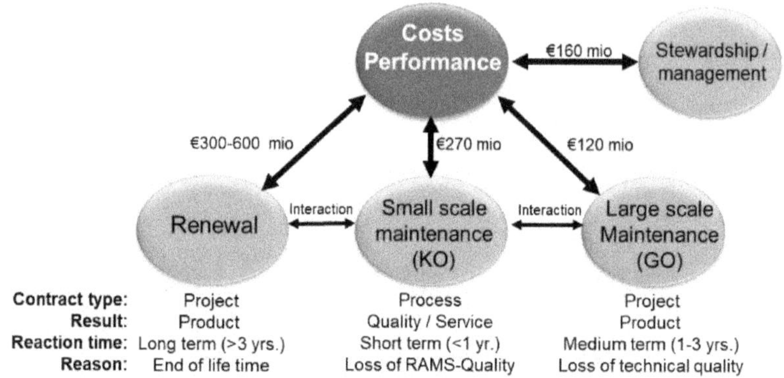

Figure 47   Types of M&R activities and their characteristics

When the TESI list was drawn up around 1998, it was recognised that certain GO activities could be better accommodated in the work package of the maintenance contractor. This created the distinction between GO P1 and GO P2 activities. The project-based P1 activities are included in the KO contract and settled on the basis of a fixed price. Subsequently, the distinction between KO and GO was made in the PGO contracts, by indicating in the objects tree with green which component renewals (GO activities) fall under the scope of the PGO contract.

Around 2000, in addition to the KO, GO and renewal activities, supervision/management activities were also distinguished as a cost category. This included all activities which enabled and secured effective and efficient operation and maintenance of rail infrastructure. These are activities for environmental- and legal management, control systems and configurations, management of infra data, taxes and insurance, utility costs, (recoverable) costs of damages, research/studies/product development and certification/release. The supervision/management is typically carried out by the central departments of ProRail. An approximate distribution among the business units is as follows: Asset Management 50%, Traffic Control 6%, Finance 4% and ICT 40%.

The M&R and supervision activities in the exploitation phase, together with the new construction activities in the investment phase, include the entire life cycle. In order to optimise the costs and performance of the assets, both phases must be connected and managed in coherence using management tools. The following section describes the why, how and what of the different management techniques and tools typical in use in a asset management system.

6.11 Management techniques for asset management

Asset management is about optimal and sustainable management of costs, performance and risks over the entire life cycle. To be able to do this, a number of specific management techniques have to be mastered:

1. Life Cycle Management (LCM)
2. RAMS Management:
3. Risk Management
4. ICT- and Information Management
5. Quality Management

The development of the five management techniques is systematically described in this section on the basis of three questions: what is the purpose of the technology, how did it develop at ProRail and what is the essence of the method? Started with life cycle management.

6.11.1 Life Cycle Management

Why LCM. Life cycle management (LCM) is a method to deploy the most optimal project approach based on a life cycle (LC) cost analysis. It helps managers and stakeholders gain insight into the consequences of choosing a certain project approach. In the case of an LC cost analysis, all costs, over the entire lifetime of an object or system, are calculated back to one moment in time whereby different solutions can be compared. It includes not only the maintenance and renewal costs but also the costs resulting from loss of performance due to failures. This is essential to demonstrate differences in complexity of solutions and effects of low maintenance costs. ProRail not only accounts for cost of performance loss, but also that of social consequences, health and environmental effects of it. It conducts durability (also called: sustainability) test as per requirement.

When life cycle costs of different alternatives are compared, decision making becomes transparent and it is possible to demonstrate the extent to which performance and costs are realised optimally and sustainably. For this, the Project and M&R organisation must be connected. In the early phase of a project, choices are made (for example, definition, alternatives and preliminary design) that determine performance and costs in the exploitation phase. Only by working together and accounting for LC cost in decision making can the most optimal choice be made. With LCM, ProRail establishes relationship between the exploitation and investment phases to optimally manage the costs and performance over the life cycle.

How LCM has developed at ProRail. It was the management consultancy firm McKinsey that, in 1989, guided the NS infra organisations to the high improvement potential of managing maintenance on the basis of life cycle costs (McKinsey, 1989-1, pp. 1-3). The realisation of that improvement was assessed as non-complex (a rather optimistic estimate as will become apparent). Organisational design requirements were: single management responsibility, availability of information and insight into different dimensions. The result of the recommendation was that the Infra Beheer department and track maintenance organisation of the Exploitation department were merged with Engineering separated and allowed to work only on behalf of the infra development department at Infra Beheer.

In February 1993, Infra Beheer organised its first symposium on life cycle management (LC-netwerk, 1993). It was an exploration of usefulness and necessity based on experiences and cases with different infra systems. The conclusions and recommendations of this symposium were as follows:
- LCM is always applicable, by and for everyone;
- Commitment and communication about LCM is necessary;
- It is important to record and exchange knowledge and experiences;
- A calculation method is selected for LCC;
- LCC comparisons only consider present and future costs;
- It is important to record historical data about costs, life time etc. ;
- We need insight into the cost-influencing factors;
- We should not wait but act.

The elaboration of these recommendations stopped with radical structural changes such as the separation of Transport and Infrastructure (1995), privatisation of Engineering (1995) and the outsourcing of maintenance (1998).

In 2000, the first version of the current LCC analysis instrument was introduced. It is a calculation model to compare costs of up to four alternatives and generate report automatically (Noort, 2014, LCM14). Input variables of the model are maintenance and renewal costs over the life span, and the costs of unplanned and planned unavailability (R&A and M of RAMS). These are the 'hard' life costs charged to the infrastructure manager. The model calculates net present value (NPV) of all costs at time t = 0 and enables comparison.

Adoption of the LCC analysis instrument was mandatory for all investment proposals above 500,000 Dutch guilders (NLG) and training was provided to about 600 staff members in the period 2001-2007. The method is mainly used to underpin renewal and investment decisions (LCM-project*, 2008-5). The instrument was later expanded step by step. Figure 48 illustrates phases of the development process and associated expansions.

In 2002, a cost database became available on the intranet, the Rail Case Base (RCB) (ProRail, 2002). The RCB has been developed to share knowledge of professional cost experts, make cost information more efficiently available, connect technology and money, and improve the quality of cost indicators. The low access threshold and high quality of RCB stimulated the use of the LCC instrument and increased quality of the analysis. For more details about the RCB, please refer section 8.2.3.

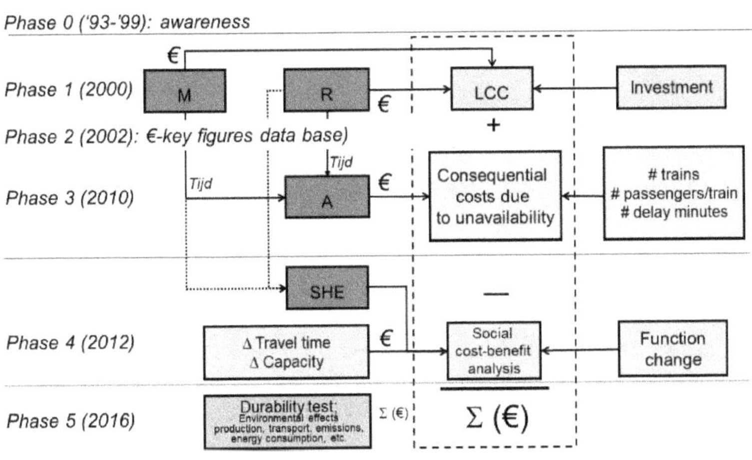

Figure 48   Principle and development process of ProRail's LCC analysis instrument

In 2008, the LCC instrument was expanded to include social costs and benefits caused by loss of travel time because of planned and unplanned unavailability. These are the 'soft' LC-costs related to train delays. The ratio between difference in income and LC costs was also estimated for each solution. The value greater than one (1) indicates positive solution and option with highest cost-benefit ratio is preferred. In the period 2010-2012, approximately 200 staff were trained and name of the LCM instrument was changed to RAM-LCC.

In 2012, the 'soft' social benefits were added to the LCM calculation model. These relate to small and large changes implemented by the network & capacity development department (V&D) and may include improvement of driving time, capacity increase or improvement of Safety, Health and Environment (SHE of RAMSHE). These 'soft' social benefits are deducted from the 'hard' and 'soft' LC-costs for RAMSHE. The name of the LCC instrument thereafter changed to RAMSHE-LCM.

In 2015, the costs and benefits of environmental qualities[38] were added to the LCC methodology (Ruygrok, 2013-1*). It indicates the effect on Health and

---

[38] Air quality, Noise & Vibration, Nature, Cultural history and Ground

Environment in the form of Durability test (D of RAMSHED) and estimates the extent to which prosperity and well-being of our natural, produced, human and social resources is maintained. By comparing the prosperity value of shrinkage of natural stock with that of the growth of produced stock, it can be checked whether the net prosperity increases or decreases with investment. In a social cost-benefit analysis (MKBA) the natural and produced stock are part of the effects on the environmental reserves. In a MKBA, these form a gauge for durability / sustainability of an investment.

What is the essence of the LCM method? The LCM methodology has developed over a period of 15 years. In this section, the method is explained in more detail with an explanation of all key concepts.

The LCM method (Noort, 2014, LCM14) compares alternatives in four standardised steps: (I) define project, (II) generate variants, (III) determine the preferred variant and (IV) report findings. The analyst is guided step-by-step through the calculation programme and can choose variants and quality of the required input data. The preparation of the report with the LCC comparison is automated. An extensive course package is available and training sessions are held annually at the Railcenter in Amersfoort. The LCM instrument is accessible through the intranet to every ProRailer and service provider who has taken the course. A specialist at ProRail AM manages and develops the method and support system, as necessary. A knowledge bank saves all LCC analyses for future use.

The LCM calculation method is based on two principles: net present value and annuity. With the present value, expenditures of future can be added by applying a discount rate. With annuity, a lump sum cash value is converted into equal annual costs over the specified period. The lowest annuity is most economical.

The interest rate in LCM instrument is fixed on the basis of information from the Ministry of Finance. Only the financial director of ProRail may instruct to change it in the LCM instrument.

Expenditure from the past, also called sunk costs, are not included in the LCM because past is accepted as is. The residual value income of an object is included.

The lifetime entered in an LCM calculation is basically that of an object or system. In case of multiple objects or systems with a different lifespans, annuity (not present value) is compared. If a complex system composed of multiple subsystems with different lifetime and costs is analysed, then subsystems with residual lifetime and value are considered and a period of 100 years is selected. The end of the period is so far in the future that the error, measured in net present value, is usually negligible.

The costs of planned and unscheduled disruptions (M and R&A of RAMS) are essential in LCC analysis because maintenance and renewal costs limit value loss caused by poor performance. Less maintenance and late renewals may lower costs but they increase failures and speed limitations; that is the price you pay for neglecting the system. The method is standardised on the basis of disruption duration, number of affected tracks and hourly rate by line value. Table 3 was integrated into the LCM instrument until about 2010 and was automatically applied on the basis of input variables. Since 2010 the costs are determined by multiplying the number of passenger delay minutes by the 'Value of Time' (VoT)

Table 3   Costs of a disruption per hour (2010)

Line value	Unplanned Disruption	Planned disruption < 9 hours	Planned disruption >= 9 hours
1 of 2	€ 2.000	€ 1.000	€ 1.500
3 of 4	€ 6.000	€ 3.000	€ 4.500
5 of 6	€ 10.000	€ 5.000	€ 7.500

The value of unplanned disruptions *(VoT)* is related to the longer travel time of a passenger caused by train service irregularities (TAO). This is done by multiplying the number of passenger delay minutes with the VoT. The VoT indicates the willingness of a passenger to arrive at his/her destination one hour earlier. This varies per travel motive: business, home-work or private. ProRail uses an average hourly rate of € 8.39 (2016) as indicated by the government (KiM*, 2013, Kim11). In case of unscheduled disruptions, the VoT is multiplied by an 'unreliability factor' of 2.0 to indicate the extra disadvantage that the passenger experiences due to unpredictability of the delay.

The value of planned disruptions is determined as that of *unplanned disruptions* but unreliability factor of 2.0 is not used and average number of passengers and delay minutes are not calculated. The difference is also that there is no calculation with an average number of passengers and delay minutes, but with ratios per hour, differentiated to working- and weekend days because they are known during planned train free working periods. Research shows that not all passengers choose the alternative offered by the train operator because passengers may choose other alternatives such as car or bicycle. The passengers who choose for alternative transport do have a disadvantage, but not as much as the passenger who accept the alternative offered. Half of the passengers are considered in determining value of disruption and this is called the 'Rule of half'.

A sensitivity analysis determines how the output responds to changes in the input. It is important when variants are close in value. The analysis is built into the LCM instrument and is performed automatically. A cost-benefit analysis assesses how benefit / ΔLCC ratio and in an LCC calculation how annuity change when one or two cost categories change. When sensitivity is low then the ranking of variants is more reliable. The sensitivity analysis is an important part in sub-stantiating choice for a variant. As a result of an audit by the TNO[39], the sensitiv-ity analysis was adapted to provide insight into the robustness of a variant to the decision-maker. It indicates likelihood for reality to deviate from the model cal-culations (J. Harmsen, 2013-2*).

LCM durability (or sustainability) test was added to the LCM instrument in 2015. Our investment decisions are sustainable when they do not diminish wel-fare and well-being of our grandchildren. This requires maintenance of our stocks, environmental capital, both natural and social. By comparing prosperity value of shrinkage of the natural stock with prosperity value of growth of the produced stock, one can evaluate whether net wealth increases or decreases due to the investment. This is the comparison made in Social Cost Benefit Analysis (MKBA), which accounts for all environmental resources. It an excellent indica-tor of sustainability of an investment (KiM*, 2013, Kim11). At ProRail, this method has been integrated into the LCC instrument by expanding the MKBA tool with additional environmental qualities (Ruygrok, 2013-1*). The principle is quite simple. For example, the production and transport of material to the con-struction site costs energy. Subsequently, material is processed and maintained till the end of technical life and then demolished. Some material is reused, some is burned and some goes to garbage dump. Environmental impact occurs in all these processes.

The best known environmental impact is release of CO_2 emissions. In addition, NOx and SOx are released, natural resources are exhausted and there are prob-lems of acidification and leaching. These negative environmental effects are rec-orded in the national environmental database (NMD) of the Building Quality Foundation (Bouwkwaliteit, n.d.). This database contains all environmentally rel-evant product information for calculation rules in the determination method. ProRail has conducted environmental life cycle analysis for many rail infrastruc-ture systems such as rails, switches and overhead lines. It has estimated emissions during lifetime of these systems. These values have been measured and are avail-able as key figures for LCC analysis.

ProRail has also developed key figures for environmental effects due to energy consumption of different types of trains. The effect on the environment can be calculated for certain increase or decrease in the number of train kilometers. The energy tool determines effects of a temporary speed restrictions on energy con-sumption. The environmental impact of this energy difference can be determined to decide about removing the limitation.

Usefulness and necessity of LCM analyses. The main advantages of an LCM analysis are as follows:

- A decision is taken only after a number of variants have been deliberately mapped out and weighed. This improves substantiation of the decision.
- The costs of entire useful life of the property are considered and this prevents sub-optimisation such as decisions based on the lowest initial investment value.
- LCM provides a simple and unambiguous method to evaluate disruptions of train service as per expenditure. This is important because the Board has proclaimed infrastructure availability as the most important product of ProRail. There is now a uniform method within ProRail to weigh this parameter for different projects.
- LCM promotes the setting of standards and key figures for future LCM assessments in similar projects. It helps ProRail justify its selection of a certain variant to third parties such as the government.
- The LCM helps ProRail demonstrate that it handles government resources responsibly and supports RAMS studies in calculating RAMS performance versus cost.
- ProRail Projects and ProRail AM work closer together because project data is required for both investment and exploitation phases.

LCM is applied at many locations within ProRail and both in the investment and exploitation phases. It is mandatory to use this method in production planning of AM. All investment and large-scale maintenance projects must today be substantiated by a LCM calculation or LCM decision rule if they exceed € 250,000 (Vernes, 2012-11*). Examples of LCM applications are:

- Release of new systems: evaluate variants for a new system.
- New construction: assess variants in solution, choice of material, facilities, execution time, duration of commissioning, etc.
- Maintenance: assess variants such as renewal/refurbishment, higher investment versus lower maintenance costs, finishing, execution, etc.

So far, the why, how and what of LCM management and the method developed by ProRail has been discussed. The LCM creates a bridge between the investment and exploitation phases, making it possible to choose the project variant with most optimal and sustainable results over the entire life span. The LCM method is entirely focused on optimising life cycle costs and it includes the loss of performance as a cost. To explicitly manage and optimise the RAMS performance in the investment phase, another management technique called RAMS management, is deployed. The why, how and what of RAMS management is described in the next section.

6.11.2 **RAMS-management**

The performance criteria of an infra manager is provision of network capability with a certain asset functionality and quality. This depends on type of transport possible on the network and ability of rail infrastructure systems. The capability and functionality are designed and installed in the project development and construction phases. The quality of capability and functionality offered to the train operators depends on maintenance quality in the exploitation phase.

Based on the four universal RAMS performances, universal quality requirements can be specified, analysed and monitored for all kind of assets / systems (CENELEC, 1999*). These are as follows:

1. Reliability: Mean Time to Repair (MTTR)
2. Availability: Mean Time between Failure (MTBF)
3. Maintainability: Mean Time to Maintain (MTTM) and
                            Mean Time between Maintenance (MTBM)
4. (Railway) Safety

ProRail added Environment and Health to the acronym RAMS and extended it to RAMSHE. Later, it added durability to performance and the acronym grew to RAMSHED. In this chapter, the three acronyms are used interchangeably either because of the period in which the chapter is written or to have the simplest form indicate performance quality of network capability and asset functionality offered to the train operators. The chapter starts with an explanation of the why of RAMS management.

Why RAMS management. Asset management is about optimising costs and performance over the lifetime. Life Cycle Management is the technique to choose the most optimal approach from a financial perspective (method described in the previous section). RAMS management is a technique to choose the most optimal approach to realise the desired RAMS performance in the exploitation phase. The European standard EN50126 (CENELEC, 1999*) describes in the 'V-model' how to deploy RAMS management. For more information about this method, please refer to section 6.13.1.

ProRail has integrated the two techniques into a RAMSHE-LCM study (Lamper, A, 2010*) because costs and performance form a two-unity. The study focuses on the project development phase because future performance and costs are mostly determined in this phase and, therefore, this phase has greatest potential for life cycle cost savings (BSL, 2000-6*, p. 46). If such a study is carried out too late then the design is already, wholly or largely, fixed with all the consequences. The study is performed in close consultation and collaboration with the Asset Management business unit because it knows the performance and M&R costs of standard infra solutions and often has ideas for improvement. The collaboration between Project and AM organisations makes it possible to choose solutions with potential for most optimal and sustainable relationship between LC costs and RAMS performance.

A quote from the RAMS guideline of ProRail: *'The real change is in the fact that the RAMS requirements are placed at the beginning of the life cycle and that compliance with these requirements is just as important as the aforementioned cases (such as: investment budgets, integration and functionality). From the beginning, the expected RAMS performance will be taken into account in the decision-making process'* (Gestel P. v., 2003-7*).

How did RAMS management develop at ProRail? In the past, there was limited contact between the engineering- and maintenance organisation. The engineering office designed and built new infrastructure, and the maintenance organisation ensured that infra continued to function within the framework of specifications and regulations. The maintenance organisation was subordinate to the engineering firm. The infrastructure organisation was also more focused on safety and reliability of various technologies and less on the performance of the entire network. This condition changed when the NS engineering office was set apart in 1990 and became independent in 1994. In that period, the Management & Maintenance Organization received assignment and space for itself and became self-aware. The development stagnated when it was decided to privatise the execution of the maintenance. The client and contractors first had to put their own organisations in order and learn how to manage and influence performance on the basis of contracts. A beginning was made on the basis of work plans, technical specifications and annual price agreements. The disadvantage of this type of contracting was that responsibility of the contractor was limited to execution of the agreed work plans and not to the result. Both organisations first had to learn to manage a contract on input and later they could progress to output/performance.

After ten years, the switch was made from input to output control. In 2007, the first Performance Focused Maintenance (PGO) contract was successfully presented. It specified and managed the RAM performance at top level, as well as Safety and Durability at the level of technical M&R specifications. For more details, please refer to section 6.8. In order to switch to performance management it was necessary to develop and implement new instruments and management techniques. This required vision and strategy, which came from an unexpected source, the construction of new lines and a new EU standard.

The awareness for performance management was stimulated by the construction of two new lines: HSL South and Betuweroute. The development of RAMS management started there as shown in Figure 49. Both projects were under development and implementation at the end of the nineties. The project management of HSL South was not at NS Railinfrabeheer but at Rijkswaterstaat (RWS). The RWS opted for an innovative contract form: Design-Build-Finance-Maintain

(DBFM). This type of contract does not focus on design but on sustainable optimisation of performance and life cycle costs of the line.

The principles used for specification and management of DBFM contract were published in European standard EN50126, which describes the process to optimally manage RAMS performance over the entire life cycle. RWS made an unusual appeal to NS Railinfrabeheer to provide experts for analysing and formulating requirements regarding RAMS performance to be delivered and preparing a maintenance concept. Employees from NS Railinfrabeheer and Projects came into contact with RAMS and risk analyses for the first time in combination with life cycle costs. They gained valuable experience in applying the methods and soon ProRail started using the EN50126 standard in its projects.

In case of Betuweroute, an investigation into the possible application of a DBFM contract for construction of the superstructure led to not selecting this type of contract but yielded knowledge and experience in the organisation. This knowledge was applied to the project development of the Hanze line, a new line between Lelystad and Zwolle. This line has been developed entirely on the basis of RAM requirements, in accordance with the principles of EN50126 (Pardijs P. , 2003-4*). The standard guided performance management in maintenance and development of required instruments. The milestones included appointment of a specialist for management and analysis of TAO failure database (2002), introduction of LCM methodology and instrument (2000), development of risk management tools (2002), first view on RAMS management for new construction (2003) and successful application in the construction of the Hanze line. Figure 49 illustrates the process.

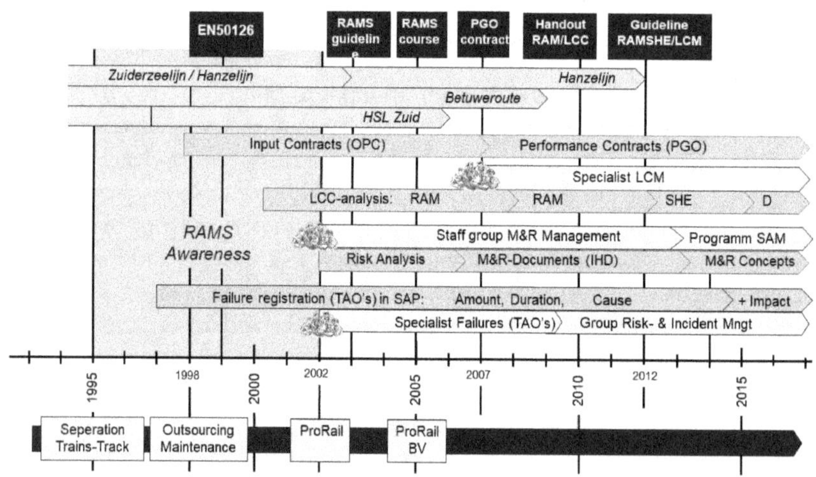

Figure 49   The development of RAMS-management at ProRail

160

The first training for RAMS management was provided to ProRail in 2005. It was a course consisting of three RAMS management modules: one for Capacity Management, Projects (Gestel P. , 2004-9*) and M&R organisation (Pardijs E. , 2005*).

The capacity management module involved applying RAMS in the practice of the 'Benutten en Bouwen' (English: 'Utilization and Building') programme. It consisted of two parts and a practical case about the railway zone in the village Elst (Gestel P. , 2004-8*).

The module for Projects focused on the usefulness and necessity of RAMS management in new construction projects, application of EN50126 with the V-model, and risk analyses. The course consisted of three sessions with practical cases (Gestel P. , 2004-7*).

The M&R management module focused on applying RAMS management from its own role. Topics were: what is it, how do you measure it, who does it and what is the connection with M&R management, Deming's quality circle, risk management, safety-case and product management (Pardijs E. , 2005*). The knowledge was applied in a practical and humoristic case about improving the poor performance of the Coyote[40] lifts and role of ProLift in it. The course started with a video film in which Anthonie Bauer, then director of ProRail Inframanagement, expresses his serious concerns about the Coyote lifts and the need for ProLift to do something about it (Pardijs E. , 2005*). The training was a success and seen as a first step on the long road from *'Talk about'* to *'Secure of'* RAMS management in ProRail.

In October 2008, a hand-out was published about RAMS / LCC for projects. It was widely distributed and the principle was promoted in lectures and training at ProRail and service providers. As a result, the RAMS thinking grew becoming part of the planning and project development process as well as project implementation. Due to advancing insights and developments, it became clear that an expansion was possible and desirable from RAMS-LCC. In particular, stimuli came from the new Safety- and Environment Management Systems, and the Sustainability programme. The Safety, Health & Environment (SHE) performance was added and durability was further elaborated in the LCM module.

The reformulation of the core processes of ProRail and increased attention to the quality of train paths have led to a broadening of control on RAMSHE performance and life cycle costs. This led to renewed guideline for RAMSHE-LCM studies at the end of 2010. This guideline is more complete and practical as the earlier version in the form of a handout. To get acquainted with RAMSHE-LCM

---

[40] A prairie wolf

and to refresh the knowledge, a training course has been developed and benefitted hundreds of ProRailers and external advisors. The project analyses were shared through a knowledge bank containing all RAMS studies for different projects. The course was moved to Railcenter in Amersfoort in 2009 and is now part of the Value Engineering (VE) course.

Since 2002, ProRail applies the RAMS/LCM methodology as a decision-making tool at various stages of projects. It is used in multidisciplinary teams which strive for cost-effective solutions for required functionality within the project. Value Engineering integrates all disciplines and specialisms in a structured multidisciplinary approach (GWW, 2013-11*) and RAMSHE-LCM fits in perfectly. The RAMSHE-LCM guide provides a complete picture of the ProRail vision on RAMS and Life cycle management, in accordance to the principles of EN50126. The project manager is responsible for applying the guideline and translating the resulting consequences in the project specifications and the design. The RAMSHE specialists at Asset Management can help the project organisation. For each project, an analysis is performed for intended and expected performances and costs, checklist of M&R facilities is applied and transfer of projects is arranged in accordance to procedure PRC00055 (ProRail, 2015*).

Introducing and applying the guideline was a success, but there is a downside. It is difficult to keep the attention for RAMS management alive in the project phase. As of 2013, there are no more RAMS courses and Project staff do not know well what to do with a RAMS analysis. In order to revitalise the process, a step-by-step plan for RAMSHE-LCM has been developed, the PRC00290. The plan emphasises collaboration between Asset Management and Projects. A project starts with identifying what the focus of RAMSHE-LCM analysis is and figuring out where to make cost/performance profit. In this way, opportunities in the project are determined and translated into requirements that are further developed in the project and avoid becoming a paper-tiger.

What is the method of RAMS management. The method that ProRail uses to optimally and sustainably manage RAMS performance over lifetime is derived from the EN50126 standard. For more details on this standard, please refer section 6.13.1 at page 189. The V-model in the standard has been applied to the business process of ProRail Projects, as illustrated in Figure 50.

The starting point of the V-model is that RAMSHED performance requirements that the new system must meet in the exploitation & maintain phase, are determined in the concept phase of a project. The principle of the V-model is that the alternatives of the project are examined in the descending branch of the V and the preferred alternative is elaborated in smaller and smaller subsystems, objects and even parts, if possible. Partial performance is assigned to all elements and constantly checked to ensure planned performance requirements of the project are met and adjusted as necessary. Performance risks are either solved in design or recorded in a risk register with solutions for management in the exploitation phase.

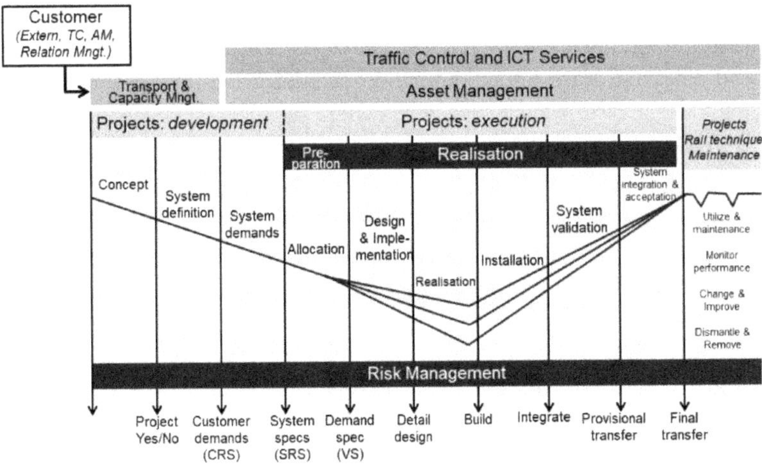

Figure 50   V-model ProRail for RAMS-management in Projects
(Source: (Lamper, A, 2010))*

Once the project choices have been made, attention shifts from safety and availability to sustainability. The design is further optimised to make new assets accessible and easier to maintain. The previously identified risks are translated into plan for initial maintenance and facilities to be built. In the upstream branch of the V, the objects and subsystems are built according to the detail design, assembled into a functioning system and eventually delivered to the AM organisation.

Both during design- and construction phases, it must be constantly checked whether the performance requirements of the system are met. The validation determines whether customer demand is met *('building the right system')* and verification determines whether (partial) specifications have been realised *('building the system right')*. In the design and construction phase, the performances to be delivered in the exploitation phase are built into the systems of the project. The capabilities and functionality can be tested before commissioning, but the RAMS quality is proven only afterwards. That is the principle and process behind the V-model, but in practice it often runs differently and is less structured than described here.

If the whole building process is carried out in accordance with EN50126, the project includes RAMS performance risk analysis, associated activities to control risks and/or maintenance instruction. This happens when standardised designs are applied because their performance in operation is known. In the case of a non-standardised system, initial performance risk analysis from design phase

informs the manager but insight and experiences from maintenance, such as occurrence of failures and investigative knowledge from major disruptions and serious accidents, provides practical experience for M&R. This is how maintenance
knowledge and experiences from management of RAMS performance is systematically recorded and made accessible. It encourages collaboration, optimisation
and continuous improvement. This is the value of risk management. The why,
how and what of it is described in the next section.

6.11.3 Risk management

Old craftsmanship in a new IT tool. Risk management is not new. Designers
and maintenance technicians used to do it earlier under the name of craftsmanship. Their considerations were often implicit. In the past, the maintenance mechanic had to rely on his feeling, hearing, practical experience and prescribed preventive measures from designers. By recording the individual old craftsmanship
in a structured way in a new risk management tool, this knowledge and information is now available for a large group of experts. This has been possible because of rapid developments in the information- and computer technology (ICT).
With ICT tools, the craftsmanship of the mechanic is no longer only in his head
(= implicit knowledge) but recorded in a structured way in M&R-Concepts (=
explicit knowledge). The role, recognition and value of maintenance has changed
considerably. What was once a craft is transformed into high-quality and management-intensive profession which positively influences results of the organisation. However, it is still a young profession in the rail sector for that reason experienced and qualified managers and technicians in risk management are still
scarce.

Why risk management? Asset management is about optimal control of costs
and performance over the life cycle. Risk management (RM) is the only technique
to explicitly establish and coherently manage the relationship between costs and
performance. The principle of risk management involves identifying and quantifying risks that threaten performance and determining control measures to optimally control these risks. Risk is an abstract concept. In asset management it is
the cause of an irregularity that leads to loss of performance because of a failure.
The knowledge and information related to risk management is recorded in a systematic and structured way in M&R concepts (IHC) by system or object type.

In its role as an infra manager, ProRail requires sufficient knowledge of maintenance. The M&R concepts are the ideal instrument to safeguard and unlock this
knowledge and thus enable LCM, lay down the relationship between costs and
performance, continuous improvement of price-performance ratio, cost calculation, management of performance contracts and railway safety. Risk management
provides the universal 'language' to connects people in different processes and
organisations.

After years of development and search, performance risk management has been anchored in processes of the Dutch rail sector. It was quite a quest because ProRail had to invent the wheel itself. There were no rail infrastructure managers with strong risk management skills and outsourcing of maintenance presented unusual and complex conditions. As a result, it was unclear for a long time what the real usefulness and necessity of risk management was for the various parties. This has changed through the tendering of performance contracts, introduction of risk management principles at management level and deployment of a safety management system (VMS). The usefulness and necessity of risk management at ProRail can be briefly described as follows:

- Guarantee safekeeping and accessibility of maintenance and renewal knowledge;
- Specify information in a structured and transparent manner;
- Specify performance quality and control at different levels;
- Establish relationship between costs and performance;
- Demonstrate control of safety.

By placing risk analysis in a central maintenance risk register (CIRR), ProRail aims to make M&R knowledge and information available to the whole sector and develop clarity about assignment to maintenance contractors *('manage these risks within these specifications')* such that the contractors prepare maintenance and inspection plans themselves *('with what activities do you control the risks')*. The CIRR became available in early 2017 but was then not (yet?) a part of contract specification.

How did risk management develop at ProRail? The development of risk management at ProRail was critical in developing professional approach for infrastructure management. Figure 51 gives an outline of the associated milestones.

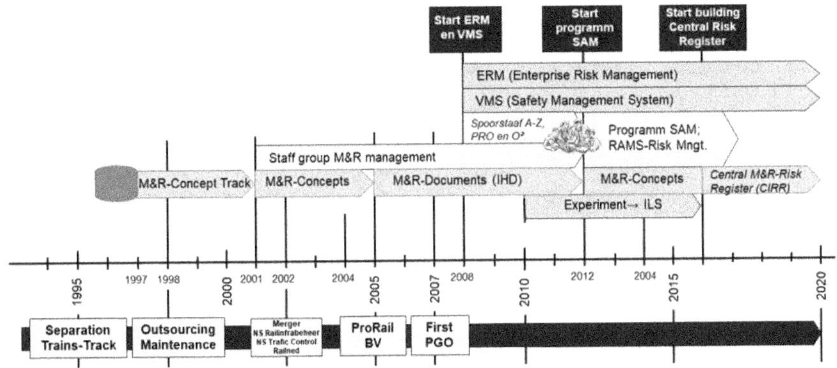

Figure 51   The development of risk management at ProRail

The risk management tool is the M&R-concept (IHC) and consists of two parts: risk analysis (RA) and associated overview with control measures (BM)[41]. The initial M&R concepts were made in 1997 by NS Railinfrabeheer to develop complete specification and job description for the new OPC contract (Swier J. , 1997*). They were called 'Instandhoudings Concept Spoorinfra' (ICS), in English 'M&R Concept Rail infra'. A small group realised that ICS is a valuable instrument for an infrastructure manager and a brochure was published to describe the versatility and value of M&R concepts (Projectteam*, 1997*).

In 2001, the business unit InfraSystems got staff in M&R Management (IHM) under leadership of an interim manager and two or three maintenance engineers were introduced per region. With lot of energy, the first step was taken in the development and implementation of the risk management tool. The first risk analyses and maintenance control measures were made for a number of object types, processed with the Optimizer+ from Baas & Roost (now known as MaxGrip) and translated into management information about availability, reliability and costs of certain object category. The aim was to do this also for entire routes by merging the risk analyses and control measures of the different systems/object types into Route Maintenance Concepts (TOC). In that period, there was some miscommunication of expectation between IHM and the management team at RIB. The management team was focussed entirely on the results of the TOCs and not on the development and implementation of the underlying instruments. The technicians didn't realized that and promised too much. When the expectations were unfulfilled, the management lost confidence in the TOCs and interest in risk management.

In retrospect, one can conclude that Railinfrabeheer was not ready: a small group of motivated and knowledgeable people had taken lead for something too big in the organisation. Nevertheless, the development of the risk management tools continued and, in the period 2002-2004, IHCs were developed for almost all systems. The details varied by system but design and structure were the same. It was quite an achievement but use of IHCs was limited to a small group of experts at IHM in Utrecht. The orientation of the maintenance engineers in the regions slowly but surely shifted to the control of the maintenance contract OPC.

In 2004, the M&R specifications (IHS) of the OPC-contract were combined with the existing M&R concepts (IHC). It became a new regulation, the M&R-document (IHD). The rationale was that maintenance concepts are a new manifestation of the old, traditional maintenance regulations and work plans but that is a fundamental mistake when you outsource maintenance. The static specification (IHS) was merged with the dynamic control instrument (IHC), and specifications for input and output were combined into one new specification. This does not

---

[41] Control measures are: maintenance, renewal, inspections, failure repair and such

work if the policy is to outsource with a focus on a switch to performance management.

The IHD was not used for contract management but to provide information through the Rail Infra Catalogue (RIC). This development had its own share of problems because there was a lack of clarity about the usefulness and necessity of risk management tools, as well as difference of opinion in specifying and managing the maintenance contracts. The technical policy department of InfraSystems was focused on traditional control principles based on maintenance regulations (read: input) while InfraOperatie had switched to innovative contract management based on performance (read: output). It took years to find the balance between technical policy with specifications in the accompanying regulations, and the method of specifying and controlling the PGO contract. These two different worlds cannot exist without each other but differ in their approach of management of costs and performance. The tension it caused in 2007 continued to date till at least 2017.

Risk management received full attention from the management when the first performance contract was put out to tender in 2007. The contract was based on performance management with the help of risk management tools. The quotation and plans for maintenance and inspection were based on risk analysis by the contractors with accompanying control measures, called FMECAs[42]. Depending on risk, performance was steered at different levels: RAM performance at reactive performance level, and safety and durability at the technical specification level for proactive control as described in section 6.8. To make this distinction between specifications, ProRail used the IHCs that had been developed in the period 2001-2004. With the introduction of risk management tools, the operational business unit within ProRail gained lead over the strategic business unit, but the latter followed quickly.

At the strategic board level, the first step in risk management was the introduction of Enterprise Risk Management (ERM). ERM is a catalyst for organisations to increase transparency, strengthen business operations and comply with new legislation. It is a new form of corporate governance[43]. ERM is based on the principle that management of business risks is delegated, coordinated and integrated over the entire organisation, taking into account the interdependencies of the business risks.

Since 2008, the ProRail management evaluates and updates the top risks annually (there were nine top risks in 2015) and delegates the management of these risks

---

[42] FMECA = Failure Mode Effect and Criticality Analysis. Strictly speaking, it is only a risk analysis, but PGO's contract experts also include the activities to control the risks.

[43] Corporate governance stands for good management and accountability to the stakeholders for the policy being pursued.

to members of the board of directors. The organisation is informed about the acceptable risk levels through a risk matrix. The board members organise risk management and further delegate the risks. The single risk that stands out in this procedure is railway safety. The EU imposes specific requirements on control of this risk through the Safety Directive 2004/49/EC, which requires asset managers to develop a Safety Management System (VMS). The VMS explicitly states the method to control safety risks and monitors effectiveness of the control measures.

ProRail has had a VMS recognised by the Minister since 2008 (Bedrijfstrategie, 2008*). It has a safety permit for the maximum validity of three years and is required to receive assessment by an independent expert following this period. The VMS is the link between safety objectives of the board of directors and realisation method adopted by the operational organisations. Figure 52 illustrates ProRail's methodology and a brief explanation follows.

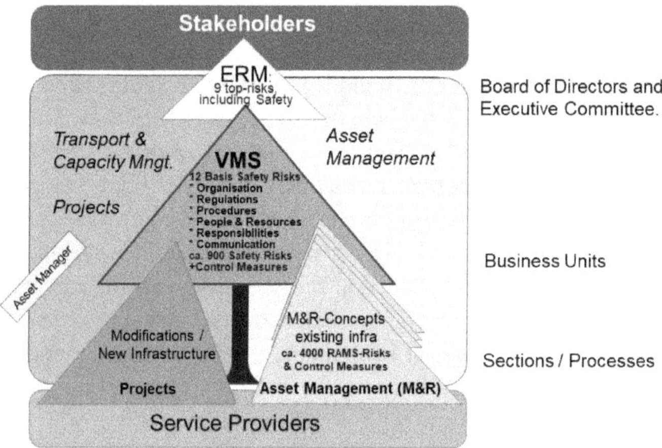

Figure 52   The method in which ProRail manages the safety risks

The VMS is based on an inventory of safety risks with associated management measures. It focuses on responsibility delegation and assurance of control in business processes, procedures as well as technical and organisational risk management measures. At the top level, the VMS of ProRail distinguishes 10 basic safety risks[44] and names a responsible director for each. For example, the director AM is responsible for 4 of the 10 basic safety risks. The directors are supported by a safety expert from the Quality department - the VMS manager - and a team that registers and investigates safety incidents and advises on the implementation of safety tasks. In order to maintain this system, risk analyses have been conducted

---

[44] The ten basic safety risks in 2015 were: derailment, collision train-train, collision train-person, collision train-object, personnel safety, electrocution, fire, hazardous substances, stations and calamities / disasters.

168

for all basic safety risks to identify organisation, processes, regulations and/or procedures necessary for management of these risks. As of date, around 900 safety risks have been identified and each of these has a designated manager and methodology for control.

At ProRail AM, M&R concepts contain all possible risks for all type of performances and objects, as well as control measures. The goal is continuously improvement of safety. This can be either be achieved by learning from mistakes or by proactively searching for improvements. The resulting measures are assigned into two groups: (1) new projects to develop and build or modify technical systems that are safer than existing systems or (2) organisational changes to make existing infrastructure safer.

In order to align VMS with the realisation, the Quality department visualised the AM core process (ProRail, 2014-5*), which identifies value-adding steps to achieve the AM goals. The development of the AM process came into a new phase with the arrival of generic process model for asset management. This model aimed to continuously improve the price/performance ratio: System Asset Management, better known as the abbreviation SAM (Smulders*, 2011*). The introduction in the SAM-report stated that system asset management is not new and even implemented partly at ProRail, but its coherence in the AM process was unclear and improvement cycle was only partially secured, if at all.

There were two projects that stimulated the development of the SAM-vision: 'Rail from A to Z' and 'PRO'. The 'Rail from A to Z' project started in 2008 to find solutions for reducing rising maintenance costs for rail construction and demonstrably guaranteeing safety. The 'PRO' project started in 2009 to establish clarity between InfraSystems and InfraOperatie about the process to contract FMECAs in the PGO contracts, particularly in the area of getting execution information from the contractor. Both projects deployed risk-based maintenance and were restarted jointly in the SAM programme around 2011.

A core team of SAM identified the weak spots in the AM process and initiated activities to tackle them. Workshops were organised and systems were audited. The IHC emerged as a weak spot in the AM process and its development was emphasised. In anticipation of the final SAM programme plan (SAM K. , 2012*), the IHCs were established in early 2012 for the 4 systems with highest failure risks and costs: track, switches, train detection and level crossing.

The SAM project also sought cooperation and coordination with the O² project. The O² project focused in particular on determining the technical need, optimizing the planning, introducing SAP LAM (Linear Asset Management) and improving the information provision in the AM process. These activities fit seamlessly into the aim of the SAM programme to set up risk-based maintenance, the core of which is formed by Deming's quality control circle. SAM involves periodic evaluation of performance and costs of a system and seeks improvement measures. There are six steps as follows:

- Step 1 - Registration and regulation in order
- Step 2 - Maintenance concept known
- Step 3 - Information need known and organised
- Step 4 - Control measures implemented
- Step 5 - Information exchanged as described in Step 3
- Step 6 - Price-performance ratio determined and process adjusted

A number of processes and associated instruments were still missing. For example, risk analyses was required with control measures (IHC) to establish object registration, failure registration, realisation information, cost information, etc. In addition, risk assessment was needed to select purchasing strategy (or purchase risk class). Figure 53 illustrates the six steps of the SAM control loop in the form of a cartoon drawing used as an illustration.

Figure 53   The SAM-control loop

A total of 13 work packages were defined, partly to elaborate parts of the circle and partly to create conditions for running the circle. Collaboration (In Dutch: "SAMenwerking") is crucial because the SAM control circle comprises various ProRail departments and maintenance contractors dependent on each other for optimum operation. To implement active collaboration for better synchronisation with the PGO contract process was an important part of the SAM programme.

In the period 2012-2015, detailed and complete IHCs were set up for 21 systems by teams of system managers, system specialists, experts and inspectors under the umbrella of the SAM programme. Later, employees of the contractors were also involved but their participation was limited to risk analysis. The management of the end products is managed by system experts and SAM team offers expert support. The IHCs were developed in Excel and made accessible through the SAM team site for internal use. The risk analysis is included in the database 'M&R Risk Analysis' (IRA) and disclosed in the Rail Infra Catalogue (RIC) for external parties.

In 2014, an awareness process was started to use risk analyses in PGO contracting. However, there was a fundamental error. Since 2007, every contractor (and ProRail itself) had made its own risk analysis to substantiate the tender, whereas in principle these are exactly the same because the assets in all contract areas correspond. The performance risks are, in fact, 'embedded' in the existing infrastructure, which is a given and starting point for the contractor. As client and asset manager, ProRail is in a position to have the most complete overview of all possible and revealed risks because of delivery information of projects, national failure registration and safety investigations. All pieces of the puzzle fall into place when ProRail gives performance risks to the contractor during a tender and asks for price to conduct maintenance and inspection for managing the risks.

In mid-2015, the MT AM agreed to develop a generic sector risk library, which was delivered in the first half of 2017 and branded Central Conservation Risk Register (CIRR). However, the introduction in the PGO contract was not forthcoming. The central management team contracting (CRC) insisted on the principle that every contractor conduct its own performance risk analysis, much to the frustration of technicians at the policy department A&T. However, the Information Delivery Specifications (ILS), derived from the IHCs and part of the CIRR, were included in the PGO contract. They provide systematic and specific information that the maintenance contractor must provide to ProRail about the work carried out.

It is clear that the entire development process of performance risk management in the rail sector was laborious and long. The first risk analysis was conducted around 1997 but the implementation of performance risk management in contracting process started around 2008 when management decided to introduce ERM and VMS. The IHC's provide know-how and expertise to manage costs and performance of assets optimally, explicitly and coherently. They are part of the AM management process, in particular the maintenance process, because RAMS performance is managed there (Swier J. , 2016-12*). In 2017, however, it was still uncertain whether the IHC would evolve from a static knowledge database to a dynamic manage- and control instrument. As long as this uncertainty exists, it is likely that tension will remain between experts in technology and those in contracting. Slowly but surely, this will weaken the position of the client; a growing risk for successful outsourcing of maintenance and performance of infrastructure.

What is the method for risk management? Risk management is about identifying and quantifying risks that threaten business goals, determining who is responsible for managing the risks and how that happens. The business goals are determined in consultation with the asset owner, train operators and other stakeholders. The business objectives specific to an infra manager are the performance risks. For rail infrastructure, these comprise capability, functionality and the RAMSHED-quality made available to the train operators. These risks are controlled by specific measures such as inspection, measurement, maintenance, renewal, etc.

Risk is defined as follows: Risk = Chance x Impact. The 'Chance' is the annual frequency of the risk event per object when no maintenance is performed multiplied by the number of objects for the entire national network. The 'Impact' is the performance lost when a risk occurs. The RAMSHED quality, reputation damage and financial consequences are some of the business goals. Risk management involves balancing of risks transparently by valuing the chance and the impact of a risk with a weight factor depending on nature of risk. Multiplication results in a risk value per risk. It allows risks to be weighed against each other and determines whether the risk is acceptable or not.

Three maintenance strategies are possible in principle: condition based maintenance (TAO), frequency based maintenance (GAO) and failure-dependent maintenance (SAO). ProRail has added function test (FT) as the fourth strategy to identify hidden failures and modification of existing system components as fifth strategy. For more details on the strategies, please refer Figure 46 at page 145 and the associated text. The choice of strategy depends on the possibilities, circumstances and size of risk. The strategies are not an object but risk-bound; every (sub)system has its own optimal mix of strategies.

To determine the weight factors, ProRail has used a risk matrix since 2008. For all company values (read: business goals or KPIs), the matrix states whether a certain combination of 'Impact' and 'Chance' is acceptable or not. For details, please refer to Figure 54. The chances are annual frequencies that increase by a factor of 10 from 0.001x to 100x each year. The impacts have a weight factor from 0 and 1 increasing by a factor of 10 to 10,000. The chance and impact combinations in the green areas are acceptable and the combinations falling in all other colours require additional risk reduction measures in accordance with the principle 'As Low As Reasonably Possible' (ALARP). Acceptance of the very high risks (indicated in red colour) is only allowed with the approval of the director or management, and that of the high risks (indicated in light brown colour) requires escalation up to the second echelon management. In this way the management oversees thoughts and action of all employees in the organisation.

The risk matrix meets all requirements set for it. It is used not only by ERM, VMS and the IHCs but also to prioritise realisation of the ProRail AM-production plan. The matrix and risk analyses thus connect the strategic goals of ProRail management with operations via planning. If CIRR becomes part of the PGO contract specification/process as a starting point for the contractor's maintenance plan, then connection is made between ProRail's business goals and activities of the mechanics (external to the organisation) to realise them.

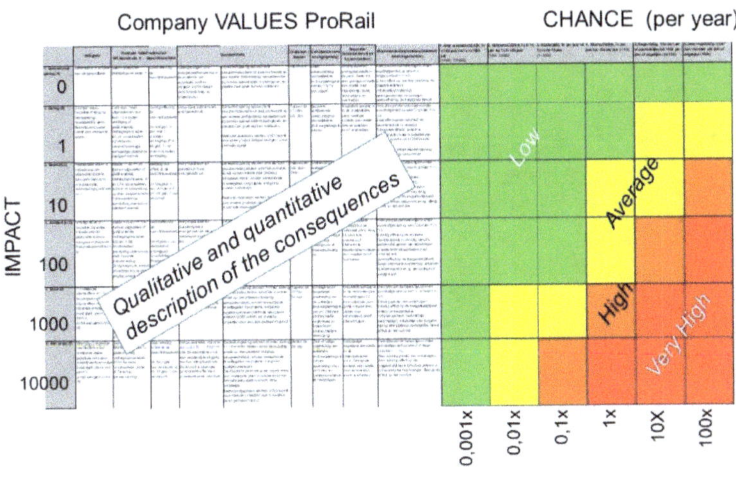

Figure 54   Risk-matrix of ProRail's board

One instrument, three functions. A professional infra manager requires risk management tools, particularly the risk register /library with information on all possible risks that can and have revealed themselves, quantification of chance and impact, as well as management strategy. The risk analysis is conducted with measures to control the risks. For each risk, a preventive and corrective measure is considered with specification to proactively manage the risk, where possible.

Risk analyses & Control measures are instruments of the risk management process and together they form the maintenance concept (IHC). All maintenance and renewal knowledge are recorded in a structured format to provide reference for continuous improvement of the maintenance process. The IHC provide overview and insight. It has three main functions: (1) management tool to manage costs and performance explicitly and in coherence, (2) knowledge tool for collecting and sharing all M&R knowledge and (3) information source to organise

173

and relate information from disparate sources[45]. The IHC is used to structure system information, test the FMECAs and/or maintenance plans of the contractors, source drafting ILSs, check completeness of M&R-specification in PGO, provide overview of M&R-specifications with associated monitoring activities, calculate maintenance costs, estimate need for train-free periods and form basis for long-term renewal plan.

With assistance from the SAM programme, ProRail AM has access to well-developed IH-Concepts for almost all types of objects. Figure 55 gives an impression of the structure, content and source information.

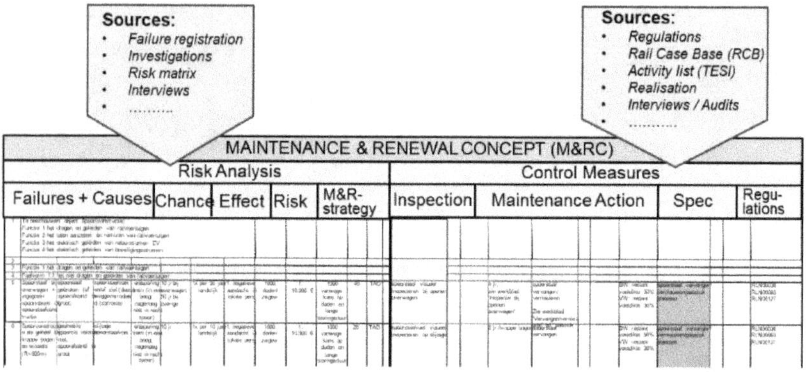

Figure 55   Structure and content of the M&R-Concept with related source information

A good failure registration system is required to keep risk analyses completed and up-to-date. In addition, (safety) investigations of incidents and interviews with mechanics and technicians are valuable sources. The risks are weighed using the ProRail risk matrix and each risk in the IHC is linked to a risk measure. Many of the measures have a unique unit code from the TESI list and cost figure in the RCB cost database. The IHC contains almost all information for cost calculations, rejection values and references to regulations and work instructions. It is also possible to model the RAMS performance with a selected risk management strategy. In short, the IH-Concept has information from very different sources, which is arranged in a logical and systematic way and brought into relationship with each other. This makes it possible to relate performance (= risks) and costs (= control measures) and manage them together, the holy grail for an asset manager.

The IHC guarantees all knowledge needed to manage performance risks optimally and sustainably. This knowledge is not only present with the maintenance contractors but now also available to the infra manager, suppliers, engineering

---

[45] Examples are: cost information in the RCB, risk information from the failure database, overview of activities in the TESI-list and unit codes, specifications and the relation with PGO specifications, etc.

firms, etc. It is the task and responsibility of the infra manager to organise and execute this process; partly it is about the quality of the organisation and management process, and partly about the quality of the information and information systems. The organisational aspects are explained in the previous chapters and sections. The following section explains the why, how and what of IT and information management, as developed by ProRail.

6.11.4 ICT- and information management

Why; the importance of information for AM. The importance of information for asset management cannot be overestimated: no asset management is possible without information. Information is indispensable to realise the business objectives of an infra manager in a predictable and controlled manner. In addition to the three main processes of strategy, tactics and operation, information is seen as the fourth main process. Knowledge and experience have always been important for management and maintenance, but development of ICT and new powerful management techniques has transformed management and maintenance from a traditional profession into a knowledge- and information-intensive industry where you can graduate from a university

How ICT and information management developed at ProRail? The application of computer technology in the office environment and technical systems grew fast. In less than forty years, it developed from nothing into an indispensable technology with huge social impact. Some more information about the impact of this technology on NS rail infrastructure and office automation is available in Appendix 14.1.4.

In the period when infra organisation transitioned from typewriters to PCs, traffic and business management process was computerised at traffic control stations through a project known as 'Transport By Train' (VPT). The VPT included systems such as traffic control system (VKL), traffic control 'Post 21', train tracking system (TNV), process control system (PRL) as well as planning systems for rail use, trains and personnel. Full computerisation consolidated traffic control at 13 posts and made the Netherlands one of the most productive and cost-efficient systems, a leader and benchmark in Europe (BSL, 2005*). The punctuality was recorded in detail by continuously comparing the plan and realisation of timetable at each service point. The commissioning of VPT in 1995 marks the beginning of strong development of the information provision at NS infra organisation, see Figure 56. There are three major milestones in the ICT development at ProRail:

I.   one PC network (1995)

II.   one ICT organisation (2005)

III.   one AM portal (2016) providing access to many AM applications for internal and external use.

The development started after Transport and Infrastructure were split in 1995 and the infra organisation had to set up its own financial administration. It required a new computer system and ERP programme from Germany-based SAP was selected to support all processes within the company. NS Railinfrabeheer started with the financial administration, object registration and fault registration. These applications were designed and built from the bottom: cost structures, cost elements, processes, functions, tasks, objects tree, information needs, and so on.

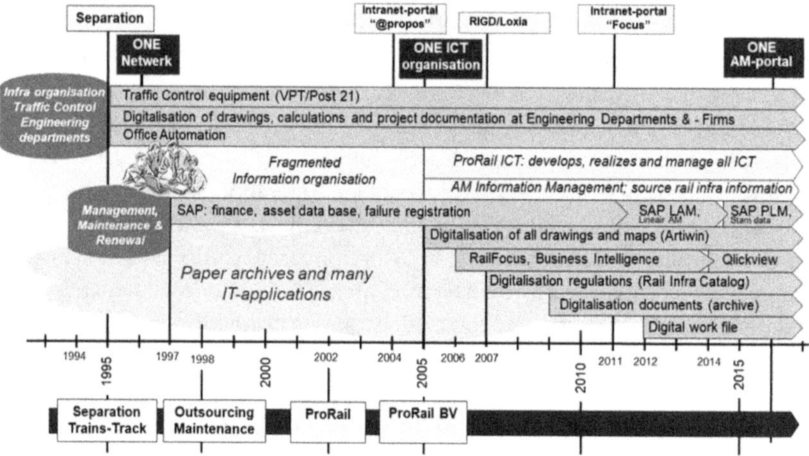

Figure 56   The development of ICT at ProRail

At the time, the infra organisation struggled with finding a single common vision for object decomposition and level of detail to store information. Improvements were made later but, in retrospect, one can determine that it was critical that work was done with single vision in single system and single structure from the beginning. The same happened with the location indication of objects. NS Railinfrabeheer opted for the familiar system of line codes and kilometers. This proved insufficient for consistency and future-proofing, but it was significant that a single location method was adopted for all IT applications from the beginning.

Around 1997, all object registers were transferred to SAP and the new financial system of NS Railinfrabeheer was in use. Thereafter, all costs were attributed to Trace Infra Clusters (TICs), business processes and cost categories; all failures were recorded in SAP and all assets were recorded in the SAP object registration. It was a big improvement but the asset database in SAP was far from complete and not very accessible till 2002 when it was realised that information can also be used for other purposes such as planning and control.

Immediately upon privatisation in 2005, the ProRail management established a company-wide vision on information management, opened an Intranet portal called @propos and founded the business unit ICT-Services (ICTS) to manage all IT systems and organizing information management at the business units. A

176

management unit for information policy was set up at the board level, and Business Information Managers (BIM) were given the role to coordinate demand and realisation by ICTS for all business units. Soon after the arrival of ICTS and BIMs, the improvement of information provision and response to the needs of users was visible.

For example, implementation of the Business Intelligence (BI) application Rail-Focus was a milestone in 2006 because it improved the accessibility and quality of AM's information provision. With this application, it became possible to present information from different data sources - financial, object and performance - on one screen and to export information into Excel for analyses. The following data and information sources were made accessible step-by-step and linked to each other:

- Revenue and costs attributed to seven cost categories (KO, GO, etc.) and eight infra-systems; from SAP
- Failure reports and registration of TAO's; from SAP
- Cost calculation OPC contracts; from M31-cost frameworks
- Soil types of ground
- Rail track alignment scores; from measuring trains
- Passed train tonnage; from QuoVadis
- Train kilometers; from the New Transport Data Bank (NVGB)
- Company-wide KPI dashboard
- Use of switches: passed tonnage, direction, number of turns, etc.
- Long-term renewal plan: reporting compiled from WebFocus on theoretical renewal requirements with cash flow planning
- TAO reference model: reporting from WebFocus with detailed trend analyses of failures and indication of recidivism per type

All of a sudden, historical and current asset information was easily accessible to all users. Data were retrievable at various levels and grouped at national level by geocodes, contract areas, regions or railway lines. For internal benchmarking, information was presented per product unit to allow easy selection and comparison of areas. Computer screens provided insight into trends and deviations from the norm. To facilitate analysis, the user could 'zoom in' on underlying detailed information and combine data from various sources. For example, a screen may combine object data from SAP (type, year of construction, switch angle, etc.), failure information from SAP and utilisation information from QuoVadis and VL systems (tonnage, switch movements, riding direction, etc.).

In 2007, the OPC budget calculations of the contractors - known as M31 formats - were made accessible through RailFocus. In 2008, a safety dashboard was added with condition information about rail and switch failures and the probability of rail buckling. In the same year, the train and tonne kilometers from the NVGB were added. In 2009, RailFocus published the complete ProRail dashboard with KPIs.

Until 2008, the focus was on the development of the system and presentation of coherent information. In 2008 to 2014, RailFocus is also used to gain a differentiated insight into the revenues, costs and performances per railway line, product and customer, and to test the realisation against an objective or standard. In 2014, the functionality of RailFocus was taken over by other systems, the business intelligence application Qlikview. It provides more options and is more users friendly than RailFocus.

The digitisation was not limited to information about costs, performance and assets but also covered drawings, maps, documents, regulations, use and technical condition of the infrastructure. In 2007, the Railinfra Data Service (RIGD) of ProRail and the engineering firm LOXIA[46] formed an alliance to upkeep data of the control systems of Traffic Control and Transport & Timetable (V&D). LOXIA developed and maintains CARE, the software that engineering firms use to design rail infrastructure. The organisation RIGD/LOXIA was formed in 2011. It creates and manages the national infrastructure data, drawings and information about network functionality, data for train management systems, signalling design documentation (SWOD), operating instructions (BVS) and road sign drawings for road vehicles (WVK). It forms the interface between ProRail's project- and asset- management business units by keeping data-carriers up-to-date and managing data exchange on projects for smooth commissioning.

Around 2012, the digital file became the new standard within ProRail so employees could become independent on place and time. The EDMS and SharePoint were designated applications to store documents. A framework contract was signed to have the entire document collections digitised as per need. Incidentally, EDMS was phased out in 2017 and the whole organisation switched to SharePoint for generic document storage and archiving.

The organisation of information provision. For the provision of information, ProRail distinguishes between ICT and Information Management (IM). ICT is responsible for architecture, development and management of all applications and IM meeting the information needs of the business processes with those applications. This is illustrated in Figure 57.

ProRail has centrally organised ICT in the business unit ICT Services (ICTS). Each business unit organises its own information management. Asset management has its own unit for information management because there is a large diversity in cohesive information facilities, information needs vary by user and the

---

[46] LOXIA is a joint venture of engineering firms Arcadis and Movares.

amount of static- and dynamic information is enormous. Around 2015, ICTS had a staff of approximately 450 employees and ProRail AM employed 120 people for information management.

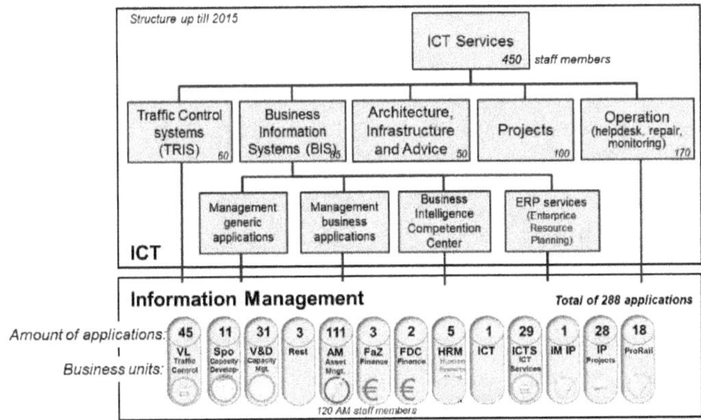

Figure 57   Organisation of ICT and Information Managemenet at ProRail (situation 2015)

ICTS distinguishes three responsibilities: (1) guarantee continuity and availability of train service and communication systems in the railway, (2) provide office automation for all ProRail and (3) support business processes of all business units within ProRail with various ICT solutions. The organisation structure is based on three core processes: operations, projects and product development. Until 2015, the three core processes were housed in five departments: Operations, Projects and three Developmental Departments, namely, Train- and Travel Information Systems (TRIS) for traffic control, Business Information Systems (BIS) and Architecture, Infrastructure and Business Advice (AI&B)[47].

When Traffic Control of ProRail was fully computerised in 1995, the TRIS department became responsible for managing applications, maintaining knowledge of relevant systems and providing insight into functional requirements of the customers Traffic Control and Transport & Timetable. The TRIS department monitors developments in the ICT market and rail sector to provide solicited and unsolicited advice to customers.

The BIS department provides cost-effective ICT solutions for business processes. It covers generic ICT such as office automation, ERP as well as project and management information systems. The construction and operational management are often outsourced to suppliers.

---

[47] From 2015, the organisation changed to comprise ICT Operations (24*7, failures and changes), Logistics (development functionality V&D and VL), Asset & Operations (development functionality Projects and AM), Infrastructure services (office automation, communication, infrastructure) and CIO-office (strategy and integrity of systems).

The AI&B department guards coherence, connection, logical structure and consistency of ICT and telecommunication facilities. It develops strategic and tactical product management and ensures that TRIS and BIS remain connected. ICTS-Architecture focuses on the link ability, continuity and coherence of the total information provision.

ICTS Infrastructure[48] is the system manager and translates all (present and future) requirements into suitable solutions. ICTS Business Advice ensures quality and efficiency of the ICTS departments through policy, professionalisation, standardisation and centralisation. It covers quality assurance, certification, business process management, implementation of uniform working methods and procedures, (internal) communication and outsourcing of vision.

The Asset Management business unit has its own department for information management as the source of all information about national rail infrastructure. The AM Information develops, manages and provides all information about the rail infrastructure in the Netherlands: configuration- and management information including physical master data, technical drawings, topographic maps, cadastral information, archives (paper and digital), technical condition, infrastructure performance and M&R activities (planned and executed).

ProRail started the SpoorData.NL programme in 2014 to provide correct, complete and up-to-date information about infrastructure to all rail sector partners. The programme makes information accessible step-by-step for all ProRail employees and recognised contractors, engineering firms and train operators. To enable information sharing in the chain, existing applications are first adapted to meet unambiguous information standards and architecture that are prerequisites for linking. SpoorData has four development pillars for information sharing:

- ***Information accessible*** ensures that all railway sector professionals have access to ready information and combines configuration and control data. The information is available online at www.spoordata.nl.
- ***Information standards*** are the foundation of SpoorData and enable good and automated information exchange between processes and chain partners. This pillar provides a uniform data model, 'Informatie Model Spoor' (= Information Model Track), for easier collaboration within the rail sector.
- ***Building Information Model*** *(BIM)* ensures that all relevant design-, construction- and management information about the life cycle of assets is shared via one common digital model for contractors, engineering firms, suppliers and other service providers.

---

[48] These include: transmission systems, network technology, data storage, data management techniques, server technology, operating systems, system security, etc.

- ***Data in order*** reorganises the existing configuration- and management data, and realises management and control organisation, process integration and IT applications in order to keep the data structurally optimized after the major clean-up.

From 2017, the railroad partners can easily consult, share and update data in various applications via an information portal. The motto of SpoorData is *'with three clicks of the button, without restriction, you have the data'*. This is possible for all employees at Pro-Rail and recognised chain partners. The Information Portal becomes the basis for all dashboards required on strategic, tactical and operational level to optimally and sustainably manage costs and performance of rail infrastructure over the life cycle.

Main structure data model for information provision. In 2008, ICTS distinguished 13 primary-, management- and support processes for providing information and grouped these into 6 main data groups: rail infrastructure, infrastructure deployment & transport, financing systems, personnel & facilities, projects & management IT resources as well as relationship management (ICTS, 2008*). Each group has its own application and data collection. Some data sets are used in multiple processes and some sets overlap. The Application Plaza contains the entire application portfolio of ProRail with a brief description of system functionality and application management. To access applications, authorisation is required for a large number of applications. The application management is at ICTS, functional management at the business units, technical management at the Generic IT Service (GID) and the construction of applications is done by suppliers.

The quality of an asset manager is partly determined by the quality of information provision, which depends on quality of the IT organisation, IT systems and data. Having an IT organisation is a prerequisite but it is also essential to have a future-proof data model that makes asset applications and information easy to combine, share and access. An asset data model consists of three elements: *'What is it'*, *'Where is it'* and *'What can it do'*, which represent physical, geographical and functional configuration of data, respectively, illustrated in Figure 58.

The physical configuration data is structured on the basis of three Basic Information Documents (BID): object structure BID00001 (A&T, 2016*), document structure BID00007 (A&T, 2016*) and characteristic structure BID00008 (A&T, 2014*). This enables identification of assets and associated information in a unique and future-proof manner. Historically, geographical configuration was based on line codes and kilometre values. However, it is not possible to describe the entire railway topology uniquely using only geocodes. Therefore, a generic rail model has been adopted that describes railway topology in terms of unique track sections, each bounded by topology drivers called nodes (Berghuis, 2016*). This is a future-proof model which links and combines data from different systems.

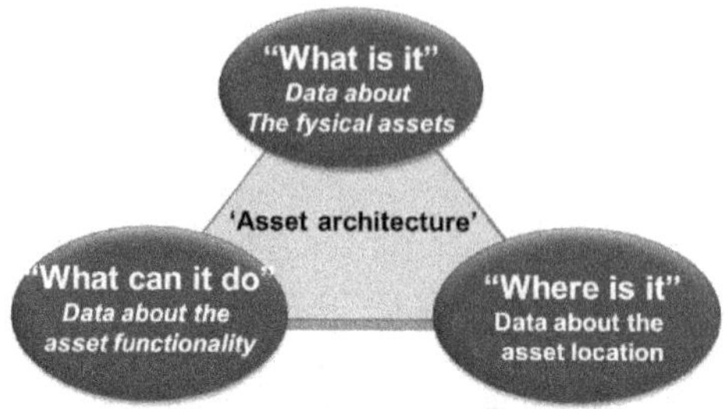

Figure 58   Main structure of the data model for asset management

The functional configuration data is combined in the Infra Atlas and managed by RIGD/LOXIA. The Infra Atlas contains railway network data that is necessary for the users. It includes survey of lines and sidings with information about signalling system and energy supply: infra-information for the operator about permissible speeds, allowed axle loads, maximum train lengths, etc. as well as VPT information for traffic controllers about functionality of installations.

The quality of data model depends on (im)possibilities to unlock, share and combine data but it is not necessary to start with a high-quality data model. Having a data model is deemed more important than having none at all. ProRail had data models for object structure, object characteristics, geography (line code/km) and network functionality at the end of the nineties, but the ambitions of SpoorData could only be realised if all the data models were radically adapted and extended. This was a huge job but it was reasonably clear in scope and doable because of the mentioned existing structures. It illustrates how valuable it is to structure an organisation from the vision of quality management; how to manage its own process and of the whole sector. In the next section, the development of quality management at ProRail is discussed.

6.11.5 **Quality management; organising the organisation**

Why quality management? Quality management focuses on control and continuous improvements of the production process to make quality of the product predictable and transparent. It is not limited to any defined area but impacts all parts of a company's management.

The quality of the product depends on the context and, in general, it concerns meeting of certain needs and corresponding specifications. The ISO9000 series is a well-known standard for guaranteeing quality of a organisation. It contains the basic principles and definitions, systems requirements as well as guidelines for performance improvements and execution of system audits (quality and/or

182

environmental management). A total of eight principles form the philosophy behind quality management. These include four relational and four instrumental principles. The relational principles are leadership, customer orientation, employee involvement and win-win relationship with suppliers. The instrumental principles are process approach, system approach, continuous improvement and fact-based decision-making.

ProRail AM has used the quality management model of EFQM/INK for establishing a development vision for the organisation, as indicated in section 6.6. The development of the organisation, control and instrumentation are described in detail in this book. This section is limited to how ProRail has integrated quality management in the organisation to control process- and product quality as well as to continuously improve it, both internally and externally within the chain.

How did quality management develop at ProRail. The organisation of rail transport has always been strongly influenced and determined by government legislation and regulations. These are general laws such as labour, safety, housing, learning, accidents and disability as well as specific railway law, with lower regulations in the form of administration measures, royal decrees and ministerial regulations.

The railroad law of 1875, together with the local rail- and tramway laws of 1900 and 1917, served as a decisive factor for the development of railways. In order to enable effective and lawful functioning of a national railway operating organisation, the company was organised and regulated similar to a military organisation from the outset. It had ranks, positions, manuals and penalties. Tasks were executed as per established procedures, guidelines and regulations. This was the practice till the NS organisation was separated into transport and infrastructure in 1995. There were standards for design, construction, maintenance, operations and organisation, with framework for functions, tasks, responsibilities and competences (FTBVs). Each standard had a specific number and colour to indicate type of regulation.

After the separation and outsourcing of maintenance, all non-technical regulations at Railinfrabeheer expired. All processes between transport and infrastructure were severed and activities of the engineering office and maintenance were privatised. In the first years, the organisation of Railinfrabeheer was based on organograms, and the knowledge and experience of employees was based on regulations from the past. The infrastructure organisation came into being after the three task organisations[49] merged. The merger was formally arranged at the beginning of 2005 and soon the Board of Directors established a process model based on one-system-company for all business units to work together in a single

---

[49] Railinfrabeheer, Traffic Control and Capacity Management

process. In this vision, ProRail transforms requirements and assignments from government and train operators into infrastructure products and services.

Thus, InfraManagement (IM) started to organise its own processes and connect them to those of other business units. The IM process plate was called *'IM à la carte'* (ProRail, 2007-5). All processes were defined and worked out in a quality management system. The Executive Board determined how this was to be done and stipulated that business units be connected to each other. The methodology distinguished the three types of processes (management, support and core) and a colour indicated the primary department. The three processes mentioned include the following management processes:

- Administrative processes: manage infra system, manage relationship and environment, and the establishment of a production plan;
- Core processes: manage operational management, determine need for maintenance, function change and third-party work, manage process-based maintenance and perform direction on infrastructure projects,;
- Supporting processes: control, administration, information, HRM, permits, archiving, etc.

Initially, the managers were required to structure their own process within the framework of the Executive Board and ensure that process activities are supported by tools such as accommodation, computers, software, guidelines, templates and such. The works that were similar were to be carried in a similar way.

What is the INTERNAL organisation of quality management at ProRail.
Managers organise their own processes with support of the quality management group. Quality management also verifies whether organisation works according to the described processes, personnel take responsibility, processes meet requirements and process descriptions are consistent.

At ProRail, more than 50 employees are active in the field of quality management. These include 18 internal quality consultants, 10 external quality consultants, 18 auditors and 8 inspectors. Their job is to guarantee quality of the organisation through a system based on continuous improvement. For example, international standards for health- and environment are met, and that risk management and life cycle management are integrated into the processes of the organisation and service providers. Quality management is not limited to internal quality but also includes external organisation quality at service providers, i.e., engineering firms, suppliers and contractors. This is essential for ProRail because all executive tasks have been privatised and outsourced.

What is the EXTERNAL organisation of quality management at ProRail.
ProRail depends on contractors to realise the goals and activities it has planned. The performance that the contractors deliver to ProRail is what the latter delivers

to its stakeholders. To guarantee external quality, general quality requirements are imposed on the organisation of service providers, who also comply with the legal requirements of their profession. While this provides a solid framework for guaranteeing quality, ProRail does more. It maintains an approval system for companies, conducts systematic performance measurements and safeguards knowledge and skills of all employees working in and around the track. An explanation of these three methods to ensure external quality are described as follows:

- **Method 1: Recognition of companies**.
  Working on the track is very risky in certain circumstances and consequences of errors and failures can be high. This is why ProRail has a recognition scheme to impose specific requirements on companies and employees working on the railway system. For example, there are tenders that are open to only companies authorised by ProRail. The qualification system is for different branches, whereby the scheme consists of a general part and specific additional parts for each branch. ProRail evaluates the financial and economic capacity of the company, in particular, for trade, management and social awareness (Procurement, 2016-7*). A recognition committee and ProRail's tender boards[50] evaluate requests for recognition.

- **Method 2: Measuring performance of production processes**.
  By measuring the performance of contractors and engineering firms, ProRail is stimulates companies to improve and align their performance with its objectives. Well-performing companies retain their recognition and have an advantage in contract award, i.e., a greater chance of work. ProRail's performance measurement is primarily aimed at recognised engineering firms, rail contractors and maintenance contractors. The method consists of a general part (ProRail, *) and specific parts for various branches. Performance measurement is also possible for non-recognised contractors with methods based on existing methods.
  The performance measurement is quarterly and includes results of interviews with ProRail employees directly involved in the management of contractor being assessed. It depends on the branch, safety incidents, availability incidents and quality measurements. The scores for various criteria are combined with a weighing factor into one number for quarterly performance. A minimum of three projects are examined per contractor.
  The quarterly performance indicator provides insight into short-term performance of the contractor and may be erratic. The weighted

---

[50] ProRail has tender boards for every business unit that seeks procurement. The boards advise on tendering procedure, act as sparring partners for project managers and make decisions on conflicting objectives.

average of quarterly performance over several quarters is a better indicator of long-term performance.

Performance measurement is also used as a revision criterion when an accreditation is renewed. It is an objective method to measure technical- and organisational suitability. In the event of poor performance, the concerned company is suspended until appropriate measures are taken.

- **Method 3: Guaranteeing professional knowledge.**
  The institute Railinfra Training (RIO) was founded in 2001 as an independent training institute and knowledge platform, housed in a foundation. Its management includes rail infrastructure companies, which keep it aligned with market developments. The mission is: *'we help your employees to develop into high-quality professionals who work on safe and reliable rail infrastructure'.* The training institute is located in Amersfoort. It has indoor and outdoor area where participants can practice with cables, signalling systems, rail construction, overhead lines, communication systems and safety. There are over 200 courses in 8 categories, namely: organisation & communication, energy supply, underground infrastructure, signalling technology, telecom systems, railway construction, safety and other learning paths. The Independent Assessment and Certification Office (BTC) certifies all courses with safety-critical functions and tasks.

  In 2016, the name of Railinfra Training was changed to Railcenter and the ambitions of the institute were expanded to be a place to stimulate cooperation and innovation among players in rail infrastructure through retention and development of professional skills, offering of test and testing centre for new systems and working methods, sharing of knowledge and creation of platform that stimulates innovation.

The recognition scheme, performance measurement and training form a trinity in which they reinforce each other. The qualification system reviews quality of the company, performance measurement reviews quality of the production process of a specific product and training guarantees quality of the employees. The external and internal quality assurance not only provides quality assessment but also informs the management about performance of business unit or process; identifies areas of improvement and advises on solutions. It seeks holistic connection and approaches of an organisation or process. These are core qualities for employees in quality management and infra management. The next chapter explains why these core qualities are important and how ProRail encourages their development.

6.12 Core qualities of an asset manager

Rail infrastructure serves rail transport operators, passengers and shippers as described in chapter 2. In order to prevent sub-optimisation, the infra manager must adopt an integrated approach such that the interests and consequences of all stakeholders are taken into account in the development and exploitation of rail infrastructure. This requires the infra manager to connect with all stakeholders.

The two core qualities that a rail infra manager must develop and control are as follows: (1) to connect people, processes and organisations and (2) adopting an integral approach such that the infra manager is present always and everywhere. The process model of the infra manager described in section 6.3 also illustrates infra manager as the connecting link between stakeholders who have needs and service providers who realise them. The infra manager has to connect six very different, coherent business processes to manage costs and performance optimally and sustainably over the entire life cycle. Because all executive tasks are outsourced, ProRail connects companies and business processes within rules of business contract.

Practice has shown that integral approach and connection are not only important at the level of companies and business processes but also at the level of employees and colleagues in the same business process. For example, an audit of the multi-year cash flow planning of the maintenance & renewal costs by the auditor PricewaterhouseCoopers (PwC) illustrated that control on life cycle costs needs to improve (PwC, 2015*). New policies are well substantiated with RAMS/LCC-analyses, but the implementation is not always as successful. Examples of this are grinding policy, conservation policy and policy to update M&R unit cost indicators. The developers of the new policy often have insufficient regard for the organisational consequences or are unable to manage implementation. To tackle this problem, four officials were appointed in 2016 to assist policy makers in organisational implementation of new policy through the star- or integral asset management approach illustrated in Figure 59.

The approach aims to map all processes that are affected and necessary for successful implementation of a new policy or other development in the organisation. It coordinates employees in the processes concerned and involves agreements. It addresses concerns such as: who is affected, who is responsible for whom, who steers what, how is the funding arranged, who does control, what are the consequences for maintenance contracts, etc. It structures the organisation by providing and securing necessary connections between employees, processes, products and/or instruments to guarantee controlled implementation of new policy or development. When people and processes are connected then people become involved and require up-to-date, complete and reliable information. Therefore, to inform is considered the third core quality of an infra manager. The why, how and what of ICT and information management is detailed in section 6.11.4.

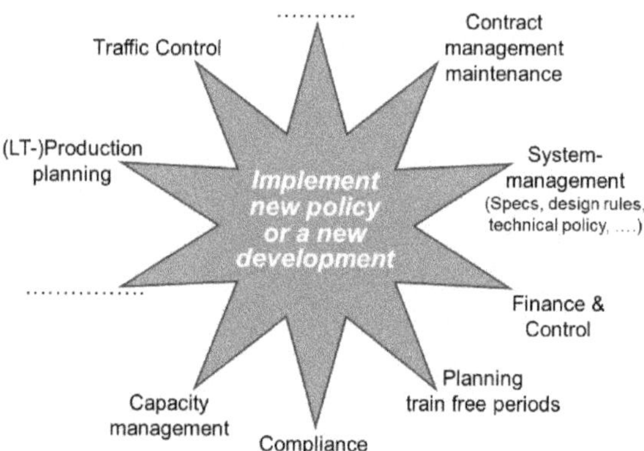

Figure 59   The star approach to implement new policies

The three core qualities can also be found in Figure 38 at page 130, an illustration of the process model of ProRail. It is no coincidence that the three core qualities – Integral approach, To connect and To inform - are also the ones necessary for effective functioning of employees of a matrix organisation. The employees must be able to develop professionally and feel 'at home' in the organisation. The matrix organisation was introduced around 2005 at the IM organisation, now known as ProRail Asset Management. For more details, please refer Figure 27 at page 83 and the corresponding text. In a matrix organisation, result-oriented line managers and employees collaborate with professional process specialists to achieve the desired results as well as implement and secure new processes and instruments. Collaboration, knowledge sharing and information availability are necessary conditions for achieving optimal and sustainable results. Without these qualities, an employee may feel isolated and disconnected in the organisation.

6.13 External AM standards and guidelines

The development of quality management principles and techniques was initiated in the defence- and aerospace industries and later adopted in the oil industry and network managers such as those for drinking water, gas, electricity and rail infrastructure. More details are provided in Appendix 14.1.5. At present, there are several standards and guidelines for asset management. The standards are:
1. EN50126 for RAMS management
2. RISMAN-method (or FMECA /RCM) for Risk management
3. PAS 55 and ISO 55000 for Asset management

NS Railinfrabeheer was only partially supported by these because the organisation was built before the standards and guidelines came into being. This chapter provides an overview of the standards, guidelines and techniques that are available for infrastructure and used by ProRail.

6.13.1 **European norm EN50126 for RAMS-management**

The European Union has approved use of generic functional safety standards for the European industry and specific standards, EN5012x, for the railway sector (CENELEC, 1999*). These include the EN50126 for railway systems in general and the EN50128 and EN50129 for electronic communication, signalling- and control systems. The standards have been available since 1999.

The EN50126 defines a process with tasks and tools necessary for realising and controlling the RAMS performance over the entire life cycle of a system. The standard describes the life cycle on the basis of the V model, as illustrated in Figure 60. The life cycle starts with the first idea for a product and then passes through design, development, commissioning, use and demolition. The process has fourteen steps.

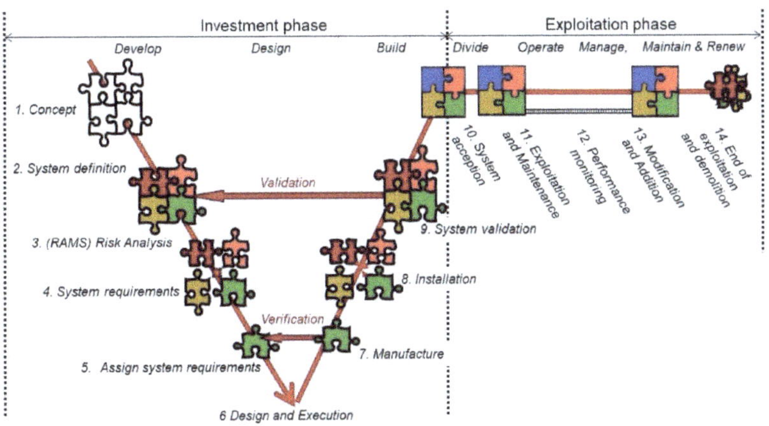

Figure 60   The V-model of the EN50126

The EN50126 is based on the principles of system theory, also called Systems Engineering (SE). The standard describes life cycle process in which a technical railway system is systematically analysed, designed, managed and demolished in subsystems covering requirements, processes and control loops by using risk management (RM) techniques. The risk analyses for new designs, systems and products enables demonstrable guarantee of the desired RAMS performance from the first phase over the life cycle. The magnitude of failure risk (= chance) and impact of consequences (=effect or impact) are estimated in analyses and compared with the RAMS requirements. In case of deviations, modifications are made to the design or maintenance concept is improved so as to comply with the requirements.

ProRail uses EN 50126 not only for development of interoperable communication, signalling and control systems but also for design and construction of new railway lines such as the HSL South (1998-2006), Betuwe route (1998-2007) and Hanze line (2003-2007). The standard has been the starting point for ProRail Projects since 2008 to meet the requirement of explicitly including RAMSHED performance and LC costs in early phase of projects. For more details, please refer section 6.11.2. This ensures the AM/M&R organization is involved from the beginning in new construction project because, together with Transport & Timetable (V&D), it specifies RAMS requirements and provides knowledge and expertise on maintenance costs, maintenance concepts as well as life cycle analyses.

The RAMS requirements, risk analyses, life time and life cycle cost analyses form the common language for effective collaboration between developers of new infrastructure and maintainers of existing infrastructure. It is a prerequisite to manage RAMS performance, risks and costs of the assets optimally and sustainably over their entire life cycle. The EN50126 is the guideline that describes process and instruments for how this is done.

6.13.2 Risk management: RISMAN (or FMECA / RCM)

The risk management aims to conduct dynamic, effective and efficient management of risks that threaten the realisation of company business objectives. ProRail Projects was the first business unit within ProRail who started to use an integrated risk control system according to the RISMAN method (RISMAN, 1998). It is a proven methodology within the infrastructure world in the Netherlands and increasingly beyond. The method is a Dutch translation of the international methods known as the risk management methods "Failure Mode Effect and Criticality Analysis" (FMECA) and "Realiability Centered Maintenance" (RCM). RISMAN was originally developed for projects but it is also suitable for exploitation processes.

The risk analysis (synonym: FMECA) systematically identifies the risks that can occur. On the basis of an FMECA process, events that may jeopardise the duration or budget of the project as well as their causes and effects are identified so the project manager(s) may take measures. The effect of measures is regularly assessed and the risks are re-inventoried. With the aid of the RISMAN method, a project manager gains insight into the most important risks for the project. All risk management methods consists of four steps:
   1.   Determining the goal;
   2.   Mapping the risks;

3. Determining the most important risks;
4. Mapping the risk control measures.

A RISMAN analysis utilises tools such as diagrams and calculation programmes.

In the development of the PGO contract, knowledge and experiences with RISMAN method in new construction projects were used. While the principles of risk management remain same, the application differs fundamentally. A project involves realisation of asset performances by selected asset solutions in the investment phase. The maintenance involves managing performance risks of the chosen asset solutions in the exploitation phase.

The performance risks of the operational phase are determined by the choice of asset solutions in the investment phase. A maintenance contractor is not distinguish by the performance risk analysis but by the effectiveness and efficiency of the control of the performance risks. However, risk management in the PGO contract was not based on this but rather on the RISMAN method, i.e., the way in which project controls the performance risks in the investment phase. The result is that every contractor and ProRail performs its own performance risk analysis. These analyses were difficult or impossible to compare even though they were about the same assets. This created inefficiency and frustration. A generic branch risk register was developed and made available in 2017 with the intention to make it a part of the PGO specification and control system. Unfortunately, the purchasing department has different ideas about this as described in section 9. and mentioned in section 4.2, at the end.

6.13.3 International standards: PAS 55 an ISO 55000

PAS55 is the first norm specific for asset management and was issued in 2008 by the British Standards Institution (BSI) (IAM, 2008*). The standard provides clear definitions and describes the management system in the form of a checklist with 22 aspects - processes, instruments and skills - required for cost-effective management of assets over the entire life cycle.

In addition to the PAS55, there is a publication of the Institute of Asset Management (IAM) entitled *'Asset Management - An anatomy'* (IAM, 2012*). It provides knowledge to operate the asset management system described in the PAS55. The *'anatomy'* is more extensive (it contains 39 subjects, not just 22 aspects in PAS55) and more accessible than PAS55 but both standards completely cover each other.

The UIC issued a guideline for the application of asset management in rail infrastructure organisations (UIC, 2010-9). The guideline is based on PAS 55 and UIC standard and provides an overview of the similarities between the two. The added value is limited

A very significant development is the publication of an ISO standard for asset management in 2014. This international quality standard is based on the PAS 55. The ISO 55000 provides an overview of AM topics and the definitions used. The ISO 55001 describes the requirements for an integrated and effective asset management system. The ISO 55002 provides guidelines for the implementation of such a system. Appendix 14.3 compares both AM-standards in relation to the five organisational boundary conditions of an organisation (please refer to section 6.6) and provides insight into the relationship among PAS 55, ISO 55000 and the EFQM/INK model.

Finally

The standards and guidelines for asset management provide insight into what is required for an effective and integrated AM system. However, they give little or no insight into the why and how it develops or what the underlying principles and starting points are. This book fills that gap. ProRail has not (yet?) been certified but when PAS55 was used as a checklist to assess whether organisational development was on course, all requirements stated in the reference frameworks/standards were found to have been filled in by ProRail (details provided in Appendix 14.3).

This ends chapter 6, which deals with the asset management system and organisation. The following chapter deals with the rail infrastructure performance and the connection with punctuality, the core quality indicator of the rail transport system. It discusses development of control and management of the RAMSHED quality of infrastructure and rail transport, and the results realised over the years. It concludes with a description of the performance dashboard of ProRail that is used for control.

7 Performance

This chapter provides insight into how rail infrastructure performance and related rail transport performance are managed, influenced and developed.

The passenger accords greatest importance to the punctuality and frequency of train service, which are determined by the performance of transport process and rail infrastructure. The infra performance are network capability and asset functionality, and the RAMS quality with which these are made available to the transport product, see Figure 61. The capability, functionality and potential RAMS quality are determined during the investment phase and the RAMS quality is realised in the exploitation phase.

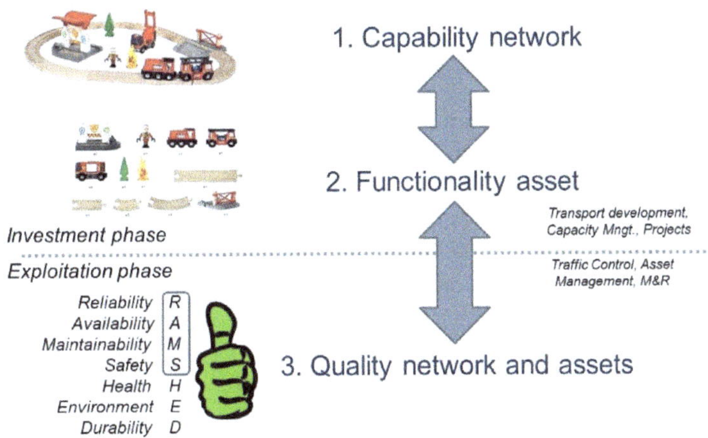

Figure 61   Cohesion between the three types of infrastructure performances

The infrastructure quality, thus, partly determines the quality of train service, the transport function. In this chapter, the relationship between the two is explained, the control of each and how performances are influenced and realised. We start with a brief explanation of capability- and functionality performance, and conclude with a detailed discussion of transport and infrastructure quality.

7.1 Performance infrastructure: capability & functionality

Without rail infrastructure there can be no rail transport and without transport needs there would be no rail infrastructure development.

The decision to build rail infrastructure always starts with the determination of the need for transport between two points and the choice to fulfil this need by means of rail transport. The next step is to determine how train operators expect to meet the transport needs and what requirements are imposed on the infrastructure: number of trains, timetable, train specifications (length, width, weight), operating speed, etc. These requirements from transport form the starting point for the rail infrastructure developers and designers. The starting point is used to identify solutions in the prescribed design regulation (OVS) and product catalogue of ProRail AM. If this does not determine the infrastructure requirement to deliver the desired performance, the design regulation and catalogue can be extended or adapted. Thus, the infra manager gets slowly, but surely, a complete picture of the infrastructure performance in terms of network capability and asset functionality, and the RAMS quality that both have to meet in operation.

7.2   Cohesion performance transport and -infrastructure

The quality of rail infrastructure, trains and train operation determine the quality parameters of the transport product such as experience of passengers and shippers as punctuality. When transport and infrastructure were separated in 1995, the management of NS Railinfrabeheer focused entirely on managing the RAMS quality of the infrastructure. The general feeling then was that punctuality is not the responsibility of the infra manager. This view no longer exists as is illustrated in ProRail's 2010 Annual Report. For the first time, the section on availability and reliability of infrastructure in the annual report also reported on realised punctuality (ProRail, 2011*, p. 23). It covered not only the impact of major infra-incidents but also the influence of Traffic Control and assistance provided by the Operational Control Centre Rail (OCCR). Figure 62 illustrates the relationship between punctuality and infrastructure quality. This relationship is also indicated in the performance matrix of rail transport (Figure 18 at page 64) and the control triangle of asset management (Figure 45 at page 144).

The connection between punctuality and infrastructure is a chain of cause and effect. If there were no disturbances in train service then every passenger would arrive on time. This ideal world does not exist. There is always some irregularity which creates chance for train delay. The irregularities are caused by rail infrastructure, trains or train operation. The exact nature of the relationship is not known in the Netherlands because more than half of the delayed trains are the result of another delayed train, known as secondary delays, and their causes are not recorded.

The proportion of the impact depends on what is measured: number of failures or train impact of a failure. Generally, the number of Train Effecting Irregularities of infrastructure (known as TAO's in the Netherlands) is much less than that of transport (proportion is about 35% : 65%), but the number of train hinderances of infra-TAOs is higher than that of transport-TAOs, with (very) large outliers that cause a great deal of hinderance. For example, in 2013, there were about 0.16% TAOs with (very) large hindrance. All of these were caused by rail infrastructure and they gave 25.2% of all TAO hinderance! For more details, please refer section 7.4 and Figure 68 at page 209.

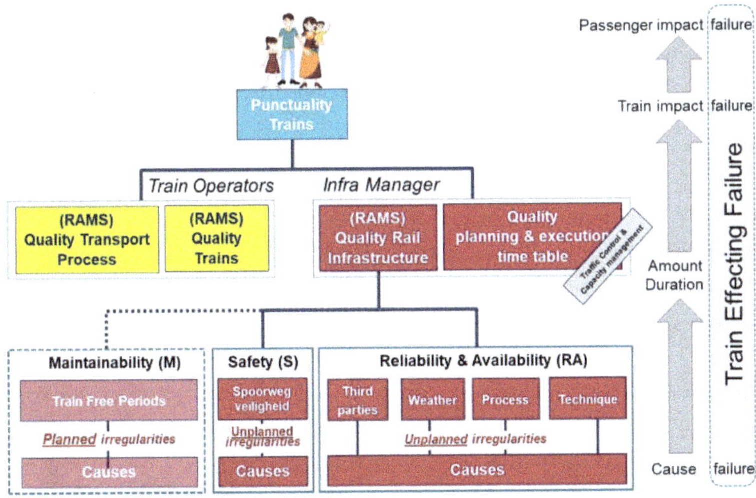

Figure 62   Coherence between punctuality and train effecting infra failures (TAO's)

The irregularities caused by train operator(s) include defective equipment, maladjusted equipment, absence of personnel, improper scheduling of personnel, problems with passengers, poor adjustment of deviation, etc. The rail infrastructure causes two very different types of irregularities: through the planning and execution of the time table or irregularities caused by the rail infrastructure.

For the first type, there are faults, imperfections or impossibilities in timetable design, or delays caused by adjustment in disrupted situations. These are TAOs allocated to Traffic Control.

For the second type, there are four types of irregularities: planned and unplanned, each with or without train hinderance. A planned irregularity is a planned train-free period to carry out track maintenance. It does not count towards punctuality because it does not always affect train service, and if they do, they are known and passengers can be informed in advance. The unplanned non-train effecting irregularities also do not influence punctuality. The unplanned train effecting irregularities, the TAOs, impact punctuality. The infra manager distinguishes four TAO-types: technology, weather, process and third party. The causes of technical-TAOs and weather-TAOs are failures caused by a technical problem whether or not caused by the weather. Process-TAOs include all unscheduled disruptions such as expiration of a planned train free period, a broken

195

maintenance machine, the consequences of bad planning, etc. Third-party-TAOs include irregularities caused by rail runners, cattle on the track, suicide, collisions on level crossings, etc.

Punctuality and irregularities are linked by a cause-and-effect chain: all delayed passengers are in a delayed train → each delayed train is caused by an irregularity → every irregularity has a cause → every cause has an underlying cause case, also called 'condition of the fault'. If you want to improve punctuality, you have to eliminate the cause of the train effecting failures. Risk management techniques help to identify causes, prioritise actions and choose an optimal maintenance strategy. A well-structured and complete failure registration is a prerequisite for managing performance and continuously improving it. It contains reliable information not only about the number and duration of failures, but also about the cause of failure and impact on transport, i.e. punctuality.

7.3 Quality of rail transport: punctuality

Development of the control of punctuality. In the Netherlands, punctuality is automatically measured since traffic control is fully computerised through the VPT process management system. VPT was the information plan to automate all processes related to train service planning, execution and adjustment. The preliminary study started in 1987 and was introduced step-by-step. The nationwide implementation was realised around 1995.

VPT includes control system of the traffic controller in which all routes for each train are pre-programmed as per the day plan. The day plans is entered into the computer system the night before and includes planned deviations and extra trains for the day. Punctuality is the public measure for quality of rail transport. It is measured by comparing realisation with the VPT plan for the day as registered at 50 representative stations in the Netherlands. A train that is late by three minutes or more is considered delayed. The computer system automatically sorts trains delayed by at least 3, 5 and 10 minutes. The method is unambiguous, simple and transparent in determining the number of trains that have been punctual.

There are countries where arrival punctuality is not measured at fixed measuring points but as delay jumps at all the timetable points[51]. This information is also available in the VPT system but is only used for in-depth analyses. It is not used to measure punctuality. The NS uses these measurements to determine the percentage of connections realised when passengers have to change trains.

---

[51] Timetable points are places on the railway network where train activities have a scheduled time in the service scheme and where possible deviations in performance are measured.

The measurements, taken both at fixed representative points and at timetable points, have their limitations. At representative fixed point, interim delays of more than 3 minutes are not measured. At timetable control points, delay is not measured if the jump is smaller than 3 minutes even though these small delays may cause the train to arrive at the arrival point with a (large) delay.

The measurements provide detailed information every day about the difference between plan and realisation for all train series at all timetable points. This information was mainly used for accountability, after the introduction of the VPT. That was about to change when Railinfrabeheer, Traffic Control and Railned merged into ProRail B.V in 2005. In the same year, the Performance Analysis Bureau (PAB) was established to measure, analyse and improve punctuality. The PAB is part of ProRail Traffic Control with an independent role as knowledge centre for information and advice in train services for the entire rail sector. The department aims to further improve the train process in collaboration with the train operators and infra manager. The PAB has acquired an indispensable place and is widely appreciated and respected. For more background information about the PAB, please refer section 10.

Results and backgrounds of punctuality measurements. The daily punctuality measurements provide a wealth of information about delays, lifted trains, number of train movements, connections made, etc. This information is provided for each day, region, traffic control post and train series. Figure 63 shows the punctuality trend in the period 1995-2015 (Swier J. , 2015*). The strongly fluctuating light-grey line is the average punctuality per week, the red line is the moving quarterly average and the black line is the moving annual average. The fluctuations are large:

- Week average: 20-30%
- Moving quarterly average: 8-12%
- Moving annual average: 0-3%

Figure 63 indicates large annual differences in the period 1995-2004 and the annually recurring difference between summer and winter. The major trend changes are related to significant developments such as separation of exploitation (NS) and rail infrastructure (ProRail) in 1995, which caused punctuality to fall from 85% to 82% and then rise to 86.4% in 1999. Thereafter, punctuality quickly went down as a result of personnel unrest at NS about work schedules, equipment shortage and increase in number of train failures due to reduction in material maintenance (Wessels, 2003).

The separation of the adjustment of timetables, trains and train personnel did not make the situation any easier and a low point was reached in 2001 when punctuality fell below 80% and the NS management was fired. The new management succeeded in gaining trust with the result that punctuality recovered in three years (2004) reaching level of the top-year in 1999. In 2005, however, situation suddenly worsened due to an unusually large number of special incidents with major impact on train service: four derailments, three notable weather changes, two large computer failures in traffic control posts and a strike. Especially the snow in the first quarter of the year and two derailments in Amsterdam halfway through the year caused major trend breaks. The year 2005 clearly illustrates that larger deviations in quarterly trend are caused by irregularities with a very high impact.

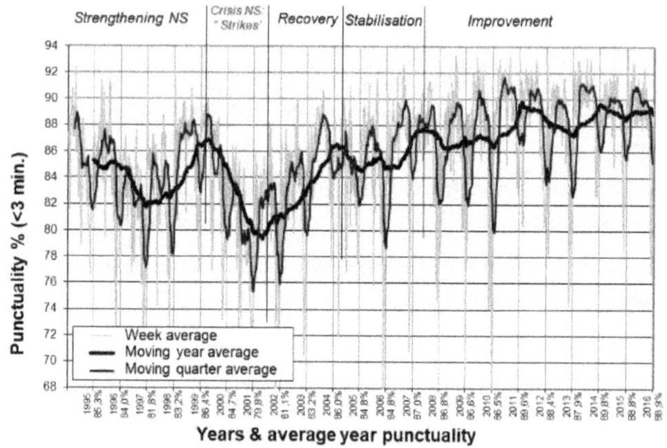

Figure 63   Development of punctuality (< 3' delay)

After 2005, the PAB made it easier for train operators and ProRail to continuously improve punctuality with many small changes in timetable and traffic management. The negative peaks in the winter periods remained, but the daily and weekly fluctuations became smaller, indicating a structurally better control of the quality of transport and infrastructure. The development can be observed when daily punctuality figures are presented in a different way, as in Figure 64.

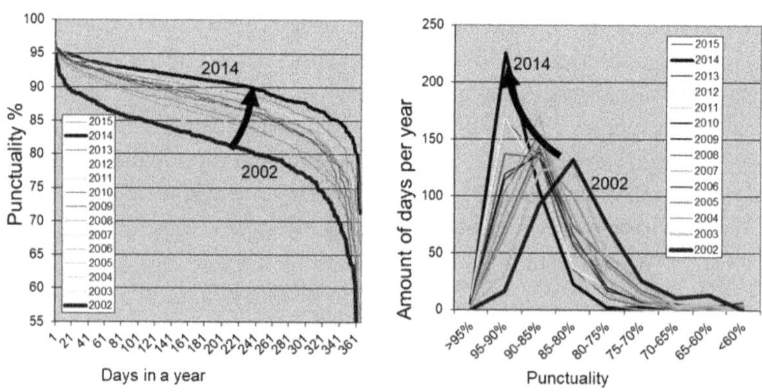

Figure 64   Development of punctuality 2002-2014: same data, different illustration

198

The day-punctuality figures of each year are plotted from high to low in the left graph and the same figures were plotted in punctuality jumps of 5% between 95-60%. The blue line is for 2014 and the red line for 2002, the two extremes in the selected period. The lines in between are those for other years. The graphs makes it evident that punctuality is more stable, spread is smaller and peak is shifted. In 2002, there were virtually no days in the group of 95-90% while in 2014 there were more than 220. In 2002, there were 24 days with a worse day-punctuality lower than 70%, while in 2014 there were none such days. The punctuality occasionally only exceeds 95%, which indicates that there is an upper limit for punctuality that can be achieved on the existing rail system in the Netherlands.

An analysis of the punctuality figures also shows that average punctuality of the two weekend days in the past was 3-5% higher than that of the five working days, as indicated in Figure 65. The improvement in punctuality in 2014 compared to 2002 was achieved especially on the working days and difference with weekend days became smaller. This is remarkable because there are fewer passengers and 25% fewer trains in the weekends. One explanation could be an increase in building and maintenance activities shifting to the weekends.

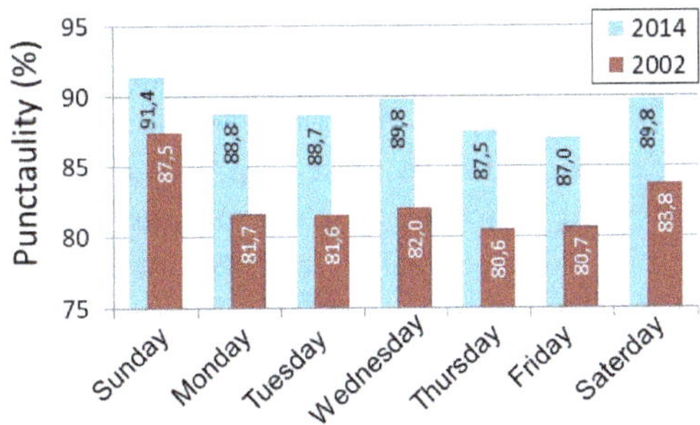

Figure 65   Improvement of punctuality per weekday in 2014 compared to 2002

The performance improvement comes from quality improvement in transport process and means of production (trains and infrastructure) as well as better design and implementation of the timetable. The project 'Benutten en Bouwen'((In English: 'Use & Build') acted as a catalyst in increasing knowledge in this area.

Change in thinking: project 'Benutten en Bouwen'. The project 'Benutten en Bouwen" was initiated by the ministry of V&W, NS, Railion and ProRail, in order to develop a joint strategic vision for dealing with anticipated large transport growth and investments requirement. In 2003, the final report was presented: Benutten & Bouwen 2003-2015 (Spoorsector, 2003*). The joint rail companies indicated that growth in rail transport can be accommodated by making better use of existing and new build infrastructure. A precondition is that the reliability of the rail system must be improved and complexity of transport process reduced.

A fundamental and radical form to realize that is by de-complication of busy lines and operate them more independent of each other. This involves less large-scale expansions of infrastructure and the result is still an increase of capacity and performance. For freight transport, the European scale is the norm with train paths also during rush hour for passenger transport, efficient use of the Betuwe route and a green signal wave for freight trains. Unfortunately, all possible, desired and expected developments were brought together under the common banner of the project 'Benutten en Bouwen'. This led to an increasing price tag which was longer in proportion to the original target. The vision of 'Benutten en Bouwen', however, remained intact: de-complicate transport process and rail infrastructure to achieve structural increase in capacity and punctuality.

In the context of 'Benutten en Bouwen', various company visits were made to Japan by mixed delegations from V&W, freight- and passenger train operators, and the infra manager. The benefit was twofold: strengthen cooperation between policy makers in the institutional triangle and develop fundamentally new insights into the possibilities and limitations to structurally improve punctuality and capacity cost-effectively. There was a growing common sense that high punctuality and capacity are interrelated and determined by the degree of complexity of the infra and transport processes, cooperation in operation and reliability of the means of production.

Cause analysis of dis-punctuality. After the 'Benutten en Bouwen' project, greater attention was paid to improving punctuality and capacity of the existing network. The potential was much greater and a number of studies were carried out around 2005 that provided insight into specific improvement areas. An overview of the most important ones:

- ProRail Capacity Management and NSR Logistics organised a research about planning standards: ONNO (in Dutch: ONderzoek naar planningsNOrmen). The most important conclusion was that generic planning standards are often unrealistic and that location-specific standards are necessary. In short: in the timetable, there were trains that could never operate on time. The dis-punctuality in the Netherlands was thus partly an ingrained planning problem and thus dissolution of this problem structurally improved punctuality.
- In 2005, ProRail carried out research into underlying causes of dis-punctuality. A detailed analysis of 33 train series was carried out to identify causes for 75% of the dis-punctuality. The identifies causes were: non-feasible planning, waiting for early or late train, too late departure in connection with a level crossing and duration of the departure procedure. It has been established that only a part of the dis-punctuality is caused by unavailability and irregularities in the means of production and processes. The quality of the plan and complexity of transport process has a greater influence on dis-punctuality. A large

part of the delay occurs on a small number of large stations. This is caused by concentration of potential conflicts in the form of over-crossings and - to a lesser extent - platform follow-up. Preventing or reducing of these conflicts would structurally improve punctuality and not require major investments. The primary cause of dis-punctuality was the Stop-Go circuit[52] at stations, which resulted in delay of 0.5 to 1.5 minutes. With an adjustment of the Stop-Go process, the problem has largely been solved.

- A study by CQM, commissioned by NSR, identified that every delay, however small, potentially allows a larger delay. A higher punctuality starts with driving the scheduled timetable as much as possible on time. It should measure deviations in seconds, not in minutes. This is a pos-sible explanation of why the timetable in Japan is planned, measured and driven up to five seconds. This principle can be illustrated with an example. In 2005, about 84.8% of the trains were delayed by less than 3 minutes. At 5 minutes, the punctuality was 94% and at 10 minutes, it was 97%. In Figure 66, punctuality data is plotted in a graph (blue line) and extrapolated (red lines). The graph illustrates a mechanism: 15% of trains with delay greater than 3 minutes is only the tip of an iceberg. It is likely that 30-40% of the trains have delay less than 3 minutes. These slightly delayed trains make the system susceptible to small disruptions, which quickly push the 3-minute limit. If a part of the group of slightly delayed trains were to become punctual then it would probably pro-duce noticeable effect on day-punctuality.

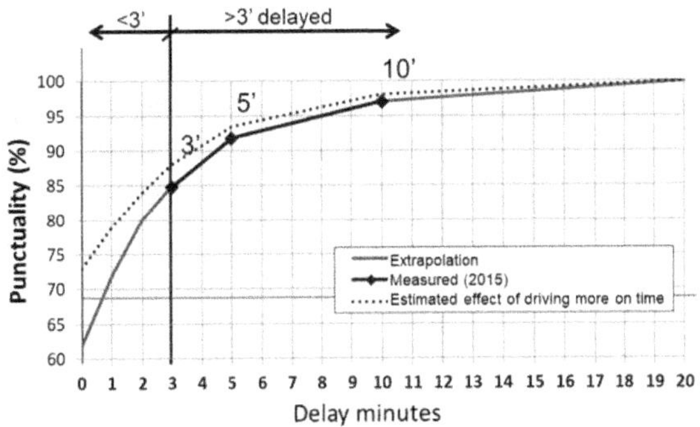

Figure 66   Possible connection between small and large(er) delays

- Upon the initiative of NSR, CQM analysed punctuality in 2005. An im-portant conclusion was that punctuality is not a measure for train delay

---

[52] In the case of a Stop-Go circuit, the train traffic controller informs the signalling at last-operated signal for level crossing, whether the train stops at the station or drives on. If the train stops then the level crossing will remain open after the station until it is activated and the train gets green light when beams are closed.

but for distribution of the realisation around planned time. Dis-punctuality is, therefore, a spreading problem and reduction in spread would improve punctuality. According to CQM, the starting punctuality of a train is essential in determining influence on punctuality. ProRail has commented on the analysis of CQM: impact of starting punctuality is estimated too high because the problem is not only driving time but also duration of stops and conflicts with other trains.

The analyses indicate various possibilities and approaches to improve punctuality and capacity of existing infrastructure. They provided new ways to substantially improve results of rail transport cost-effectively. This led to improvement projects and concrete improvements in results.

Improvement projects for punctuality and capacity. The 'Benutten en Bouwen' project and dis-punctuality cause analyses have ensured, or at least stimulated, many notable improvements in operations, timetable and process cooperation since 2003. An overview of this most remarkable project:

- A large number of major ICT failures in the VPT traffic control system led to the decision in 2003 to make the whole traffic control system redundant. These type of failures generally have a very big impact on train service and, therefore, on passengers. In 2008, all 13 traffic control posts were equipped with new hardware and redundant facilities. In 2010, a twin computer centre was put into operation to allow mutual diversion of and between posts. The effects were visible when in the period 2007-2011, the number of ICT failures with major impact on train service decreased from 286 to 54.

- A number of large infrastructure failures in 2005 led to the establishment of the Operational Control Centre Rail (OCCR). In that year, passengers were either stranded or arrived at their destination with great delay. Analyses showed that in case of disruptions and calamities there are too few people who have an overview of the larger picture and that the operational processes of operators, traffic control and maintenance contractors are not integrated to allow decisive actions in situations of disturbance. In the following years, the concept was elaborated and all parties were aligned to adopt principle of 'develop by learning'. This implied that the OCCR was built on the basis of knowledge and experience of all participants by trying and refining ideas. At the end of 2010, the OCCR was operational and delivered from one large control room. In 2013, the Operational Information Centre Infra (OBI) was added to OCCR with the merging of four regional Switch & Report Centres (SMC) into a single national centre for the control of the catenary system and handling of irregularities. The image gives an impression of the OCCR

OCCR Source: Wikipedia

- In 2007, a multidisciplinary team came together for a week to answer the question whether 20% growth is possible for the existing network and to determine requirements to facilitate substantial growth. The answer was: yes, even with a limited package of measures, if generic solutions were not chosen but measure packages were adopted per railway line. There is a lot of air in the existing system: large margins in planning standards, combination of stop-intercity-freight trains, cross-traffic and (freight) train paths that are planned but not used much (team, 2007*). The chosen form of multidisciplinary task force was found to be valuable.

- The recommendations of the multidisciplinary team were elaborated in a vision to enable growth by dealing with capacity differently. The ambition was expanded to run more trains per line without a timetable and create new train paths for freight. For this purpose, the usual way of thinking and doing had to end to enable better utilisation of capacity of the existing network. A railway line has theoretical capacity of 30 trains per hour per track, but in practice there were no more than 12 trains per track on the Dutch network. It was considered possible to increase capacity at considerably lower costs. The better utilisation of capacity meant that the sector had to work *'three times different'* [53]: Different plans and execution, different distribution of capacity and different ways to increase capacity (Verstegen, 2007*). The project got the name 'Triple A'. The 'Triple A' brochure at the time led to a conflict with the train operators about the approach and costs. This was because of insufficient tuning and lack of communication. The Ministry of Transport was confused. 'Triple A' quickly disappeared from the

---

[53] 'Different' means in Dutch 'Anders', hence the project name 'Triple A'.

table but the ideas remained intact. In the end, a joint memorandum was published for the entire rail sector: 'Ruimte op de Rails' (English: 'Space on the Rails'), with the ambition to increase the capacity on track by 50% for 2020 for a maximum of € 4.5 billion. This vision has been elaborated in the 'Program Hoogfrequent Spoor' (PHS, in English: 'High Frequency Track') based on consultation with all parties involved. New working methods were successfully applied. For example, ProRail regularly brought together all relevant disciplines in design workshops to make an inventory of measures per workflow, exchange information and involve stakeholders in the process. Intensive work conferences were held between train operators and ProRail to break down traditions, make compromises and gain mutual confidence. As the owner of infrastructure and financier, the government made the plan. A good role fulfilment in the institutional triangle of Government, Train Operating Companies (TOCs) and ProRail created the necessary support among regional authorities. ProRail and the TOCs presented the facts without any opinion or preference, the municipalities expressed their wishes and the central government decided because it paid. While the new division of roles in the institutional triangle was an improvement, the PHS showed that there was room for improvement in the interpretation of roles. In mid-2010, however, the Council of Ministers agreed with the PHS plan. It was a huge victory considering the complexity of the subject with the secondary result of a better relationship between ProRail and all sector parties.

- In the project development period of PHS, regular mixed delegations visited Japan under the motto 'first see, then believe' and 'play together, share together'. In Japan, there was a temporary employee of ProRail who assisted delegations on part-time basis and maintained a blog to share his experiences. This resulted in a wealth of knowledge and experiences in the form of 25 stories about why Japanese railways perform so well (Hofstra, 2010*). It described not only the operation of rail transport and development of rail infrastructure, but also about the underlying conditions and circumstances.

We have now gained insight into punctuality, the quality parameter of rail transport, which connects quality of train service and rail infrastructure. In the next section, we will delve deeper into the development of control of infrastructure quality and realised results.

7.4   Quality infrastructure: Availability and Reliability

Development of asset quality control in the Netherlands
Measuring is knowing and a condition for control. Punctuality and failures have been measured for a long time. The measurements were initially recorded on

paper and since the end of the eighties also in computers. Looking back, we can conclude that, in the nineties, measuring was limited to registration of performance in order to justify their existence. As long as the maintenance organisations in the districts ensured that infrastructure functioned safely and well, it was good. This began to change after Transport and Infrastructure were separated and maintenance was outsourced. The management of different organisations made agreements about deliverables and wanted more control over the realisation. The interest in 'measuring & knowing' punctuality and infra performance grew quickly and more attention was paid to connect the two. Figure 67 illustrates the development and this section provides the details.

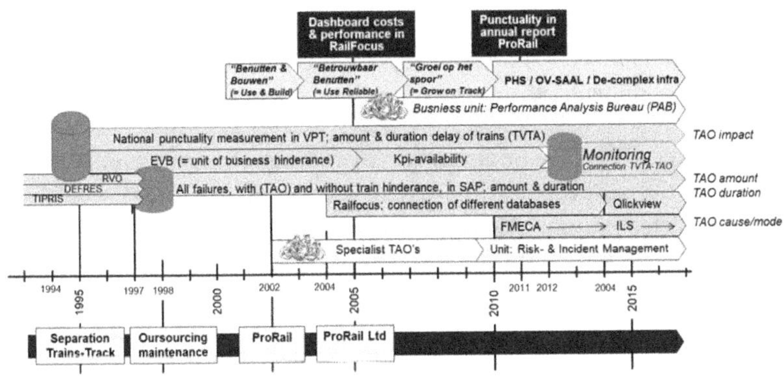

Figure 67   Development of control on the coherence of punctuality and infra failures

In 1990, asset information was managed by the NS organisations responsible for technical systems. The information was on paper or in a mainframe or standalone computer. The failure information was recorded in systems such as DEFRES[54], Tipris, Geeltje and the Report of Irregularities (RVO). Different systems had different piece of information and there was overlap.

After the separation of Transport and Infrastructure in 1995, NS Railinfrabeheer started preparations for implementation of the ERP system SAP. This became the system for recording all asset information, failures and the financial administration. In a single system, information was available on *'what do we have'*, *'where is it'*, *'how does it perform'* and *'what does it cost'*? Implementation of SAP was completed in 1996/1997. This was a huge improvement but the downside was that SAP-knowledge and -experience were required to enter and retrieve information. The comparison was made of the storage of a milk bottle in a safe while one needed a refrigerator.

---

[54] DEFRES = DEFects Registration of Energy supply and Signalling

In 2001, Railinfrabeheer published a report with analysis of the failure information for the period 1998-2001 (Swier J. , 2001-06). The report was prepared to meet increasing demand for knowledge and information about availability and reliability of Dutch infrastructure. The demand came from very different parties and with very different objectives: standards for performance contract between Transport and Infra, model to predict availability and reliability of new lines, standards for product specifications, management information and data for UIC benchmark study. The report became a source of knowledge and inspiration. The management attention grew to improve the quality of failure information and use of it for performance improvement. A professional specialist was appointed with this task in 2002 and became an indispensable knowledge centre and booster for other ProRail departments through evaluation and trend analyses. The professional specialist ensured continuous improvement of the performance registers and the connection with other information systems.

The 'Benutten en Bouwen' project made an important contribution in focussing management on performance improvement (Spoorsector, 2003*). Within the framework of this project, a delegation went to Japan in March 2002 *'to find out what makes it possible for Japan to have a much higher punctuality of trains and a twice as high degree of utilization of a rail infrastructure that is largely in terms of technology comparable with ours'* (Velde, Japanse Horizon (Vel02), 12-2002*, p. 7). It was a mixed delegation with representatives from NS, Railion, V&W, Railned, Rail Traffic Control and Railinfrabeheer. The visit was organised and supervised by Didier van de Velde of the Erasmus University in Rotterdam. It concluded that *'the crux of Japanese success lies in the unambiguous choice of the Japanese management for quality of the infrastructure, trains and the personnel'*. In summary, it was concluded that the quality in Japan is guaranteed by:
- Customisation in infrastructure; signal compaction, passing tracks, etc.
- Homogenisation: customisation in rush hour on busy routes;
- Reliable infrastructure, equipment and personnel: very high availability;
- Route-based deployment of equipment: avoiding expanding consequences of delays to other lines and areas;
- Monitoring punctuality: at 10-15 seconds, accurate driving of service;
- Maximum communication: integrated train service control at single location.

It was found that corporate culture and management attention play important roles and these had to change in the Dutch rail sector to enable delivery of transport performance as in Japan. In November 2002, a small delegation from Railinfrabeheer went to Hong Kong and Japan to seek for strategies to significant improve rail infrastructure availability. This trip was made again in the context of 'Benutten en Bouwen' project. The learning points of the delegation were:
- Examples of better technical solutions and adjustments;

- No failures with a long duration exist due to intensive cooperation;
- Delays on a line do not affect other lines due to separation of lines and low complexity;
- There are less technical failures due to closed quality circle, low complexity and consistent learning from breakdowns;
- More attention is given to robustness, redundancy and simplicity.

The epilogue of the report states: *'An important explanatory factor for the high punctuality of train service and availability of rail infrastructure seems to be found not so much in technology but in the simplicity of the system and the processes, both in Hong Kong and Japan. The network is not cross-linked, the organization works as a whole, processes are well controlled and railway lines are separated as much as possible from each other. Everything and everyone is focused on the execution of the train service'* (Swier J. , 2002*, p. 47). The study trip has stimulated communication and focus within Railinfrabeheer on improving infrastructure availability and reliability. More attention was paid to reducing breakdown time because *'It is clear that this (= influence on train service) is not so much because infrastructure is less frequently disturbed but because infrastructure is less disturbed for a long time'* (Swier J. , 2002*, p. 43).

At the end of 2003, a policy note on asset management was published (Lamers, 2003*). The management of ProRail wanted a long-term vision in asset management and formed a platform for conducting reconnaissance study. It was established that rail infrastructure management cannot do asset management professionally because the processes and associated skills are lacking. Many improvements were underway but incoherent. The proposal was to make projects coherent on the basis of the five-phase growth model of the INK, while starting with the basics: development of product and process orientation at the M&R-organisation. The challenge was to become transparent, put the foundation of M&R organisation in order and continuously improve on the basis of measurements and process control.

For control, the business objectives must be linked to processes and the processes must be further linked to decision models. Based on the mission and business goals, a target Key Performance Indicators (KPI)-tree should be defined as the baseline, with KPIs for TAOs, Function Recovery Time (FHT), Temporary Speed Restrictions (TSB), failure impact (EVB) and Train Free Periods (TVP). There was now a vision for performance management which determined where to start and why. Measuring is knowing and the basis for improvement. A dashboard was needed to directly link to the source and make information accessible to everyone in the organisation.

At the end of 2003, Loyds Register and Horvat & Partners (LREHC) introduced an analysis of the measurability and manageability of technical quality and rail infrastructure performance (LREHC, 2003*). The basic principle was that Pro-Rail must control process transparently to achieve required performance effectively and efficiently, both at the level of network performance, and of objects and components. This required improvements in the management of technical quality, outsourcing and performance; attention to repetitive failures and optimisation of measurement techniques. With regard to the RAMS performance, LREHC recommended improvement of the management and registration of the TAOs, FHTs and Safety incidents, as well as annual evaluation and adjustment of the policy. The importance of LREHC analysis was that it demonstrated coherence between performance and technical quality, and indicated how these are specified and monitored at different levels. For more information, please refer section 6.8 at page 138.

In 2004, ProRail informed the Minister of Transport, Public Works and Water Management about the performance of rail infrastructure (ProRail, 2004*). It was established that number of failures decreased while punctuality, number of trains and maintenance costs increased: higher quality and capacity came at a price. The presentation ends with the text: *'Our ambition: to become the best rail infrastructure manager in Europe. We are on track.'*

Manage failure numbers, duration and impact. The broad attention to reduce TAO's decreased considerably in 2006 when ProRail management decided not to steer on the KPI's failure number and failure duration anymore, but rather adopt a new KPI 'Availability'. It is a calculated percentage according to the formula: Availability = Function recovery time (FHT) * line section value * number of affected work zones. The value of KPI was between 99% and 100% and was given with three decimal places. At the same time, the 'Eenheid van Bedrijfshinder"(= EVB = 'Unit of Business Annoyance') was retired. The EVB was a simple but valuable KPI to gain insight into the impact of TAOs on train service.

The KPI Availability did not bring any improvement. The percentage was meaningless and the KPI did not provide insight into relationship between failures and punctuality (Jenma, 2010, Jen10). A manual processing was required to present the figures. In 2012, this KPI was stopped and replaced with the number and duration of TAOs. The EVB was replaced with a new and better KPI, the 'Te Verklaren Trein Afwijking' (= TVTA = 'To be Explained Train Deviation').

The TVTA stands for the number of trains delayed because of a failure. These are monitored by Traffic Control and registered in the monitoring system. If a train makes a delay of three minutes or more, is cancelled, moved or diverted, the system generates a TVTA. The traffic controller then assigns the TVTA to a cause. The monitoring system of Traffic Control was linked to the TAO registration system of ProRail AM in 2012. From 2013 onwards, every TAO has a known impact, measured in the number of delayed and cancelled trains.

In 2014, the number of delay minutes per TVTA and TAO was added as a parameter, based on weighted delays in eight monitoring categories[55] and four weight categories[56]. The focus shifted from reducing the number of TAOs to reducing the number of TAO's with major customer hinderance. After the presentation of the 2015 Annual Report, the CEO of ProRail, Pier Eringa, said: *'... It is easier to rectify minor failures and then proudly proclaim that the number of failures is decreasing. That is the exercise for beginners. But we are more advanced and want to focus on issues that have a lot of consequences for our customers'. (V*ries, 2016 *). Figure 68 illustrates Eringa's message.

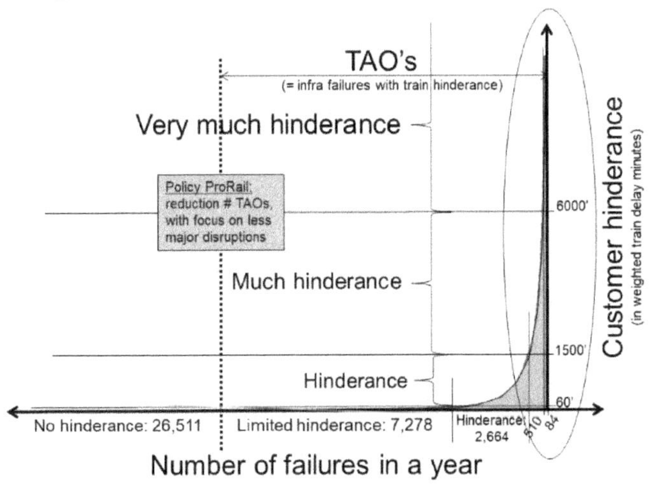

Figure 68   Relationship of number of TAOs and customer hindernace in 2016 (on scale)

When the number of infrastructure failures in 2016 were plotted in relation to customer hinderance, measured in train delay minutes, it was observed that of the 37,047 failures in the year, a total of 10,536 affected train services, i.e. TAOs. Of these, 594 (6%) caused much-to-very-much train hinderance, about 68% of all hinderance. Therefore, a total of 9,942 TAOs (94%) cause the remaining 32% hinderance. Reducing the number of TAOs with much-to-very-much hinderance yields an average of 35x higher return than that of TAOs in the two lower categories. The TAOs with greatest impact are generally the most difficult to tackle. Very often the cause is not technology but circumstances such as the weather, process or third party.

In 2015, the NS prepared for the first time a customer hinderance report, which provided insight into number of disrupted journeys because of larger disruptions on route section, i.e., the number of passengers in delayed trains. It indicated

---

[55] The 8 monitor categories in are: 1'-3' | 3'-5' | 5'-10' | 10'-20' | >20' | Divert | Cancel | Reroute
[56] The 4 weight categories in minutes are: Light: <60' | middle: 60'- 1500' | Heavy: 1500'- 6000' | Ultra: >6000'

whether specific customer support was provided in the form of replacement bus transport, extra staff and/or a cup of coffee. The report is under construction. In 2017, customer hinderance data was not linked with monitoring system and TAO registration. If that link is established then customer hinderance can be measured not only in train delay minutes but also in passenger delay minutes.

Management of TAO impact reduction is possible when concerned organisations use basic principles of RAMS performance management. To achieve decrease in number and duration of failures, the organisations required complete and reliable failures registration. The work was under way since 2002 with dip in the period 2006-2012 when ProRail management used KPI availability but resumed thereafter when this KPI was abolished.

A TAO reduction programme was launched in 2012 with the assignment: *'Reducing TAOs, by having ProRail Asset Management (AM) work as intended'*. The programme provided a platform to identify obstacles in reduction. These obstacles included technical, organisational or contractual aspects. Examples of TAO-reducing actions are exchange of light bulbs for LED, creation of knowledge tables in various fields and the introduction of TAO incentives in OPC- and PGO contracts. The programme improved focus; exchange of knowledge and experience; as well as development of effective and unambiguous methods to collect information about failures. Much importance was accorded to cooperation among parties involved. To stimulate collaboration, the *'TAO-hunk'* was created. It was a trophy awarded to employees of two different departments or organisations that together provided tangible and demonstrable TAO reduction. Partly as a result, employees from trace teams worked together with contractors every two weeks to discuss measures to reduce disruptions and failures (recidivism) with lot of train hinderance. They evaluated underlying influences and improved the process as well as making adjustments in the management concept and modifications to prevent failures. The infra performance of the past week was discussed weekly in the regions. In the meantime, the share of technical TAOs dropped from around 50% of the total number of infra failures to about 32% (2016). The programme emphasises preventing TAOs with a great impact for passengers and shippers.

In 2012, the 'Systeemsprong Wissels' (= in English: 'System Leap Switches') programme was established to specifically reduce the number of switch failures in Amsterdam, Schiphol and Utrecht by 50% and formulate a vision for the entire network based on these experiences. After a year, remarkable results were achieved because of the following:
- Weekly consultation;
- Attention to maintenance engineering;
- Publishing and sharing of performance information;

- Stimulating improvement;
- Tuning maintenance to age, use and importance of object;
- Attention for recurrences;
- Better information about condition of switches;
- Reduced interface problems caused by splitting and outsourcing.

The experiences were shared with other regions and contractors, contributing to reduce the number of technical TAOs.

In order to reduce the number and impact of failures, employees of infra manager and maintenance contractors must have good understanding of the circumstances and causes of failures. Realising that good failure and cause registration is essential, a pilot project started in 2013 in the Gelre contract area of Asset Rail. It brought many improvements that reduced the number and duration of TAOs in Gelre. The improvements included the following:

- Linking failure registration of ProRail and maintenance contractors;
- Failure app for the technician;
- Real-time insight into process;
- Data entry at the source;
- Handling of failures directly in the ProRail system;
- Standardisation of failure modes and -causes in the registration system;
- Structural consultation between ProRail and PCA about improvement.

The Information Supply Specifications (ILSs) from the maintenance concept (IHCs) of the SAM programme proved to be an indispensable platform of knowledge and information for systematically standardising all failure modes and -causes in the failure app of the failure technicians. The experiment was a success! At the start of 2016, BAM Rail and VolkerRail were connected to the failure management system and their technicians gained access via the failure app. Strukton and Asset Rail joined later. This fulfilled all basic conditions to reduce the number and duration of failures as well as their impact.

Development of the rail infra quality in the Netherlands. In the period 1995-1999, the total number of TAOs of rail infrastructure had increased by 47%. The biggest increase was caused by technical TAOs, which increased by 53% from 5,563 to 8,490, as indicated in Figure 69 (Swier J. , 2015*). This increase in number of failures was the price paid for the decision to outsource maintenance. In that period, attention and focus of personnel and management were on safeguarding their job and facing radical organisational changes with personnel consequences. There was extra work, unrest and uncertainty.

When everyone was settled in the new role, the focus returned to restoring infrastructure performance. The total number of TAOs dropped from 15,960 to

13,308 in three years and the technical TAOs dropped from 8,490 to 6,116. This decline continued when, from 2002 onwards, OPC+ increased focus on reducing the number of TAOs. The performance of railway infrastructure sector started to improve in 2004, before the separation of trains and track, even though train intensity had increased.

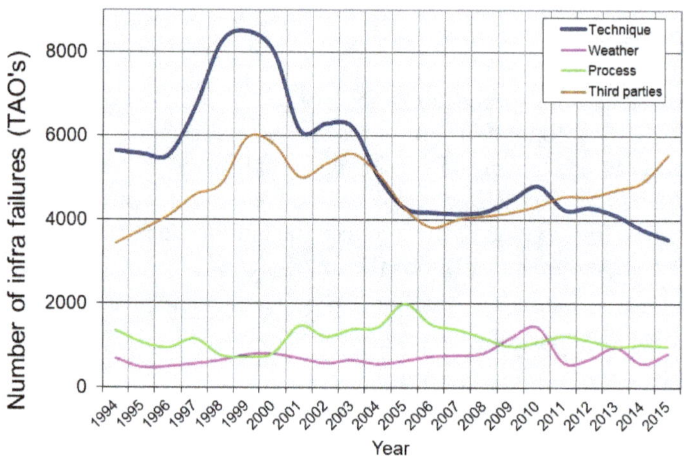

Figure 69   Development of the number of train effecting infra failues (TAO's)

The cause of worry at this stage was the continuous increase in number of third-party TAOs, indicated in green line in Figure 69. The third-party failures included road accidents, suicides, cattle on track, passers-by along track, etc. This group was difficult to influence until a task force of 'Buitengewone Opsporing Ambtenaren' (= BOA = in English: 'Extraordinary Investigation Official') was launched in the South region. The introduction of this approach in other regions (2004) reduced the third-party TAOs by approximately 25% in two years. When a major break was realised in the trend, the formation of ProRail AM was expanded by approximately 50 persons with the role of BOA. This move however failed to stop the decline. The number of third-party TAOs started to rise again after 2006 and exceeded technical TAOs in 2011. It seems that social conditions changed faster than influence of the measures taken.

7.5   Quality infrastructure: Maintainability & Health

Maintainability is, according to the EN50126, the number and duration of planned train free periods to carry out maintenance, as also illustrated through decomposition of infrastructure performance in Figure 62 at page 195. The Dutch network has many of such periods because all maintenance is done during shutdowns. Maintainability and personal safety are thus considered as a two-part concept in this book and therefore described in the same section.

Safe work on track was part of the Railways Act until 1992 and under safety legislation thereafter. The risk number[57] in construction industry was around 0.81 and that in track works was 3.6 (Koster, 2008*). The new Minister for Social Affairs and Employment (SZW) mandated a working group in 1994 and proposed new regulations in June 1995, the 'Reglement Veilig Werken'(= RVW. In English: 'Safe Working Regulations') on rail infrastructure.

In the same year, there were three accidents in which five track workers were killed: one in Heiloo on April 11, 1995; three at Mook on May 31, 1995; and one at Gouda on May 31, 1995. The shock was enormous and subsequent review of the safety process brought far-reaching changes through the RVW which came into force on January 1, 1996. The regular inspections and maintenance were no longer permitted between running trains, but only in shutdowns, known as train free periods.

In the five years thereafter, the number of train free periods rose sharply and in 2002, the risk figure dropped to 2.8. The effect of RVW was assessed inadequate and ProRail approached track worker safety differently with the arrival of the Standards of 'Normenkader Veilig Werklen'(= NVW. In English: 'Safe Working Framework') that came into effect on January 1, 2005. The NVW describes how personnel safety must be organised and guaranteed during infrastructure works. It involves setting clear requirements for organisations, people, resources and processes to achieve and maintain acceptable and demonstrable safety level. The NVW uses the method of risk inventory and risk assessment. ProRail is required to determine risks, desired safety level and security method.

On January 1, 2008, the NVW management was assigned to RailAlert, the foundation to which ProRail, maintenance contractors and engineering firms are affiliated. This enabled the NVW to emerge as a collaborative initiative, not as some client-imposed condition, thereby improving quality and acceptance. The NVW is in line with the philosophy of the Working Conditions Act: on a case-by-case basis, an appropriate package of safety measures is compiled after inventorying the risks. The NVW mainly contains *'goal rules'* and minimises *'do rules'*. There is a preference for functional specification over technical; a safe workplace is required but its form is flexible. This is based on the premise that people should not blindly follow rules but rather think for themselves about the purpose, risks they face and strategies to manage the risks.

A train free period creates the safest conditions to work, but it is not always necessary because the situation on site, type of work and safety measures have impact. According to the NVW, a new way of securing workplace may be adopted if safety analysis deems it safe. A hierarchy of safety measures is provided as

---

[57] Risk number = number of fatal victims per 10,000 persons

indicated in Figure 70. It is determined what maintenance can be carried out where with which safety measures, without the need of a train free period. Controlled authorisation (BT), physical protection and guaranteed warning (GW) are measures that qualify with the condition that protective measures exist and safety is guaranteed.

Prevent / Eliminmate	Train free periods
	Controled admission
Restrict / Isolate	Physical shielding
	Demarcation
Collective protection	Garanteed warning
	Personal observation
Individual protection	Single person

Figure 70   Hierarchy of measures in the safe working standard framework (NVW)

The consequence of risk approach was that there was rapid growth in need for train free periods. The number of ad hoc applications for Small Incidental Withdrawals (KIOs) rose sharply. A structural Maintenance Schedule (OHR) was needed to increase predictability of train free periods and limit the administrative tasks. Because maintenance was about to make a structural claim to limited infra capacity, it became a serious competitor of train service. This was a new phenomenon because until that time maintenance used the 'leftovers' of unused capacity. In order to find a good balance, the OHR was developed and implemented incrementally. It started in 2005 and became nationwide in 2008. In a few years' time, the distribution of day and night work in small scale maintenance (KO) changed significantly, from 63/27% in 2005 to worst case of 31/69% in 2008 (Swier J. , 2008*). This increased costs of the OPC contracts but to a limited extent because the shift only influenced direct maintenance hours in train free periods.

In 2014, a new maintenance schedule was launched. The historic schedule had become a patchwork that no longer matched needs of train operators and asset management. The train planning requirements were tightened in response to the train-train collision at Amsterdam, as were the NVW regulations due to increase in number of near-collisions with track workers.

In order to better manage safety risks, double-track train free periods were needed. With the new OHR-2014 came five nights (Sunday/Monday night through Thursday/Friday night) and double-track train free periods spread across the country. Exceptions in the form of alternative routes were provided for select freight main routes and the NS night network. As illustrated in Figure 71,

214

personnel safety increased significantly. The risk number for the period 2006-2010 lowered to 0.6, well below the goal of 1.0. The drastic changes in policy, organisation and work processes had produced the desired effect.

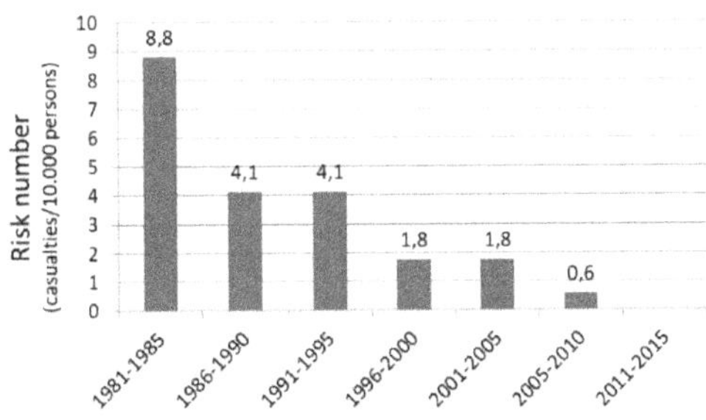

Figure 71   Risk number for track workers (1981-2015). Source: (W. Kruidhof, 2014-4)

7.6   Quality infrastructure: Safety

The highest priority in rail transport is the safety of train passengers, train staff and public in the railway environment. Safety has always been a priority for railway companies, and they fulfilled it through failsafe signalling, detailed regulations and strong hierarchical control based on a military organisation structure. The possibilities to manage safety proactively grew with the emergence of risk management. This development is described extensively in section 6.11.3. Risk management was initially deployed at the operational level of NS Railinfrabeheer in the nineties of the last century but it really took off with the introduction of Enterprise Risk Management (ERM) and the Safety Management System (VMS) in 2008 at ProRail. These provided the right conditions for broad implementation of risk management.

There are two methods for managing safety risks of existing rail infrastructure: maintenance and improvement projects. Sections 6.11.2 and 6.11.3 explain how safety risks are optimally and sustainably managed with maintenance. Maintenance concerns the improvement of processes, procedures, inspections, etc. If higher requirements are set, improvement projects can enable changes in asset functionality. To illustrate with example, this section describes three improvement projects that ProRail realised in recent years:

a.   ***Increasing safety on level crossings.*** In 1992, NS proposed a new level crossing policy to implement Rail-21 plans for level crossing safety (Swier J. e., 1992). For the first time, risk management technique was used. It involved identifying and quantifying level crossing risks, analysing control measures, calculating costs and prioritising action items. This was the start of various improvement programmes financed by national- and local authorities to significantly improve safety on level crossings:

- AKI safety bottleneck programme, 1999-2006 (approximately € 50 million annually);
- PVVO-old, 1999-2010 (First Framework Document on Rail Safety);
- PVVO new, 2005-2010 (Second Framework Document on Rail Safety, € 480 million);
- National Improvement Program Level Crossings (LVO), 2014-2018.

The programs were successful in reducing the number of victims by around 80%. In 1986, there were 68 persons who died in an accident and in 2015 this number reduced to 12 victims. The number of accidents also decreased: from 180 in 1986 to 29 in 2015. The following approach has led to success:

- ***Safer level crossings.*** The share of secured crossings has risen from around 50% in 1986 to around 80% in 2015. All Automatic Flash light Installation (AKI) are replaced with Automatic Half Beam Level crossings (AHOB), which are much safer. Their wooden beams are also replaced with aluminium beams and LED lighting. The strategies to influence road user behaviour for safety are being investigated. These include better recognition of level crossing by reducing distracting objects in the area and clear marking of (un)safe zones.

- ***Less level crossings.*** The number of crossings has reduced from 3,306 in 1991 to around 2,500 in 2015. In consultation with municipalities and provinces, the crossings are either being eliminated or replaced with a tunnel and no level crossings are permitted on new railway lines anymore.

- ***Safer use of level crossings.*** Action is taken against use of private level crossings for public use such as recreation or route shortcut. The public is alerted to the dangers of risky behaviour at level crossings and encouraged to comply with the rules. Cameras record violations and action is taken against offenders.

- ***Risk-based improvement.*** In 2012, a safety monitor was deployed to assesses all level crossings in road register on the basis of 20 characteristics, including train frequency, traffic intensity, number of tracks, close time and facilities for preventing slalom. The score for characteristics leads to risk assessment value between 2 to 16 points per crossing. The top 50 crossings are the risky crossings selected for improvements. This risk-based scale can also determine impact of new timetable or road situation change.

b. ***Improve visibility of signals.*** At the end of 2012, the project MOOS ('With the Eye on Signals') was launched to improve placement and visibility of signals on the basis of reports from train drivers and conductors. A number of these 'users' at NS were asked to indicate potential improvements on a specially-designed web forum. This resulted in about 3,000 cases in three years. A team of signalling- and safety- experts from NS Reizigers, ProRail AM and Project Management assessed each situation, remediation technique and implementation. Approximately half of the cases were handled by AM within regular maintenance. Small functional changes were put out to tender in clusters per region by Project Management. Major functionality changes required infrastructure projects. The results were reported back via the web forum. In the period 2012-2015, 66%of the reports were resolved (Rhee, 2016-nr 2).

c. ***Reduce Stop Showing Signal passages.*** A Stop Showing Signal (STS) passage is the unauthorised passing of a red signal. This can have major consequences: collision with another train, traffic on level crossing or railway worker, switch damage, derailment, or run into water in case of an open movable bridge. Despite the Automatic Train Control (ATB), an STS passage can take place because the ATB does not work at speeds below 40 km/hr. The ATB was not installed in railway yards because maximum speed was limited to 40 km/hr and ATB could not add value.

In order to reduce the total number of STS passages, the ATB-Improved-version (ATB Vv) was introduced in 2008 at 1,151 locations with risky signals. The trains were also made suitable for the system. ATB Vv was an addition to the existing ATB system and used three beacons for the signal, lying at 120-, 30- and 3-metre distance. If a train passes the first beacon too quickly, the equipment in the train intervenes and stops the train. The addition reduced STS number from 265 in 2003 to 173 in 2012.

In 2012, there was a train accident in Amsterdam because of STS passage and a passenger death happened for the first time after 24 years. The switch involved in the accident was not equipped with ATB Vv because location was not considered risky in normal use. With changes in track use, risk profile of the location had changed but this change was unnoticed. After this accident, more attention was paid to follow-up of modified track use to reduce the chance of red signals and improve departure procedure of trains. With the implementation of these measures, high punctuality of trains and new 2014-timetable, the number of STS passages dropped to 112 in 2014.

The construction of ATB Vv has cost around € 70 million so far. The number of STS passages are stabilising because most risky locations have been tackled. Further investment is expected to be of little use because it concerns signals that are never passed after a stop showing signal. In order to further reduce STS passages, ERTMS and warning system ORBIT developed by NS are planned to be implemented. The ORBIT system warns the driver if it approaches a red signal too quickly. It compares the position of the train and the signal based on GPS. By combining this information with the speed of the train, ORBIT calculates whether the train can stand still in time for the red signal. If this is not possible then the train driver receives two types of warning signals to apply brakes immediately.

Function change projects improve safety substantially but cost money. The infra manager develops policy and implementation plans, but the government, with role of asset owner, decides about implementation because the payer decides. Looking back, it can be concluded that the costs incurred have demonstrably led to a safer rail transport in the Netherlands.

7.7 Quality infrastructure: Durability & Environment

Sustainability[58] is a container concept for everything related to socially responsible living, environment, ecology and future-oriented thinking. The World Commission on Environment and Development of the United Nations uses the following definition in the report 'Our Common Future' (1987): *'Sustainable development is the development that meets the needs of the present without compromising the ability of future generations to meet their own needs.'*

There are many ways to enhance sustainability. The aim is to limit use of new raw material and dump or incinerate old ones. This can be realised through maintenance; reuse of products and parts as well as raw material recycling. Figure 72 illustrates the principle of the circular economy. The smaller the circle, the smaller is the loss of raw material and larger the contribution to sustainability.

Environment and sustainability have been explicit business objectives at ProRail for a long time. The innovation programmes such as noise hinderance were launched initially but soon the sustainability programme followed (ProRail, 2010-11*). The latter put sustainability as focus and established company policy which was visible in the behaviour of employees and company results. As of 2012, ProRail has emphasised continuous sustainability of rail network as a business

---

[58]ProRail AM uses the word 'Durability' in the context of RAMSHED business goals because 'S' is already used for 'Safety'.

objective. The sustainable travel, -life and -work approach was adopted in the Multi-Annual Plan for Sustainability 2013-2015 (Directie, 2013-6*).

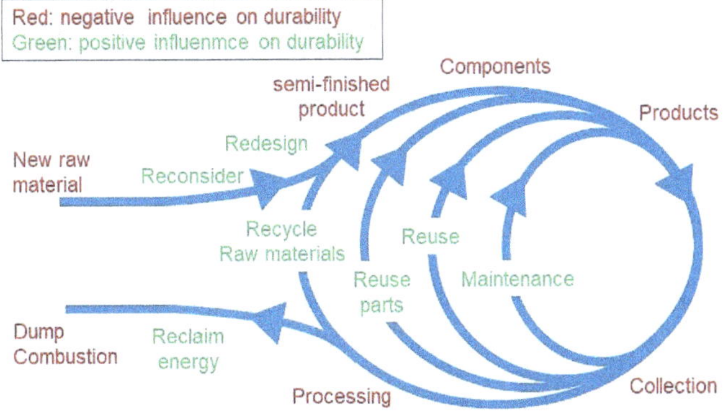

Figure 72   The circular economy

Sustainable travel involves reducing the CO_2 footprint of the rail sector. Sustainable living involves better integration of railway into the environment with fewer adverse effects of noise, vibrations and waste/raw material on people, flora and fauna in the immediate track environment. Sustainable work involves increasing transparency and involvement of employees in sustainability measures and dialogue with stakeholders. Some of the company-level sustainability measures are as follows:

- ProRail is the initiator of the CO_2 performance ladder (Duin, 2010-12*). Since December 1, 2009, it rewards climate-conscious producers. Contractors and suppliers receive a fictitious discount on their tender price when they offer demonstrably sustainable products (works, services and deliveries) and conduct sustainable business operations (Nieuwsbrief, 2010-12*).
- Research into use of owned land for sustainability objectives. For example, planting rapeseed along the track or installing solar panels.
- Research to increase catenary voltage from 1500V to 3000V by making adjustments to rail infrastructure and trains. For example, traction energy savings of 20% are feasible and 250,000 tonnes CO^2 annually.
- Sustainable lighting and heating of offices and stations by switching to energy-saving LED or fluorescent lighting as well as automatic switch off of lights when no work is done.

ProRail Asset Management focuses on making management and maintenance of existing rail infrastructure more sustainable. Examples are:

- Design requirements and -measures to keep noise hinderance within legal frameworks and standards through noise barriers, wheel rail conditioning, larger mass of the rail, etc.

- Fundamental research into vibrations and lowering of their environmental impact

- Re-use of raw material, parts and objects such as switches

- Replacing light bulbs in signals with LEDs, which are safer (provide more light for working), more durable (consume less energy, longer life time) and are more reliable (reduce failures).

- Make sustainability part of RAMS-LCC analysis. For each project of value more than € 500,000, an LCC analysis must be conducted for substantiation of renewal and investment decisions. In addition to the maintenance and renewal costs, LCC includes costs of infrastructure performance and its effect on society in terms of failures, travel time loss, driving time improvement and capacity increase. In 2015, a sustainability test was added to the LCC methodology. It estimates extent of prosperity and welfare generating capacity of our natural, produced, human and social resources, and determines impact of investment on prosperity. For more details, please refer section 6.11.1 on LCC management. In the PGO contract for maintenance, requirements for Safety and Durability have been added to the specifications for availability, reliability and maintainability. The durability specification optimises lifetime by controlling wear and tear. Its main structure is a specification tree with breakdown of objectives as indicated in Figure 73. This main structure has been elaborated in specification requirements with reference to regulations and standards.

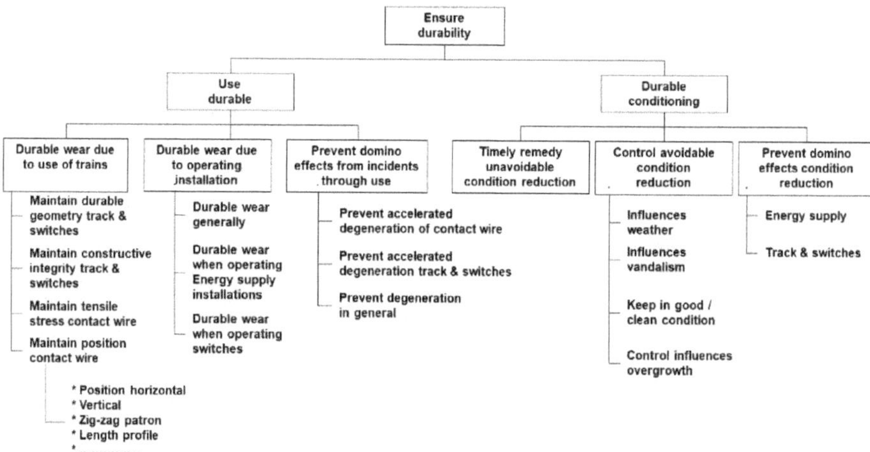

Figure 73   Durability specification tree of the PGO-contract

Rail is one of the most sustainable forms of transport. ProRail aims to improve sustainability by making it a natural part of all business processes not only in its own organisation but also in all other parties including train operators, authorities, suppliers, contractors and engineering firms.

7.8 Dashboards for managing rail infra performance

Measuring is knowing. Without goals and realisation measurements, we cannot manage effectively. A dashboard with performance targets provides focus and direction to steer the course to the goal.

At ProRail, the first dashboard was introduced in 2005 when a new railroad law came into effect and ProRail received management concession for rail infrastructure. The concession includes performance standards agreed to with the Ministry of Transport, Public Works and Water Management (V&W) and agreements for financing. Key Performance Indicators (KPIs) were set with limit values, which were re-established annually. The KPIs are SMART, i.e., Specific, Measurable, Ambitious, Realistic and Time-bound. The minister will receive an overview of progress every quarter. At the time, core performance was in top KPIs and in one or more Further Performance Indicators (NPIs). The core performance in the management plan is supplemented by two internal KPIs for staff and innovation. The whole forms a dashboard (ProRail, 2005*) indicated in Figure 74 with KPIs, NPIs and control limits.

KPI/NPI	Dashboard Items	Target value (internal regulation limit 1))	Internal regulation limit 2	Threshold value 2005 (Agreement Ministry of Transport)
1	**KPI Availability**			
1.1	NPI-Unplanned non-available (TAO (#) *(FHT (hours))	14.200*	[illegible]	N/A 2005
1.2	NPI Planned non-available (TVP (#))	344	[illegible]	N/A 2005
1.3	NPI Weighted unplanned non-available (TAO (#) *(FHT (hours)*BVW)	In development		N/A 2005
2	**KPI Transfer**			
2.1	NPI Appreciation social safety (daytime)	84%	78%	76%
2.2	NPI Appreciation social safety (night-time)	45%	[illegible]	[illegible]
2.3	NIP Appreciation cleanliness	48%	47%	47%
3	**KPI Adjustment**			
3.1	NPI Information provision in accordance with agreements	98%	[illegible]	[illegible]
3.2	NPI Adjustment in accordance with agreements	92%	[illegible]	[illegible]
3.3	NPI number of irregularities in route setting	1.075	[illegible]	N/A 2005
4	**KPI Use**			
4.1	NPI Successful appeals Netherlands Competion Authority (NMa)	40%	[illegible]	N/A 2005
5	**KPI Safety & Environment**			
5.1	NPI System safety	In development		N/A 2005
5.2	NPI Work safety	In development		N/A 2005
6	**KPI Finance**			
6.1	NPI Overhead costs	15.0%	16.3%	N/A 2005
6.2	NPI Costs per train km (costs including capital costs)	€ 8.23	€ [illegible]	N/A 2005
7	**KPI Personnel (internal KPI)**			
7.1	NPI Absenteeism due to sickness	5%	5.80%	N/A 2005
7.2	NPI RGB appraisals held (planning and evaluation meetings)	90%	75%	N/A 2005
7.3	NPI Employee satisfaction	73%	[illegible]	N/A 2005
8	**KPI Innovation (internal KPI)**			
8.1	NPI Innovation	In development		N/A 2005
	The following NPIs are information items for the Board of Directors**			
1.1.1	NPI Availability due to unplanned withdrawal (TAOs (#))	Information item		N/A 2005
1.1.2	NPI Average functional repair time for a TAO (FHT (hours))	Information item		N/A 2005
2.3.1	NPI Cleanliness (objective measurement)	Information item		N/A 2005

Figure 74   Dashboard and control limits (2005)

The introduction of the top KPIs was an important step in the professionalisation of ProRail and the 2005 dashboard was the initial step. For every NPI, a plan was prepared with process agreements about management, expansion and change. The aim was to have the dashboard complete and operational in 2008 to fulfil precondition to switch to output steering by government. The dashboard was developed such that KPIs are limited and feasible for implementation. With improvements in information provision, the dashboard was developed further and made online via RailFocus as indicated in Figure 75. Many KPIs and NPIs remained the same, few changed and new ones joined. For example, the complex KPI Availability changed into three less complex NPIs: number of TAOs, function recovery time and number of delayed trains. Also a KPI was added for punctuality and passenger impact.

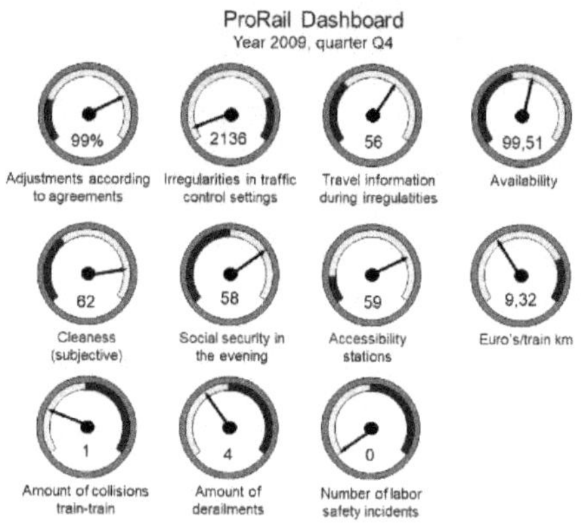

Figure 75   Dashboard in railFocus

The presentation of the top KPI/NPI dashboard changed from Railfocus to Qlikview, a Business Intelligence (BI) instrument that easily convers data into information. With the arrival of Qlikview, the reporting and presentation options expanded considerably. For example, for the KPI Punctuality, a dashboard was provided with extensive reports for specific target groups and various levels of detail.

The dashboard with top KPIs and NPIs is the tip of a dashboard pyramid. Every business unit has (or get) its own departmental dashboard with technical and process-related KPIs. All ProRail dashboards form a coherent structure with top KPIs as the final piece. An example of this is the specification and control triangle used by ProRail AM and described in section 6.8. The triangle indicates requirements for controlled management and realisation of RAMS goals through risk analysis, rejection standards, condition reports, production plans, task plans, work plans and the execution. For all activities in the realisation process, KPIs either exist or are established to manage progress and cohesion. It forms the relationship between strategy, planning, and operation, and as well as performances and required activities to realise them.

The dashboards continue to develop. Around 2012, they came under the Business Intelligence Competency Centre (BICC), a team that deals with all ProRail-wide BI issues from 'analysis' to 'management'. Business Intelligence is the collection and structuring of business data to gain information and managing processes. The four product groups under BICC are as follows:

- SpoorKompas - analytical BI environment of ProRail
- SpoorRadar - operational BI environment of ProRail
- SpoorTuin - explorative ad-hoc BI environment of ProRail
- BICC legacy systems - predecessors of the current BI environments

For example, BICC supervises the Spoordata.NL programme that makes available all static- and dynamic information about assets to the industry through a portal. An example of a project it made feasible was a reporting tool on *The state of the infrastructure'*. A new reporting tool had to be created because no one was satisfied with the old one with which ProRail reported every four years to the government about the state of the infrastructure. A satisfactory new tool became possible after the introduction of Spoordata.NL. The Network Condition Report (NCR) developed by the Swiss Infra Manager (SBB0 inspired ProRail. The NCR provides a dashboard for all systems to monitor four performances - availability, remaining lifetime, safety and technical condition - that give good insight into state of infrastructure even for someone who is not a technical expert. The method also provides structure and overview to determine availability and need of information for optimal and sustainable management of rail infrastructure performance at all levels. The development of such a reporting tool is only possible when very different asset databases can be linked to each other, and the BICC with Spoordata.NL takes care of that.

Resume

Rail infrastructure is a means of production. It costs money and has to function. Only then a train 0perators earn money with rail transport. The service provided by rail infrastructure manager is availability of network capabilities with certain asset functionality and RAMS quality. Performance is the goal and money the means to realise it.

The capability and functionality of rail infrastructure is determined in the investment phase. With use and aging, the infrastructure wears out and increases chance of inadequate network capability and functionality. The quality is controlled through a dynamic maintenance and renewal process during the 24/7 exploitation phase to manage availability, reliability, maintainability and railway safety (RAMS). This process, initially known as management of Maintenance & Renewal, is now often called Asset Management.

The RAMS performance of infrastructure directly influences the performance of rail transport, i.e., the interests of passengers and shippers. The infrastructure manager is also responsible for performance that relates to personnel safety, environment and durability. These are goals that result from social responsibility and specific legislation. Together with the RAMS parameters, they form the acronym RAMSHED.

For each performance targets, a specific process for realisation as well as responsible manager and specialists are required. The processes need and influence each other. To realise them they must be Specific, Measurable, Ambitious, Realistic and Time-related (SMART), an important task of the strategy department in the organisation. The optimal and sustainable realisation of goals involves planning and consideration for conditions and circumstances. It involves management of process, techniques, instruments, analysis and interpretation of a lot of information.

The performance targets are not achieved at the reactive top level but at the pro-active level where technical quality and failure modes & causes are controlled with maintenance and renewal activities. Both levels are necessary to manage performance optimally and sustainably over the entire life cycle. Therefore, coherent dashboards at all management levels are indispensable for connecting people at different management levels who need each other to set goals and achieve them.

With this discussion, we have completed the chapter on performance. The next chapter provides insight into all aspects that have to do with the costs of the assets and the way in which they have developed at ProRail.

8 Costs

The model for asset management shows that performance and costs are managed by managing risks with activities, under the constraints of the conditions that affect them. This chapter provides insight into the development of management and control of costs (at ProRail) and the factors that influence them.

Introduction

After the separation of trains and track as well as the outsourcing of maintenance, the focus of infrastructure management had to shift from formations and budgets to performance and costs in the late nineties. A necessary condition was set up of a new financial system in SAP in which all costs are accounted for by business unit, cost type and asset. The short-term and long-term cash flow planning, cost standards, cost calculations, etc. are also required to manage and control expenses. The chapter deals with the development and design of these instruments. It starts with an overview of where the money comes from and where it is spent. It concludes with an overview of the development of ProRail's total expenses and maintenance costs in particular.

8.1 Activities, financing and expenses

ProRail distinguishes three types of activities:
- Maintain function, which covers operations, management, maintenance and renewal of the existing rail infrastructure;
- Change of function, which covers modification of existing infrastructure; and
- Extension function, which covers creation of new infrastructure.

ProRail manages three networks:
- Mixed main rail network;
- Freight line Betuwe route; and
- High Speed Line South (HSL Z).

It is noted that the Betuwe route was managed by Keyrail until 2015 but is now part of the main rail network. For HSL South, ProRail does contract management and facilitates operations.

ProRail is funded from three sources:

- Infrastructure fund of the Ministry of Infrastructure and the Environment (I&M);
- User charge for the mixed network, Betuwe route and HSL South; and
- Work commissioned by local authorities: provinces and municipalities.

Figure 76 illustrates the activities, networks, funding sources and budgets in 2015.

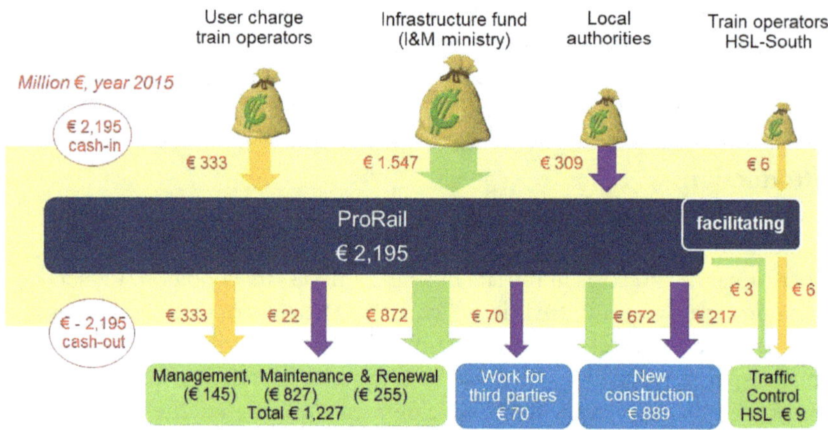

Figure 76   Overview of activities and their funding sources (Source: Evert Hetebrij)

ProRail allocates all costs by business unit, cost type and route infra cluster. Every business unit is responsible for its own finances. The cost types are distinguished as: small-scale maintenance (KO), large-scale maintenance (GO), stations, management, exploration & innovation, depreciation, net equipment costs and financing costs. The route infra clusters comprise nine systems[59] that create a rail network divided into about 300 geocodes. The allocation to geocodes is a problem not for projects but for maintenance because maintenance costs are invoiced per contract per month. In order to account for KO contract costs, ProRail uses fixed percentages per geocode.

For more information on costs by system, please refer Figure 81 at page 241 for maintenance costs and Figure 85 at page 248 for investment / depreciation costs. The cost overview in Figure 77 at page 231 provides information about all costs and revenues of ProRail in a year.

---

[59]Substructure, Track & Switches, Bridges & Tunnels, Energy supply, Signalling, Level crossings, Communication, Operation (traffic control), Stations.

8.2 Development of the cost insights

In 1995, the employees of Railinfrabeheer experienced a major change in having to manage costs instead of formations and budgets. They had managed formation, work hours and budgets, but costs were responsibility of the finance department. An initial challenge was fair allocation of regional maintenance budgets to contract areas. A standard cost model was developed for this, based on quantities, asset parameters and weighing factors. The principle of the model became the starting point of an extensive cost matrix, which had maintenance and management costs broken down to the level of infra elements on the basis of quantities and key costs.

Soon after the outsourcing of maintenance, there was need to build knowledge about the influence of cost drivers, such as utilisation, ratio of day/night work, and ineffective working time, not only for maintenance & renewal (M&R) but also for new construction, especially the HSL South and Betuweroute. To meet this demand, maintenance costs were modelled using new insights and information from the European benchmark study LICB started in 1996. The model was used for prognosis of maintenance costs of new and existing lines. It was later extended to model renewal costs and, from 2010 onwards, user charge to determine variability and marginality of the M&R costs.

Modelling is a useful tool but best cost insights came from realisation and calculation. SAP provided knowledge about realisation costs. Cost calculation knowledge was mainly concentrated with the AKI[60], a staff group with experts from contracts, tendering, purchasing, costs and performance measurement. To share this knowledge, a database, Rail Case Base (RCB), was set up with cost indicators. The RCB, the use of which is natural today, created conditions for implementation of Life Cycle Management (Section 6.11.1) and development of a transparent and reliable multi-year renewal plan (MVP).

This chapter deals with the instruments developed to forecast and plan the M&R costs. The following instruments an developments are described more in detail:
1. Norm cost model for maintenance in OPC contracts.
2. Cost matrix maintenance and management costs.
3. Cost data base: Rail Case Base.
4. Unlocking cost information in SAP through RailFocus.
5. Long Term Plan Function Enforcement.
6. Cost driver-model for maintenance and management costs.
7. Modelling the variability of renewal costs.
8. Cost development ProRail.
9. Cost development maintenance costs.

---

[60] AKI was called 'Procurement' from 2014 onwards.

8.2.1　**Norm cost model for maintenance in OPC contracts**

This model was developed in 1997/1998 to attribute the annual maintenance budget to 37 OPC maintenance contracts and four regions (Swier J. , 1998*). The principle of the model is based on a proportional distribution of available budget per system over the contract area. The distribution is based on quantities and impact factors per subsystem. The factors are diverse, based on experience and collected from internal and external sources.

The standard costs per system and contract were calculated through the following steps:

> ➢ Total available budget was divided into budget factors (% distribution) among the systems based on past experiences.
> ➢ System budgets were allocated to sub-systems based on quantities and chosen weight factors by experiential experts.
> ➢ The budget per sub-system was divided proportionate among the 37 OPC contracts based on the quantities per sub-system.
> ➢ The system budget for track and switches was corrected with an extra weight factor for differences in utilisation.

With the current insights, other choices would have been made for budget- and weight factors, but at the time, this model included input from many people and provided a transparent method. With proportionally distribution of the nation-wide network budget, any increase in budget of one sub-system implied an equal reduction in budget of another sub-system(s).

8.2.2　**Cost matrix maintenance & management**

The standard cost model KO provided a matrix of cost indicators per subsystem and per OPC contract. It provided the total the total spent budget in a year. The cost matrix for management & maintenance went a step further in detail with framework and content development best described as *'as soon as new insights arose, they were incorporated in the matrix'*. Sources were the OPC norm cost model, TESI list, policy documents, MVA administration, AKI cost information, UIC benchmark information, etc.

The initial cost matrix was an evolving list of available cost information and knowledge (Swier J. , 2002*). It was an Excel worksheet. The vertical axis listed more than 150 subsystems and system types covering the entire rail system. The horizontal axis provided quantity, lifetime and costs for construction, renewal, maintenance, management, and ratio of maintenance costs to renewal costs.

The reliability of the matrix was secured by means of a square count: all the added costs per (sub) system - a multiplication of quantities and cost values - had to correspond with the known realised costs. The matrix forms a coherent system whereby a higher cost figure for one system always had to be compensated with a lower cost figure for another system. In case of disagreement between system experts, there was discussion, analysis and, where necessary, adjustment. In this way, errors were limited and there was a shared concern for costs and indicators.

The extensive cost matrix generated knowledge and cooperation but could not be managed well because of its person bound and evolving nature. It was succeeded by a focussed version with quantities and maintenance of cost indicators for approximately 75 subsystems and system types issued annually by AKI (AKI, 2011*). The list is available on the website of the Rail Case Base (RCB) under the tab 'Tools'.

8.2.3   Cost data base: Rail Case Base (RCB)

Why a cost database? The focus of employees at Railinfrabeheer was slowly but surely widening from budgets to infrastructure costs. As a result, there was a growing demand for cost information mainly focused on new construction- and renewal projects. This knowledge was concentrated with a small group of experts; strongly person- and workplace-related; and difficult to maintain and access. To overcome this problem, a database called the Rail Case Base (RCB), was developed with cost indicators. It was made accessible to all ProRail employees accredited for its use.

How the RCB was developed and structured? AKI (now known as: Procurement) developed the design and structure of RCB in 2004 and manages it since. The RCB gradually evolved into a complete cost database with clear structure. In principle, each cost indicator has its own Excel worksheet. All worksheets are stored in a database such that information can be searched quickly and in a structured manner. Users can consult the RCB via an intranet environment. Search uses the following four options:

- Use of search engine (free search terms).
- Feature layer: track system, signalling system, energy system, etc.
- Type of indicator: generic, unique, maintenance, renewal, etc.
- Combination of above-mentioned options.

The cost figures have universal structure: Context | Unit | Price. The context provides the circumstances for which the cost indicator applies such as execution method, material, decommissioning, etc. The unit is the quantity for indicators such as kilometers, meters, pieces, etc. The price is the result of cost calculation related to context and units. All cost indicators have a price level. The RCB has a chapter 'Tools', which covers cost-related topics such as indices, time norms, key rates, engineering costs, etc.

The cost indicators are indexed every five years after calculation on the basis of composite CBS figures. The calculation is critically assessed and adjusted where necessary. If the context of an indicator changes, the justification or entire calculation is adjusted. The employees keen to use the RCB undergo a half-day training, which covers theory, design and use of cost indicators and the RCB.

What's in the RCB? The RCB contains cost indicators including technical and contextual information. It covers new construction, maintenance and renewal, and all processes and phases in the life cycle: project development, investment requests, tendering, planning, life cycle analysis, management, etc.

The cost indicators in the RCB are of two types: generic and unique. The generics are based on pre-calculation based on average values and the circumstances. The unique indicators are available for specific realised projects. The starting point for the cost indicators is the economic value; the influence of market forces has thus been removed.

The key figures can also have different levels of detail. For example, key figures with a low level of detail can be applied in plan studies, and that with a high level of detail in budgets and preliminary calculations of contracts. There are cost indicators for activities in small-scale maintenance and the Fictive Infrastructure Units (FIE) model tests maintenance offers for small-scale maintenance based on circumstances such as track load and operational possibilities.

8.2.4   Unlocking cost information in SAP through RailFocus

The Business Intelligence application RailFocus was installed in 2006 to improve accessibility of the cost information in SAP. It collects information from disparate data sources on one screen and exports it to Excel. It provides access to all underlying costs and revenues by simple click on an amount in the matrix of the overview screen.

Figure 77 illustrates the overview screen of 2013, with allocation of EUR1.494 billion to all activities on the horizontal axis as well as business units and systems on the vertical axis. This allows detailed cost analysis with data from SAP. For example, the level of detail in small-scale maintenance is very limited because it is invoiced monthly as per total contract volume without any details.

The model for asset management shows that performance and costs are managed by managing risks with activities, given the conditions that affect them. This chapter provides insight into the way in which the management and control of the costs has developed at ProRail and what influences it.

Landelijk

2013 Kw artaal 1 t/m 4, bedragen zijn absoluut (Euro)

	Opbrengsten Totaal	Gebruikers Vergoeding	Kosten Overige Opbrengsten	Bijzondere Opbrengsten	Totaal	KO	GO BRV	Transfer	BEH	Verkenning &Innovatie	Afschr.	Netto Apparaat	Finan. kosten
Totaal ProRail	1.494.931.086	263.203.445	-848.840.829	-382.886.813	1.656.894.081	266.184.635	148.618.400	70.490.698	164.037.573	16.246.800	657.498.228	316.358.066	17.459.682
Totaal Operatie	-1.082.241.204		-699.628.718	-382.612.485	22.723.651						-418.373	22.097.303	1.044.722
Directie & Staf	-1.062.241.204		-699.628.718	-382.612.485	22.723.651						-418.373	22.097.303	1.044.722
Totaal AM	-12.333.937		-12.333.937		1.219.673.787	266.209.273	75.615.502	70.490.698	84.957.422	6.343.230	657.916.601	67.118.390	22.640
Baan					495.905.198	171.022.137	48.296.226	1.848.964	7.615.331	31.623	267.329.025	-249.614	11.497
Spoor													
Wissel													
Overig													
Kunstwerken					101.942.585	11.014.593	4.631.479	-6.848	731.564	1.460	85.605.935	-48.164	12.566
Energievoorziening					126.031.142	23.415.950	3.715.945	54.481	30.043.190	4.887	69.000.832	-204.143	
Beveiliging					108.131.179	33.651.158	5.187.100	13.935	589.810	1.976	68.682.478	4.722	
Overwegen					27.662.355	5.396.470	586.141	-25.752	68.707		21.636.474	1.737	-1.422
Posten					25.180.828	194.746	286.611		117.043	361	24.736.260	-156.192	
Telecommunicatie					56.069.286	5.962.531	1.099.392	-2.936	204.761	1.085	50.804.309	144	
Stationscomplex					158.063.875	720.239	9.813.729	68.778.854	8.805.195	692	70.121.288	-176.121	
Overig AM	-12.333.937		-12.333.937		116.687.320	13.831.451	1.996.879	-170.000	36.781.822	6.301.146		57.946.022	
Projecten	-30.679.445		-30.679.445		94.790.767	810.561	73.497.222		4.476.199	2.498.153		6.781.533	6.726.999
Verkeersleiding	-1.548.609		-1.548.609		75.514.801	17.700	26.551		460.601			74.482.949	525.000
Vervoer en Dienstregeling	-278.648.285	-263.203.445	-15.444.840		21.553.946	147.000	39.435		572.644	3.816.404		16.978.462	
ICT Services	-10.533.930		-10.533.930		120.898.193		-914.935		66.397.641	1.589.013		53.823.893	2.580
Totaal RvB & Staven	-78.945.677		-78.671.349	-274.328	101.738.967		352.624		7.173.066			85.075.537	9.137.741
RvB & Staven	-39.268.856		-39.268.856		56.176.047		187.469		7.444.464			47.544.114	
FENS	-75.196		-75.195		-695.944		111.050					-806.994	
Human Resource Management					8.250.814							8.250.814	
Facilitaire Zaken	-1.414.125		-1.414.125		9.427.996		54.105					9.373.891	
Communicatie	-10.000		-10.000		4.339.300							4.339.300	
Bedrijfsstrategie	-7.119		-7.119		2.893.860							2.893.860	
Corp. finance & Control	-38.170.382		-37.896.054	-274.328	21.293.024						-271.399	12.426.682	9.137.741
Audits					1.053.869							1.053.869	

Figure 77   Overview of all costs and revenues in RailFocus

8.2.5   Long Term Plan Function Enforcement (LT cash flow)

Why LTP FH?

The government finances the maintenance and renewal of rail infrastructure. For this purpose, it prepares financial budget of ten years. The budget is adjusted annually on Prince's Day (budget day in the Netherlands). The Management Plan provides the financial range for 'function enforcement' (FH), which are expected costs for maintenance and one-to-one renewals. For substantiation, ProRail has developed a Long-Term Plan Function Enforcement (LTP FH). A difference between financial series in the government budget and the ProRail management plan indicates potential problem and is to be solved together. A reliable LTP FH is indispensable for discussion and opinion formation.

How is the LTP FH developed? Around 2003, a need was identified to prepare an integrated infrastructure M&R plan. This was a consequence of the project *'Opening balance ProRail'* which mapped the financial implications of the new Railways Act. A long-term plan was required for consideration of the Mobility policy memorandum from the Ministry of Transport, Public Works and Water Management in the Lower House.

In the beginning of 2004, a project group started to prepare the Long-Term Renewal Plan (MVP) for entire rail infrastructure. Initially, a 'QuickScan' was created on the basis of the depreciation database and then started with the analysis for the first MVP. ProRail's system experts were involved in the realisation of the plan from the beginning because they were to become responsible for quality and management of the LTP-series.

In the end of 2004, ProRail introduced the first MVP 2005-2025 (Swier J. e., 2004*). It included a cash flow plan and calculation of the current renewal value. Detail and background information were included in a separate report (J.Swier, 2004-12*). The MVP 2004 was made up of 17 partial plans divided over nine systems. The robustness of cash flows was tested. It depended on the quality of information and organisation, and was assessed on the basis of the 'push-button content' of the cash flows. A consideration was made for reliability of the information about building years, lifespan and renewal year, and quality of cost indicators. Uncertainties were taken into account in technology development, utilisation intensity, unforeseen project risks and extra efficiency gains. The robustness was expressed in a bandwidth and reached + 10% to − 20%.

The quality of the MVP 2004 was assessed at the time by Booz Allen Hamilton (BAH). The assessment indicated that the plan was complete, provided good insight but estimated on the high side because of missing details, high cost figures and insufficient integration and optimisation of the sub-plans. In 2005, BAH conducted an audit of the Management Plan 2005. There were 10 recommendations, two of which related to the MVP. They involved improving robustness of the long-term budget and updating modelling information.

By the end of 2008, there were various reasons to update the MVP 2004: there was a financial gap between plan and realisation, ownership among the managers of the MVP series was insufficient, and the government wanted to update the series and gain insight into the improvements achieved following the recommendations in the BAH audit in 2005

During updates, another project organisation was added and the scope was extended to a cash flow plan for the entire function enforcement: KO, GO, management and renewal of rail infrastructure, including ICTS computer infrastructure. In mid-2009, the final report was available (Schouten, 2009*) with details and background information in an appendix, and results presented to members of the AM management team (MT AM). The name of the MVP 2004 was changed to Long-Term Plan Function Enforcement 2009 (LTP FH), which provided realised cost development over the period 1995-2009 and forecast for the period 2010-2030.

The LTP 2009 provides an up-to-date, was well-founded, transparent, complete and gave a reliable insight into the financing requirement, but the assurance of the LTP FH process should receive more management attention. There were demonstrable improvements in the recommendations of BAH:

- The Material & Fixed Assets (MVA) administration was completely redesigned with quantities directly from SAP and cost indicators based on actual renewal value and selected depreciation periods in relation to the theoretical technical lifetime. Management was well assured in the process.

- The most important cost drivers of KO, GO and Maintenance were modelled. The management was well anchored in a group known as SPA-office (now part of Finance).
- ICT and information management were reorganised with strong organisation, new object structure, management information per line, accessibility and higher quality data, etc.
- The three defining MVP series were modelled directly from SAP object registration: track, switches as well as bridges & tunnels. The series were accessible through an application in Webfocus. The management was regulated but still insufficiently anchored.

The management and development of the LTP FH is better structured after 2009 in the business unit Architecture & Technology. The system managers behaved as owners of their series and an LT-planner was appointed in the group Planning & Programming to conduct annual consolidation on all (sub) system series. The group had overview to assess series quality. Where possible, the series were modelled directly from the asset database. The government periodically engaged independent external expert to assess series quality.

The most recent audit was in 2015 by PwC (PwC, 2015*). It concluded that the system was logical, series were reliable and slightly too high, there was no backlog in maintenance, processes could be better defined, and proposals were needed to reduce tension between government's M&R budgeting of and ProRail's LTP FH.

Content LTP FH plan and realisation. The LTP FH comprises long-term cash flow planning for management, maintenance and renewal of nine systems: rail & switches, substructure, level crossing, bridges & tunnels, signalling, energy supply, stations, traffic control equipment and telecom. The renewal costs are modelled on the basis of building or renewal year, theoretical technical lifetime in the asset database and cost indicators from the Rail Case Base (RCB). For systems with little reliable information, personal expertise is used to estimate renewal costs. Where necessary, renewal series supplied by project organisation such as ERTMS are used.
References from the MVA are composed as a test. They provide financial LTP prognosis from the perspective of finances. A difference with cash flow in the LTP FH prognosis can always be explained by difference analysis of the input. Incidentally, an MVA series is also used in the LTP FH if there is insufficient information in the asset database to model a series.

Figure 78 illustrates structure of the LTP FH 2009. The renewal plan comprises 82 sub-plans, clustered into 25 renewal plans divided over eight rail systems. The stations have their own plan and series. On the basis of best- and worst- case scenarios, a bandwidth of -20%/+15% was established to account for uncertainties about lifetime extension, cost changes and program realisation.

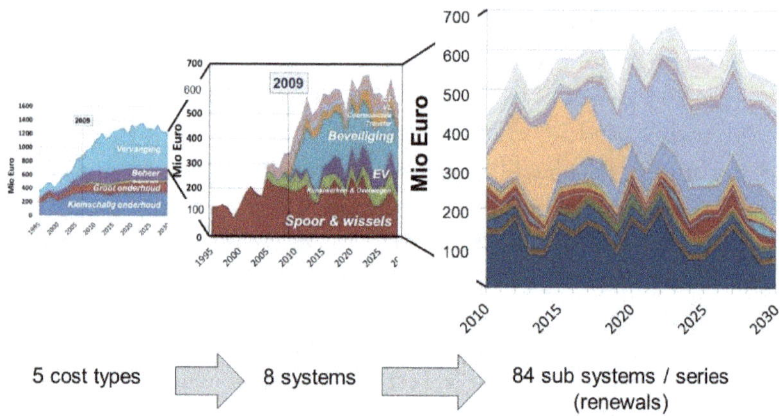

Figure 78   Long term cash flow plan 2009 and structure of renewal series

The renewal series are modelled from the asset base as much as possible. The M&R and management series are based on analysis of the realised contract costs for OPC / PGO contracts and the related mutants, and an inventory of the expected mutants in the future with a cost forecast. The influence of mutants is based on the business model, experiences from realisation and specific calculations.

The Management costs were (also known as 'Steward' costs), for the first time, separated around 2000 and then expanded to the current level. The management cost forecast is fairly stable from 2009 onwards. It comprises cost of the following organisations: AM Management, Financial Management (PcP), Traffic Control, ICT Traffic Management, ICT Communication, IT Generic and costs to connect to the TenneT electrical network.

The LTP is based on average theoretical renewals and expected mutants. The actual renewals for the short term are in the production plan (PP) and based on actual technical requirements. They often show a wide spread compared to the average theoretical need, both downwards and upwards. There are, therefore, substantial differences between the LTP and PP in the level of detail, especially for rail and switches, but the differences can be managed at the total cash flow level.

In the next phase, Projects makes an implementation plan for production. This can lead to adjustment of budget planning because of problems such as

234

inadequate production capacity or lack of train free periods (preventing planned projects in production plan from continuing).

Apart from the need to coordinate cash flow in Management and LT plan, it is necessary to account for the connection of LTP FH to the production and execution plans. One complicating factor is the overflow from planned production to the subsequent year, through which expenditure of a released annual budget is spread over two years. A difficult-to-manage risk is the under-spending due to godsend in tenders, too high estimates in production plan or inadequate implementation capacity. Government funding does not allow big financial fluctuations in following years.

8.2.6   Cost driver-model for maintenance & management costs[61]

In 1996, a benchmark study was initiated by the Union Internationale des Chemins de fer (UIC) to compare the costs of M&R and new construction projects across European countries. The study started with six companies and eventually covered 16 European railway companies. It also received contributions from railway companies in East Asia and North America. It concluded in 2002 and was structurally secured in the Lasting Infrastructure Cost Benchmark (LICB).

From the beginning, ProRail (then: NS Railinfrabeheer) was involved in the study. There was an interesting voyage of discovery in the uncertain time immediately after the separation of transport and infrastructure, and the privatisation of engineering and maintenance. These radical organisational changes stimulated implementation of the UIC benchmark study results because ProRail confronted new challenges and questions. The new knowledge and insights of the benchmark study provided useful answers. A few examples of the questions are as follows:

- Trace manager was confronted with cost claims from a maintenance contractor because about 20% more trains used a line. Further, more maintenance teams were forced to move to the night. The trace managers wanted to gain insight into the relationship between costs and utilisation, and the shift from day to night work.

- The project manager for construction of HSL South needed a forecast for maintenance and renewal costs of the new line. The forecast had to be flexible in design to account for different scenarios.

- The project management of the Betuwe route required a well-founded cost forecast for maintenance and renewal over a period of 25 years after commissioning. This was necessary for development of an effective

---

[61] This issue was previously published in an article in the *Railway Gazette International* (Swier J. , 2004*). The article has since been expanded with new information about renovation cost modelling and variability of maintenance and renewal costs.

payment and penalty regime, calculation of the financial effects of utilisation scenarios, sensitivity analyses for user fee and a long-term budget planning.

- Under the influence of European regulations, user fee was introduced in 2000. The fee could not exceed variable costs and was utilisation dependent. The management of ProRail wanted to gain insight into the relationship between costs and utilisation, distribution of fixed/variable costs and the risk level.

With the benchmark study, Railinfrabeheer not only gained insight into cost position of the Netherlands compared to European colleagues but also received detailed documentation regarding costs, complexity, use and cost drivers from different countries facing different circumstances. This turned out to be a valuable source of information to answer questions within the organisation.

Benchmark M&R costs. The UIC benchmark working group collected and analysed large amount of cost data, covering not only European companies but also companies from the United States, Hong Kong and Japan. It soon became clear that costs varied greatly across companies and according to circumstances. The main causes of the differences were:

- Purchasing power;
- Wage costs;
- Switch density;
- Degree of electrification;
- Quantity of single track[62];
- Utilisation intensity.

To make the M&R costs of participating European countries comparable, a method was developed to harmonise the original cost data step-by-step with correction factors accounting for differences in conditions and circumstances as per a chosen reference situation. The correction factors came from detailed analysis of the available cost data. The result was a life cycle cost (LCC) benchmark limited to annual operating costs required for rail infrastructure M&R. It included maintenance, renewal and organisation (overhead) costs, both from the organization and contractors. The benchmark results were anonymised and presented as a histogram with cost column for each participating country, see Figure 79 (ProRail = H). The figure indicates substantial cost differences across European countries and even larger differences across the three continents. The costs in the United States are about 20% of those in the Netherlands and those in East Asia are about 100-200% higher.

---

[62] Later, it turned out that this cost difference was negligibly small, measured in costs per km / main track. This influence has since been scrapped as a cost driver.

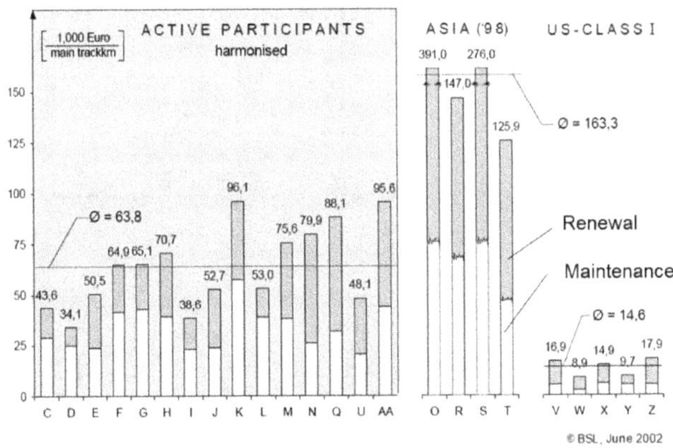

Figure 79   Result of the first UIC study on rail infrastructure cost benchmark (UIC, 2002)*

In the first benchmark study, life cycle costs were presented only as per kilometer of main track. Later, this figure was extended to three perspectives, each with its own benchmark unit:

- infra manager: LCC / km main track
- train operators: LCC / train km
- commercial perspective: LCC / transport unit[63]

The differences in LCC/km main track largely disappear when Life Cycle Costs were compared from the perspective of train operators, i.e. the LCC/train km. From the commercial perspective (LCC/Transport Unit), however, infrastructure costs in both East Asia and North America are lower than those in Europe. The large cost differences among the three continents were surprising and eventually attributed to differences in circumstances.

Costs, utilisation and cost drivers. The benchmark study yielded a wealth of knowledge and new insights. A remarkable insight emerged when the same LCC costs per km main track were plotted against both the realised train-km and the gross tonne-km, illustrated in Figure 80. The graph with train kilometers shows an approximate directly proportional relationship, with the three continents clearly distinguished and in succession. The graph with gross tonne kilometers illustrates a very different picture with the three continents still recognised as groups, but in completely different relative positions when compared to the former graph.

---

[63] Transport Unit = TU. One TU = one passenger km and one net tonne km for freight. Because they share a common unit, the commercial products of passengers and freight can be added for a cumulative total.

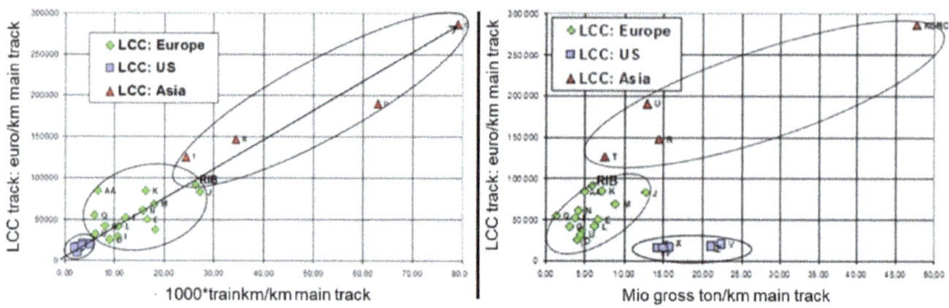

Figure 80   Same LCC data plotted per train kilometer (Left) and tonne-kilometer (Right)

Company visits, made for collecting benchmark information, had made it clear that there are more similarities than differences across the continents from a technical asset point of view. The rail systems comprising rail, switches, signals, bridges, overhead lines, etc. and the experience of technical staff were similar. It was concluded that there were no fundamental differences in rail technology to explain the large cost differences. Table 4 was prepared after analysis of rail systems and provided the required clarity in this matter.

Table 4   Difference in rail transport systems

	US	Europe	East Asia
Transport type	Freight	Mix	Mix
Transport distance	Long	Short/Middle	Short/Middle
Train intensity	1-10 per day	2-16 per hour	2-24 per hour
Punctuality	Hours per day	85% <3 min.	98% <3 min
Train length	>2.500 m	50-350 m	50-350 m
Train weight	>7000 tonne	100-700 tonne	100-700 tonne
Switch density	<0,3 /km	1 per km	1 per km
Signal distance	>5.000 m	1.000 m	500 m
Energy supply	Diesel	Electric	Electric
Work period	Day	Day/Night	Day/Night
Train-free periods	Long	Short	Short

The US mainly has very long, heavy, slow-moving diesel freight trains over long distances. There are few trains every day. These deliver low train-kilometers but very high gross tonne-kilometers. The infrastructure is simple with relatively few switches, signals and level crossing, no overhead line and relatively simple traffic control. The punctuality of freight trains does not have to be too high; a longer transport time (> one day) is acceptable if known well in advance. As a result, most maintenance and renewal activities can be carried out during the day in long train free periods.

Compared to the US, rail transport is very different in Europe and Asia. There is a mix of freight- and passenger trains. Transport of passengers is decisive for the design of network. Trains run frequently, according to a fixed timetable with relatively short, light, fast-moving and electric railcars. There is need for stations with several platforms. As a consequence, the number of trains and train-kilometers are high but gross tonne-kilometers figures are relatively low because passenger trains are much lighter as an average freight train. The infrastructure of mixed trafic networks is therefor complex with many switches, signals, level crossings, overhead lines and sophisticated traffic control. The network faces high demands for reliability because the schedule is constrained and has many dependencies. The train free periods are typically only possible at night and work time during the day can only be brief. As a consequence, the maintenance is expensive and working time is less. In countries such as Japan and Hong Kong, high quality is paramount and costs are not the highest concern because the trains carry 2 - 8 times more passengers than those in European countries such as Switzerland and the Netherlands. The challenge was to model the influence of utilisation, complexity and working conditions to explain the biggest cost differences. The first step was to prepare a checklist of cost drivers, as indicated in Table 5. The available information was examined and modelled. The cost drivers marked in light gray were selected for modelling influence on the maintenance and management costs.

Table 5   Checklist cost drivers

Aspect	Cost drivers	Cost driver details	Source	Modelling method
Money	Ko, GO, Beheer		Realisation SAP	Realised ciosts
	Man hours		M31 / RCB	%
	Materials		M31 / RCB	%
	Machines		M31 / RCB	%
	Indirect		M31 / RCB	%
Scope		Amount	SAP	Variabel in model
		Complexity	In kwantities	In kwantities
		Capacity		Complexity & Use
		Load (tonkm)	SAP: QuoVadis	Relation graph / system
		Intensity (treinkm)	SAP: QuoVadis	in tonkm
		Train type	Capacity mngt.	with fictive day tonnage
	Functionality	Train axle load	In load	In fictive day tonnage
		Train length	In load	In fictive day tonnage
		Train sped	SAP: Infra Atlas	In fictive day tonnage
		Energy supply	SAP: Infra Atlas	Yes/No catenary
	Use quality	Reliability		Implicit in costs
		Availability		Implicit in costs
		(railway) Safety		Implicit in costs
Conditions	Technical quality	Divers en specific	Party in use	Partly in utilisation
	Purchasing Power	(PM)		Implicit in costs
	Law	Environment		Implicit in costs
		Labor Safety		Implicit in costs
		Health		Implicit in costs
		Social law(s)		Implicit in costs
		Working hours		Implicit in costs
	Train Free Period	Maintainablity	M31 / RCB	Effective work time
		Effective work time	M31 / RCB	Difference with a shift
		% Day/Night	M31 / RCB	Difference hr-costs
Time	To build		NVT	NVT
	To maintain		M31 / RCB	Part of KO/GO costs
	To renew		RCB	Part of renewal costs
	Lifetime		SAP, MVA, ...	Standards

Principles for modelling. The rail infrastructure cost model for small-scale maintenance (KO), large-scale maintenance (GO) and management excluded stations because the latter form a separate system with its own cost drivers. The starting point for rail infrastructure cost model was costs incurred in the previous year as allocated to 16 (sub) systems. These costs converged in a cost matrix, indicated in   Table 6, which formed foundation of the model. The matrix was limited to 16 (sub) systems which were well recognised, covered the entire rail infrastructure system and had relevant differences in costs and variability. The telecommunication system station and marshalling yard were excluded because the former does not belong to the rail system and the latter is a unique to Betuwe route.

Table 6   Cost matrix maintenance & management costs; input M&R business model

Systems	Quantities	KO	GO	Management	Total	Cost indicators
		Cost matrix; input for calibrating the model			Realisation: 2011	
Substructure	2794 Km trace	€ 25.66	€ 8.03	€ 11.23	€ 44.92	€ 16.078 /km line
Main track	4952 km main track	€ 70.14	€ 46.96	€ 10.39	€ 127.49	€ 25.747 /km track
Side track	829 km side track	€ 3.22	€ 1.27	€ 0.84	€ 5.33	€ 6.431 /km
Switches in main track	4187 pieces	€ 94.44	€ 3.13	€ 10.11	€ 107.68	€ 25.718 /switch
Switches in side track	2445 pieces	€ 9.53	€ -	€ 1.12	€ 10.66	€ 4.359 /switch
Marshalling yard system	1 yard	€ 0.92	€ 0.22	€ 0.56	€ 1.70	€ 1.697.156 /yard
Level crossing, road part	68166 m' road	€ 9.49	€ 0.13	€ 1.12	€ 10.74	€ 162 /km level crossing road
Level crossing, signaling part	1660 piece crossings	€ 6.33	€ 2.98	€ 1.12	€ 10.43	€ 6.285 /level crossing
Bridges & Tunnels	163395 m'	€ 9.03	€ 12.12	€ 2.81	€ 23.96	€ 147 /m' bridge & tunnel
Energy supply, electric	5974 km catenary	€ 21.24	€ 21.09	€ 30.35	€ 72.67	€ 12.165 /km catenary
Energy supply, diesel	20 tank plate	€ 0.02	€ -	€ 0.03	€ 0.05	€ 2.335 /tank plate
Signalling	20546 sections	€ 25.54	€ 14.10	€ 2.81	€ 42.44	€ 2.066 /track section
Telecom, stations	19524 speakers	€ 5.86	€ 0.27	€ -	€ 6.13	€ 314 /speaker
Telecom, rail infra	2794 km trace	€ -	€ -	€ 44.24	€ 44.24	€ 15.833 /km trace
Trafic Control	73 workplace	€ -	€ -	€ 19.20	€ 19.20	€ 263.010 /workplace
Rail related buildings	691.0 pieces	€ -	€ 1.69	€ -	€ 1.69	€ 2.441 /building
Sub total rail infra		€ 281.42	€ 111.97	€ 135.93	€ 529.32 million	€ 106.897 railinfra/ km main track

Graphs were created for all 16 (sub) systems to describe the relationship between utilisation and costs. The fictive day tonnage was chosen as unit for utilisation as per UIC leaflet 714 (UIC, 1989*). The influence of train type and speed on static daytime tonne was processed with an impact factor, which accounted for speed, driveability and axle load.

The average impact factor for the Dutch network is determined at 1.344 (Swier J. , 2011*, pp. 13 en 5-7). The variety of sources used to prepare the relationship graphs included historical and current realisation information, UIC cost benchmark (LICB, 2007*), UIC leaflet 715 (UIC, 1992*) and estimates based on expert opinion. The relationship graphs of different system added up into a single graph that described the relationship between utilisation and maintenance costs, as indicated in Figure 81. The small red square on the relationship graph represents the current situation, referred to as scenario R. It is the intersection of the average fictitious day tonnage and average maintenance costs per kilometre main track. Its cost-index value is 100. The graph indicates variation in costs with change in utilisation. The network complexity is directly related to costs because cost per kilometre of main track is provided for all Dutch railway systems. The relationship chart indicates the impact of two cost drivers on costs:

- *Influence of utilisation*: upper thick black line
- *Influence of complexity*: height of the black line

240

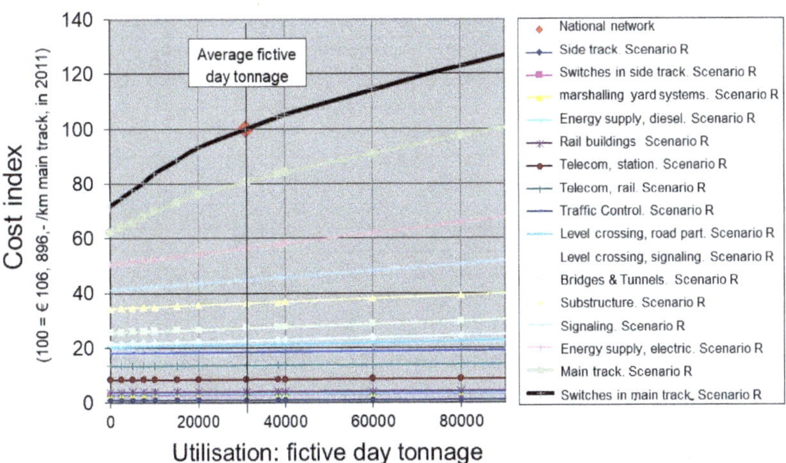

Figure 81   Costs-utilisation relationship graph for the Dutch rail network

The relationship graphs for (sub)systems were based on a standard, partly derived from realisation or benchmark information and partly estimated (Swier J. , 2011*). The maintenance costs of 12 of the 14 systems are either not or little influenced by utilisation: 8 relationship graphs are flat, one has a small slope and 3 have a very small slope. The angle of inclination of the 12 relationship graphs is based on expert judgment. Because slope is flat and costs are relatively low, the impact of estimation error in angle of inclination is negligible. The maintenance costs of rail and switches are mostly influenced by utilisation. This is also substantiated by the UIC leaflet 715 (UIC, 1992*), tested and adjusted as per realisation information from ProRail or the UIC benchmark study.

The cost matrix and relationship graphs enable prediction of cost consequences for change in infrastructure and/or utilisation. This principle is applied to change in working condition of maintenance mechanics working on tracks; more trains mean less time for maintenance and less work during the day. Finally, the following two influences have been incorporated into the model:

- *% day work.* Difference in costs of day, night and weekend service. The increase or decrease in day work, when compared to a reference situation, translates into change in costs.
- ***Effective working time.*** The time that people actually work in a service. The increase or decrease in working time, when compared to a reference situation, translates into change in costs.

In order to model the influence of working conditions, the cost for each system is divided into labour-hour-, material- and machine costs, as well as into indirect and direct costs, as indicated in Table 7. For this purpose, OPC contract tender information is in the M31 format.

Table 7   Breakdown in costs for labour, material and machines

		Costs KO+GO+ Management	Labour hours costs OFF track	Labour hours costs IN track
KO	Fixed	15%		
	Materials	6%		
	Machine	6%		
	Labour	23%	2%	21%
GO	Materials	6%		
	Machine	6%		
	Labour	10%	3%	6%
Management		28%		
Total		100%	5%	27%

Initially, the model assumes that influence of circumstances is limited to direct labour-hour costs in the track. Table 6 shows that 5% of the total costs are spent on direct man-hours off the track and 27% in the track. This ratio is estimated by weighted addition of respective figures per maintenance system (KO, GO).

Figure 82 is the rate-matrix used to model the influence of working conditions. It indicates cost impact of working time in services. A distinction is made between executive day service independent of train service (D, OT) and that dependent on train service (D, AT). The initial point is that a mechanic is paid according to the collective agreement for an eight-hour shift and that hourly wages for day- (OT & AT), night- and weekend services (DDNW) differ as per tariff factor.

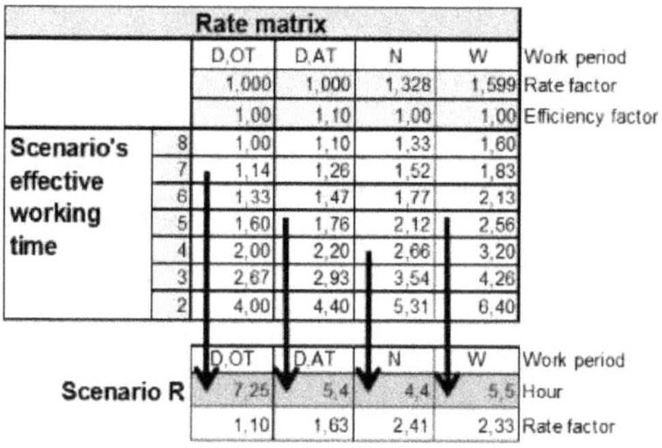

Figure 82   Rate-matrix with scenarios and rates (Swier J. , 2001*, p. tariefmatrix)

The cost differences between hourly wages are modelled with factor for DDNW services being 1x, 1.1x, 1.33x and 1.60x, respectively. Therefore, a weekend service is 1.6 times as expensive as day service. With an in-efficiency factor, it is possible to increase the cost of service. The rate-matrix has factor of 1.1 for all D and AT services because effective working time is always lost in passing of trains or to obtain train-free period on a certain track section.

The personnel is paid per service but the model estimates effective working time per service. If effective working time decreases then the number of services to carry necessary maintenance increases. In the tariff matrix, this effect is processed by multiplying rate factors of DDNW services with the difference between service time and effective working time in a service. For example, a service lasts 8 hours and the effective working time is 2 hours. The tariff factor of the service is then increased by a factor $(8/2 =)$ 4x.

The average effective working time on the Dutch network for DDNW services was 7.25, 5.1, 4.4 and 5.5 hours, respectively. Using the rate-matrix, the corresponding cost factors were calculated for effective working time in a service. For the national network, the average rate factors for DDNW in scenario R are 1.1x, 1.63x, 2.41x and 2.33x. It is indicated as bottom block in the rate-matrix.

In order to determine changes with respect to reference situation, the ratio for DNW work has been determined for various scenarios. For KO, the ratio was determined from tender information of the maintenance contractor. For GO, the ratio was determined based on an expert estimate. The day hours without train hinderance are also estimated. On the basis of these insights, a weighted national average was compiled for KO and GO from the DDNW percentages per system.

The DDNW ratios determined for the average national network are 10, 47, 29 and 14 (total = 100). These are represented in a simplified way as DNW = 57, 29 and 14. Of the direct man hours, 57% is made during the day and 43% during the night and in the weekend.

According to the Working Hours Act, an employee can be on duty for up to 36 nights in a duration of 16 weeks. Therefore, a maximum of 36 night shifts and a minimum of 44 shifts is possible in 16 weeks. This leads to minimum day/night ratio of 55/45. If night work rises above 45% then model adds extra capacity for the surplus.

Relationship graph. The section above describes the components of the model. With the model, it is possible to forecast maintenance costs of lines, other networks or changing conditions, as well as to account for the differences in complexity, utilisation and working conditions. The output of the model is a table with figures or a relationship graph in which the situation is presented with reference being the national rail network. Table 8 and Figure 83 provide an example with input and output data for a fictitious railway line of the Dutch network. The asset quantities per system are not listed and the modelled line has less switches and crossings for simplicity.

The input shows that the fictional line is used more intensively but has less favourable working conditions and is less complex than the average national network. In the output, the red dotted line runs through cost index 100 and comprises relationship graph for the average national network. It is the reference situation R.

	National network	Fictitious railway line
Cost index	100	To determine with the model
Costs / km main track	€106,900	To determine with the model
Utilisation	30,274 Tf	65.285 Tf
% Day work	58%	52%
Effective working time DDNW	7.25 | 5.4 | 4.4 | 5.5	7.25 | 5.1 | 4.0 | 5.0
Complexity = Quantities	ProRail netwerk	Far less km main track, side track, switches and level crossings

The fictitious line is less complex and, therefore, less expensive. In Figure 83 the cost index drops with difference 'a', from 100 to 77. Because the utilisation intensity is higher, the maintenance costs increase with difference 'b', from index 77 to 91.1. The working conditions are slightly less favourable so the costs increase with difference 'c' such that cost prognosis for the line comes to a cost index of 96.2.

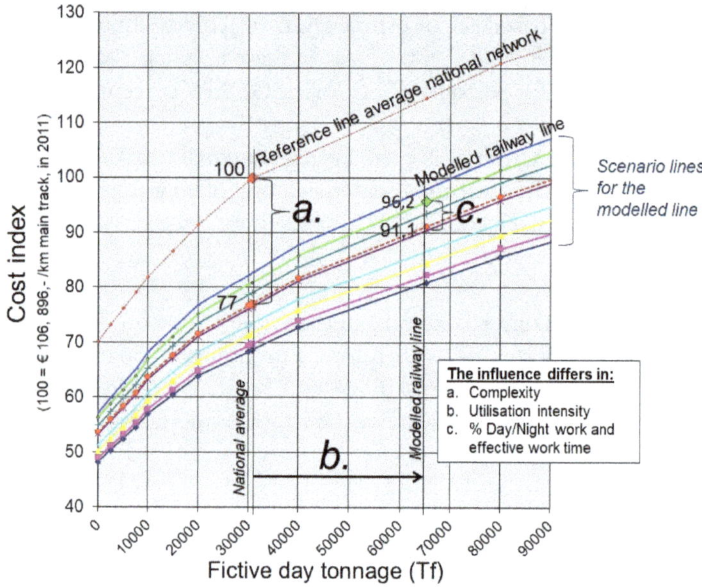

The model shows that increase of 4.6% is caused by less effective working hours and 0.5% by less day work. The annual maintenance costs per kilometre of main rail are known for the average Dutch rail network. By multiplying these by the modelled cost index for the fictitious line, the maintenance costs are determined at: € 106,900 * 96.25 = € 102,426 per kilometre main track.

Cost analysis United States and East Asia. The model can also be used to assess networks of other countries. We can calculate costs for the Dutch network under conditions same as in other countries. A comparison was done for the networks in Hong Kong and Japan as well as a first class rail company in the US.

244

By adjusting the variables step-by-step, a residual group of influences remained that could not be quantified with the model. This influence was partly assessed and partly explained by other sources. Figure 84 illustrates the result of the difference analysis of the US and Japan with the Netherlands.

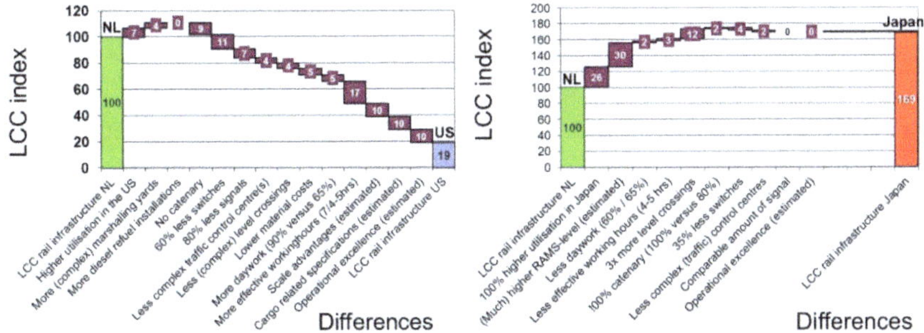

Figure 84   Difference analysis for US-NL (left) and Japan-NL (right)

The maintenance costs of rail infrastructure in the US are approximately 80% lower than those in the Netherlands. The most important explanations are:

- Higher users fee;
- Less complex infrastructure; fewer switches, less signals, no catenary;
- More favourable conditions such as day work and effective work time;
- Lower material costs;
- Differences in purchasing power;
- Economies of scale (estimated);
- Lower technical specifications for freight transport (estimated);
- Higher professionalism (estimated).

The difference can be explained by the model (more than 50%), other sources (<20%) and estimates (>30%).

The cost difference between the Netherlands and Japan is about a factor 2 and is explained by the following:

- More intensive use;
- Less favourable conditions, more night work;
- Differences in purchasing power;
- Higher RAMS performance (influence is estimated).

The difference can be explained by the model (more than 50%), other sources (25%), and estimated (25%).

A difference analysis with Hong Kong is similar to that of Japan but cost difference is about a factor 3x. This is explained by the extremely high utilisation of the network in Hong Kong: about 8x of the Netherlands!

The development and interpretation of such analyses is possible only with knowledge of the local situation. Initially, there may seem more similarities than differences between the rail infrastructure in Japan and the Netherlands. Upon closer inspection, the Japanese network is found to be not cross-linked, operating with matched schedules, managed by well-controlled organisation, measured for quality improvement and preventive maintenance, and maintained through in-house works.

A transport system that is used intensively and has high quality (high punctuality) is fully focused on performance. It is more expensive not only because of differences in technology, working conditions, process complexity, use of infrastructure, as well as strategy and priorities.

The cost driver model described above was known for a long time as the QM4C-model[64] and is called the 'Business model costs' since 2008. It is managed by the finance department and used to forecast maintenance costs for new or modified lines, calculate consequences of a new policy, and determine impact on user charge. A supplemental model was needed to determine variability of the renewal costs. This model is described in the next section.

8.2.7　Modelling the variability of renewal costs

The variability of maintenance costs can be determined with the 'Business model costs' described previously. When user fee was introduced, it had been assumed that all renewal costs are fixed. Around 2010 that insight changed. ProRail AM had to investigate the extent to which renewal costs depend on utilisation. To account for changes in renewal costs, a cost model was developed. The goal was to determine variability in relation to utilisation such that an annual average is added to model output for management and maintenance costs.

Preface. In order to model the relationship between renewal costs and utilisation, the system has to be specified with dependency of depreciation periods on technical lifespan and utilisation. With track and switches, increase in utilisation increases need for renewal. The lifespan of other systems is not or little affected by utilisation[65].

Relationship graphs for each system has to be developed for renewals with on the horizontal axis the fictive day tonnage and the vertical axis the average annual depreciation costs. Not the realised renewal costs because they fluctuate strongly over the years due to differences in building- or renewal year, construction type and utilisation.

---

[64] QM4C = Quality, Materials, Machine, Man hours, Methods and Costs = QMforSee
[65] The contact wire of catenary is subject to wear and tear but life time is relatively long (20-30 years) and costs are low compared to track and switches.

The determination of depreciation costs was based on investment costs and average lifespan. This information was available in ProRail's fixed assets administration (MVA) as balance sheet item and related items on balance sheet, and profit & loss statement.

The relationship graph was utilised in three steps:
Step 1:   Determine average depreciation period (average lifespan) and depreciation costs of systems to be modelled. Information source: MVA.
Step 2:   Convert lifespan of track and switches into lifespan graphs. Information source: lifespan matrix in superstructure renewal policy (BBV) and derived average lifespan graph for track and switches.
Step 3:   Convert lifespan graphs with annual depreciation costs into relationship graphs with average annual depreciation costs plotted against utilisation

Step 1: Determine average depreciation costs and depreciation periods.
The MVA has renewal values, amortisation periods, annual depreciation and book values for all systems and basic objects. The modelling focuses particularly on track and switches because they are variable. In the MVA, both systems are part of the guidance system and include rail brakes on yards and monitor systems. The latter two have been set aside in the model because their costs are fixed.

The starting points for the model are as follows:
- Total national network managed by ProRail includes Betuwe route but excludes HSL South
- Annual renewal value of all systems with the exception of the Transfer System (= Stations)
- Only costs for rail and switches considered variable; annual depreciation costs of the other systems considered fixed and taken directly from the MVA
- Side track and switches in side-track considered to have fixed costs and separated from the switches in main tracks; this provides key figures for renewal costs, depreciation periods and depreciation costs
- Average (financial) life span determined for rail and switches based on renewal values and annual depreciation costs
- Modelling is based on assets in-depreciation; renewal costs of assets already fully depreciated not taken into account

The renewal- and depreciation costs have been set for rail and switches, so both in- and out of depreciation. The variability of renewal costs is determined for all in-depreciation constructions. Subsequently, the split was made between main and side tracks and the switches therein. This was based on quantities and average cost indicators for (switches in) side-track. The result is summarised in Figure 85.

Year 2015		Renewal value	Average lifetime	In-depreciation/yr
Main trackl	5379 km	€ 5.611.591.936	33,6	€ 140.963.528
Side track	989 km	€ 791.120.000	45,0	€ 15.913.778
Switches in main track	4451 pc	€ 1.212.658.324	25,2	€ 34.863.447
Switches in side track	2673 pc	€ 534.600.000	38,0	€ 11.436.842
Substructure and Buildings		€ 2.830.953.684	79,0	€ 28.773.349
Bridges, Tunnels & Level Crossings		€ 12.081.171.317	72,5	€ 138.871.377
Energy supply		€ 4.772.550.083	39,6	€ 68.706.381
Signaling		€ 3.127.560.257	26,2	€ 76.096.255
Remains of the group track & switches		€ 96.133.613	10,0	€ 1.365.864
Traffic control		€ 671.936.071	11,3	€ 34.298.765
Communication systems		€ 898.764.008	11,8	€ 44.680.694
Equipment & Industrial equipment		€ 50.196.157	5,1	€ 821.978
Sub totaal		€ 32.679.235.452	41,5	€ 596.792.257
Stations		€ 4.803.547.760		
Totaal		€ 37.482.783.212		

Figure 85   Investment cost information of ProRail (Source: MVA, (Swier J. , 2017))

Step 2: Develop relationship graphs for lifetime use. The lifespan of track and switches depends on design type and use intensity. ProRail has saved this knowledge in BID00020 (A&T, 2015*). The theoretical expected life span for all kinds of track and switch is included for six utilisation intensities as per UIC category classification. The UIC classification of railway lines (UIC, 1989*) assumes a static train weight converted into dynamic, fictive tonnage or Tf (= Tonnage fictive) with a bump factor. The groups are as follows:

Group 1:		> 130.000 Tf
Group 2:	80.000	- 130.000 Tf
Group 3:	40.000	- 80.000 Tf
Group 4:	20.000	- 40.000 Tf
Group 5:	5.000	- 20.000 Tf
Group 6:		<5.000 Tf (= side track)

The lifetime in track and switch renewal matrices are plotted for some of the most relevant construction types. These trend lines describe relationship between utilisation and lifetime. For very heavily loaded lines in the UIC class 1 and 2, detailed estimates are provided. This is because there are no lines in UIC class 1 in the Netherlands and only very few in UIC class 2.

For rail, the types NP46, UIC54 on wood, and UIC54 and UIC60 on concrete have been chosen. For switches, the UIC54 types on wood, UIC54 on concrete, NP46 on wood and double diamond UIC54 on wood, have been chosen. ProRail policy aims to change all constructions to UIC54 on concrete. The UIC60 is only used on the Betuwe route. Both types of rail have equal life and decisive cost rating. The average lifetime graph for rail and switches is derived from different lifecycle graphs per type. In doing so, it is ensured that average lifetime at national average utilisation intensity corresponds to average depreciation period in the MVA. For switches, the lifetime graphs are derived directly from policy matrices. For rail, an additional modelling was required because the system consists of three structures each of which has different lifetime: rail, sleeper (including fastening) and ballast. The lifespan graph for rail comprises a weighted addition of components on the basis of average renewal costs per structure. Figure 86 illustrates the principle for track UIC54 on concrete. The graph shows that the lifetime of rail (steep, blue line) is related to utilisation and that wear of sleepers (upper, red line) and ballast (lower, green line) are less dependent on utilisation. The dotted line is the composite lifespan graph for rail. It is based on a weighted average of renewal costs per part.

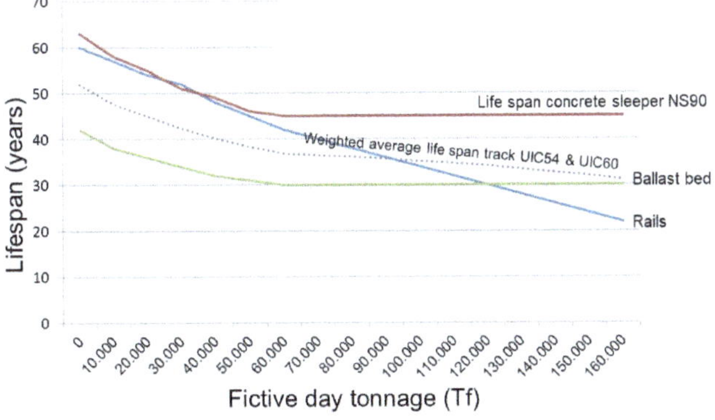

Figure 86   Compound lifespan graph for track part

With the life-time graphs for the various construction types, average life-time graphs have been determined for track and switches, see Figure 87. The dotted lines are the averages, calibrated on the average lifetime for those constructions from the MVA, which is the same as the average depreciation value. For the different construction types the spreading of track life is smaller as for switches. A heavier rail type has a longer lifetime saving for switches as for rail, and constructions on concrete have a considerably longer service life as on wood. The average lifespan of switches is lower than expected because it is calibrated with the average lifetime in the MVA with average use, an indication that there are relatively few switches on concrete at the time of modelling or that the depreciation periods in the MVA may be slightly too short.

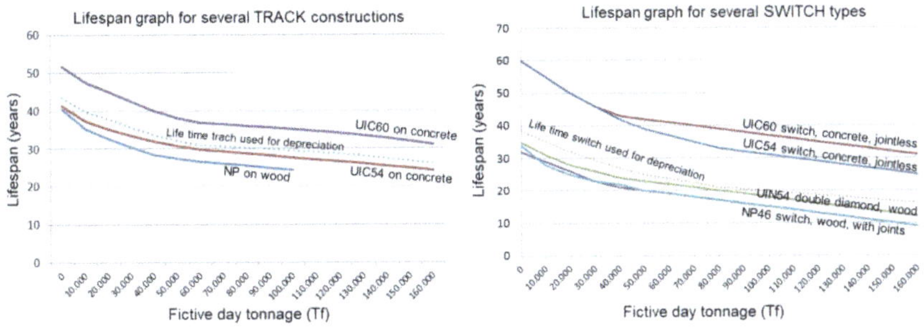

Figure 87   Lifespan graphs for the most relevant track- and switch types

249

Step 3: Relationship graph for depreciation costs versus utilisation. The
variability of maintenance costs is determined with the cost driver model (please
refer paragraph 8.2) based on a relationship graph, with the fictional day tonnage
on the x-axis and the annual costs per kilometre of main line track on the y-axis.
The same axes are used for renewal costs with the exception that annual depreciation costs from the MVA are plotted on the y-axis. For this purpose, the annual
depreciation costs are combined with lifetime graphs by dividing average renewal
values for rail and switches by lifetimes and taking the part that is in-depreciation.

A distinction has always been made between depreciation costs and lifetimes for
(switches in) main- and side track, because costs of (switches in) side track are not
variable (low speed → low load → hardly wear). The result is the relationship
graph in Figure 88 with relationship graph lines for main track (blue), switches in
main track (red), side track (green) and switches in side-track (purple). It is clear
that the renewal costs of (switches in) main track are variable and that of (switches
in) side track are fixed.

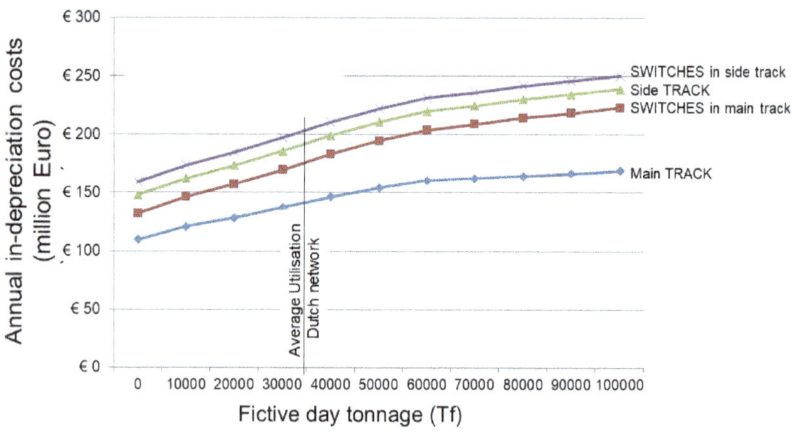

Figure 88   Relationship graph of average renewal need of the Dutch network

To determine cost variability of renewals, the relationship graph with annual depreciation costs of rail and switches was combined with MVA's annual depreciation costs for other systems, and divided by kilometre per main track. The result
is the relationship graph of Figure 89.

The distribution of fixed/variable for renewal costs of rail and switches is
78.4%/21.6% (year 2015). The distribution of fixed/variable for total renewal
costs of rail infrastructure (excluding stations) is 92.7%/7.3% (year 2015).

250

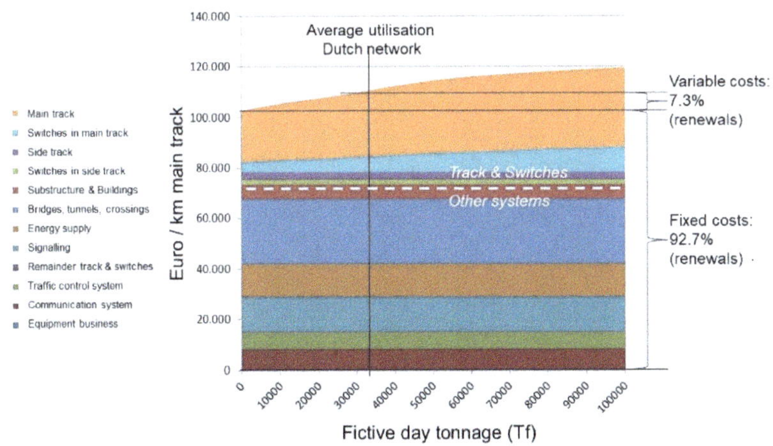

Figure 89   Relationship graph renewal costs and utilisation

Combined relationship graphs for maintenance and renewal costs. To determine variability of annual M&R costs, the relationship graphs for renewals and maintenance were combined. For maintenance, the 'Business model costs' described in the previous section was used. Both activities have the same unit for horizontal axis; the fictional day tonnage (Tf). By normalising all costs to costs per kilometre main track, the costs for maintenance and renewals can be added to create the relationship graph in Figure 90.

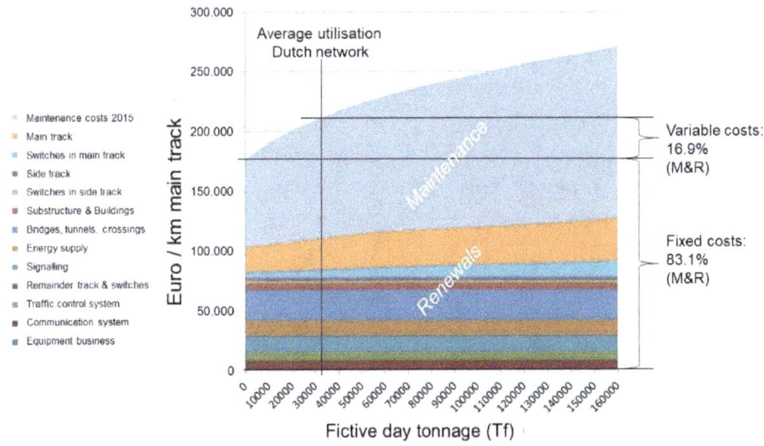

Figure 90   Relationship graph for M&R-costs and utilisation

The distribution of fixed/variable for M&R costs of total infra, excluding stations, is 83.1%/ 16.9% (year 2015).

8.2.8 Cost development ProRail

The M&R costs for rail infrastructure have risen from around € 600 million to around € 1,600 million in ten years, as indicated in Figure 91. A further analysis shows that the increase is mainly due to changes in organisation and accounting practices for depreciations, not so much by costly maintenance and/or renewal.

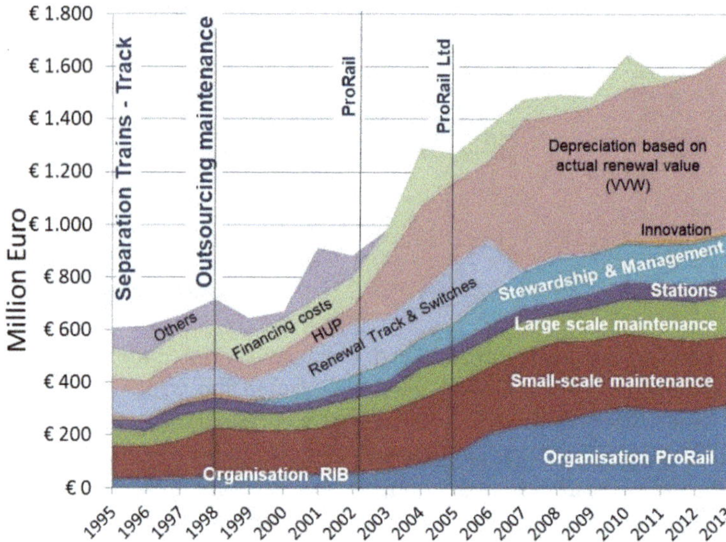

Figure 91   Development of infra maintenance-, renewal- and management costs (Swier J. , 2016)*

The main reason for increase in costs is change in accounting for depreciation. The remaining costs have increased slightly due to inflation, more intensive use and/or unfavourable conditions and circumstances. Earlier, depreciation was based on historical spend prices (HUP) combined with 'a fond perdu' financing of track and switch renewal. This method was changed in 2006/2007 into depreciation based on renewal value (VVW). All actual renewal investments are financed 'à fond perdu'.

The second major break in the trend was increase in organisation costs because of merger of the three task organisations and privatisation of ProRail into a Limited.

The third reason was increase in stewardship and management costs. These costs cover taxes, insurance, ICT, traffic control equipment, national electricity grid connection, etc. These costs were part of NS's accounting but with the separation of NS and ProRail, and the merger of the three task organisations, they became costs for ProRail.

Conclusion: After the separation of transport and infrastructure, and the privatisation of all service provider activities, the allocation of costs to rail infrastructure changed drastically. The organisation grew as costs were attributed to it and method of depreciation changed fundamentally. With this background knowledge, the increase in costs can be explained.

8.2.9   Development of maintenance costs in the Netherlands

ProRail distinguishes two types of maintenance: process-based small-scale maintenance (KO) that is outsourced through OPC / PGO contracts and large scale maintenance (GO) put out to tender every year. Figure 92 indicates how KO and GO costs have developed for rail infrastructure excluding stations. The total maintenance costs for the period 1994-2013 increased with a factor of 2.3x from € 181 million to € 414 million (Swier J. , 2016*). The KO costs increased with a factor of 2.3x and the GO costs with a factor of 2.2x.

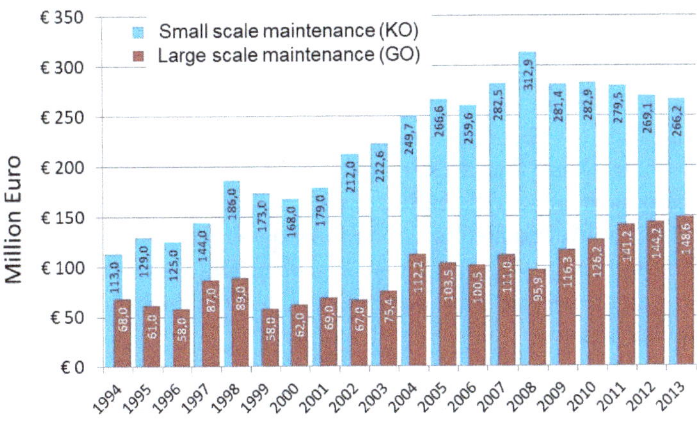

Figure 92   Development of maintenance costs (KO and GO)

The rise in GO costs has not been analysed but can largely be explained by fluctuations in necessity, expansion of work package and autonomous price increases.

The causes of KO cost development have been analysed. The sudden increase in costs in 1998 by a factor of 1.3x was because of outsourcing. The labour agreement (CAO) of the maintenance contractors, in particular, the costs for pensions and holiday payment was expensive (Swier J. &., 2001*). The cost reduction that followed was because of realisation of an agreed efficiency improvement.
The KO costs increased by a factor of 1.5x over the period 2001-2005 and 1.23x over the period 2004-2009 (Schouten, 2009*). This increase has been attributed to price rise, stringent safety regulations, and quality improvements such as reduction in number and duration of train effecting failures and rail contact fatigue (RCF).

For the period 2004-2008, the causes were diverse and as follows:

1. Extra safety measures because of the NVW: + 4.7%
2. Maintenance schedule for night work: + 5.7%
3. Maintenance increase due to noise reduction: + 1.1%
4. Operational property management: + 1.2%
5. Indexation: + 11.7%
6. Utilisation increase: + 2.0%
7. Infrastructure development: + 1.0%
8. Infrastructure reduction: Europoort, Randstadrail and Zoetermeer-line: - 4.9% +/-

Total period 2004-2008   + 23.1%

After 2008, there was a break in trend of KO cost development. The costs dropped by a factor of -0.15x from € 312 million in 2008 to € 266 million in 2013, despite price increases. This decrease has been attributed to the gradual transition from input-driven OPC contracts to performance-based PGO contracts.

With competition and performance management, the contract prices decreased by at least 25% because of risk-driven, condition-based maintenance, in particularly for track and switches. The traditional frequency-based maintenance strategy and input control were found less efficient and effective. The performance contracts gave opportunity to the contractors to work in a risk-driven manner and only do maintenance required to deliver the requested performance. In 2019, all KO contracts are required to be put out to tender. This is expected to reduce the total KO even further but it has become clear that 'the market' has also become more unpredictable.

Conclusion: After the separation and privatisation of service provider activities, the maintenance costs rose sharply by about a factor of 2.3x. This was partly the direct result of outsourcing maintenance. The increase was mainly caused by all kinds of external mutants even though input control and adherence to traditional maintenance also had their price. The KO cost reductions realised after 2008 were due to tendering of performance contracts.

8.3   Insights and experiences

The knowledge of cost development is a prerequisite for cost management. In the period that NS did maintenance on its own, it was able to manage labour hours and budgets. The cost knowledge was with the financial department and cost experts. At the time, the focus was mainly on financial control and not cost management. This changed after the separation of transport and infrastructure as well as privatisation of all service provider activities. With these developments, relationships were formalised; explicit agreements were made about costs for activities and products; and cost knowledge was required for financial planning, tendering, and new management techniques such as life cycle management. The fast-growing demand for cost experts could not be met.

The initiatives that have ensured cost knowledge develops among the ProRail employees include the following:

- ***Financial administration and accounting.*** A new system was set up in which costs were allocated to Trace Infra Cluster (TICs), types of activities and business units. The financial administration was made accessible through RailFocus for all employees in the organisation.
- ***Cost matrix:*** In order to develop cost indicators for each product unit, the realised annual expenses were allocated to asset and M&R activities in a cost matrix. The costs were provided by the financial administration or estimated at a detailed level. By dividing costs with corresponding asset quantities, many unit cost figures were obtained. The allocation was based on a system of communicating vessels, i.e., too high estimated costs in one system were corrected in other systems such that the cost matrix continues to reflect the total expenses incurred in a year
- ***Cost knowledge database (Rail Case Base).*** Cost calculations and indicators are provided in a structured and systematic way for all employees trained in theory and methodology.
- ***Modelling.*** The influence of changing conditions and circumstances on costs can be modelled. Similar to the cost matrix, the model is based on the principle of what we know and what we derive. Examples include utilisation-cost relationship, increase in night work and inspections, reduction in train free periods, etc.

It is about the knowledge and feeling for the costs per unit product; the maintenance costs per switch, the renewal costs per level crossing, the inspection costs of track and the like. It is not necessary to set up the entire financial administration for this. This gives an enormous administrative burden and the level of detail has little or no added value. Cost indicators are reliable averages and you can calculate and deduce them very well within the framework of a less detailed financial administration. A condition is, however, that the financial department also coordinates administration and accounting with the needs and wishes of the business units.

The employees at ProRail are increasingly focused on sustainable optimisation of performance and costs over the life cycle. It is noteworthy that approximately 15% of the financing comes from the user fee and 85% from the government through tax revenues. The former source of income has direct relationship with commercial revenue from sale of transport product. The latter depends on economy, politics, realisation of plans and budgets, and relationship between the government and ProRail. Government decisions are based on extensive studies, alternative research, substantiation, explanations, audits and political decision-making. The realisation of the decisions depends on many uncertain external factors. The investment and exploitation processes are, therefore, quite complex, slow and syrupy.

Despite the uncertain circumstances, many expansion and change projects are realised satisfactorily every year and ProRail is able to improve performance of an increasingly intensively used network for about the same costs. This is because the entire sector is gaining capability of managing risks associated with performance and costs, with activities as per the given conditions. The next chapter describes how this happens.

9 Activities, Conditions and Risks

Costs and performance are managed by controlling risk causes with activities, given the conditions that affect them. The previous chapters have explained how the organisation manages performance and costs and how they have evolved. This chapter provides insight into the influence of the activities and conditions on performance and costs, and how risks are the connecting link between them.

Managing Activities

The activities are necessary to realise new infrastructure and to maintain existing ones. They are very diverse: design, build, maintain, inspect, manage, etc. Depending on the type of the contract, the infrastructure manager, the engineering firm or the contractor can choose the activities to control the performance risks. In new build, the most extreme contract type is the Design-Build-Finance-Maintain (DBFM) contract. The contractor makes all choices to realise the performance specified by the client, and is responsible for financing the project. Another extreme contract type is that the client does everything on its own. Further, all kinds of intermediate forms of contracts are possible. ProRail has outsourced all engineering, maintenance and renewal activities and uses Design-, Build-, Design & Build- and Maintain contracts. It has never put a DBFM contract on the market[66] and uses DBM contracts only for very specific installations.

In maintenance, it is common practice for many infrastructure managers to outsource renewals and large-scale maintenance as a project. The contractor is often responsible for engineering, work preparation, material supplies and execution. At the railways, it is still very common for the infrastructure manager to perform maintenance itself. ProRail is one of the few infrastructure managers in Europe, and even in the world, who has outsourced maintenance. The reticence to outsource is because maintenance is a continuous process and the result is not a tangible product but a quality. A contractor must have continuous care for railway safety and the reliability of the infrastructure for which it is responsible. The client must be able to rely on that quality of service even though it cannot be easily arranged within a contract. This is the reason railway companies often stick to the tradition to do the maintenance themselves. Railinfrabeheer, the predecessor of ProRail, did not had that choice. The government and board of directors of NS made the choice for that organisation in the nineties and decided to privatise the

---

[66] HSL South was a DBFM-contract but the Dutch government was responsible for the project management and ProRail contributed to the project as a consultant.

execution of maintenance. The consequence of this decision was that around 2,800 NS infra staff members were transferred to three existing rail contractors. Both, the client Railinfrabeheer and the contractors, had to learn how to manage maintenance by means of contracts. Ten years after privatisation, the maintenance sector was able to award and manage performance contracts, thereby improving performance and lower costs. This development is described in detail in chapter 4 how the execution of the maintenance is optimally and sustainably managed in a controlled manner. This description also applies to organisations that have their own maintenance department. The only difference is that with a contract the preconditions and management principles of maintenance execution is very sharp. When the organisation is doing the activities itself the activities are often more diffused but the control principles are exactly the same.

Very important for the successful outsourcing of maintenance by ProRail was the transition from an input-driven OPC contract to an output-driven PGO contract. The OPC contract is based on yearly fixed work plan for which a price has been agreed. The failures are settled afterwards in relation to the work plan. The disadvantage of this type of contract is that the contractor is not responsible for the performance but for carrying out the fixed work plan. The contract type does not stimulate ownership for result of the efforts. The mechanics had to do what they were told and often limited themselves to it. The contract is driven by turnover, little attention is paid to efficiency and too much attention is paid to extra work. Of course, an OPC contractor also wants to perform better, but in order to achieve this, new processes or more people are often added to the existing organisation. As a result, the size and complexity of the organisation grows, the costs increase and the results hardly improve. By securing the PGO performance contract, the contractors started looking for a different way of steering. They learned that the optimisation had to come from the execution and not from a planning office.

The PGO contracts give the contractor the opportunity to make their own choices about how the best performance can be delivered. The preconditions and control principles are fundamentally different from those of the OPC contract. The contractor offers a fixed price for the specified performance requirements and determines which maintenance activities will be carried out. However, explicit process requirements are imposed with regards to quality control, applicable regulations and risk management techniques for management and control of the performance. In principle, however, the requirements are constructive and give the contractors the freedom to make their own choices. The award of the PGO contract is also not based on the lowest price but the Economically Most Advantageous Tender (EMVI) and depends on the offered price and the offered performance such as the number of train-free periods, number of train effecting failures (TAOs) and the function recovery time. For the award of the contract, the discount rates offered and the adjustment of the technical condition also apply.

There are bonuses, malus and discounts if the contractor performs better or worse. Summarising: the costs are fixed and the contractor is responsible for realising the services offered. Performing better than offered is rewarded and worse is punished. This is the design of the PGO contract and the ideal condition. With award of performance contracts, the client loses some control and may face negative consequences.

For a PGO contract, the focus has to shift from payment of units to managing the usefulness and necessity of the money spent. That's a big change and takes time. Practice has shown that one maintenance contractor succeeds faster and better than another. The core of the change lies in having small fixed maintenance teams with short lines of communication to work preparation, planning and the contract manager. The roles and responsibilities must be clear to everyone in the process. Everything revolves around creating ownership with the fixed management teams for daily performance, and an integrated approach to technology, logistics, railway safety, personnel safety, work preparation and planning. An open communication and cooperation with the client is a condition, as is an attitude in which the contract states the rules that both parties adhere to. That is not self-evident. Due to competitive pressure, the lagging behind of the results and / or rising penalties, tensions arise that impede good cooperation and open communication between the client and the contractor. This is a dangerous development for the stability and continuity of the maintenance process. To gain insight into this, the control process of the PGO contract is explained in more detail.

An effective and efficient PGO process is not task-driven from the planning side (='push') but demand-driven (='pull') from the need and execution side. A prerequisite is a well-organised and transparent process, with the maintenance team in a steering role, supported by a maintenance engineer, work preparator and planner. Figure 93 illustrates the process of specifying performance as well as preparation and support of maintenance execution. In case of ProRail, a service provider performs maintenance engineering and planning; however, in other cases, maintenance can also be the executive organisation of an infrastructure manager. The process remains the same, except that there is no contract.

The difference between OPC and PGO starts with the specification. It is different in structure and content. OPC specifies work plans and technical M&R specifications while PGO specifies the intended performance, technical M&R specs and gives a set of requirements for the process control of the contractor. The performance in the PGO contract is specified at different levels, depending on the type of risk: the RAM performance on a reactive top level, safety and durability on a proactive level with technical rejection standards and, mandatory risk control measures. More details can be found in section 6.8. The break-up and elaboration of the intended RAMSHED performances in PGO specification trees, along with corresponding contract requirements and references to regulations, was made on the basis of the generic performance M&R-Concepts available at Pro-Rail. The PGO contract steering is based on the performance specification trees and performance requirements. ProRail provides the underlying generic risk analysis to the branch through the Rail Infra Catalogue (RIC) in the form of Maintenance Risk Analysis (IRA). As of Spring 2017, the IRAs and accompanying control measures are placed in a database, the Central Infra Risk Register (CIRR) are added and shared after assessment. If the contractor manages all the risks, he will control the performance and costs.

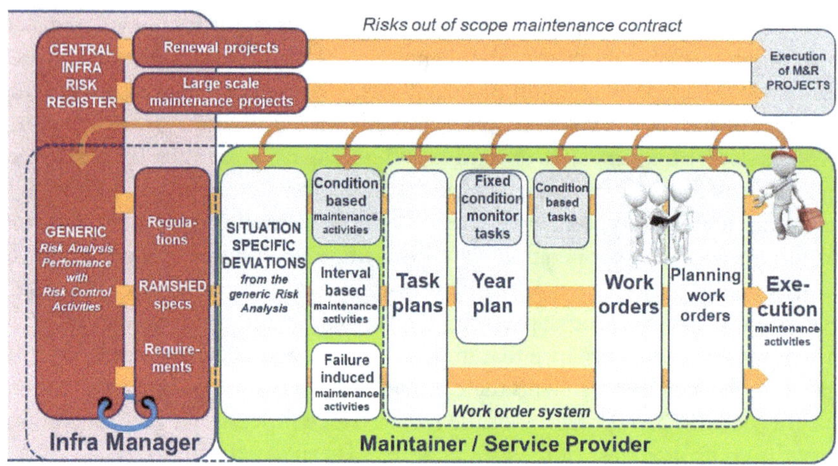

Figure 93   The process for optimally contracting and managing the maintenance execution

The maintenance contractor provides a contract-specific maintenance plan for an offered performance output. The starting point is generic risk analysis with risk control measures in the IRA/CIRR, possibly supplemented by contract-specific and risks missing by the contractor[67]. For safety and durability, ProRail prescribes technical, condition based, rejection specifications with associated monitor activities and, if these are not available, interval based activities.

If the contractor acquires the contract then he puts all activities with a fixed periodical character in an annual plan. These are all activities with a fixed interval

---

[67] It is not organised that way (yet??). ProRail and the four maintenance contractors each have their own performance risk analysis and risk control measures. These differ from each other while the assets and performance risks are exactly the same. They are also incomparable because ProRail AM considers function failure as the performance risk and the PGO contractors (+ProRail Procurement) the not realised specifications. Consequences: (i) a lot of extra and unnecessary work (ii) contractors not connected to the safety management system of ProRail, and (iii) contractors and system managers not connected because they do not speak the same 'risk language'. Unnecessary distance is created where cooperation is desired. The solution: make generic M&R-Concepts part of the contract specification. The assignment is then to manage the risks in the M&R Concepts within the given technical specifications. That is the starting point for the maintenance plans drawn up by the contractor for inspections, measurements and maintenance activities. These may deviate from the generic IH-Concept from ProRail if supported by a contract area specific risk analysis or explanation of the deviation from the generic strategy / control activity.

(GAO) and partly also condition based maintenance activities (TAO) such as inspections and measurements with a fixed frequency. Failures with a failure induced maintenance strategy (SAO) are accepted and therefore no preventive measures are planned. It means that many activities are already planned and fixed a year in advance. Most at signalling and the least at rail & switches. During the year, the activities in the annual plan are supplemented with condition-based activities planned on the basis of the degradation of the technical condition and the corresponding rejection specifications.

All activities are elaborated in task plans. These contain a description of the work, the documents needed, time estimate, material and equipment requirement, need for service to hire, etc. The task plans are location specific in work orders and the work orders are then sent to the planner who plans execution by coordinating a large number of variables such as availability of mechanics, qualifications, shift schedules and day/night rhythms, material deliveries, machine availability, train free periods, etc. This results in preparation of weekly plans per line and team. These contain all the maintenance activities to be carried out and all preconditions arranged. The team leader receives maximum support. He/she knows the current situation and needs; has direct influence on execution because he/she is in direct contact with the work preparator, planner and maintenance engineer; and has the option to create work orders. It means that the ownership for the performance is at the right place and the maintenance process is fully optimised and controlled. Maintenance is only done when it is really needed, and the need is determined by the people who can determine it. This explains why the costs of the PGO contracts are substantially lower than those of OPC (>-25%) and the performance is better. This also explains why employees in well-established PGO contract areas do not want to return to the OPC contracts: they have influence and are involved so there is satisfaction and joy at work. Whether that will remain so is uncertain. Here is an intended and desired situation realised by a number of maintenance contractors. There are, however, signs that the cost / performance ratio is out of balance due to the growing competition to deliver better performance at lower prices. Attention seems to have shifted from better performance to financial survival. That is an insidious, dangerous development.

Managing Conditions

Maintenance activities are needed to control the performance risks to identify potential failure causes and remove them in time. These activities cost money and the amount of money depends on the conditions and preconditions in which the activities are carried out. Examples of this are: the amount of infrastructure, intensity of use, technical condition, available effective working time, amount of night work, legislation, collective agreements and so on. The influence of the conditions on the activities, and thus on the costs, can almost always be modelled. The conditions with the greatest influence have already been identified and quantified in earlier chapters. This section is limited to a brief overview of the conditions with an explanation and reference to the sections with more information:

- ***Quantity and type of assets.*** The impact on costs is great. Illustrative of this is the difference in M&R costs between the Netherlands and the United States. In the US, these are only 20% of what is spend in the Netherlands. It is due to the difference in infrastructure complexity: fewer switches, fewer level crossings, fewer signals, no overhead lines and easier traffic management. For more details, reference is made to the Cost Driver model for M&R costs (sub-section 8.2.6 at page 235), the Long Term Plan Function Enforcement (sub-section 8.2.5 at page 231) and the cost development of maintenance (sub-section 8.2.9 at page 253).

- ***Utilisation intensity and influence.*** Track and switches are directly loaded by the trains and thus wear out the fastest. They determine the cost variability. Approximately 27% of the maintenance costs and about 9% of the renewal costs are variable. For more details, reference is made to sub-section 8.2.6 at page 235. The utilisation intensity and the costs vary by line. Internationally, infrastructure managers share the same category classification for the taxation of railways, taking into account differences in train type, speed and axle load. More information can be found in the UIC leaflet 714 and 715.

- ***Effective working time.*** According to the collective social agreement, an employee is paid for a service of eight hours regardless of the actual working hours available. For work next to the track, this usually does not impose any restrictions, but in the track it is different. There work can only be done in a train free period and that is almost always much shorter than regular eight hours. In addition, to get a train free period takes time and that is at the expense of the remaining effective working time. It is not uncommon for services to be effective for only four hours. In order to do the same job, two services are required and the costs are (at least) twice as high. The influence is large but is limited to the executive services in the track. This influence is modelled in the maintenance business model . For the current network, this is approximately 6% of the maintenance costs (KO, GO and Management). The influence increases if the track is used more intensively. More information on this can be found in section 8.2, the sub-sections about the cost driver model for maintenance and management activities (sub-section 8.2.6 at page 235).

- ***Ratio day/night work.*** More intensive train traffic not only impacts the effective working time but also the period during which work can be done. Trains mainly run in the period between six o'clock in the morning and one o'clock the following morning. An increase means that there is a shift from day to night work and often also from working days to weekend days. That affects the costs. Night and weekend services are a factor of 1.4x and 2x higher than day services, respectively. The influence of the ratio of day / night work to the executive services in the railways is also limited, and that is also modelled in the business model. They are approximately 5% of the current maintenance costs for KO, GO and Management. The influence increases if the track is used more intensively. More information in sub-section 8.2.6.

- **_Legislation._** The influence of legislation has a diffuse effect on the M&R costs and performance. Consideration must be given to the influence of legislation, in particular, on the environment, working conditions and safety. Examples of the effects are: measures against noise pollution, remediation of contaminated soil, prevention of environmental pollution, demands on working conditions and safety provisions, protection and removal of level crossings, limits on the amount of night work and so on. The legislation mandates companies to take measures. It may cost extra but it delivers higher performance of rail infrastructure or rail transport as well as higher quality of society and the environment.

- **_Collective labour agreement (CAO)._** The collective labour agreement contains binding agreements between the employer- and employee-organisations on wages, holidays, working hours, secondary employment conditions, job evaluation and so on. The costs of a service and the limits imposed on its implementation are partly from legislation and largely from the collective labour agreement. The agreement determines the costs of the activities needed to manage the performance risks.

- **_Technical quality._** The technical quality of the Dutch railway network is good. It meets at least the minimum standards and requirements that are set for it. This is because sufficient money was available to carry out all necessary maintenance and renewal activities. Insufficient money would sooner or later have a negative effect on the technical quality. The number of disruptions and speed limitations would increase and the effect of this is reflected in the transport performance: structurally longer travel times and more train delays. This effect is visible in other countries such as the former Eastern European countries, and countries such as France. In these countries there is awareness about managing technical quality of rail infrastructure but funding is insufficient. The technical quality is regarded as a condition because it is dependent on funds available and the ability to carry out necessary M&R activities. The effect of technical quality is demonstrated in the quality of performance delivered. The technical quality is measured through a complex set of requirements and standards for very different systems. The necessity of an activity is based on the degradation rate of technical standards and requirements.

Managing Risks

Outsourcing of design, construction and renewal is very common. It is project-based work with a clear end and start. There are experienced commissioners and contractors and there is a lot of competition. However, ProRail also outsourced the maintenance of the rail infrastructure. This is unusual. Maintenance is a service, a continuous process until the demolition. There were no experienced contractors but ProRail performed successfully with the maintenance contractors. The performance improved and costs fell. The reason for this is not in outsourcing but in the set-up of a new maintenance process. This process is no longer geared to the controlled execution of maintenance regulations and work plans, but to the prevention of irregularities, better known as 'failures', which threaten the desired performance. This can only be done by carrying out maintenance that is aims to control failure causes and the underlying mechanisms, a selective choice of risk control strategies based on an estimate of the probability and impact of a potential failure. This is risk management, a fundamental management technique for professional asset management. The principles and development of risk management are described in detail in section 6.11.3. The shift from carrying out fixed work plans to controlling causes of failure and underlying mechanisms has led to a revaluation of the task of the foreman and his gang. Fixed maintenance teams are the best in knowing the situation of a line and when this knowledge is combined with information from inspections and measurements, it becomes an art. This can be achieved by having the foreman and his gang collaborate with a permanent team of a work preparator, a work planner and a maintenance engineer. *An effective and efficient maintenance process is not order-driven (= 'push') from the planning side but demand-driven (= 'pull') from the performance and knowledge side about the degeneration of the quality, source of risks and cause of malfunctions.*

Based on the experiences with input-driven OPC contracts, the maintenance contractors and ProRail have learned the hard lesson that maintenance costs and performance are not optimised by centralising the planning and rationalising the execution. Instead, optimisation is achieved by creating ownership among the employees in the maintenance process for the performance of infrastructure and use of operational knowledge and experience. This requires a very different attitude for management and their staff. It is quite difficult to implement when pressure is high to deliver better performance at lower costs. Letting go is difficult and takes time but it is worth the effort because not only the results improve but also the managers and employees work with greater pleasure and satisfaction. It is uncertain whether this will remain so. There is a growing tension due to the effects of tendering and competition. It is becoming increasingly difficult for maintenance contractors to make a profit and that is a precondition for trust, stability, satisfaction and long-term cooperation.

10 Examples of integral asset management

Asset management is a technique that makes it possible to optimally and durably improve the asset results over the entire life cycle, in accordance with the requirements and wishes of the stakeholders. An indispensable characteristic needed for this is the ability to connect people, processes and organisations such that they function as single organism with same purpose. In this chapter, some examples are given that illustrate what is possible if the realisation of a business goal is not dealt with in isolation but in an integral way, and how that is implemented in practice.

Performance improvement of the Utrecht junction

With the railways, large transport flows can be processed safely with only small scarcity in our country. Government and train operators expect that transport will continue to grow in the coming years. To cope with that and to improve the quality of rail transport, the 'Programma Hoogfrequent Spoor' (PHS) program was developed. On the basis of a planning study conducted by ProRail, the government decided to start 'timetable-free' driving in the conurbation of Western Holland with six Intercity trains and six regional trains per hour per direction. The capacity of the existing track had to be increased for this purpose. An important hub for this was Utrecht. Expansion of the number of tracks was not an option here due to limited space, major potential impact on the environment and financial limitations. In order to solve the bottleneck at Utrecht, the government decided to transform Utrecht into Flow Station Utrecht (DSSU), see Figure 94.

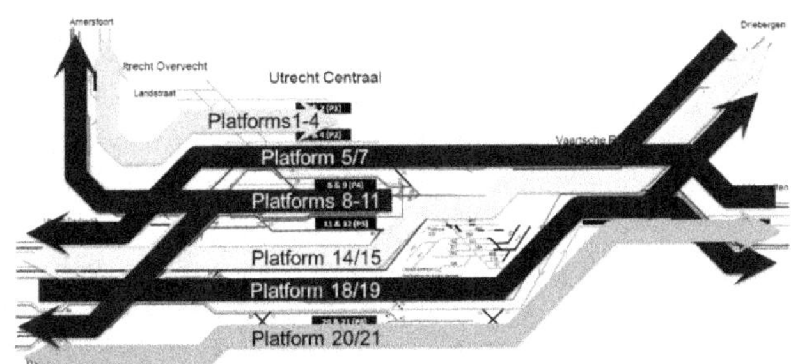

Figure 94   *Flow Station Utrecht (DoorStroomStationUtrecht = DSSU)*

Flowing through is achieved by eliminating crossing, conflicting train traffic and handling train service over fixed, conflict-free corridors. As a result of these changes, around 70% of all switches disappeared, including all double diamond switches that limit the maximum speed at the yard to 40 km/hr. By eliminating switches, straightening tracks and reducing signal distances, passenger trains can follow each other with shorter distances ('2 instead of 3' distance between two trains) and the maximum speed on the entire Utrecht junction increased from 40 km/hr to 80 km/hr. This means that one to two minutes of driving time savings per train is realised and it is possible to schedule 2 * 6 trains per hour per direction. Reducing the number of switches makes shunting difficult, but the positive side effect is a reduction in M&R costs and an improvement in the RAMS performance of the rail infrastructure. Complexity is reduced not only because of fewer switches but also because of lesser associated catenary-, signalling- and traffic control systems.

More capacity and quality for lower life cycle costs is the holy grail for every infrastructure manager. It may seem very logical and simple to reduce the number of switches, but it is not. It is a big step to change the design goal of the main junction in the network from maximising flexibility[68] to maximising performance. Traffic control and NS initially did not want to do this but the budgetary and spatial restrictions forced them to think of this option. To choose the best solution, ProRail worked in design workshops and discussed infra alternatives with all internal and external stakeholders on driving the desired train service, shunting, maintenance and emergencies. Every change was judged on usefulness and necessity and that ultimately led to the final layout realised. The capacity and quality of the solution is much better than those of the old, partly due to the reduction in the number of switches by 70%. A result that involved all stakeholders: government, train operators, traffic control, capacity management and asset management. All parties contributed in this textbook example of integral and professional asset management: *optimal and sustainable management of expenses, risks and performances over the entire life cycle with the aim to realise the strategic plan of the organisation in accordance with the requirements and wishes of the stakeholder* (IAM, 2008*).

It is now customary to host a design workshop when a large switch renewal is needed at a railway yard. For example, the capacity of Enschede, Den Bosch, Amsterdam Zuid, Zevenaar and Arnhem has increased similar to that of Utrecht, and Amsterdam CS, Uitgeest, Den Haag CS, Nijmegen, Amersfoort, Leiden and Haarlem are being worked on. Optimisations do not always succeed because, for example, preparations may have started too late or problems with financing may have occurred. However, the approach and working methods are integrated to continuously improve the price-performance ratio of rail infrastructure and rail transport.

Performance improvement with high speed switch

Until recently, ProRail had two types of high speed: 140 km/hr and 160 km/hr in a curve and, therefore, an angular ratio of 1: 34.7 and 1: 39.1, respectively. The switches are complex because they have very long tongues with several drive rods and control points as well as a movable frog, which according to international

---

[68] That vision was known as the 'open layout' vision. This meant a railway yard design on which all desired train movements could be made, to any rail or platform.

regulations is necessary with an angular ratio of 1:30 or more. Due to the large length and many control points, the alternating performance is highly dependent on the stability of the substructure. As a result, the high-speed switches have, on average, 10x more failures compared to standard switches. Despite modifications and improved maintenance concepts, the high-speed switches continued to perform poorly. It was decided to develop a new type, the 1: 29 high speed switch, that does not have a movable frog and can still be used at 140 km/hr in a curve. At the time, it was decided to fully outsource construction, drive and control, so that the integration is realised by one party. The VAE group, of which Railpro Voestalpine is a part, provided the design according to ProRail's specifications. The 1: 29 change is 135 meters long and is longer than the current switch 1: 34.7. This is because the curve in the switch has been optimised such that it begins to faint and gradually becomes sharper. It is also for the first time in the Netherlands that hydraulic drives are used to move the tongue as in Germany and Austria.

The development of the 1: 29 high speed switch is a good example of professional asset management. It is an improvement of the asset performance based on a clear specification by an experienced external party who also did the full integration of the different sub-systems. Thanks to an integral tendering procedure, maximum use has been made of European knowledge and experience. For the development and manufacture of the new switch, companies throughout Europe had to work closely together. The result is a high-speed switch that performs better, requires less maintenance and, therefore, has (much) lower life cycle costs than the old high-speed types.

Performance improvement in rail transport process

In 2006, the Performance Analysis Bureau (PAB) started at Traffic Control to gain more insight into the train process. The Bureau offers the entire rail sector information and advice in the field of train service to help operators, shippers and ProRail colleagues to improve the train process. The PAB has made significant achievement in reporting and analysing performance data as well as giving advice for business, management and adjustment of train process. This has led to structural improvements in train punctuality, rail capacity and travel time.

Today, the period of structurally low train punctuality is behind us and other problems require attention. These include reducing the impact of major disruptions, busy trains, missed connections and red-light passages. In performance, attention has shifted from train punctuality to passenger punctuality. Increasingly, improvements are being made in the underlying processes and freight traffic is getting more attention in the work package of the PAB. The improvement advice of today focuses on the following terms and domains:

- Short term with lead time of several weeks: focused on execution. For example, roadway setting Traffic Control, stop / go timers, Asset Management and instructions for train drivers.

- Medium term with lead time of about one year: focused on the timetable, especially planning time and use of rail and equipment. Something more fundamental is the change of planning standards or driving time calculations.
- Long-term with lead time of several years: focused on rail infrastructure, often on unbundling and / or the realisation of driving time gains.

Every day, the PAB collects more than twenty gigabytes of planning and realisation data from various computer systems with cryptic names such as TROTS, PRL, VOS, ISVL, Donna, Monitoring and GPS. With its analysis tool 'Sherlock', the PAB makes cross connections between these different systems and provides an integral overview of what has happened per train per day such that both structural and incidental problem situations can be analysed. It is expected that, in the near future, an ever larger proportion of the dis-punctuality and dropout of trains will be automatically explained, and research will be conducted to improve simulation models by better use of realisation data. PAB's work package today consists mainly of:

- Providing standard and customised reports on train service, including punctuality overviews, KPI scores, monitoring data, freight performance, annual compliance report data, noise production ceilings and billing data for rail infrastructure users;
- Advising on current and future timetables, adjusting the train service, development and use of steering indicators, etc.;
- Introducing practical knowledge and analysis capacity in improvement projects (including timetables, infrastructure), Regional Chain Consultations (RKOs), Concession teams (of regional train operators) and Corridor teams (freight);
- Developing, improving and managing analytical tools and management information systems;
- Answering ad hoc questions from colleagues, train operators, shippers and third parties.

In 2013, ProRail PAB and NS Knowledge Center decided to examine one bottleneck every week to look for a structural improvement and communicate broadly on improving train process. The solutions for the 'Point of attention of the week' are varied and include adjusting planning, other routing, more favourable signal images, placement of signals, stop position of train, etc. All these small improvements add up for noticeable and structural improvement of punctuality.

The three examples illustrate how optimal and sustainable result improvements can be realised by connecting all stakeholders in working together on the solution. A common goal and shared analysis based on the same information are important ingredients for success.

11 Benchmarks; results of ProRail in perspective

Rail infra managers are monopolists. To assess their results, they depend on comparisons with other infrastructure managers. For the first time, a cost benchmark was implemented in 1996 by six European infrastructure managers at the initiative of the Union International des Chemins de fer (UIC). The presentation of the initial results led to strong reactions from a few participating countries who disagreed with the results; questioned the methodology and data; and saw benchmark as a condemnation rather than an opportunity to learn from better-performing infra managers. After sometime, the resistance weakened because of the anonymous presentation of the results and because people became familiar with the phenomenon of 'benchmarking' and its use. A benchmark makes it possible to compare the organisation with others, seek better-performing companies to learn from, and help transition from budget-based management to result-based management.

ProRail has participated in the UIC benchmark from the beginning. It also carries out additional benchmarks on its own initiative and uses benchmarking as an instrument for making internal comparisons between regions, lines, projects, etc. This chapter provides insight into the results of various international benchmarks and the position occupied by ProRail and the Dutch rail transport system. Finally, an assessment is made of the performance of ProRail as seen from this international perspective.

11.1 Results of seven international benchmark studies

Introduction

The honest comparison of railway companies and infra managers is quite a complicated task because of differences in circumstances, impact of conditions and data quality on the outcome as well as interpretation of the benchmark outcome. We should consider the influence of purchasing power and differences in utilisation or network complexity on the basis of cost and/or performance comparison. Differences in definitions and methods can also provide comparisons that do not give a correct picture. The value and meaning of a comparison may change completely due to the benchmark unit used: it makes a lot of difference whether one shares the costs by kilometers track, train kilometer, tonne-kilometer or the number of inhabitants in a country.

For example. The UIC has developed a method to compare costs by harmonising infrastructure maintenance costs based on the influence of main cost drivers. The original costs per kilometer main track are corrected by factors for differences in purchasing power, switch density, utilisation intensity (in tonnes), electrification percentage and ratio of double/single track. This method is a good basis for cost comparison but it is quite complex to understand. After years of comparison, it appeared that a comparison based on the original costs per train kilometer, harmonised only for differences in purchasing power, showed about the same outcome. In order to compare costs between regions and lines, ProRail uses not only the costs per kilometer main track as a benchmark unit but also the costs per train kilometer. For international comparisons, ProRail mirrors itself to the Switzerland's SBB, which is comparable in terms of network size and utilisation, and recognised for good performance. ProRail can learn about lowering of maintenance costs from SBB and SBB can possibly learn about lowering of renewal costs from ProRail.

Conclusion: *Benchmarking is the only way a monopolist can assess the results. It is essential to demonstrate to stakeholders and outsiders how to perform, where and how to transition from budget-based to result-based performance. Making good, reliable comparisons is a profession.*

To assess the results of rail transport and infrastructure in the Netherlands and to place them in perspective, I have summarized the results of seven benchmark studies, namely:

1. National ProRail-benchmark rail transport: page 270
2. Benchmark transport performance: page 271
3. ProRail-benchmark of costs and performance: page 272
4. UIC-benchmark of costs and performance: page 273
5. EIM-benchmark costs and performance: page 274
6. UIC-benchmark safety: page 276
7. Benchmark BCG: influence of the chosen method and unit: page 277

1. National ProRail-benchmark rail transport

The easiest way to benchmark is to compare a company's results over the years with circumstances and conditions remaining the same. Table 9 provides a comparison of rail transport systems in the Netherlands.

Table 9   Development of the transport and infra results in the Netherlands

	Unit	1995	2005	2014	Source
Train operators	Amount	1	>30	>30	Annual reports
Passenger transport	Mio train km	119	123	145	Figure 5, (Swier J. , 2016*)
Freight transport	Mio net ton	20,5	35	38,9	
Punctuality	%	85,3	84,8	89,8	Figure 63, (Swier J. , 2015*)
TAO's, technical	Amount	5.563	4.270	3.769	Figure 69, (Swier J. , 2015*)
TAO's, third parties		3.766	4.274	5.500	
TAO's, weather		481	641	579	
TAO's, process		1.075	2.001	1.030	
Cost ratio transport/infra		0,672	0,595	0,494	(Swier J. , 2016*)

TAO = Train Effecting Irregularities

Compared to 1995, passenger and freight transport in the Netherlands has grown sharply in the approximate 20 years. The average annual punctuality has increased from 85.3% to 89.8%, the number of technical TAOs has dropped by 33%, third-party TAOs have risen substantially, process and weather TAOs have remained about the same, and the cost ratio of transport/infrastructure has improved by 24%.

Conclusion: *With the exception of third-party TAOs, all the results of rail transport in the Netherlands improved substantially after the separation of trains and tracks in 1995.*

2. Benchmark transport performance

Apart from Switzerland, the Netherlands has the most intensively used rail network in Europe as measured in train kilometers per kilometer line, see Figure 95. It is more than 2.6x higher than the European average, excluding Greece. Measured in tonne-kilometer per kilometer line, the Netherlands has fourth-highest utilisation intensity in Europe.

Conclusion: *The Dutch rail network is among the most intensively used in Europe.*

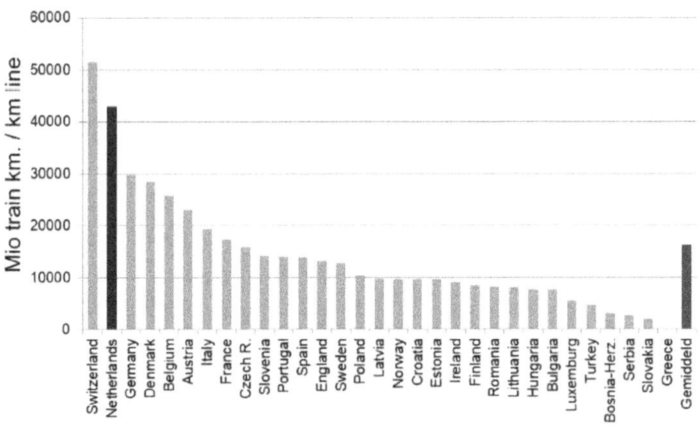

Figure 95   Benchmark utilization. Source: UIC Statistics (Swier J. , 2011*)

In 2014, the NS carried out a benchmark study for transport concession (NS, 2014*). The study contained various benchmarks about performance, including punctuality. According to the report, punctuality cannot be separated from the operational context. For example, it is more difficult to realise high punctuality with a more intensive network; a train with delay causes delays on other trains. In Figure 96, the punctuality is shown relative to rail traffic on the basis of the punctuality threshold <5 ' delay. The figures are indicative due to possible differences in the measuring method or measurement quality, but the order of magnitude is correct.

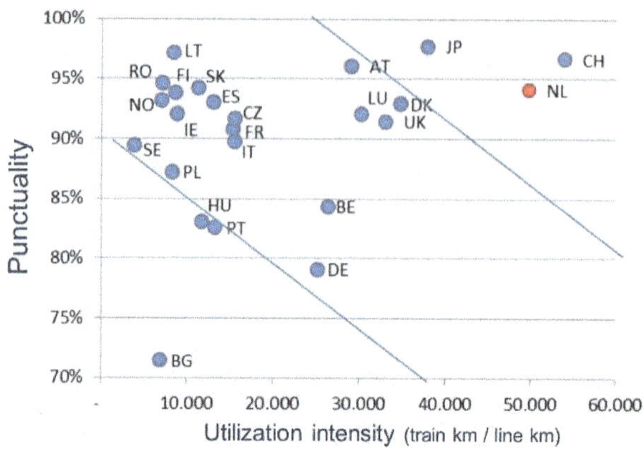

Figure 96   Benchmark punctuality. Source: UIC, ERADIS, 2012 (NS, 2014)*

Conclusion: *Given the high intensity of use, NS and SBB score significantly better on punctuality than the railway companies of other European countries.*

3. ProRail-benchmark of costs and performance

The management concession terms state (I&M M. , 2014-12*) that ProRail must compare its performance every four years with at least five comparable countries and/or areas. That should have happened again in 2015, but postponement was granted until 2017 to do the infrastructure benchmark in the same year as the benchmark from the train operator NS. Due to this delay, the most recent infra benchmark covered in this book is that of year 2011 (CFC, 2011-8*). The most important conclusions from the infrastructure benchmark 2011 are as follows:

- The Netherlands has a complex rail network, which has grown in length by 3% since 2001 and the number of switches has dropped by 12%.

- It has the second highest utilisation of track among the European peers, with an upward trend over the years.

- Life cycle cost per train kilometer remained virtually unchanged despite inflation, while it has increased in other countries. As a result, ProRail generally scores higher on costs, while being above average in 2006.

- Availability has increased compared to 2007, but due to winter weather and fire in 2009 and 2010, respectively, it was lower than that in 2008.

- On the busiest track, ProRail scores average in terms of costs, use and breakdowns. On the regional railway line, ProRail has higher costs but higher than average utilisation.

- In the field of punctuality, ProRail has risen from position 3 to 2 in the peer group.

272

- ProRail delivers above-average punctuality and utilisation at average LCC costs. Compared to other European peers, more trains on the Dutch network have a high punctuality.

- The number of collisions and derailments on the track has decreased in recent years.

- There are only few serious accidents in the Netherlands among employees on the railway.

- The Netherlands has to deal with the largest number of suicides per train kilometer.

- Winter weather not only affects the Netherlands, but also European peers.

Conclusion: *Compared to the peer group, ProRail performed above average in 2011.* In the years that followed, performance improved and maintenance costs decreased further.

4. UIC-benchmark of costs and performance

The UIC started a cost benchmark in 1996, which it has updated every year since. The benchmark is now known as the 'Lasting Infrastructure Cost Benchmark' (LICB). It started with six European companies, including NS Railinfrabeheer, expanded to fifteen, but has twelve active members since 2015. The costs that are benchmarked are those for maintenance and renewal, including organisation or overhead. To make the costs comparable, they are harmonised for the most important cost drivers. Figure 97 illustrates the cost comparison made in 2010. In the nineties, ProRail was 118-130% above the group average, in the years 2000-2010 it varied between 123-104% and in the period 2011-2015 it was between the 117-110%.

Conclusion: *ProRail is about 15% more expensive than the average of European peers after harmonisation for the most important cost drivers.*

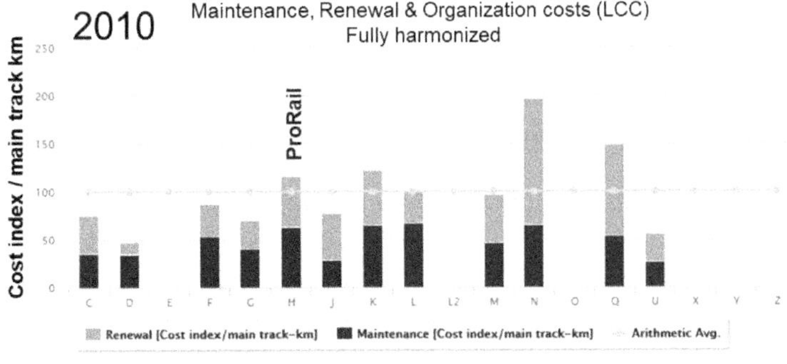

Figure 97   LICB cost benchmark (2010)

In 2010, the LICB also launched a benchmark of the number of train service-related technical failures. It started with seven companies and there were six participants in 2015. Figure 98 illustrates the results. ProRail represents the group of six best companies. The low number of failures in signalling, traffic control and telecom equipment is striking. The number of switch failures is slightly higher.

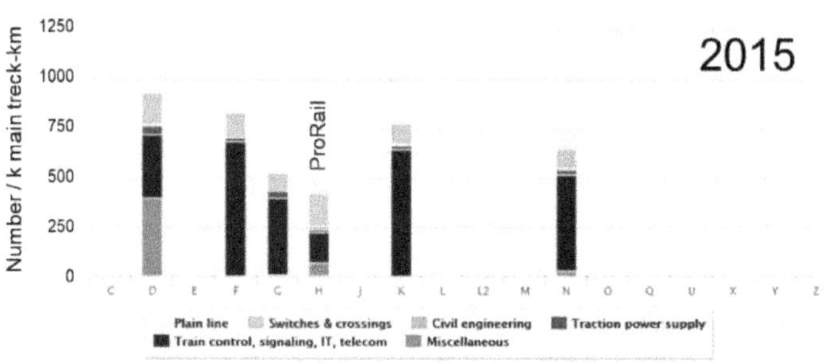

Figure 98   LICB benchmark technical train effecting infra failures (2015)

Conclusion: *ProRail provides the best infra performance among the peer group, measured in terms of the number of technical failures per kilometer main track.*

5.   EIM-benchmark costs and performance

The European Infra Managers (EIM) in Brussels carries out benchmarking in the area of infrastructure costs and -performance for its members. The benchmark differs from others by making infrastructure comparisons for various transport segments, namely: High-speed, Intercity, Regional and Freight, all divided by intensity levels high, medium and low.

In 2012, EIM published a report with cost benchmark per transport segment - low, medium and high (EIM, 2013-6*). Figure 99 illustrates the results for Intercity transport and the two dark green balls represent ProRail.

The cost comparison concerns all maintenance costs and renewal costs of rail and switches. The benchmark unit is track kilometers. The costs are plotted against train intensity, measured in terms of the number of trains per track kilometer on a weekday. In the EIM report, the results of ProRail are briefly summarised as follows:

- The cost difference between ProRail and the average of the peer group is less than 10%.
- The cost difference between ProRail and the lowest costs of the peer group is limited by just over 15%.

- Given the small size of the cost differences and the possible consequences of performance differences, it is not (yet?) possible to conclude that ProRail has a good or bad cost / performance ratio.

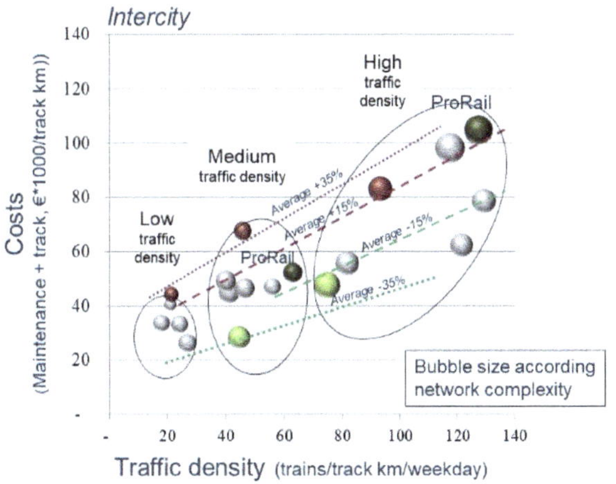

Figure 99   EIM cost benchmark (dark green = ProRail)

The EIM started a performance benchmark directly after the cost benchmark (EIM, 2017-1*). Of the ten infrastructure managers who participated, the data quality of six was sufficient, namely: Network Rail (Great Britain), Trafikverket (Sweden), SNCF (France), ProRail, Infraestructuras de Portugal (Portugal) and Jernbaneverket (Norway). The following method has been used:

- The performance is compared on the basis of the number of failures per track kilometer and impact measured in delay minutes per failure.

- The comparison has been made despite differences in the definitions:
  - Delay thresholds for incidents are not the same (3', 4', 5' or 6').
  - Allocation of failures: infra related, direct and indirect delay minutes.

The result of the EIM benchmark is a comparison of the number of train service effecting failures per track kilometer per transport segment. The performance per transport segment is weighted and put together to determine an overall network performance benchmark. The result is shown in Figure 100.

Comment rapporteurs: *'In view of network breakdown by segment, if ProRail presented average performance among its peers for each segment then its rate of asset failure would be 59% higher and its average delay per failure would be 15% lower'.*

Based on the average performance of other peers, one would expect 59% more failures at ProRail and 15% fewer delay minutes per breakdown. That longer failure time is not a surprise and can be explained by the extra time needed to take the track out of service if there is failure repair in or nearby the track, in the profile of free space (PVR). This does not happen in other peer group countries because the policy places fewer demands on this condition.

Conclusion: *The performance of ProRail is above average compared to the peers.*

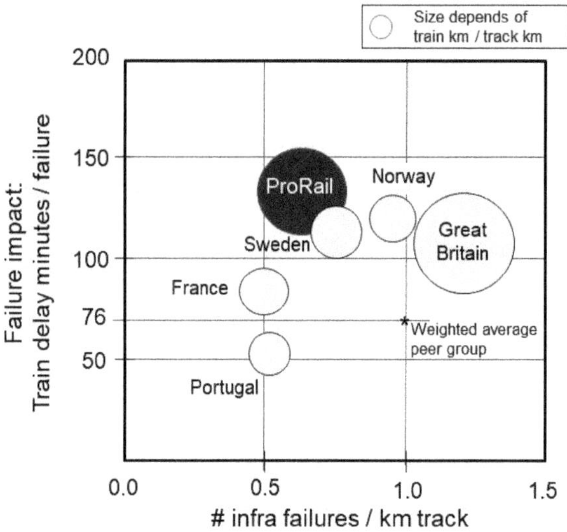

Figure 100   Network performance benchmark

6. UIC-benchmark safety

The UIC prepares an annual confidential safety report in which safety performances of the member countries are compared in benchmark. The report is confidential because this was the condition for many infrastructure managers to participate. The purpose of the report is that infrastructure managers can learn from each other regarding frequency, type and causes of accidents. For this purpose, fifteen indicators are used, whereby the number of accidents or incidents is related to the number of passenger train kilometers on the network.

The report for 2014 shows that the Netherlands/ProRail performs well in relation to most indicators, sometimes considerably better than average (UIC, 2015). The benchmark unit used is the number per billion train kilometers. In Table 10, the scores of ProRail are compared with the UIC average. The Netherlands has 156 million kilometers of train travel annually and, therefore, the numbers may seem large.

Table 10   UIC benchmark safety figures: ProRail and UIC average

	ProRail # per billion train km	**UIC average** # per billion train km
Level crossing accidents	83	104
Accidents	141	445
Deadly victims (excl. suicide)	58	221
Derailments	13	31
Collisions	32	44
Collision with person (incl. suicide)	1,3	1,3
Amount STS-passages	>UIC average	Pm

A public version of the report, in which confidential information is omitted, is available on the UIC website and includes participating infrastructure managers.

Conclusion: *ProRail has a high level of safety.*

7. Benchmark BCG: influence of the chosen method and unit

The Boston Consulting Group (BCG) published a benchmark in 2015 on the performance of the railways in twenty-five European countries (BCG, 2015-3). This benchmark differs somewhat from the previous one because it illustrates pitfalls caused by the method and / or benchmark unit used, and the effect these have on the outcomes and conclusions.

BCG has developed a 'Rail Performance Index' (RPI) for the benchmark. It measures performance in three dimensions with eight variables, and aggregates them on the basis of a percentage distribution. The dimensions and variables are as follows:

- Use: passenger kilometers and net freight kilometers per inhabitant;
- Service quality: punctuality of regional trains (<5 'delay), punctuality of long-distance trains (<15' delay), share of high-speed services and price of a train ticket;
- Safety: number of accidents and fatalities per train kilometer.

BCG's conclusion with regard to the Netherlands: *'With a score of 5.2, this country has a very good safety level, but its good rating for intensity of use stems from low freight utilization. Its quality-of-service rating is poor.'* According to the BCG, the Dutch railway network scores high on safety, but the score is far behind the dimensions of use intensity and service quality. That's strange. Switzerland and the Netherlands have similar network size and both have the highest user intensity and punctuality in Europe.

According to the BCG, Switzerland with an RPI of 7.1 is on position one and the Netherlands with a RPI of 5.2 is on position ten. The explanation for this ranking is in the benchmark units used. Switzerland has fewer inhabitants and proportionately more freight transport. In service quality, the Netherlands scores worse because there is almost no high-speed transport and there are no long-distance trains whose punctuality is measured on the basis of <15 'delay.

BCG has also analysed the cost-effectiveness of the railways. The RPI is compared with government expenditure on the railways. The results indicate that for every euro of public money that the Dutch government invests in rail transport and ProRail, the consumer gets the most value and cost-effectiveness is lowest. That is logical because the Netherlands is the most densely-populated country in Europe and use of train is relatively less per inhabitant.

Conclusion: *Due to the benchmark units and method used, the BCG benchmark study does not provide a good insight into the cost-effectiveness of rail transport and infra.*

11.2 Overall assessment of ProRail performance & costs

The value of a benchmark depends on the method and benchmark units. The benchmarks may differ because of their goal and target group. However, it is quite possible to draw a general conclusion on the basis of previous benchmarks with regards to the costs and performance of transport and infrastructure. *The utilisation intensity of the network and punctuality of transport in the Netherlands are, together with Switzerland, among the highest in Europe. The rail infrastructure is of high quality and the maintenance and renewal costs that are 10-15% above the European average.*

Third Part

Reflection and Closing

Change is natural

Change is often seen as a difficult process. Managers benefit from this. Change makes their task difficult and they are well paid. However, the truth is that people do not find it very annoying to change because is in our inherent nature and we automatically adapt to the circumstances. Fear of change is a myth, as per Professor Hans Wissema. He discovered that people want to change themselves, they just do not want to be changed. (Starren, 2016, p. #43)

Part III: REFLECTION and CLOSING

12 Lessons learned and future forecast

The previous two sections of the book describe the process through which a fragmented and internally-oriented infrastructure organisation within the railway company NS developed into an independent, commercially operating, externally-oriented infrastructure manager with a well-functioning asset management system. This last part reflects on the evolution to summarise the main lessons learned and forecast future trajectory. We realise only one thing is certain: change. The world is constantly changing and we need to respond to it sooner or later.

12.1 Lessons learned

This section deals with the lessons that ProRail has learned in implementing an asset management system. There are seven lessons that deal with the following aspects:

1. Major influence of role separation and interpretation. Page 281
2. Organic growth of an AM-system; *the journey is the goal*. Page 284
3. Start by putting the M&R house in order. Page 286
4. Master specific AM-techniques. Page 288
5. Core qualities: integral approach, connecting and informing. Page 289
6. Sharing and securing information and knowledge. Page 290
7. *Man is the measure* and good leadership a condition. Page 292

For each aspect, the lesson is first briefly summarised and then explained, with references to background information. The lessons also summarise the contents of the book. For example, the first lesson deals with the subject covered in the first chapter of the book: the circumstances, in particular, role separation and role fulfilment.

1. Major influence of role separation and interpretation

The government has major influence on the development of an asset management system. The way in which it allocates various roles and the process it determines for communication, affects the relationships of role players. It takes time, attention and leadership to build an environment where people collaborate professionally.

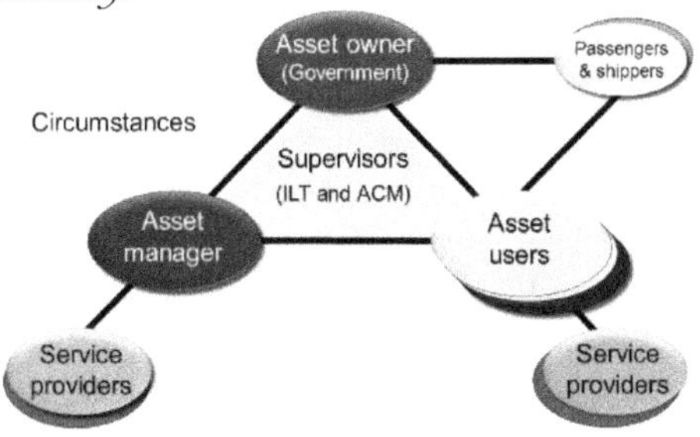

Today, ProRail is an independent infrastructure manager that is increasingly able to manage the costs and performance of rail infrastructure optimally and sustainably over the entire life cycle of the assets. This is expected but success is not self-evident. The organisation's development had decisive influence on the results. When we look at the way in which transport and infrastructure are separated in Europe, we can observe the consequences of role allocation, positioning of traffic control and privatisation of service providers.

Two examples for illustration: Great Britain and France. In Great Britain, transport and infrastructure were separated in the 1990s, the infra was listed on the stock exchange and maintenance was outsourced on the basis of performance contracts. Within ten years the infra organisation was a public company and the maintenance was done inhouse again This was because the circumstances that were created provided the wrong incentives, the result of which was that infrastructure deteriorated and performance declined. In France, transport and infrastructure were separated in the 1990s, but in a very modest way. The maintenance department was not part of the infra manager RFF but rather stayed with the train operator SNCF. Traffic control was the function of independent organisation SNCF and capacity management was the function of independent organisation RFF. In about 2015, it was decided to merge operations and infrastructure again. The rail infra manager had weakened by poor division of roles, the rail transport sector was divided and connections between organisations were under tension. The examples illustrate the extent of the influence of the circumstances on the development of an infrastructure manager.

In the Netherlands, many radical and fundamental choices were made during the period of railway restructuring. Roles were separated incrementally and converged to form an institutional triangle, execution tasks were assigned to service providers and the links between the role players were developed. The seed for this development was laid in the sixties, when rail transport started to make structural losses and the network was declared unprofitable. The government became increasingly involved in the management of rail transport by providing an annually increasing subsidy, and grew into an essential role player who ultimately developed the Rail Road Act and an institutional triangle. In the intervening period of about thirty-five years, several decisions were made that were instrumental in creating the suitable conditions for the infrastructure manager ProRail. The intermediate milestones of this period are as follows:

- 1969. The Netherlands railway network declared unprofitable and the government performs role in financing the railways deficits.
- 1988. NS director Ploeger decides not to include the Rail21 plan in the NS strategy and to leave this choice to the national government who establishes policy and pays for transport. Ploeger put the government in a new, correct role.
- 1989. On the basis of an analysis by McKinsey, the NS management opts for bundling of infrastructure-related business units and

privatising the engineering firm. This was an important first step in shaping the role and task of the infra manager.

- 1992. The government rejects the advice of the Wijffels Commission and opt not for an administrative separation of transport and infrastructure, but rather an economic and legal one. The roles of 'asset user', 'asset manager' and 'asset owner' are consequently separated.

- 1994. Quite unexpectedly, the Minister of Transport, Public Works and Water Management (V&W) announces an initial public offering (IPO) of NS. This caused uncertainty regarding future of the organisation and unrest among the employees. The IPO was cancelled in 2002. The announcement of the IPO is an example of an impulsive, incorrect and poorly-timed policy intervention with negative consequences for passengers, operators and industry.

- 1995. Privatisation of the NS engineering firm, which resulted in a clean separation of the roles of 'asset manager' and 'service provider'.

- 1998. Privatisation of all executive activities and companies in infrastructure. NS Railinfrabeheer becomes the sole asset manager and service providers are responsible for execution of M&R activities. The companies were new, often without any experience with contract management. There were questions about the approach and timing, but the choices ultimately worked out well.

- 2002-2003. Project "Benutten & Bouwen (English: Utilize & Build) was launched by the Ministry of V&W to develop a vision for managing transport growth together with all parties in the rail transport sector. There was a joint proposal to improve use of existing infrastructure and the project contributed to the design, development and collaboration of new roles and business processes.

- 2003. Due to a deterioration in the maintenance of infrastructure, a recovery plan was required. ProRail AM presented three cost-benefit scenarios to the government. It was the first time that the government had options to choose from: different network performances with corresponding price tags. This approach gave shape and substance to the roles of the government and infrastructure manager. It was well-timed because the infrastructure organisation was able to implement one of the scenario's.

- 2005. In the first management concession, targets were not set for improving the results but for the organisation quality, which was expressed in the form of four conditions to be able to switch to 'output' management. This was a powerful incentive for ProRail to set targets to improve its organisational quality.

- 2008. The ProRail management decides to gradually introduce Enterprise Risk Management (ERM) as the guiding principle for management, which is based on knowledge, transparency and accountability.

This turned out to be an important condition for further development of the asset management system.

- 2010. The management establishes a manual for safety management system Veiligheid (VMS) based on risk management principles and techniques. This was an important stimulus for development of the asset management system.
- 2012. ProRail AM starts the SAM programme for the development of performance risk analyses and control measures. These were partly developed, but the introduction had stalled because purpose was not clear and the organisation was not prepared for it. The introduction of ERM and VMS created the policy incentive for AM puzzle pieces to fall into place.

The rail transport sector was divided into several independent organisations in the period 1990-2005 on the basis of roles. This division created many interfaces and it took fifteen years to establish ways to make the system work. That may sound as a long period but it was transformational in developing new forms of cooperation and change of culture. In hindsight, it can be said that it was prudent to separate the roles fully and provide time to organisations to establish base before pursuing higher goals. One wonders if the timeline could have been shorter or the process better or if the current governance model could be chosen immediately. Opinions are divided. Today, there are more formal interfaces because of the separation and outsourcing. It makes it more complex but also make opposing business interests visible to everyone. This can be explained positively but also negatively. The results are better than before all changes, organizations are developing well and employees are generally satisfied; what more do we want?.

2. Organic development AM-System; the journey is the goal

The development of a professional asset management system is a journey that is organic, passes through coherent orientation phases and leads to total quality control such that performance, risks and costs can be optimally and durably managed over the entire life cycle.

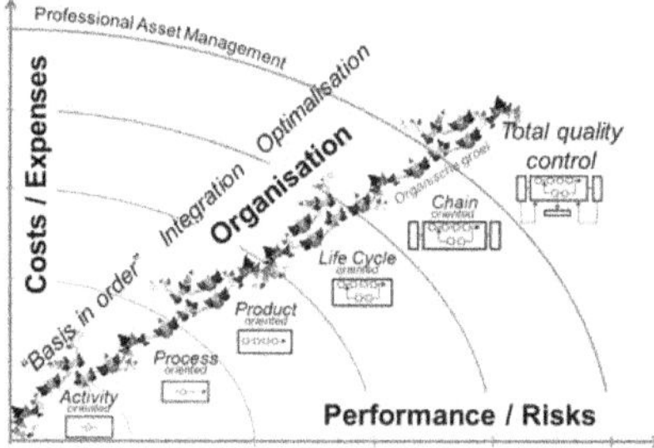

It took more than ten years for the asset management system to take shape at ProRail. This seemingly long time was partly due to unfavourable conditions experienced in the initial phase and partly because changes involved touched the entire value chain and culture of all the organisations involved. The development can be seen as an organic growth process that comprised coherent phases involving many large and small changes. None of those phases could be skipped. In each stage, the quality of the organisation went higher, employees gained more control and self-confidence in improving process and results, and the stakeholders became more satisfied. Time is relative when the journey is the goal. A highly ambitious performance target puts excessive pressure on the people involved, requires lot of energy and can lead to false expectations. When the goal is the journey then we create conditions that encourage people to work together and processes to develop naturally. As a result, people's confidence grows, they perform better and the organisation function more efficiently. Such change is an organic growth process where the road to the goal paved with many small intermediate results. Railinfrabeheer adopted the journey as the goal because it was the only way to survive. Nobody at Railinfrabeheer, at the M&R contractors and other infra companies could accept high and abstract targets at the time. The aim was to develop missing tools and skills and to make connections between people, processes and products, starting with those that were most needed.

In the period between the separation (1995) and privatisation (2003/2005) of NS Railinfrabeheer, the foundation was lain for the M&R organisation at ProRail AM. The organisation structure was good, tools and information systems were appropriate, and the people gained control of costs and performance. The development of the AM system then proceeded to the next phase, in which all lifecycle processes were integrated to establish a link between the investment and operating phases. Initiatives were already underway in this area, but they had to be elaborated organisation-wide and implemented in the work processes. The introduction of lifecycle-, risk- and RAMS-management, as well as the safety management system (VMS) throughout the organisation were important milestones. In that period, the relationship with stakeholders and service providers began to develop and conditions were optimised across the entire chain. The orientation of the organisation grew step-by-step: from activity to process, from process to product, from product to lifecycle and finally to control of the whole chain. This growth in orientation and focus is illustrated through four examples:

1. After the separation and privatisation of all executive activities, Railinfrabeheer's focus was on developing tools and managing budgets, tasks and malfunctions. There was a shift in this strategy when ProRail management commissioned three result scenarios in 2003 to improve performance. It initiated transition from management of budgets to management of performance and costs. It was a risk but the timing was suitable because the necessary insights and instruments had been developed. For more details, please refer section 3.1, period 2002-2005.
2. Before the separation, Railinfrabeheer was highly technical and internal oriented. In order to make the change to an organisation focussed on performance control, it was essential to register failures properly.

Railinfrabeheer grew its fairly simple database to a well-managed SAP application with an increasingly complete and superior recording of all failure information: numbers, duration, causes, circumstances and consequences for train service. The failure registration now connects ProRail with the contractors and train operators. It is a cornerstone in the foundation of the asset management system. For more details, please refer section 7.4.

3. The first performance risk analyses were made in 1997. It was only after the introduction of risk management at the Board level in 2008, that ERM and VMS were introduced. Shortly thereafter, the System Asset Management (SAM) programme was initiated to develop performance risk management in the AM processes and the necessary instruments. For more details, please refer section 6.11.3.

4. Outsourcing of maintenance started with input-driven OPC contracts based on work plans, an open budget and annual price agreements. Both parties developed instruments, knowledge and information to manage maintenance. After ten years, ProRail was ready to award the first performance contract (PGO) based on output specifications, process control and risk management principles. The contract presented a huge change for the client and contractors. It caused tensions, even lawsuits and temporary suspension of tenders because some contractors did not want or could change from an input-driven to an output-controlled contract so suddenly. As a result, the implementation took about four years longer than planned. For more details, please refer chapter 4.

The examples illustrate how the focus of the people in the organisations shifted incrementally: from technology to performance, objectives to functions, input to output and failures duration to failure causes and impact. It is challenging to choose the right pace, timing, process and setting. Good leadership is needed to make choices in an environment of constant tension, balancing needs, options and expectations. Changing circumstances have an impact that cannot be underestimated and partly determines the route of the journey to professional asset management. In summary, the most important lesson to draw from the development of the asset management system at ProRail: *the journey to a professional AM system is the goal, man is the measure, course-seeking leadership is indispensable and good timing of milestones crucial.*

Developing a properly functioning asset management system takes years. It fully depends (and therefore starts) with the professionalization of the maintenance & renewal organization. That is where the core, continuity and assurance of (rail) asset management is located. To do this, start by setting up a good asset and failure registration and learn from each failure: find out the cause, determine the severity and determine whether and how the failure can best be

> prevented in the future, so what the best maintenance strategy is. Do only what is demonstrably necessary to realize the wanted performance. By doing this systematically and structurally record the results, you are busy developing and implementing performance risk management, a fundamental technique for optimizing performance, risk and costs over the life cycle, so asset management.

3. Start by putting the M&R organisation in order

Start by putting 'the house' of the management M&R organisation (now known as ProRail AM) in order as a process-oriented organisation, which controls performance and costs, has the right tools, and orderly organized ICT and information provision.

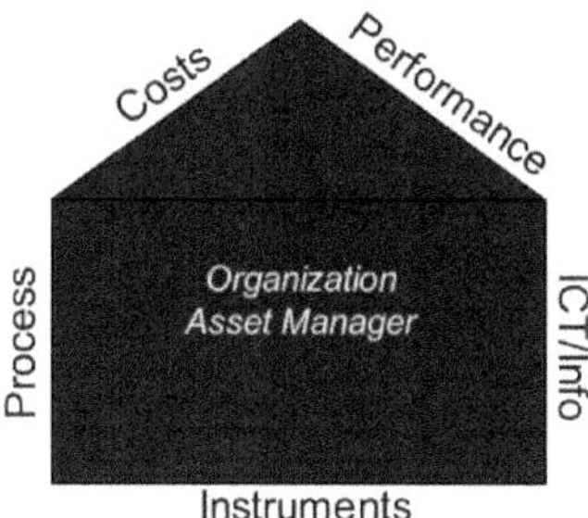

The development of ProRail started with the privatisation of NS-engineering in 1990. The M&R organisation had to take over tasks, which became complicated when it was decided to privatise all executive maintenance activities. The traditional, internally-oriented M&R organisation had to evolve with specific attention to five developments:

1. Management of task to processes,
2. Management of technique to performance of railway lines,
3. Change in financial focus from budget to cost,
4. Implementation of management techniques and tools
5. Organization of ICT and information management

The M&R organisation thus changed into an asset management organisation, the basis for a well-functioning asset management system and capable of managing the costs, risks and performance optimally and sustainably over the entire life cycle of the assets. The development of the AM system started after NS Railinfrabeheer, NS Traffic Control and Railned came together under the trade name ProRail in 2003 and merged in 2005 into ProRail Ltd. The following milestones mark the development of the M&R organisation and AM system:

- 1990-1994. All engineering firm activities are privatised. For more details, please refer sections 1.3 and 3.1
- 1994-1998. All executive maintenance activities are privatised. For more details, please refer chapter 4.

- 1995. The M&R organisation changes the structure from technical systems to processes. For more details, please refer sections 3.1 and 6.7.

- 1995-2005. The focus of the M&R organisation shifts from budgets and regulations to costs, performance, specifications and work plans. Missing instruments are developed and implemented. These include a failure registration, a production plan, technical policy, a financial administration, maintenance contracts, specifications, long-term renewal plan, etc. For more details, please refer chapters 3 and 4.

- 2005. There is a company-wide vision on information: one ICT organisation and information management system per business unit. For more details, please refer section 6.11.4.

- 2006. With the business intelligence application RailFocus, it becomes possible to estimate costs, performance and objectives from a wide range of data sources and bring them together on one computer screen. There are online dashboards for availability, reliability and safety. For more details, please refer section 7.8.

4. Master specific AM-techniques

In order to manage costs and performance optimally and sustainably over the entire life cycle, a link must be established between the investment and exploitation phases, and between the business goals and the realisation. The organisation must master specific management techniques, such as life cycle management, risk management, RAMS management, maintenance management and information management.

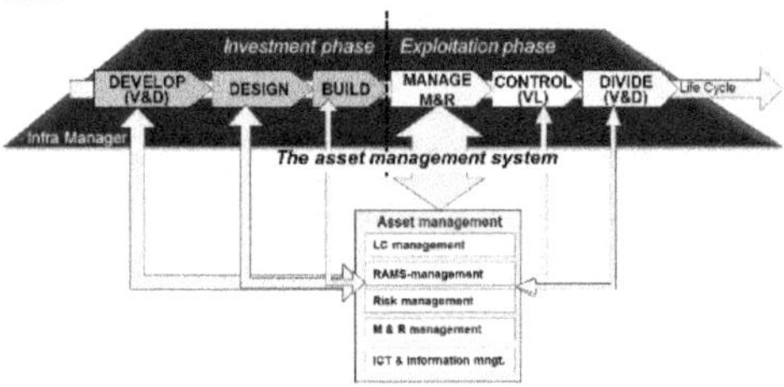

The aim of asset management is to optimally and sustainably manage the costs, risks and performance of the assets over the entire life cycle. For this the link must be established between the exploitation and investment phase and between the intended goals and their realisation. There are various instruments for making that connection and each has its own intrinsic value. The instruments mentioned are the core skills to be mastered for professional asset management. For more details, please refer chapter 6.

- ***Life Cycle Management*** supports decision-making by providing insight into the financial consequences over the entire life cycle of multiple project solutions and comparing them. The LC-cost includes the costs of loss of quality because of failures and other incidents, and associated social consequences. It connects the processes in the investment and exploitation phase with the goals to be realised.

- ***RAMS management*** is the process and method to explicitly manage the RAMS performance over the entire life cycle based on system engineering and risk management principles. It connects the processes in the investment and exploitation phases with the performance targets.

- ***Risk management*** is the process and method to systematically establish the relationship between risks that threaten performance and the most optimal method for managing the risks. It safeguards all maintenance knowledge, structures information and manages costs and performances explicitly and in coherence. It connects the processes in the investment and exploitation phase, and the cost and performance targets to be realised.

- ***M&R management*** is the process and the method to choose the most optimal M&R strategy in the exploitation phase. It connects the maintenance and renewal process, and the cost and performance goals to be realised.

- ***ICT & Information management***. No asset management system can exist without a good ICT organisation and information management. It is a cornerstone in the establishment of an AM-system.

5. Core qualities Asset Manager: integral, to connect and to inform

An asset manager is the connecting link between stakeholders expectations and services of providers, i.e. between strategic goals for the network and operational activities to be realised. This requires an integrated approach and the ability to connect all actors and stakeholders across the entire life cycle.

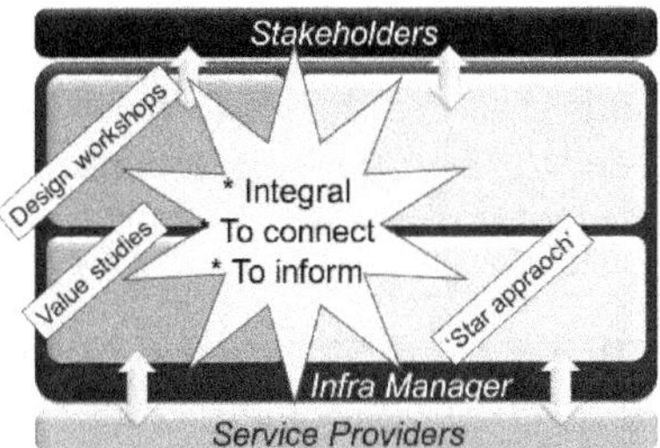

An independent infrastructure manager such as ProRail has a special task and position: managing a production tool commissioned by the national government, used by several train operators, and full outsourcing of executive activities. ProRail is the connecting link between stakeholders expectations and activities realised by the service providers. It is the tactician who determines how the asset goals of the stakeholders are realised in the most optimal and sustainable way. It is the infrastructure manager who realises new transport capacity by designing and commissioning new assets with the desired functionality and capabilities.

In the operational phase, the infrastructure manager delivers performance in the form of RAMS quality based on the network made available to the train operators. From its role and position, the infra manager determines the effectiveness of the entire infra process (*'Do I do the right things'*) and the efficiency of the service providers (*'Do I do things right'*). To choose the most optimal and sustainable solution, the integral approach to issues is a core quality that an infrastructure manager must have. It involves a trade-off between the requirements and interests of different stakeholders and the technology. Issues need to be approached and optimised from multiple angles. It is achieved by connecting stakeholders, specialists and decision-makers with each other and coordinating efforts. At ProRail, this happens in different ways in project development. For example, the 'value studies' in which all interested parties examine why a project is needed, which solutions are possible and what is the most optimal solution. Another example is 'design workshops' in which all organisational units analyse the most optimal and sustainable layout of existing railway yards and lines, and are advised on the possible adaptation of these options. An appealing result of a design workshop is the "Flow Station Utrecht"(in Dutch: DoorStroomStationUtrecht; DSSU), where more capacity has been created with fewer switches within a limited budget. For more details, please refer section 0. In order to select the most optimal project approach, an integral life cycle analysis is conducted and connection between people in the investment and exploitation processes is established.

ProRail Asset Management has developed its own working method for the development and implementation of new policy. This method is called the 'star approach'. It was needed because policy developers were often unable to manage the implementation process. An AM-colleague organises the 'star' by bringing together all parties and coordinating implementation. The parties identify consequences, align interests and plan implementation to control quality. For the three different working methods - value study, design workshop and star approach - an integral approach is needed to realise goals and connect all parties involved. These are the core qualities of an asset manager.

6. Sharing and securing information and knowledge

Organise the safeguarding and sharing of data, information and knowledge. Data models are essential for exchanging and combining information. To store and transfer knowledge, documentation must be easily accessible and professional training should be provided.

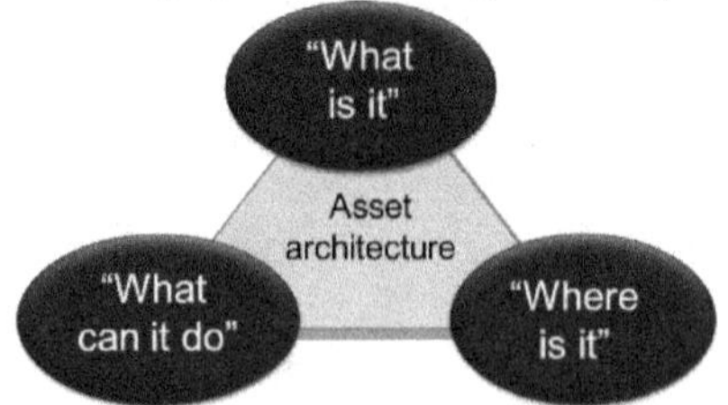

No asset management is possible without information sharing. The value addition depends of the quality and accessibility of the information. It is essential to record data at the source to be able to share and combine it. Technology exists to link networks, but an asset information model is needed to exchange and combine asset data. The asset information model describes the way in which specific asset characteristics and values are recorded. The master data has information about the object ('what is it'), location ('where is it'), function ('what can it do'), architecture and logical coherence of the asset in the network. ProRail deploys the "spoortakken model" (= 'track branch model'). With consistent use of the information model, very different databases are linked and data is exchanged and combined. The experience is comparable to that of speaking a common language. With an asset information model, not only can data be revealed, exchanged and combined but also all asset-specific knowledge and documentation such as drawings, calculations and regulations can be made accessible. The following is an overview of milestones achieved in the development of the asset information model and safeguarding of knowledge at ProRail:

- By privatising the engineering firm, Railinfrabeheer was forced to standardise substantial integral technical and administrative knowledge. Agreements were made about the ownership of the archives and the transfer of drawings and documentation.

- When it was decided to outsource small-scale maintenance, the scope of work had to be clearly demarcated. For this purpose, a TESI list was prepared with all types of activities and grouped according to type of system and object as well as method of financing. The list is a necessary data model used by AM planning and AM Operations.

- An object (or asset) tree was created to implement SAP information system (1998). It ensured that Railinfrabeheer used an asset data model from the beginning for 'What is it'. Unfortunately, the model was not compulsorily imposed on the maintenance contractors, as a result of which the direct exchange of information was not possible. On both sides, however, the need grew to be able to do so. The programme 'Spoordata.NL' (2014-2017) ensures structural regulation by introducing asset-information models for the entire industry.

- Around 2005, the management decided to have a dashboard for steering processes and controlling quality. The underlying data had to be made accessible to the entire organisation to enable further analyses. The business information application RailFocus was purchased to link and combine data sets by costs, performance and assets. This was a quantum leap in the development of asset management. The process was not optimal but it opened a door and paved the way for an effective unlocking and use of information.

- Since the beginning, the NS Railinfrabeheer used line codes, kilometers and rail numbers as data models for geographical identification. This was perfect when there were no computers but it was inconsistent for digital recording and linking of databases. The rail model was introduced and a recording based on x-y-z coordinates was adopted to connect to external reference systems. The line code/kilometers are still maintained as a secondary model to connect with geographic data in earlier documentation.

- At ProRail, there was a growing need to gain insight into maintenance because it was being outsourced. This was only possible when M&R Concepts became available and a methodology was developed to derive 'Information Supply Specifications' (ILS) from the M&R concepts. The ILS's are now included as a specification in the PGO contract.

Safeguarding and sharing of knowledge and information is a core task for every asset manager. If all executive activities are outsourced then higher requirements are imposed because several parties are involved. Knowledge and information about the assets are not only guaranteed and passed on through the information systems but also imparted as part of the vocational training courses for the employees of service providers and ProRail. In 2001, 'Railinfra Opleidingen' (RIO), the institute for rail infra training, was established as an independent training institute with representatives from across the industry in the board. Its mission is: *'We help your employees to develop into high-quality professionals who work on a safe and reliable rail infrastructure'*. In 2016, the name 'Railinfra Opleidingen' was changed to 'Railcenter' and the objective was expanded to create a place where all players in the rail infrastructure sector can meet to stimulate cooperation and innovation. In order to facilitate the development of knowledge and expertise, ProRail started the learning environment 'ProLeren' in 2015. It provides an overview of all external training suppliers with which ProRail has agreements. It makes searching, booking, recording and evaluation easier and interactive.

7. Man is the measure and good leadership a condition

The employees in the organisation determine the results. To function properly, they must be empowered, in safe and supportive organisational conditions. Good managers create such conditions and make the best use of the capabilities of their employees by setting challenging yet achievable goals at the right time and they provide the right attention.

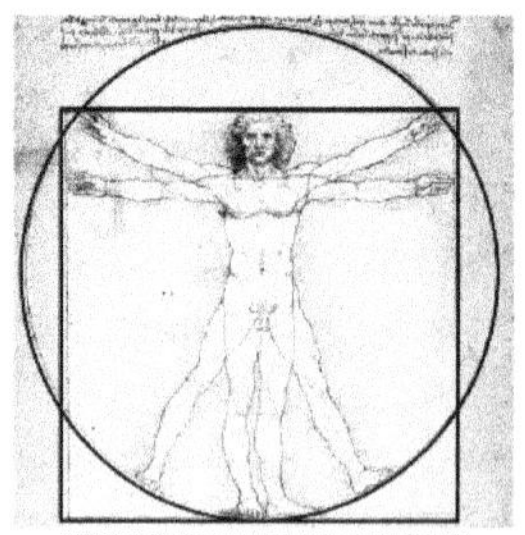

Vitruviusman of Leonardo da Vinci

In this book, the development of the infrastructure manager ProRail and the asset man*agement system is explained on the basis of structures, systems, processes and evolution. It is a fairly mechanistic approach. The advantage is that it provides insight in a structured, systematic way into the suitable conditions and development of an AM organisation. However, it is the people and the interaction between them that determines the results. People require a safe and enabling working environment with respect and appreciation for each other, work that offers sufficient challenge and supportive organisational conditions. The way in which managers guide, use qualities and talents of, and train employees plays a crucial role. It is important to develop clarity about the evolution of the organisation, establish binding values, and pay attention to changing circumstances and new developments.

For employees to function effectively, it is essential to feel safe, satisfied at work, and motivated to achieve challenging goals at the right time. Research shows that successful leaders are capable of inspiring, motivating, connecting and clarifying employees about the course to adopt and the higher goals to pursue. In the initial years after the separation and outsourcing of maintenance, this was not easy. The people lacked knowledge, experience and basic control instruments to fill in the new role of infra manager. The attention of the M&R management of Rail-infrabeheer was focused on their development during that period. This gave something to hold on to. Slowly, but surely, confidence level grew and a new identity emerged. With the establishment of ProRail in 2003/2005, people and organisation grew in their role. They started to look for connections with other business units, and as a result of this, asset management function began to develop into an asset management system. Management was successful in connecting with the stakeholders and service providers. In the beginning, communication was often forced by the circumstances and there was dissatisfaction in dealing with each other, accessing information or achieving cooperation. A bureaucratic infra manager had to learn about customer service. In 2009, an article was published in the magazine 'Binnenlands bestuur': *"PrutsRail wordt ProRail."* (English: 'PotterRail becomes ProRail"). It was a signal that the company culture and orientation were really changing. Without inspiring, effective and course-seeking leadership that would not have been possible. The employees also experienced this and their appreciation is outlined in the results of four SKOOP studies. ProRail conducts this study every two years to measure employee satisfaction. In short, an outline of the outcomes is as follows:

- *SKOOP 2010.* Response 78%. ProRailers are satisfied and involved, but expect that the process be more effective and efficient. Most employees value their supervisor and are satisfied with their development opportunities.
- *SKOOP 2012.* Response 72%. ProRailers are very involved in the organisation but simultaneously look for their role within the company. High involvement, motivation and loyalty are positive. Many

employees also indicate that the working atmosphere and dealing with direct colleagues is pleasant. Many ProRailers express low satisfaction about customer focus, operations efficiency, performance and role clarity.

- *SKOOP 2014.* Response 74.1%. Scores are high for satisfaction but significantly lower for work experience. Lower ratings were achieved for involvement, enthusiasm, development opportunities, job security, confidence in management and openness for different opinions.
- *SKOOP 2016.* Response 81.8%. ProRail secures appreciation on almost all themes except efficiency. Trust in management increased considerably but assessment of efficiency and effectiveness remained low. This was because time, energy and focus are too fragmented.

Employees are satisfied, safe, appreciated and well informed. Today they are once again proud of their company. It is clear, however, that employees expect the organisation to become more effective, efficient, and customer-oriented. They expect the process to be better, but they also understand that it is complex, requires team effort and dependent on the environment. ProRail is well on its way but has not yet reached its final destination.

The lessons that ProRail has learned are universal in character. They are about creating the right conditions under which the AM system will grow organically the organisational basis; developing the core qualities and speaking common 'asset management language' in the sector. However, man is the measure, and the circumstances and leadership determine the path followed and goal achieved.

12.2 Future expectations

Future expectations are not facts and analyses but personalised estimates. This subject has been added to make it clear that the development of the asset management system will continue. This is because circumstances change, stakeholders set new requirements, and there is innovation in products and management techniques. Future expectations are provided for developments at three coherent levels: circumstances, organisation and the AM system.

Circumstances

The question is what changes in circumstances have an impact on rail transport and how will the change be like. There may be changes in road transport because of electric and autonomous driving, a development that is set in motion and not likely to stop. When cars become electric, they become more environmentally-friendly like trains and when cars are autonomous, they are more attractive especially over medium and long distances. Such vehicles are safer due to fewer accidents, faster due to less traffic jams and more comfortable. In order to remain competitive, rail transport needs to become more reliable, faster and comfortable. The capacity of infrastructure and trains must be increased, the vulnerability to disruptions should be reduced and the layout of the trains must be customised as per the needs of passengers and shippers. Japan and Hong Kong may show the way: well-protected non-intersecting lines with fixed combinations of train and personnel, and possible use of autonomous driving trains. That is a lot for rail infrastructure and transport. It is not possible with small incremental steps but requires a jump in innovation of the entire system. The big question is who takes the initiative: government, infrastructure manager or train operators. Given the separation of transport and infrastructure, and the role and position of the government it is a task for all. But as policymaker of (public) transport and financier of the rail infrastructure, the government has a stimulating and coordinating role and must challenge the sector to come up with solutions.

Organisation

The further splitting up and combining of roles and processes is always possible, but it does not seem very likely because the current division of roles is fundamental, and no developments are anticipated that give rise to major process adjustments. Of course, they can always come from the political side, but that is beyond consideration here. While there are no expectations with regards to structural changes, there may be changes in people and culture. By outsourcing all executive tasks in an environment of growing complexity of the asset management system, there is the threat that organisations will withdraw in their own tasks and processes, even though an integrated approach and connection with other organisations is necessary. Continuity and trust are important preconditions for this. A few examples of the conflicts are as follows:

- By delivering in accordance to performance contracts, contractors may lose contracts and incur significant fines. These risks have a negative influence on the relationship between client and contractor.
- Technological developments are fast, particularly in maintenance. With a contract term of five years, there is little chance for contractors to invest in cost-saving innovations themselves because the payback period is (too) short.
- By outsourcing maintenance, not only technicians but also contract experts and lawyers become part of the maintenance process. Parties have different interests and that gives rise to conflicts. A healthy balance is needed in this case.

My future expectation is that new contract forms will be introduced that stimulate people, processes and companies to cooperate and work from an integral perspective. Contracts not only optimise performance and costs but also the quality of relationship. They must stimulate cooperation and transparency through continuity, trust and win-win situations. It requires a different way of thinking and leadership to realise that.

Asset Management System

In the area of optimal and sustainable management of asset costs and quality, there are many developments that could affect the future of rail infrastructure. For example, there is a report from the Innotrack project (Innotrack, 2010) which includes a list of 135 results to be implemented in the field of rail, switches, contracting and management techniques. Part of it are innovations and part of it are applications of existing innovations. The report is limited to innovations in the field of rail and switches and leaves other systems out of consideration, such as signalling, energy supply, communication, bridges, tunnels and so on. It is merely the tip of an innovation iceberg and yet it shows that much is being invested in rail technology. How does it impact the asset management system? A comparison with other industries can help. An extreme example is the aircraft industry. Aircrafts are assets and require optimal and sustainable management of costs and performance. This industry is able to continually improve performance and reduce life cycle costs through technological innovations, full process control and the use of better management techniques. New devices deliver better performance and have become more cost-efficient through better designs, quality control, better material and more sophisticated instruments. The RAMS quality in the exploitation phase continues to increase because of more effective and efficient maintenance execution, which has significantly increased aircraft revenues and reduced life cycle costs. There are at least two explanations for the quality improvement in maintenance of aircrafts: (1) consistent communication of operational experiences to the designers and (2) ability to monitor degradation of the condition of all kinds of systems on the aircraft, continuously and from a distance with telemonitoring systems. The circumstances are essentially different for rail infrastructure, as are the risks and the control thereof. Nevertheless, the aircraft industry can very well be used as an inspiration for innovations in the rail assembly management system when adapted for the circumstances in which rail transport operates.

A trait of the railway people is that they are generally conservative: they tend to stick to proven techniques. That is understandable and it has brought them far, but times are changing. Promising innovations tend to remain too long on the shelf. The Innotrack report writes about this: *'Railways also endure various other problems: they have to be far from ambitious and expensive to maintain. At one of the latest world congresses of rail research, it was claimed that two-thirds of all railway research is undergoing significant innovation in products and services offered by the industry. However, the time to market and the need to be significantly reduced in R&D by the supply industry."* The big challenge is not that service providers should become more innovative, but that infra managers, such as ProRail, should sponsor innovations more actively, test faster, take the initiative and implement innovations. The innovator must also be rewarded because innovation grows only when there is a win-win situation for innovators and the client.

To stimulate innovations in the field of rail asset management, ProRail has set up a network platform: InnoRail. All partners in the industry can join in: contractors, engineering firms, suppliers, advisors, universities and so on. The objective is to improve the performance of the rail infrastructure in an optimal and sustainable manner by promoting technical and process-based innovations in the field of rail asset management. The network platform contributes to this by making developments proactively negotiable, bringing parties together and exchanging knowledge and experiences. InnoRail strives for the professionalisation of its affiliated companies and their professionals in asset management and innovation. It is a partner of the Railcenter, the training institute for the rail sector. It is a home port where people regularly meets to discuss developments, share knowledge, find sponsors and test innovations.

ProRail has also started a research programme under the name ExploRail, together with the Netherlands Organization for Scientific Research (NWO) in the field of social and behavioural sciences and with the Technology Foundation STW. The three entities finance doctoral research aimed at reducing disruptions and optimal cooperation in the rail sector. Two research themes have been formulated: 'Self-thinking Track' and 'Whole System Performance'. The 'Self-thinking Track' leads to a rail infrastructure that informs when, how and where maintenance is needed. This involves themes such as measuring degeneration, choosing the most optimal maintenance strategy, gaining a better understanding of the technical situation by combining data, better predicting the breakdown duration and developing more sustainable material. The 'Whole System Performance' creates a robust rail system by influencing the interplay of stakeholders with different interests.

Innovations come anyhow, but it is human ability to extract and implement what is valuable. It involves creation of an environment and organisation in which people feel involved, safe, empowered and connected with internal and external colleagues to work together on continuously improving performance and costs. A lot has been achieved in that area in recent years. For the future of the sector, it is necessary to strengthen and further expand the positive innovation climate.

13 Epilogue

The organisation of the asset management system differs by branch. In the aircraft industry, it is the designer and builder who organise and control the asset management system. They inform when, how and with which material and machines the aircraft must be maintained to perform safely and reliably[69]. In case of national networks such as rail, electricity, roads and drinking water, designers and builders determine the capacity and functionality of the network, and M&R organisation manages the performance in the exploitation phase. This was strongly dependent on the knowledge and experience of maintenance teams but it has changed due to mechanisation, rise of ICT and asset management goal to sustainably optimise performance and costs over the entire life cycle. Asset management has therefore become a complex, management-intensive expertise. In the railway sector, the complexity has been strengthened by separating transport and infrastructure, and privatising all executive activities. It took the infrastructure industry at least fifteen years to adapt to the changed circumstances. During that period, the focus of employees and managers shifted from technical to business, internal to external, informal colleagues to formal contacts and execution to management and collaboration. This happened gradually, in an almost organic way. There was no master plan to optimally optimise performance and costs over the life cycle. On the contrary, the goal was vague and the route towards it was already determined on the basis of the changed circumstances, as well as the possibilities and limitations of people: the journey was the goal and man the measure. It is an example of course-seeking leadership; a form of management necessary when the ultimate goal is vague, circumstances are changing rapidly and the people need a common cohesion and connection in a fragmented sector.

The circumstances are very decisive for the development of a company. In rail transport, politics has always had a big influence because it determines the transport and mobility policy and thus the future of rail companies. Look at the history of rail transport in the Netherlands. Conscious and unconscious, desirable and undesirable, positive and negative, politics were always involved in rail transport. Due to rapidly increasing deficits in the 1950s and 1960s, it was even inevitable that the government would become part of rail transport management. This was a far-reaching reform that took effect over a long period of time before transport and infrastructure were separated. It took more than ten years to choose a governance model. The development of the infrastructure manager ProRail started more than ten years earlier than the arrival of the first international Asset Management standard PAS55. The company has sought its own way to put the

---

[69] Due to changing laws and regulations, a change has been set in motion. The owner of the aircraft will be responsible for its maintenance. The manufacturer's manuals and maintenance schedules are advisory (and are taken as a starting point). National CAMO's (Continuing Airworthiness Management Organisations) supervises the development of maintenance programmes, organisation or coordination of necessary modifications, repair and maintenance. Other activities are technical inspections and management of technical documentation of aircraft.

organisation and management in order, assisted by insights from the quality standard EFQM/INK. It is remarkable, but also not surprising, that today Pro-Rail almost completely covers the reference frameworks in the AM standards. ProRail, however, has not developed asset management as an AM system based on an AM standard, but as a step-by-step development of necessary process specialisms like information-, traffic- and project management, concentrated in the 'old' M&R organisation. The fundamental difference is that an AM standard, such as PAS55 or ISO55000, assumes a single quality circle, namely the life cycle, and that ProRail assumes two cycles, namely the life cycle and the annual operating cycle. According to ProRail's approach, the intended life cycle optimisation is best initiated and stimulated from the cyclic asset management process in the exploitation phase, the M&R / AM organisation. It is the continuous factor, oversees the whole life cycle process and has the most to gain. It has led to a well-functioning AM system at ProRail. Ten years after its founding, ProRail is performing better than ever and, together with Switzerland, the best in Europe. ProRail is now a leading asset management organisation for national and international companies that come to gather knowledge, experience and inspiration.

The positive development of the organisation and results was not judged and appreciated by the press, politicians and the public. That was not surprising when things got worse, but the criticism persisted even when things got better. It shows that it is very difficult to get rid of a negative image, but there is more to it. A public service is always critically assessed and the valuation of the performance depends on the experiences of the users. Anthonie Bauer, former director of Pro-Rail AM, used the metaphor of *water from the tap*. There are countries where residents do not get water from the tap temporarily on average once a month. If a drinking water company succeeds in making it once every two months, everyone is happy. Should that happen in the Netherlands, then the whole country will be in turmoil. What matters is that people form reference of what they are used to. The better a company performs, the harsher criticism it faces when things go wrong. In addition to the fact that most Dutch people love their car much more than public rail transport, the criticism of rail transport persists even though it is among the best in Europe. Managers and employees in the rail transport sector must learn to deal with this and they may also be less modest and cautious. The negative news comes naturally in the newspaper and on TV, and it is an art to bring the (many) positive news to attention. This has been increasingly successful given the more positive media coverage in recent years: fortunately and rightly so. It is also good to see that there is no happy leaning backwards, but that the train operators, government and ProRail are working together constructively to continuously improve the performance of rail transport. Not in a spectacular way, but slowly, certainly and with perseverance because the path to the goal fits the character of the sector and the circumstances in which it operates.

Part four

ANNEXES, INDEX and EXPLANATIONS

- Annexes
- Index with keywords
- Abbreviations: Dutch and English translation
- Quoted works

Part IV: ANNEXES, INDEX and EXPLANATIONS

14 Annexes

14.1 Developments

14.1.1 Development of circumstances of rail transport in the Netherlands

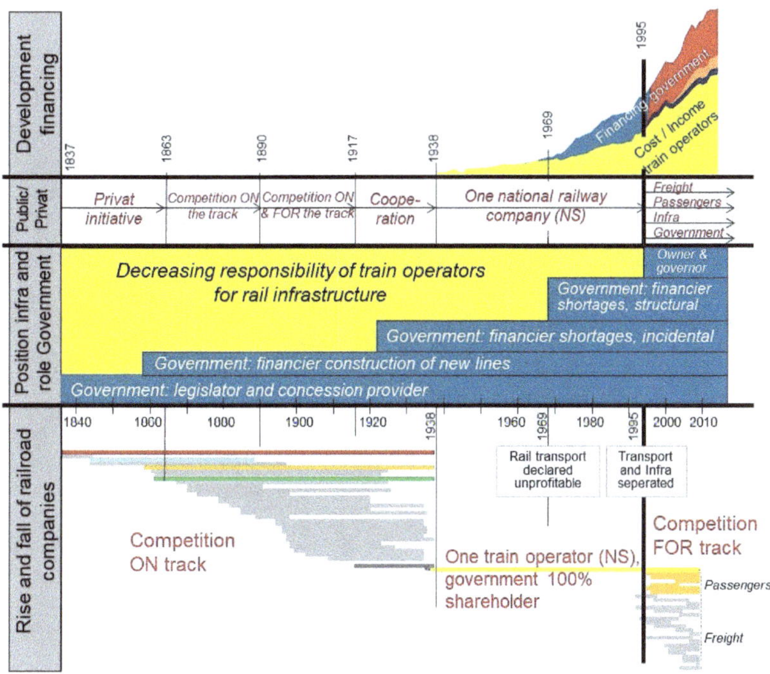

Figure 101   Development circumstances for rail transport and role of government

The government has always played a role in the management of rail transport in the Netherlands and this role was related to money and the use of the rail network. Figure 101 provides an overview of the developments, which started with the construction of the rail network. The main network was constructed by and for the national government. This was not the preferred choice. The government wanted to leave construction entirely to the private sector, but when it did not work because the financial risks were too high, the government took the initiative. As soon as the lines were ready, the maintenance and operations were transferred to the largest private company that used the system. It was expected that the investment would soon be repaid from the income from transport but that assumption was far too optimistic. The revenues were sufficient to pay for infrastructure maintenance but not enough to pay the depreciation costs, so not at all to pay the initial construction investment. On the contrary, in times of recession the government had to make regular financial contributions to cover the shortages. Competition lowered fares and increased train frequency. Companies had to work together to survive or were taken over to prevent bankruptcy. After the First World War, the rapidly rising competition from road transport and the big depression caused a halving of the revenues and an increase in the shortages. A reorganisation was inevitable. In 1938, the existing railway companies were liquidated and merged into a national railway company, the NV Nederlandse Spoorwegen (in English: Ltd Dutch Railways).

In the early 1960s, the costs started to rise faster than income due to rapidly rising labour costs experienced with the strong economic growth after the Second World War. Because of the social importance of rail transport, the state government started structural subsidy and became actively engaged in management. This created an administrative institutional triangle that turned out favourable in the long term. After the split in 1995, the revenues from transport increased faster than the costs of transport and infrastructure because use increased (there was need to avoid traffic jams), investments in network quality and transport service, and user fee from other train operators upon opening of the network.

14.1.2 **The institutional triangle**

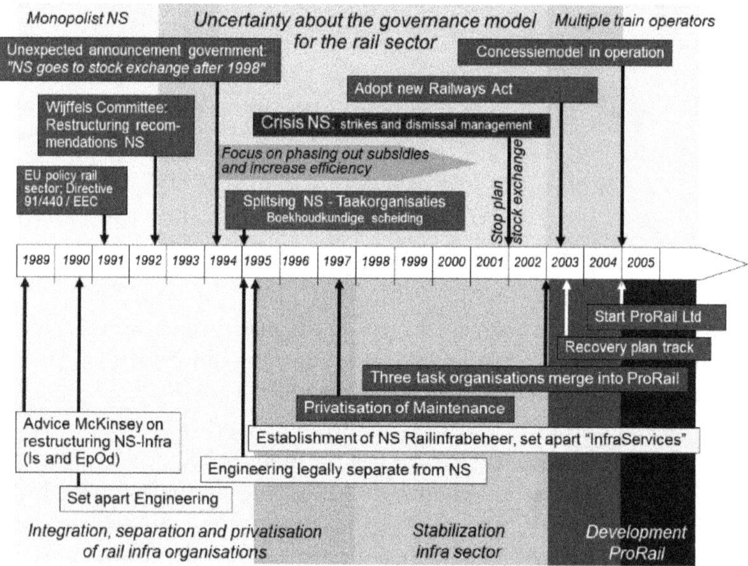

Figure 102   Milestones in the restructuring process of the rail transport sector (1989-2005)

No one is positive about the change process for the separation of Transport and Infrastructure. The path could also have led to wrong results. There were

304

conscious and unconscious large risks taken in the realisation of ProRail. The risks were not because of the splitting of Transport and Infrastructure, but mainly because of the lack of vision on the restructuring of rail transport and the outsourcing of maintenance while there was no maintenance market for rail infrastructure at all. Figure 102 provides an overview of the relationship between the changes at NS and the Rail Infrastructure Organizations. It shows that there was a period of at least 10 years of uncertainty about the rail sector organisation and drastic changes at NS and NS Railinfrabeheer (now ProRail). In 1992, the NS knew that the three infra/task organisations would be relocated but this did not actually happen until the end of 2002. At that time, decisions were taken for NS Railinfrabeheer that did not aim to establish a strong asset management organisation. On the contrary, NS Railinfrabeheer was the remains of a split up and divided operation, as evidenced by the long list of tasks that were privatised: design and management of new infrastructure, maintenance, fibre optic network, material procurement and logistics, training, personnel safety and commercial station activities. The starting position of NS Railinfrabeheer in 1998 was outright bad; a large part of the necessary management skills and instruments was missing. The organisation was not at all ready for its new task as an asset- and contract-manager and there was no market for maintenance at all. Rail maintenance was to be built as a completely new industry. The development of infrastructure management got off to a good start only when the three task organisations from NS Holding were merged in the beginning of 2005 into ProRail Ltd with central government owning all the shares. With this merger, space was created and attention was given to improve cooperation with other parties and companies, including the NS.

In the period 1999-2001, the NS experienced difficulty due to various factors, including, staff uncertainty about privatisation, a growing number of equipment disruptions because of excessive cuts in equipment maintenance and unrest among staff on duty rosters, leave arrangement, security and information provision. The result was instability, declining performance and strikes. Ultimately, this led to the resignation of the NS management on January 2nd, 2002. The new management restored confidence, and it helped when the plan was abandoned to go to the stock exchange early in 2002. The adoption of the new railway and concession law in 2003 was the start of a new course that was formalised in 2005. After that, NS also started exploring options to build constructive cooperation with other companies, including the infra manager ProRail.

14.1.3 Mechanisation and automatization of track maintenance

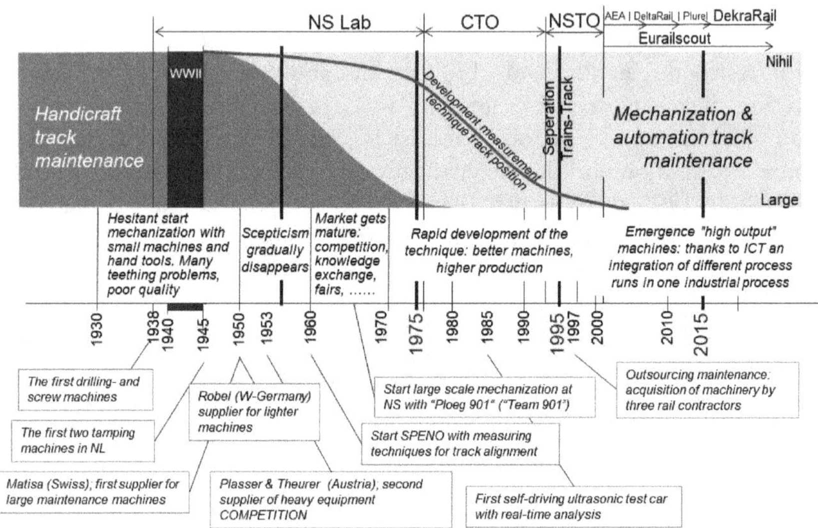

Figure 103 *Development mechanisation and automation of track maintenance. Derived from information source* (Strukton, 2004-12)

Most of the maintenance was and continues to be in track and switches. Before the Second World War began, almost all maintenance was carried out manually. The maintenance needs were relatively higher because the connection between rails was made with bolts and plates and not with termite welds. The first two tamping machines came to the NS immediately after the Second World War. It was not an immediate success. The machines had many flaws, quality was worse than manual works and there was resistance because machines were seen as a threat to employment. The fact that these machines would reduce heavy labour did not matter then. However, there was a turnaround in the second half of the fifties. The machines and delivery quality improved and there was a shortage of labour because of rapid economic growth. The real breakthrough came in the early sixties. Machine builders, constructors and railroad technicians exchanged knowledge and experiences at trade fairs and thus stimulated the development of machine quality. The mechanisation of track maintenance in the Netherlands was energetically taken up by mechanising the nationally operating 'Vliegende Ploeg 901' (English: 'Flying Team 901') of track workers. In the mid-seventies, the machines became indispensable. Due to the mechanisation as well as introduction of longitudinal welded rail and crushed stone as ballast, the number of man-hours in track maintenance decreased by > 65% in the period 1955-1975 (WO, 1987*), the working conditions improved enormously and so did the quality of the track. The quality and productivity subsequently increased rapidly given the possibilities offered by ICT in the area of automation and information provision. The Centre for Technical Research (CTO) of the NS began in the seventies of the last century with use of measurement vehicles for measuring track position and conducting other specialised technical research work. All these activities were privatised around 2000. The measuring services were partly taken over by Eurailscout and technical expert research by AEA Technology, later continued by DeltaRail and Plurel, and finally taken over by DekraRail in 2015.

14.1.4 ICT-infra and office automation

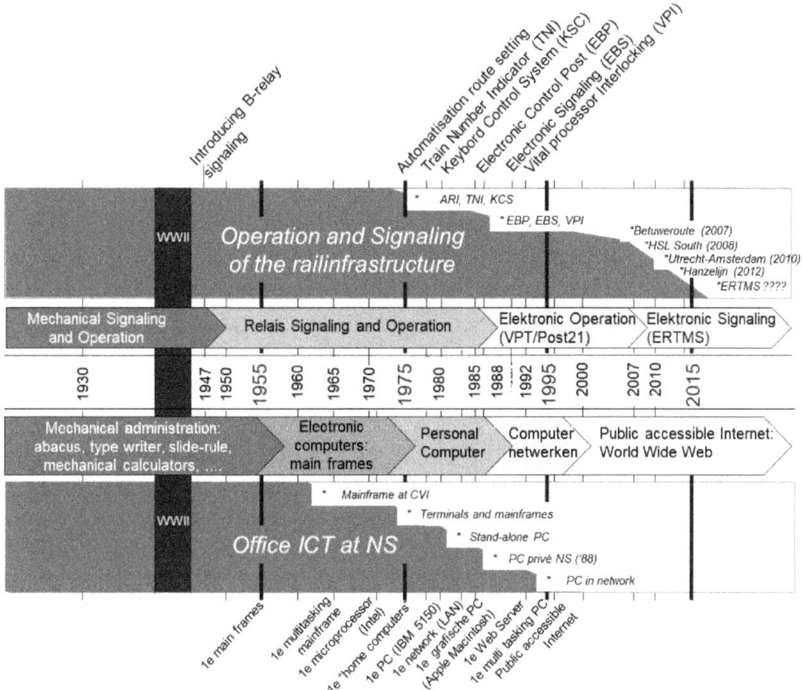

Figure 104   Development of ICT global and atthe NS

The office automation at NS started in the sixties with the introduction of the first main-frame computer, a large computer where data was centrally entered with punched cards and magnetic tapes. Its use at NS was mainly focused on applications in business administration. The Centre for Information Services (Dutch abbreviation: CVI) was established for management and train operations.

At the end of the seventies, terminals were connected to the mainframes and the information was decentralised. The output was supplied by the CVI on continuous paper, a folded pack with holes in the edges for printer feedthrough and perforated folds for easy separation of sheets.

The first Personal Computer (PC) appeared in the late 1980s. With its arrival, the administration switched from electric typewriters, typing rooms and paper archives to standalone PCs with Word Perfect as the word processing software, fixed memories and portable floppies that were later replaced by floppy disks. To promote and stimulate use of PCs, a private project was launched in 1988 and followed by a second project few years later. In the beginning, office PCs were used by several employees; but in the mid-nineties, there was one PC on each desk and these PCs were also connected to a network. Windows 95 became the standard software and in the late nineties, e-mail was introduced for the written communication between the employees.

After the Second World War, relay signalling was introduced. Partly for signalling (with type J-relay) and partly for protection (with type B-relay). The first form of electronic signalling was the Automatic Traffic Control (Dutch abbreviation: AVL) Amsterdam. It was a tested from 1974 to 1978. In that period, the Train Number Indication (TNI) and Train Number Tracking system (TNV) were introduced. In 1980, the first Keyboard Control Systems (KCS) from Siemens came with an Integra viewing panel, keyboard and pre-programmed routes. They quickly replaced all traditional control panels. The next step was to replace the signalling circuits on a few railway yards with electronics: the Electronic Control Station (Dutch abbreviation: EBP). After the EBP, safety circuits were replaced with the Electronic Security Simis (Dutch abbreviation: EBS) system. Because EBS is too large for simple railway yards, the Vital Processor Interlocking (VPI) has been developed in combination with the EBP. A new development was the introduction of PLC Interlocking / Eurolocking (programmable logic controllers, developed by Movares) in 2012.

With the arrival of the first European Rail Traffic Management System (ERTMS) on various lines, not only a standardised interoperable train signalling system is deployed but also a standardised train control system.

14.1.5 **Asset management principles and techniques**

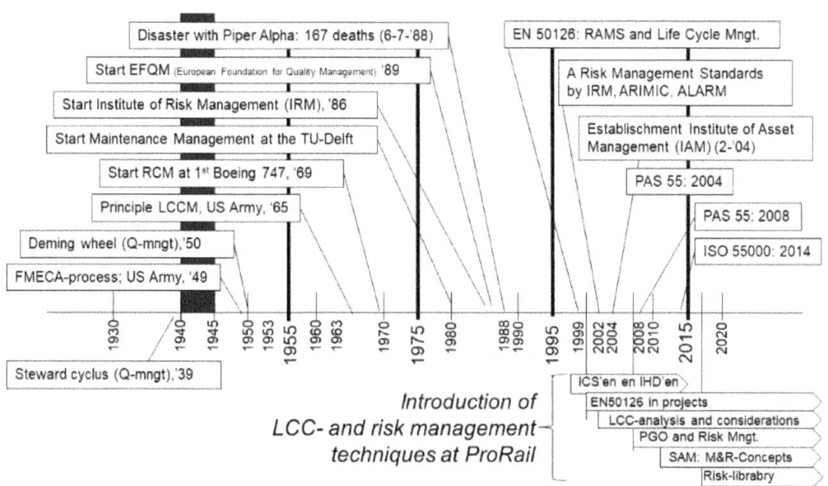

Figure 105   Development of AM-principles and techniques

The systematic reflection on the improvement of products started when Dr. Walter A. Stewart, in 1939, established the 'Steward-circle', the connection between a scientific method and pragmatic thinking about quality. This was the beginning of quality management. In 1949, the US Army used the first risk management principles from the financial world to improve the reliability of their equipment. Deming and the Japanese car industry were then the main promoters of continuous improvement with the PDCA, later also known as the PDSA circle[70]. The aircraft industry developed the Reliability Centred Maintenance (RCM) method to significantly improve the reliability of aircraft components with goal-oriented maintenance. This technique was applied successfully for the first time to the new Boeing 747 at the end of the sixties and is widely adopted thereafter. The methodology is now leading in the field of maintenance- / risk- / asset management.

Risk management for projects was introduced in the 1970s. In 1986, the Institute of Risk Management was established in England. In 1988, the Piper Alpha disasdisaster led to a shift in thinking about safety in the oil industry. The prescriptive regulations of the government gave way to an objective for companies. Risk management principles were introduced to realise the performance goals in a controlled and demonstrable manner.

In 1999, a first European standard for the railways was published to explicitly manage the RAMS performance over the entire life cycle based on risk management techniques and system engineering principles, the EN50126. The IRM

---

[70] PDCA = Plan-Do-Check-Act   PDSA = Plan–Do-Study-Act

came up with risk management standards for the industry in 2002 and 2009. A milestone was the introduction of PAS55 in 2004, the first AM standard to manage the performance, costs and risks of physical assets explicitly and in cohesion, using various management techniques such as risk-, quality- and Life Cycle Cost Management. The IAM standard was replaced by the ISO 55000 standard in 2014.

ProRail started at the end of the nineties with the development of Risk Management (RM) and LCM instruments, and the application of the EN50126 in projects. RM became the foundation of PGO control in 2007. In 2010, the SAM-programme was established to perform risk analyses and prepare risk management concepts (Dutch abbreviation: IHC) for all systems, together with the maintenance contractors. In 2017, a Central Infrastructure Risk Register (CIRR) was put into use in which all IHC's are managed by ProRail A&T and made accessible to the entire industry.

14.2 Input transport in business model Transport & Infra

Source: (Swier J. , 2016*)

Input passengers

	A Km line = 2831 km	B NS Passenger	C Regional TOC's	D TotalPassenger NL	
1	Gross ton passenger				
2	Costs	€ 1.601 (Annual report)	€ 160 (B1*C4)	€ 1.761	mio
3	Passenger kilometers (Tranport Unit = TU)	16.180 (Annual report)	1.618 (B3*C4)	17.798	mio TU
4	NS Passengers/Other TOC's	90%	10% (10%, educated guess)	100%	
5	Earnings train operation	€ 1.775 (Annual report)	€ 165 (Assumption)	€ 1.940	mio
6	Users charge paid	€ 168 (Annual report)	€ 16,8 (B6*C4)	€ 184,8	mio
7	Profit	€ 174 (Annual report)	€ 5	€ 179,00	mio
8	Unit: Earnings Passengers			€ 0,109 (M5/M3)	/ TU
9	Unit costs: income (Km line= 2831)			€ 685.270 (M5 / 2831km)	per line km
10	Unit: utilization	5.715.295 (B3/2831km)	571.529 C3/2831km)	6.286.824 Som	TU/line km
11	Unit costs: users charge Pass.			€ 0,0104 (D6/D3)	/TU
	Earnings Passengers			€ 0,109 (D5/D3)	/TU
	Earnings, stations & real estate	€ 629 (Annual report)	0	€ 629	mio
	Profit, stations & real estate	€ 120 (Annual report)		€ 120	mio

Earnings Freight+Passengers		€ 0,089	/TU
Combination of figures from annex 1 and 2			
User charge Freight+Passengers		€ 0,0079	/TU
Combination of figures from annex 1 and 2			

Input freight

	A Km line = 2831	B DB Schenker	C Schenker NL	D Other Freight TOC	E Total Freight NL	
1	Gross ton freight		11.341 (E1*E4)	3.544 (E1*F4)	14.885 ProRail (V&D)	mio
2	Net ton freight		32 DB Schenker	10 Calculated	42 ProRail (V&D)	mio
3	Volumes sold (mio net tonkm) (Tranport Unit = TU)	113.630 Annual report	5.670 (G3*E4)	1.772 (G3*F4)	7.442 (G 1/2)	mio netto tonkm
4	Schenker / Other TOC's		76,2% (E2/G2)	23,8% (F2/G2)	100% Som	
5	Earnings train operatio	€ 4.654 Annual report	€ 232,2 (E3*G8)	€ 72,6 (F3*G8)	€ 304,82 Som	mio
6	Users charge paid		€ 10,89 Calculated	€ 3,40 Calculated	€ 14,30 ProRail (V&D)	mio
7	Profit	€ 307 Annual report	€ 19,30 (G7*C4)	€ 6,03 (G7*D4)	€ 25,33 Assumption (high)	mio
8	Unit: Earnings Freight				€ 0,041 (D3/D5)	per net tonkm
9	Unit costs: income				€ 107.672 (G5/2831km)	per line km
10	Unit: utilization		2.002.953 (C3/2831 km)	625.923 (D3/2831km)	2.628.875	TU/line km
11	Unit costs: users charge				€ 0,0019	/TU
12	Earning freight				€ 0,041 (E5/E3)	/TU

Earnings Freight+Passengers		€ 0,089	/TU
Combination of figures from annex 1 and 2			
User charge Freight+Passengers		€ 0,0079	/TU
Combination of figures from annex 1 and 2			

14.3 Coherence of reference frameworks and AM guidelines

NS Railinfrabeheer, and later ProRail, has developed the Dutch version of EFQM based on insights and structures from the organization reference framework INK. Later, more specific guidelines for asset management became available. In this appendix, a comparison is made based on the aspects (processes, instruments and/or skills) that are distinguished see Table 11 (Source: (Swier J. , 2016*)). The comparison is made between the following reference frames:

1. EFQM / INK model.
2. ProRail processes and instruments.
3. An Anatomy of PAS55.
4. PAS55
5. ISO55000.

'An Anatomy of PAS55' is the most detailed and used as a frame of reference for comparison. The others are added to make the list complete.

Conclusion:
The processes and instruments developed by ProRail cover the aspects mentioned in the reference frameworks. This is an indication that ProRail meets all the requirements that are set for an asset management system. It is not surprising because the organisation performs well. It has developed organically on the basis of necessity and possibilities, starting with the demands and wishes of stakeholders and increasingly capable to manage assets in optimal, sustainable and transparent manner.

EFQM- / INK-model	ProRail Processes and instruments	PAS 55; An Anatomy 6 subject groups	39 subjects	PAS 55 22 AM system requirements	ISO 55000 24 AM system requirements
Strategy	Vision	AM Strategy & Planning	1 AM policy	1 AM policy	4.1 Gain insight into the organization and context
Strategy	Strategic plan ('Beheerplan'), Technical Policy		2 AM strategy	2 AM strategy	5.2 Policy
Strategy	V&D: developments, plans, bottlenecks, 'Tafel van Vergroting'		3 Demand Analysis	3 AM Objectives	4.2 Gain insight into the needs and expectations of stakeholders
Strategy	Strategy plan V&D, Projects, AM, TC		4 Strategic Planning		4.3 Determine the scope of application of the AM system
Strategy	Life Cycle-, RAMS-, Risk, M&R-management, Quality managment, VMS, ...				4.4 Asset Management System
Strategy	Investment projects (MIT), Long Term Renewal plan, 'Beheerplan', ...		5 AM Plans	4 AM Plans	
Resources	Business Case, MKBA, RAMS/LCC	AM Decisions Making	6 Capatal Investement Decision Making		
Resources	Risk Mngt. / Project Mngt.		7 Operation and Maintenance Decision Making		
Resources	Life Cycle Cost analyses, Value engineering		8 Life Cycle Cost and Value Optimalisation	15 Life Cycle Activities	6.2 Asset Management goals and plans to realize them
Resources	Projects: long term M&R plan and Investment plan		9 Resourcing strategy and Optimalisation		
Resources	Distribution capacity for Trains and Track, maintenance schedule,....		10 Shutdowns and Outige Strategy and Optimalisation		
Resources	Long Term Renewal plan		11 Aging assets strategy		
Resources	Technal Poilicy, Rules, Regulations, ...(RIC)	Life Cycle Delivery Activities	12 Technical standards & Legislation	13 Legal and other requirements	
Resources	Stragegic plan V&D: developments, botlenecks, ...		13 Asset Creation & Acquisition		
Resources	Risico Mngt., RAM-mngt., system engineering, value engineering		14 Systems Engineering		10.3 Continue improvement
Resources	Infra atlas, Infra architrectuur, Infraconcepten,		15 Configuration Management		
Resources	OPC/PGO		16 Maintenance Delivery		8.1 Operational Planning and Control
Resources	Maintenance Engineering, IH-mngt, risico mngt.,		17 Reliability Engineering & Root Cause Analysis	18 Investigation of asset related failures, incidents, ...	9.1 Monitor, measure, analyse and evaluate
Resources	Traffic Control		18 Asset Operations		
Resources	Facility Services ProRail, contractors, Railpro, ...		19 Resource Management	16 Tools, faclities and equipment	
Resources	Maintenance schedule, distribution capacity for infra,		20 Shutdown/Outige Management		
Resources	OPC/PGO-contract/process, regulations failure repair, performance risk analyses, ...		21 Incident Response		10.1 Deviations and corrective measures
Resources					10.2 Preventive measures
Resources	Bottleneck analysis, design ateliers, technical policy, environmental policy, ...		22 Asset Rationalisation & Disposal		

Continued on the next page

EFQM- / INK-model	ProRail Processes and instruments	PAS 55; An Anatomy		PAS 55	ISO 55000	
		6 subject groups	39 subjects	22 AM system requirements	24 AM system requirements	
Resources	ICT and information policy	Asset Knowledge Enablers	23 Asset Information Strategy	10 AM System Documentation		
Resources	Information prescriptions (BID1, 2, 7, 8,...)		24 Asset Knowledge Standards	11 Information Management	7.5	Requirements for information
Resources	ICT systems		25 Asset Information Systems		7.6	Gedocumented information system
Resources	Information management AM and other business units		26 Asset Data & Knowledge			
Organisation	OPC/PGO, Projects, ...	Organization and People Enablers	27 Contract & Supplier Management	7 Outsourcing of AM-activities	8.3	Outsourcing contracts
Culture	MT, Board, Scope inquirey, top 100 meetings, "forest"-days, ...		28 Asset Management Leadership	14 Management of change	5.1	Leadership and involvement
Organisation	Quality Management; VMS, MMS,		29 Organizational Structure & Culture	6 Structure, authority and responsibilities	5.3	Roles, responsibilities and competences
Culture	HRM, communication, Table of division, LOCOV, ...			9 Communication, participation and consultation		
Man	HRM, Quality Management, ProLeren, RailCentre, ...		30 Competence & Behaviour	8 Training, awareness and competence	7.1	Man and resources
Mana					7.2	Competence
Man					7.3	Awareness
Man					7.4	Communication
Resources	Risk Management	Risk and Review	31 Criticality Risk Assessment & Management	12 Risk Management	6.1	Measures to address the AM system risks and to seize opportunities
Resources	M&R-management, Traffic Control,..		32 Contingency planning & Resilliance Analysis	5 Contingency planning		
Strategy	Environment Management Systeem, Sustainability		33 Sustainable Development			
Strategy	analysis, Environment and sustainablity policy, ...		34 Weather & Climate Change			
Resources	Condition Monitoring, RAMS-dashboard, Failure registration, Health-registration, Safety inquiries, ...		35 Assets & Systems Performance & Health Monitoring	17 Performance and conditions monitoring		
Resources	Technical policy, 'Star-approach', innovations, InnoRail, Railcentre, ...		36 Assets & Systems Change Management	21 Improvement actions	8.2	Management and changes
Organisation	Internal auditing		37 Management Review, Audit and Assurance	20 Audit	9.2	Internal audit
Organisation	Finance; P&C		38 Accounting Practices	19 Evaluation of Compliance		
Strategy	Board of directors, Account management V&D, Compliance officer, Enterprise Risk mngt.		39 Stakeholder relations	22 Records	9.3	Management review
Appreciation by customers	Yearly realtion days, ...					
Appreciation by employees	SKOOP inquiry					
Appreciation by customers	Passenger inquiry NS					
Overall results	ProRail DASHBOARD					
Learn and Improve	PDCA-process, improvement goals, RGB, audits, Railcentre,.....					

Index with keywords

EU directive 1191/69, 27
EU directive 91/440, 31, 34
Eurailscout, 150, 322
European Union, 48, 71, 99, 193
ExploRail, 312

F
Faber, 16, 27
FMECA, 170, 173, 177, 195
France, 42, 59, 126, 289, 296
FTBV, 112, 125
future, 309

G
Germany, 47, 59, 179, 280
Great Britain, 40, 59, 93, 289
growth model AM, 116, 120

H
Hofstra, Klaas, 53, 55
Holland Railconsult, 32
Horvat, 145

I
ICT, 68, 179, 303
IHS, 141
ILT, 107, 144, 145
information delivery spec (ILS), 108, 175, 307
Infra '96, 71
Infra Services, 72, 73
InnoRail, 312
Innotrack, 311, 312
institutional triangle, 29, 30, 36, 39, 65, 125, 295
integral, 278, 304
ISO55000, 122, 135, 315, 327

J
Japan, 49, 244, 255, 310
Jonckers Nieboer, 16, 17, 24, 27

K
Key figures

maintenance costs, 249
knowledge, 305

L
leadership, 11, 15, 28, 136, 169, 187, 295, 301, 308, 314
lessons learned, 295
LICB, 235, 243, 250, 287
life cycle costs, 65, 121, 133, 142, 154, 160, 163, 192, 245, 279, 311
Life cycle management, 131, 153, 303
LOXIA, 182, 186

M
M&R management, 119, 164, 303, 308
maintenance strategy
    GAO, 273
    SAO, 273
    TAO, 273
matrix organisation, 102, 193
McKinsey, 29, 37, 69, 136, 154, 297
mechanisation, 30, 68, 150, 314, 321
ministry, 34, 108, 137, 157, 234, 240, 297
MKBA, 61, 156, 158
Movares, 32, 73, 182, 323

N
Nederlandse Spoorwegen (NS), 25, 319
Norway, 289
NVW, 143, 265

O
OPC contract, 97, 139, 141, 270
OPC+, 95, 99
organisation
    conditions, 135
    structure, 29, 37, 132, 183
outsourcing maintenance, 93

Abbreviations in Dutch and the (English translation)

ACM	Autoriteit Consument & Markt (Authority Consumer & Market)
AHOB	Automatische Halve Overwegbomen (Automatic half barrier level crossing)
AI&B	Architectuur, Infrastructuur & Bedrijfsadvies (Architecture, Infrastructure & Business advice)
AKI (1)	Aanbestedingszaken, Kostenmanagement & Inkoop (Procurement matters, Cost management and Purchasing)
AKI (2)	Automatische Knipperlicht Installatie (Automatic Flashing Light Installation)
ALARP	(As Low as Reasonably Possible)
ALI	Abnormaal Lage Inschrijving (Abnormally low offer)
AM	Asset Management (Asset Management)
ARBO	Arbeidsomstandigheden (Working Conditions)
ATB	Automatische Trein Beïnvloeding (Automatic Train Control)
ATB Vv	ATB Verbeterde versie (Automatic Train Control Improved version)
AVPO	Algemene Voorwaarden Prestatiegericht Onderhoud (General Conditions for Performance-Oriented Maintenance)
BAH	Booz Allen Hamilton (Name of an organisation)
BBV	Bovenbouwvervanging (Renewal of track & switches)
BCG	Boston Consulting Group ()
BI	(Business Intelligence)
BICC	(Business Intelligence Competence Centre)
BIM (1)	(Business Information Manager)
BIM (2)	Bouw Informatie Model (Building Information Modelling)
BIS	Bestuurlijke Informatiesystemen (Administrative Information Systems)
BM	Beheer Maatregel (Management Measure)
BOV	Beheer, Onderhoud, Vervanging (Management, Maintenance, Renewal)
BR	Betuweroute (Betuwe Route)
BSI	British Standard Institution (company name)
BTC	Bureau Toetsing en Certificering (Office Testing and Certification)
BVS	Bedien Voorschrift (Operate Prescription)
CAO	Collectieve Arbeid Overeenkomst (Collective Labor Agreement)
CAPEX	(Capital Expenditures)
CC	(Corporate Control)
CFC	(Corporate Finance & Control)
CIRR	Centraal Infra Risico Register (Central Infra Risk Register)

CRC	Centraal Regieteam Contractering
	(Central Control Team Contracting)
CTO	Centrum Technisch Onderzoek (Centre for Technical Research)
CVI	Centrum Voor Informatieverwerking (Centre for Information Processing)
DBFM	(Design, Build, Finance, Maintain)
DDNW	Dag, zonder treinhinder | Dag, met hinder | Nacht | Weekend (Day without hindrance | Day with hindrance | Night | Weekend)
DEFRES	DEFecten Registratie Energievoorziening en Seinwezen (DEFect Registration Energy supply and Signaling)
DNW	Dag | Nacht | Weekend (Day, Night, Weekend)
EBP	Electronische Bedien Post (Electronic Control Post)
EBS	Electronische Beveiliging SIMIS (Electronic Signalling SIMIS)
EFQM	European Foundation for Quality Management (Name of an organization)
EG	Europese Gemeenschap (European Union)
EIM	European Infra Managers (company name)
EKOM	Exploitatie Kosten Model (Exploitation Cost Model)
EMVI	Economisch Meest Voordelige Inschrijving (Economically Most Advantageous Tender)
Ep	Exploitatie (Name of an organization)
ERM	(Enterprise Risk Management)
ERP	(Enterprise Resource Planning)
EU	Europese Unie (European Union)
EUR	Euro
EV	Energievoorziening (Energy Supply)
EVB	Eenheid Van Bedrijfshinder (Unit Of Company hindrance)
FBTV	Functies, Taken, Bevoegdheden, Verantwoordelijkheden (Functions, Tasks, Competences, Responsibilities)
F&C	(Finance & Control)
FH	Functie Herstel (Function Recovery)
FHT	Functie Herstel Tijd (Function Recovery Time)
FIE	Fictieve Instandhouding Eenheid (Fictive Maintenance & Renewal Unit)
FMEA	(Failure Mode Effect Analysis)
FMECA	(Failure Mode Effect & Criticality Analysis)
FT	Functie Test (Function Test)
GAO	Gebruiksduur Afhankelijk Onderhoud (Frequency (or Time) Based Maintenance)
GB	(Great Britain)
GBI	Groep Bedrijven Infra (Group Businesses Infra)
GCB	Grand Central Belge (company name)

GID   Generieke IT Diensten (Generic IT Services)
GO   Groot Onderhoud (Large-scale Maintenance)
GPS   (Global Positioning System)
HRM   (Human Resource Management)
HSL   Hoge Snelheid Lijn (High Speed Line)
HSM   Hollandsche Spoorweg Maatschappij (company)
HIJSM   Hollandsche IJzeren Spoorweg Maatschappij (company)
HUP   Historische Uitgave Prijs (Historical Spend Price)
IB   Ingenieursbureau (Engineering Company)
IAM   Institute of Asset Management (company)
ICS   Instandhouding Concept Spoorinfra (M&R Concept Rail infra)
ICT   (Information & Communication Technology)
ICTS   (ICT Services)
If   Infrabeheer (a company name)
IFO   Inrichting, Formatie en Ontwikkel plan
             (Layout, Formation and Development plan)
IH   Instandhouding (Maintenance & Renewal; conservation)
IHC   Instandhouding Concept (M&R Concept)
IHD   Instandhouding Document (M&R Document)
IHM   Instandhouding Management (M&R Management)
IHS   Instandhouding Specificaties (M&R Specifications)
ILS   Informatie Levering Spec (Information Delivery Specification)
ILT   Inspectie Leefomgeving & Transport
             (Inspectorate Human Environment & Transport)
IM   (Infra Management)
INK   Instituut Nederlandse Kwaliteit (Institute Dutch Quality)
I&M   Infrastructuur & Milieu (Infrastructure & Environment)
IRA   Instandhouding Risico Analyse (M&R Risk Analysis)
IRSE   (International Railway Signal Engineers)
Is   Infrastructuur (company name)
IS   Infra Services (company name)
IT   (Information Technology)
IVW   Inspectie Verkeer & Vervoer (Inspectorate Traffic &
             Transport)
IW   Interventiewaarde (Intervention Value)
KCS   (Keyboard Control Systems)
KO   Kleinschalig Onderhoud (Small-scale Maintenance)
KPI   (Key Performance Indicator)
LC   (Life Cycle)
LCC   (Life Cycle Cost)
LCCM   (Life Cycle Cost Management)
LICB   Lasting Infrastructure Cost Benchmark (name of a UIC-group)
LREHC   Lloyds Register En Horvat & Partners (company)

LTP FH	Lange Termijn Plan Functie Handhaving (Long Term Plan Function Enforcement)
LTSA	Lange Termijn Spoor Agenda (Longe Term Track Agenda)
LVO	Landelijk Verbeterprogramma Overwegen (National Improvement Program Level crossings)
MKBA	Maatschappelijke Kosten Baten Analyse (Social Cost-Benefit analysis)
MMS	Milieu Management Systeem (Environment Management System)
MOOS	Met het Oog Op Seinen (With the Eye on Signals)
M&R	(Maintenance & Renewal)
MT	(Management Team)
MTBM	(Mean Time Between Maintenance)
MTBF	(Mean Time Between Failure)
MTTR	(Mean Time to Repair)
MTTM	(Mean Time to Maintain)
MVA	Materiële en Vaste activa Administratie (Material and Fixed assets Administration)
MVP	Meer jaren Vervanging Plan (Multi-year Renewal Plan)
NCS	Nederlandsche Centraal Spoorweg Maatschappij (company)
NLG	Dutch guilder
NRS	Nederlandsche Rhijnspoorweg Maatschappij (company)
NS	Nederlandse Spoorwegen (company name)
OAW	Onmiddellijke Actie Waarde (Immediate Action Value)
OCCR	Operationeel Control Centrum Rail (Operational Control Centre Rail)
OHM	Onderhoudsmanagement (Maintenance Management)
OHR	Onderhoudsrooster (Maintenance Schedule)
ORR	Office of Railway Regulation
OPC	Output Proces Contract (Output Process Contract)
Od	Onderhoud (company name)
Odh.	Onderhoud (Maintenance)
ONNO	ONderzoek naar planningsNOrmen (REsearch about planning STandards)
OPEX	(Operational Expenses)
O&V	Onderhoud & Vervanging (Maintenance & Renewal)
OV	Openbaar Vervoer (Public Transport)
OV-SAAL	OV-Schiphol, Amsterdam, Almere, Lelystad
OW	Onderhoudswaarde (Maintenance Value)
PAB	Prestatie Analyse Bureau (Performance Analysis Bureau)
PC	(Personal Computer)
PCA	Proces Contract Aannemer (Process Contract Contractor)
PDCA	(Plan, Do, Check, Act)

PGO	Prestatie Gericht Onderhoud
	(Performance Aimed Maintenance)
PHS	Programma Hoogfrequent Spoor
	(Program High-frequent Track)
PLC	(Programmable Logic Controllers)
PP	Productieplan (Production Plan)
PRL	Procesleiding (Process Management)
PSO	(Public Service Obligation)
PVR	Profiel van Vrije Ruimte (Free Train Profile)
PVVO	Programma Verbeteren Veiligheid Overwegen
	(Program Improvement Safety Level crossings)
PwC	PricewaterhouseCoopers (company name)
RA (1)	Risico Analyse (Risk Analysis)
RA (2)	(Reliability, Availability)
RAMS	(Reliability, Availability, Maintainability, Safety)
RAMSHED	(RAMS + Health, Environment, Durability)
RBV	Registratie Bijzondere Voorvallen (Registration Special Events)
RCB	(Rail Case Base)
RCF	(Fail Contact Fatigue)
RIO	Rail Infra Opleidingen (company name: Rail Infra Training)
RPI	(Rail Performance Indicator)
RIB	Railinfrabeheer (company name)
RIC	Rail Infra Catalogus (Rail Infra Catalog)
RIT	Railinfratrust (Rail Infra Trust)
RM	Risico Management (Risk management)
ROSCO	(Rolling Stock Leasing Company)
SAM	Systeem Asset Management (System Asset Management)
SAO	Storingsafhankelijk Onderhoud (Failure Induced Maintenance)
SAP LAM	(SAP Linear Asset Management)
SCE	Service Centrum Electrotechniek
	(Service Centre Electro technique)
SE	(Systems Engineering)
SKI	Samengestelde Kwaliteitsindicator(Compund Quality Indicator)
SMART	Specifiek, Meetbaar, Ambitieus, Realistisch en Tijdsgebonden
	(Specific, Measurable, Ambitious, Realistic and Time-bound)
SPA	Scenario en Prestatie Analyse
	(Scenario and Performance Analysis)
SS	Staats Spoorwegen (company name)
SSC	(Shared Service Centre)
STS	Stop Tonend Sein (Stop Showing Signal)
Sw	Seinwezen (Signalling)
SWOD	Seinwezen Ontwerp Documentatie
	(Signalling Design Documentation)

TAO (1)	Toestandsafhankelijk Onderhoud (Condition Based Maintenance)
TAO (2)	Treindienst Aantastende Onregelmatigheid (Train service Impairing Irregularity
TEB	Techno Economisch Beheer (Techno Economic Management)
TEN-T	(Trans-European Transport Network)
TESI	Technisch Economische Stuurinformatie (Technical Economical Management information)
Tf	Tonnage fictive = Fictief dagtonnage (Fictional Day tonnage)
TIC	(Tracé Infra Cluster)
TNI	Trein Nummer Indicatie (Train Number Indication)
TNV	Trein Nummer Volgsysteem (Train Number Tracking System)
TOC	Tracé Onderhoud Concept (Trace Maintenance Concept)
TSB	Tijdelijke Snelheid Beperking (Temporary Speed Restriuction)
TRIS	Treindienst- en Reis Informatie Systemen (Train service & Travel Information Sustem)
TROTS	Trein Observatie en Tracking Systeem (opvolger TNV) (Train Observation and Tracking System)
TU (1)	(Transport Unit)
TU (2)	Technische Universiteit (Technical University)
TVP	Trein Vrije Periode (Train Free Period)
TVTA	Te Verklaren Trein Afwijking (To Explain Train Deviation)
UB	Ultrasoon Bedrijf (Ultrasonic Company)
UIC	Union Internationale des Chemins de fer (= company name)
UPGE	Uitvoering Programma Geluid op Emplacementen (Execution Program Sound on Yards)
V&D	Vervoer & Dienstregeling (Transport & Timetable)
V&W	Verkeer & Waterstaat (Traffic- and Water Management)
VKL	Verkeersleiding (Traffic Control)
VL	Verkeersleiding (Traffic Control)
VMS	Veiligheid Management Systeem (Safety Management System)
VoT	(Value of Time)
VPI	(Vital Process Interlocking)
VPT	Vervoer Per Trein (Transport by Train)
VTW	Verzoek Tot Wijziging (Request for Change)
VVW	Vervangingswaarde (Renewal Value)
WBS	(Work Breakdown Structure)
Wf	Weegfactor (Weighing factor)

Quoted works

(sd).

A&T. (2014*). *BID00008. Generieke en algemene kenmerken (BID08).* Utrecht: ProRail A&T.

A&T. (2015*). *BID00020. Levensduur verwachtingen ten behoeve van vervangingsplannen (BID20).* Utrecht: ProRail A&T.

A&T. (2016*). *BID00001. Objectenstructuur en basislijst objecten (BID01).* Utrecht: ProRail.

A&T. (2016*). *BID00007 (BID07) Documentvragen.* Utrecht: ProRail T&A.

AKI. (2011*). Instandhoudingskosten Objecten/Systemen (KO+GO+Beheer) 2011 (RCB11). Rail Case Base (RCB), op het netwerk van ProRail AM en beheert door AKI.

B.Hedeman, G. v. (2015). *Projectmanagement op basis van Prince2.* Zaltbommel: Van Haren Publishing.

Bauer, A. (2003*). Beheer & Instandhouding (Bau03). *Presentatie vaste commissie voor Verkeer en Waterstaat* (p. 14). Utrecht: ProRail.

BCG. (2015-3). *The 2015 European Railway Performance Index. Exploring the Link Between Performance and Public Cost (BCG53).* BCG.

Beckum, P. v. (1992). *Ploeger op het spoor.* Utrecht: Boekhoven Bosch bv.

Bedrijfstrategie. (2008*). *Handboek Veiligheid Management Systeem (VMS89).* Utrecht: ProRail.

Berghuis, S. (2016*). *Productomschrijving Generieke Spoortakken (Tak16).* Utrecht: ProRail.

Bouwkwaliteit, S. (sd). Opgeroepen op maart 9, 2016, van Nationale milieu database: https://www.milieudatabase.nl/index.php?id=basisinformatie

Bruin, H. d. (2002). *Prestatiemeting in de publieke sector.* Boom Lemma uitgevers.

BSL, R. e. (2000-6*). *The Cost of Railinfrastructure. Investment and Maintenance/Renewal (BSL06).* BSL Management Consultants en R+R Burger und Partner.

BSL, R. e. (2005*). *Infrastructure Operations Performance Analysis (IOPA). Summary report (BSL05).* Hamburg: BSL en R+R.

Capgemini. (2004*). Verbeteren efficiency back-office (Cap46). *3e bijeenkomst werkgroep 'asset management'* (p. 12). Utrecht: Capgemini.

Caralp, R. (1951*). L'evulation de l'explatation de ferroviair en france (pdf en excel) (Car12). *National Geografic,* 321-336.

CBS. (2001). *Tweehonderd jaar statistiek in tijdreeksen 1800-1999.* Voorburg/Heerlen: Stichting Beheer IISG.

CENELEC. (1999*). *EN 50126 Spoorwegtoepassingen – De specificatie en het bewijs van de betrouwbaarheid, beschikbaarheid, onderhoudbaarheid en Veilgheid (RAMS) (CEN99).* Brussel: CENELEC.

CFC, P. (2011-8*). *Internationale Benchmark 2011 (pro18).* Utrecht: ProRail.

Dalen, J. v. (2005*). *"De waarde van publieke belangen" (Dal05).* Utrecht, ProRail: Internal report ProRail.

Dehornoy, J. (2011*, november 21). *The evolution of public funding to the rail sector in 5 European (Jul11)*. p. 17.

Descheemaecker, M. (2014-3). *Dwarsligger.* Amersfoort: Wilco.

Dijkstra, G. (2002*). *Japanse Horizon: Fata morgana of Nederlandse realiteit? (Ger02).* ProRail: NS Raiolinfrabeheer.

Directie. (2013-6*). *Meerjarenplan duurzaamheid 2012-2015 (Dir36).* Utrecht: ProRail.

Duck, R. D. (2016-1*, januari 22). Donald Duck. *Donald Duck, Disney (Red61). Een vrolijk weekblad,* pp. 5-15.

Duin, L. v. (2010-12*). *Nieuwsbrief. Samen zorgen voor minder CO2 (Lis12).* Utrecht: ProRail.

EIM. (2013-6*). *Cost and Performance comparison 2012. ProRail version update. (EIM26)* . Brussel: EIM.

EIM. (2017-1*). *Performance comparison workstream (EIM71).* Brussel: EIM.

Empel, F. v. (1997, Februari 18). *Retro.nrc.nl.* Opgeroepen op januari 20, 2015, van http://retro.nrc.nl/W2/Lab/Spoorwegen/970218.html.

EU. (1969-6*). *REGULATION (EEC) No 1191/69 OF THE COUNCIL (EU96).* Brussel: EU.

EU. (1991*). *Richtlijn 91/440 (EU91).* Brussel: EU.

EU, C. (2008*). *Guide to Cost-Benefit Anlysis of investment projects (EUR08).* Brussel: Directorate General Regional Policy.

Eurostat. (2014*). *EU transport in figures. 2014 (Eur14).* Belgium: Publication office of the European Union.

Faber, J. (1989). *Het spoor. 150 jaar spoorwegen in Nederland.* Amsterdam: Meulenhoff.

Factsheet. (2013*). *Dagelijks spooronderhoud. "Positieve effecten prestatiecontracten spooronderhoud" (Com31).* Utrecht: ProRail.

Gestel, P. (2004-7*). RAMS in de praktijk. Module Nieuwbouw. Deel 1, 2 en 3 + praktijkcase Zevenaar (Ges42). (p. 108). Utrecht: ProRail.

Gestel, P. (2004-8*). RAMS in Praktijk. Module Capaciteit Management. Deel 1 en 2 + praktijk case (Ges41). (p. 44). Utrecht: ProRail.

Gestel, P. (2004-9*). *Module RAMS in praktijk. Nieuwbouw. Deelnemersmateriaal (Ges04).* Utrecht: ProRail.

Gestel, P. v. (2003-7*). *RAMS leidraad Nieuwbouw (RAM03).* Utrecht: ProRail.

Gomez-Ibanez, G. d. (2006). *Competition in the railway Industry.* Northampton, Massatusetts, USA: Eadward Elgar Publishing Limiited.

Graaf, G. d. (2006-12). *Sporen van verandering.* De Alk BV.

GWW, W. L. (2013-11*). *Leidraad voor System Engineering binnen de GWW-sector (SE11).* GWW-sector Nederland.

Hofstra, K. (2005*). *Systeemkosten en opbrengsten Nederlandse Spoorwegnet (Hof05).* Utrecht, ProRail: Internal report ProRail.

Hofstra, K. (2010*). *Blogpost. Interne website ProRail (HOF10).* Opgehaald van Onze man in Japan.

Hofstra, K. (2010*). *Japan, blog Klass Hofstra; verzameling van 25 blog's over de ervaringen van Klaas Hofstra in Japan (Hof02)*. Utrecht: ProRail.

Hoogen, H. v. (1997). *Uitbesteden van onderhoud*. Utrecht: Bariet.

Horvat. (2014*). *Onderzoek veilige berijdbaarheid (Hor14)*. Rotterdam: Horvat.

I&M. (2012*, Juni 8). Kabinetsreactie op onderzoek Tijdelijke commissie onderhoud en innovatie spoor. *Kabinetsreactie op onderzoek Tijdelijke commissie onderhoud en innovatie spoor (Min12)*. Den Haag: Ministerie I&M.

I&M, M. (2011-9). *Reizen zonder spoorboekje. Programma hoog frequent spoorvervoer (minpt)*. Den Haag: Ministerie van Infrastructuur en Milieu. Directie Spoorvervoer.

I&M, M. (2012, juni 8). *Kabinetsreactie op onderzoek tijdelijke commissie onderhoud en innovatie spoor*. Den Haag.

I&M, M. (2014-12*). *Beheerconcessie 2015-2025 (Min12)*. Den Haag: Rijksoverheid.

IAM. (2008*). *PAS55. Part 1: Specifiaction for the optimized management for physical assets (IAM55)*. London (PAS08): Britush Standards Institution (BSI).

IAM. (2012*). *Asset Management - An anatomy(IAM22)*. Bristol: Institute of Asset Management.

ICTS, I. e. (2008*). *Hoofdgegevensgroepen en authentieke bronnen ProRail (ICT08)*. Utrecht: ProRail, Informatiebeleid en ICT Services A&P.

ILT. (2012*). *Quick Scan Beheer Onderhoud ondehoud hoofdrailinfratsructuur ProRail. RV12-0119 (ILT26)*. Den Haag: ILT.

ILT. (2013*). *Prestatiegerciht Onderhoud van de Nederlandse Spoorweginfrastructuur. RV13-0017 (ILT12)*. Den Haag: ILT.

Innotrack. (2010). *Concluding Technical Report*. Parijs: UIC.

J. Harmsen, O. K. (2013-2*). *Toets LCM-tool ProRail (TNO32)*. Delft: TNO.

J.Swier, M. P. (2004-12*). *Meerjaren vervangingsplan 2005-2025. Detail- en achtergrondinformatie (MVP12)*. Utrecht: ProRail.

Jenma, R. (2010, Jen10). *Het verband tussen beschikbaarheid en punctualiteit (JEN10)*. Utrecht: Stageverslag.

Jonckers Nieboer, M. D. (1938). *Geschiedenis der Nederlnadse Spoorwegen 1832-1938*. Rotterdam: Nijgh & van Ditmar N.V.

Jongma, J. J. (1992). *Geschiedenis van het Nederlandse wegvervoer*. Drachten/Leeuwarden: FPB Uitgevers.

KiM*, K. v. (2013, Kim11). *De maatschappelijke waarde van*. Den Haag: Ministerie van Infrastructuur en Milieu.

Koster, J. (2008*). De trein moet rijden (Joy08). *NVVK info*, 4.

Kuiken. (2012*). *Parlementair onderzoek onderhoud en innovatie spoor (Kui12)*. Tweede Kamer, Parlementair onderzoek. 's Gravenhagen: Tweede Kamer.

Lamers. (2003*). *Beleidsnotitie Asset Management (Lam01)*. Utrecht: ProRail.

Lamers. (2008). *Expliciet werken*. Amersfoort: Dialoog.

Lamper, A. (2010*). *Leidraad voor RAMSHE-LCM-studie (RAMS1)*. Utrecht: ProRail.

LCM-project*. (2008-5). *Gebruik Life Cycle Management binnen ProRa*. Utrecht (LCM85): ProRail / Inframanagement.

LC-netwerk. (1993). *Life Cycle management bij Infra Beheer.* Utrecht: NS Infrabeheer.

LICB. (2007*). *10 years op benchmarking 1996-2005 (LICer).* Parijs: UIC.

Loving, R. (2006). *The Men Who Loved Trains. The Story of Men Who Battled Greed to Save an Ailing Industry.* Bloominton and Indianapolis: Indiana Universaty Press.

LREHC. (2003*). *Analyse meetbaarheid en behersbaarheid van techniische (basis) kwaliteit en functionele prestatie van de railinfrastructuur (LRE22).* Rotterdam: LREHC.

LREHC. (2004*). *Deel II 'Doelmatigheid'. Analyse doelmatigheid van processen, organisatie en activiteiten Beheer & Instandhouding railinfrastructuur. Deelproject II "Doelmatigheid" (LRE41).* Rotterdam: LREHC.

LREHC. (2004-12). *Deelproject IV 'Kostenniveau'. Analyse ontwikkeling en opbouw alsmede sturing en beheersing van de kosten B&I railinfrastructuur (LRE31).* Den Haag: LREHC.

Marcelis, W. (1984*). *Onderhoudsbesturing in ontwikkeling (Mar84).* Deventer: Kluwer.

McKinsey. (1989-1). *Naar en meer Bedrijfsmatig en Doorzichtig Functionerend Infra-Proces (Kck89).* McKinsey & Company.

NASH, C. (2010). The Effectiveness of EU Rail Policy – an overview., (p. 13). Brussel.

NEN-ISO. (2014*). *Assetmanagement – Managementsystemen – Richtlijnen voor het toepassen van ISO 55001 (NEN14).* Delft: Nederlands Norm Instituut.

Nieuwsbrief. (2010-12*). *Samen zorgen voor minder CO2 (Nie12).* Utrecht: ProRail.

Noort, M. v. (2014, LCM14). *Handleiding Life Cycle Management - Rekentool.* Utrecht: ProRail.

NRC, H. M. (2012, Februari 16). Weeffouten trekken wissel op het spoor. *NRC,* p. 25.

NRC, K. B. (2011, Oktober 2). Een goede toezichthouder wordt gehaat". *NRC,* pp. Economie, blz. 4.

NRC, M. V. (2007, december 4). Hereniging exploitatie en beheer. *NRC,* pp. Opinie, blz 6.

NS. (2009*). *Jaarverslag 2008 (NS09).* Utrecht.

NS. (2014*). *NS Benchmark Hoofdrailnet. Eindrapportage benchmark 2013 (NS14).* Utrecht: NS.

Oosterhaven, P. e. (2003). *Transportkosten, locatie en economie.* Onderdeel van preadviezen 2003: locatie en concurrentie.

OPC+, W. c. (2005-3). *Visie OPC+ 2006.* Utrecht: ProRail.

Overdijk, C. (2009-4*). Prutsrail wordt Prorail (Pru09). *Binnenlands Bestuur,* 2009, aflevering 14.

OVG/SORT. (1992*). *Evaluatie ODIS-Veranderingsproces (OVG92).* Utrecht: NS Nederlandse Spoorwegen.

P/SA, C. t. (2013*, augustus 26). Convenant Prestatie Geicht Onderhoud Spoor in Nederland - naar een toekomstbestendig model (Con13). *PGO 3.0.* Utrecht.

Pardijs, E. (2005*). *Module RAMS in de praktijk Instandhouding. Deelnemersmateruiaal (Par051)*. Utrecht: ProRail.

Pardijs, E. (Regisseur). (2005*). *ProLift. Samen aan de top (ParF52)* [Film].

Pardijs, E. (2005*). RAMS-management in praktijk Instandhoudingsmanagement (Par05). *Opleiding RAMS-management in praktijk Instandhoudingsmanagement* (p. 88). Utrecht: ProRail.

Pardijs, P. (2003-4*). *Omgang vaststellen RAM-eisen voor de Hanzelijn (Par03)*. Utrecht: ProRail.

pm. (2010*). *Handleiding voor LCM (LCM02)*. Utrecht: ProRail.

Procurement, P. F. (2016-7*). *EP2016. Erkenningsregeling van ProRail (Ep267)*. Utrecht: ProRail.

Projectteam. (1995*). *De plattegrond van Railinfrabeheer (Pro95)*. Utrecht: ProRail.

Projectteam. (1997*). *De rode draad van Besturing Instandhouding (Pro97)*. Utrecht: NS Railinfrabeheer BV.

Projectteam. (1997-4*). *De veelzijdigheid vasn INSTANDHOUDINGSCONCEPTEN*. Utrecht: NS Railinfrabeheer.

Projectteam. (1998-1*). *Sturen op Output (OPC98)*. Utrecht: NS Railinfrabeheer BV.

Projectteam*. (1997*). *De veelzijdigheid van Instandhoudingsconcepten (Pro74)*. Utrecht: NS Railinfrabeheer.

ProRail. (*). *Basisrapport prestatiemeten. Algmeen deel (ProPm)*. Utrecht: ProRail.

ProRail. (2002). *ProRail/@propos (Pro02)*. Opgeroepen op maart 9, 2016, van "Werken met de RailCase Base": http://rcb.prorail.nl/

ProRail. (2003*). *Plan van aanpak beheer en onderhoud Spoorwegen. Herstelplan spoor (Pro03)*. Utrecht: ProRail.

ProRail. (2004*). Inzicht prestatie infra (Inz04). (p. 23). Utrecht: ProRail.

ProRail. (2005*). *ProRail Top-KPI's en NPI's. Hoe en Wat 2005 (Pro06)*. Utrecht: ProRail.

ProRail. (2005-11*). *Inframanagement in 2008 (Pro08)*. Utrecht: ProRail.

ProRail. (2007-5). *IM a la carte (Pro75)*. Utrecht: ProRail.

ProRail. (2010*). *ProRail jaarverslag 2009 (Pro10)*. Utrecht: ProRail.

ProRail. (2010-11*). *Duurzaamheid bij ProRail, Factsheet (Pro101)*. Utrecht: ProRail.

ProRail. (2011*). *Jaarverslag 2010 (Pro10)*. Utrecht: ProRail BV.

ProRail. (2012*). *In samenspel naar een vernieuwd Nederlands spoor. Onze opdrachten voor 2012-2015 (Pro121)*. Utrecht: ProRail.

ProRail. (2012*). *Jaarverslag 2011 (Pro12)*. Utrecht.

ProRail. (2014-5*, mei 16). *teamsites*. Opgeroepen op maart 16, 2016, van ProRail, Focus (Pro14): https://teamsites.prorail.nl/teams/Operatie_AM_TenA/Gedeelde%20documenten/PDF%20Kernproces%20AM%20v1.0.pdf

ProRail. (2015*). *Procedure PRC00055 (PRC55)*. Utrecht: ProRail.

ProRail, D. (2014-12*). IJken strategie uitbesteden kleinschalig onderhoud (Dir12). (p. 26). Utrecht: ProRail.

PwC. (2015*). *Doorlichting van de financiele meerjaren reeksen BOV spoor (PWC15)*. Amsterdam: PwC.

PwC, d. A. (2015-6*). *Covering letter onderzoek aanbesteding ProRail (PwC15)*. Amsterdam: PwC.

Rechtbank, d. (2013, februari 13). *de Rechtspraak*. Opgeroepen op april 18, 2014, van www.de rechtspraak.nl.

Rechtbank, m. N. (2016*). *Vonnis in kortgeding van 8 januari 2016 (Rec16)*. Utrecht: Civielrecht, handelskamer.

Rechtbank, m. N. (2016-7*). *Vonnis in kortgeding uitspraak 8-7-2016. Zaak C/16/413830 / KG ZA 16-298 (Rec167)*. Utrecht: Civielrecht, handelskamer.

Rhee, G. v. (2016-nr 2). Zichtbaarheid seinen sterk verbeterd. *Proloog*, 8.

RIB. (2000*). *InstandhoudingsSPECIFICATIES Spoor infra (RIB00)*. Utrecht: NS Railinfrabeheer.

RISMAN, b. u. (1998). *De RISMAN-methode*. Twijstra Gudde.

Roest Crollius, A. (2010-1*). *Multi annual maintenance plan for NRIC Bulgaria. Final report (Roe01)*. Zoetermeer: NEA.

Ruygrok. (2013-1*). *Aanvulling MKBA-tool ProRail met extra omgevingskwaliteiten (Ruy31)*. Deventer: Wiiteveen en Bos.

SAM. (2014*). *SAM handboek. Handleiding Systeem Asset Management. Versie 2 (SAM42)*. Utrecht: ProRail AM. Bedrijfsbibliotheek HLD00039-002V.

SAM, K. (2012*). *Systeem Assetmanagement (SAM). Project initiatie document (SAM26)*. Utrecht: ProRail.

Schouten, J. (2009*). *LT-plan 2009. Hoofd rapport (LTP10)*. Utrecht: ProRail.

Schouten, J. (2009*). *LT-plan Functiehandhaving, details en achtergronden (LTP09)*. Utrecht: ProRail.

Schöyer, H. o.-h. (2006*, juli 7). Zo gaat het zonder technici aan de top (NRC06). *NRC*, p. Opinie.

SMC, C. (2014*). *Summary report: SMC Benchmark (SMC01)*. Brussel: SNCB.

Smulders*, J. (2011*). *Systeem Asset Management (SAM). (Smu11)*. Utrecht: ProRail.

SPA, P. (2007-12*). *Inzicht in prestaties en kosten bij ProRail (SPA01)*. Utrecht: ProRail.

Spoorsector. (2003*). *Benutten en Bouwen PLan van de spoorsector (Spo03)*. Utrecht: NS, ProRail, Railion.

Spoorsector. (2003*). *Benutten en bouwen, het plan van de spoorsector (Desug)*. Utrecht: Spoorsector.

Starren, H. (2016). *Think like a manager don't act like one*. Amsterdam: BIS Publishers.

Strukton, M. R. (2004-12). *Zwaar materieel op de sporen van de Lage Landen (Str12)*. 's-Hertogenbosch: Strukton Railinfra.

Swier, J. &. (2001*). *Ontwikkeling onderhoudskosten railinfra in de periode 1994-2000 (Swi14)*. Utrecht: ProRail.

Swier, J. (1997*). *Instandhoudingsconcepten Sporinfra (ICS) & Opdrachtomschrijving Procescontracten (OPC) (Swi97)*. Utrecht: Railinfrabeheer.

Swier, J. (1998*). *Model voor het berekenen van normkosten PROCESCONTRACTEN (Swi98)*. Utrecht: NS Railinfrabeheer.

Swier, J. (2001*). *BMK.Nivo 2&3.Odh.LIJN,gemodelleerd (Swi11)*. Utrecht: ProRail.

Swier, J. (2001-06). *Beschikbaarheid & Betrouwbaarheid. Realisatie 1998-2001 en het R&A-model (Swi01)*. Utrecht: Railinfrabeheer.

Swier, J. (2002*). Kosten matrix beheer & instandhouding (Swi21). Bronbestand Jan Swier. File: Kosten matrix. QM4C.mod.1.NSnet2001.

Swier, J. (2002*). *Studiereis Hong Kong & Japan (Swi11)*. Utrecht: ProRail.

Swier, J. (2004*). Exposing the infrastructure cost drivers (Swi19). *Railway Gazette International*, Page 34-36.

Swier, J. (2006*). *Hogere capaciteit en punctualiteit door decompliceren (Swi23)*. Utrecht: ProRail.

Swier, J. (2008*). *De samenhang tussen OHR, nachtwerk en infra-kwaliteit (Swi82)*. Utrecht: ProRail.

Swier, J. (2010*). How to increase cost efficiency of rail infrastructure (Sw24). (p. Presentation of 16 pages). Utrecht: Rail-Tech conferentie.

Swier, J. (2011*). *Bedrijfsmodel onderhoudskosten. Onderbouwing relatiegrafieken en uitgangspunten (SWIni)*. Utrecht: ProRail, intern rapport.

Swier, J. (2011*). Benchmark database 2010 (Jan11). Utrecht.

Swier, J. (2012*). Railway Business captured in a single model (Swi12). Brussel: 5th CRNI Conference.

Swier, J. (2012-4*). A Business Case in a Nutshell (Swi18). *Railway Gazette International*, 64-66.

Swier, J. (2015*, Mei 1). Punctualiteit 1995-2015 (Swi15). Bronnen proefschrift, Originele bron: PAB en Storingsregistratie AM.

Swier, J. (2016*, mei 16). KostenDekkingsGraad spoorlijnen (Swi20). Utrecht, Excel bestand.

Swier, J. (2016*). Ontwikkeling spoorwegen, gebruik, kosten (Swi16). Utrecht.

Swier, J. (2016*). *Overzicht kosten ProRail. 1994-2013 (Swi13)*. Utrecht: ProRail.

Swier, J. (2016*). *Samenhang PAS55, EN50126, ISO5500, ... (Swi17)*. Utrecht: ProRail.

Swier, J. (2016-12*). *Spanning tussen A&T en CRC over de specificaties en risicoanalyse in PGO (Swi32)*. Utrecht: ProRail A&T.

Swier, J. (2016-2*). Historie van lijnen en bedrijven (Jan17).

Swier, J. (2017, mei 4). Bedrijfsmodel vervangingen 2015.v016 (Swi26). Utrecht.

Swier, J. e. (1992). *Bouwstenen voor een nieuw overwegenbeleid (Swi92)*. Utrecht: NS Infrabeheer, If5.3.

Swier, J. e. (2004*). *Meerjaren Vervangingsplan 2005-2025. Vervangingswaarde en cashflowplanning (MVP04)*. Utrecht: ProRail.

Swier, J. i. (1994). *Borging van Technische kennis voor de kerntaken van Railinfrabeheer*. Utrecht: Leider projectgroep Infrabeheer; A.v. Niekerk.

team, M. (2007*). Samen groeien. Capaciteitsmanagement 2012 en verder, de rek eruit ?! (Mul07). (p. 95). Leusden/Utrecht: ProRail.

UIC. (1989*). *Classefication of lines for the purpose of maintenance (UIC714)*. Parijs: UIC.

UIC. (1992*). *Factors that effect maintenance costs and their relative importance (UIC715)*. Parijs: UIC.

UIC. (2002*). *Infra Costs. The costs of rail infrastructuire (UICne)*. Parijs: UIC.

UIC. (2007*). *10 years of Benchmarking. 1996-2005. Glossery, page 137 (LICB01)*. Paris: UIC.

UIC. (2010-9). *Guidelines for the application of Asset Management in Railway Infrastructure Organizations*. Paris: UIC-org.

UIC. (2015). *UIC Safety Report 2015. Significant Safety Accidents 2014. Public report*. Parijs: UIC.

Uitvoering, P. B. (4-1994). *Adviesaanvraag BE Uitvoering (Adv94)*. Utrecht.

V&W. (2005*). *Beheerconcesiie 2005 (Min05)*. Den Haag: Ministerie V&W.

Veenendaal, G. (2004). *Spoorwegen in Nederland*. Amsterdam: Boom.

Velde, D-. (12-2002*). *Japanse Horizon (Vel02)*. Rotterdam: Erasmus Universiteit (Vel02).

Velde, D. (2012-11*). *EVES-Rail Economic effects of vertical seperation in the railway sector (Vel11)*. Amsterdam: CER and inno-V.

Veraart, M. (2007). *Sturing van publieke dienstverlening, Privatiseringsprocessen doorgelicht*. Utrecht: van Gorcum.

Veraart, M. e. (2011, januari 7). Een spoorboekje voor de toekomst van ProRail en NS. *Infrasite.nl*.

Vernes, M. (2012-11*). *Basisafspraken totstandkoming productieplan asset management. Productieplan 2014-2018 (Ver11)*. Utrecht: ProRail AM P&P.

Verstegen, C. S. (2007*). *Meer groei mogelijk maken door anders om te gaan met capaciteit (Chr07)*. Utrecht: ProRail.

Vries, T. d. (2016*, mei 10). ProRail-directeur: We moeten af van grote storingen (Met16). *Metro*.

W. Kruidhof, d. M.-T. (2014-4). *RAMS / LCC analyses SAAL cluster C*. Utrecht: Movares.

Werkgroep. (2013*). *RAMSHE-LCM dossier (RAM12)*. Utrecht: ProRail.

Wessels, K. (2003). *Verkeerd spoor. De crisis bij de NS*. Amsterdam/Antwerpen: L.J. Veen.

Wester & Berkhout, J. &. (2011, Oktober zaterdag 1& zondag 2 oktober). "Een goede toezichthouder wordt gehaat". *NRC*, p. 4/5 Economie.

WO. (1987*). *Ontwikkeling manuren WO (WO87)*. Utrecht: EpOd.

www.ingramcontent.com/pod-product-compliance
Lightning Source LLC
Chambersburg PA
CBHW061503120726
48001CB00004B/1191